Building States and Markets After Communism

Does democracy promote the creation of market economies and robust state institutions? Do state building and market building go hand in hand? Or do they work at cross-purposes? This book examines the relationship between state building and market building in twenty-five postcommunist countries from 1990 to 2004. On the basis of cross-national statistical analyses, surveys of business managers, and case studies from Russia, Bulgaria, Poland, and Uzbekistan, Timothy Frye demonstrates that democracy is associated with more economic reform, stronger state institutions, and higher social transfers when political polarization is low. But he also finds that increases in political polarization dampen the positive impact of democracy on reform by making policy less predictable. He traces the roots of political polarization to high levels of income inequality and the institutional legacy of communist rule. By identifying when and how democracy fosters markets and states, this work contributes to long-standing debates in comparative politics, public policy, and postcommunist studies.

Timothy Frye is the Marshall D. Shulman Pr⌐f   -Soviet Foreign Policy in the Department ⌐f Political Science   Director of the Harriman Institute ⌐   ısly taught at Ohio State University   the World Bank, the European Ban   nent, the U.S. Agency for Internatio   ...berg Foundation. He is the author of   ...crats: Building Markets in Russia (2000), which w⌐   ... 2001 Hewett Prize from the American Association for the Advancement of Slavic Studies. His articles have appeared in *American Political Science Review*, *World Politics*, *American Economic Review Papers and Proceedings*, *American Journal of Political Science*, and *Comparative Political Studies*, among other journals.

Cambridge Studies in Comparative Politics

General Editor
Margaret Levi *University of Washington, Seattle*

Assistant General Editors
Kathleen Thelen *Massachusetts Institute of Technology*
Erik Wibbels *Duke University*

Associate Editors
Robert H. Bates *Harvard University*
Stephen Hanson *University of Washington, Seattle*
Torben Iversen *Harvard University*
Stathis Kalyvas *Yale University*
Peter Lange *Duke University*
Helen Milner *Princeton University*
Frances Rosenbluth *Yale University*
Susan Stokes *Yale University*

Other Books in the Series

David Austen-Smith, Jeffry A. Frieden, Miriam A. Golden, Karl Ove Moene, and Adam Przeworski, eds., *Selected Works of Michael Wallerstein: The Political Economy of Inequality, Unions, and Social Democracy*

Andy Baker, *The Market and the Masses in Latin America: Policy Reform and Consumption in Liberalizing Economies*

Lisa Baldez, *Why Women Protest: Women's Movements in Chile*

Stefano Bartolini, *The Political Mobilization of the European Left, 1860–1980: The Class Cleavage*

Robert Bates, *When Things Fell Apart: State Failure in Late-Century Africa*

Mark Beissinger, *Nationalist Mobilization and the Collapse of the Soviet State*

Nancy Bermeo, ed., *Unemployment in the New Europe*

Carles Boix, *Democracy and Redistribution*

Carles Boix, *Political Parties, Growth, and Equality: Conservative and Social Democratic Economic Strategies in the World Economy*

Catherine Boone, *Merchant Capital and the Roots of State Power in Senegal, 1930–1985*

Continued after the Index

Building States and Markets After Communism

The Perils of Polarized Democracy

TIMOTHY FRYE
Columbia University

CAMBRIDGE
UNIVERSITY PRESS

CAMBRIDGE UNIVERSITY PRESS
Cambridge, New York, Melbourne, Madrid, Cape Town, Singapore,
São Paulo, Delhi, Dubai, Tokyo, Mexico City

Cambridge University Press
32 Avenue of the Americas, New York, NY 10013-2473, USA

www.cambridge.org
Information on this title: www.cambridge.org/9780521734622

First published 2010

Printed in the United States of America

A catalog record for this publication is available from the British Library.

Library of Congress Cataloging in Publication data

Frye, Timothy.
Building states and markets after communism : the perils of polarized democracy / Timothy M.
Frye.
   p. cm. – (Cambridge studies in comparative politics)
Includes bibliographical references and index.
ISBN 978-0-521-76773-6 (hardback) – ISBN 978-0-521-73462-2 (pbk.)
1. Nation-building – Economic aspects – Former communist countries.   2. Capitalism – Political
aspects – Former communist countries.   3. Free trade – Political aspects – Former communist
countries.   4. Privatization – Political aspects – Former communist countries.
5. Post-communism – Economic aspects.   6. Democratization – Economic aspects – Former
communist countries.   I. Title.
JZ6300.F79   2010
338.947′– dc22   2009036451

ISBN 978-0-521-76773-6 Hardback
ISBN 978-0-521-73462-2 Paperback

Contents

List of Tables and Figures		*page* viii
Acknowledgments		xi
	Introduction	1
1	The Political Logic of Economic and Institutional Reform	21
2	Political Polarization and Economic Inequality	48
3	The Pace and Consistency of Reform	70
4	Political Polarization and Economic Growth	104
5	Political Polarization and Policy Instability: The View from the Firm	122
6	Nationalism and Endogenous Polarization	144
7	Russia: Polarization, Autocracy, and Reform	168
8	Bulgaria: Polarization, Democracy, and Reform	192
9	Poland: Robust Democracy and Rapid Reform	213
10	Uzbekistan: Autocracy and Inconsistent Gradualism	229
11	Conclusion	244
References		255
Index		283

Tables and Figures

Tables

I.1	Predictions	*page* 3
1.1	Economic and Institutional Reform in a Democracy	31
1.2	Economic and Institutional Reform in an Autocracy	34
2.1	Average Annual Polarization Score, 1990–2004	55
2.2	Polarization and Income Inequality, 1987–1988 to 1993–1994	61
2.3	Accounting for Polarization and Income Inequality	62
A2.1	Examples of Partisan Factions	64
3.1	Dimensions of Economic and Institutional Reform, 1990–2004	73
3.2	Reform Index, 1990–2004	75
3.3	Polarization and Reform	76
3.4	Average Scores on the Reform Index	77
3.5	Polarization, Democracy, and Reform	81
3.6	The Marginal Effect of a One-Unit Increase in Democracy on the Reform Index Conditional on Polarization	83
3.7	Inconsistent Reforms, 1990–2004	89
3.8	Polarization, Democracy, and Inconsistent Reform	91
3.9	The Marginal Effect of a One-Unit Increase in Democracy on the Inconsistent Reform Index Conditional on Polarization	93
3.10	Transfers	97
3.11	Polarization and Transfers	98
A3.1	Correlation Matrix of Economic and Institutional Reforms	99
A3.2	Descriptive Statistics	100
A3.3	Correlation Matrix of Variables of Interest	101
A3.4	Reform in Presidential and Parliamentary Regimes	102
A3.5	Interpreting the Impact of Polarization and Democracy	103
4.1	Economic Growth in the Postcommunist World, 1990–2004	110
4.2	Accounting for Growth	113
4.3	A Different Take on Economic Growth	117

A4.1   Quantitative Studies of Economic Growth in the
       Postcommunist World at a Glance   120
  5.1 Polarization and Reversals of Reform   126
  5.2 Polarization and Perceptions of Policy Unpredictability   131
  5.3 Obstacles Faced by Business   131
  5.4 Polarization and Policy Instability   132
  5.5 Accounting for Perceptions of Policy Unpredictability   135
  5.6 Accounting for Investment   139
A5.1   Variable Definitions from BEEPS Data and Descriptive
       Statistics   141
A5.2   Average Responses by Country   142
A5.3   Two-Step Analysis: Polarization, Policy Instability, and
       Investment   143
  6.1 The Roots of Political Polarization   158
  6.2 The Determinants of Polarization   161
  6.3 Instrumental Variable Estimate of Reform   165
  8.1 Heads of Government, 1990–1996   193
  8.2 Campaign Platforms   197
 10.1 Revenue as a Share of GDP   240
 10.2 Public Expenditure as a Percentage of GDP in the 1990s   240

Figures

A1.1   Policy Choice: The Sequence of Decisions   44
  3.1 Polarization, Democracy, and Reform   84
  3.2 Polarization, Democracy, and Inconsistent Reform   94
  7.1 Polarization and the Government Bond Market   176
  8.1 Business Climate in Bulgaria   211
  9.1 Warsaw Stock Exchange Main Index, 1991–2004   218

Acknowledgments

The development of states and markets in many postcommunist countries has taken longer than expected. So has this book. I have worked on the manuscript on and off for about a decade and received comments and encouragement from many quarters. The first inkling of the argument took shape during the summer of 1999, while I was working with Joel Hellman at the European Bank for Reconstruction and Development. I am indebted to Joel for encouraging this line of research and to colleagues at the EBRD for providing much of the data for this project.

I thank participants in seminars at Columbia University, Harvard University, Ohio State University, Princeton University, Rutgers University, Yale University, and the Center for the Study of Democracy in Bulgaria. I am especially grateful to Herbert Kitschelt, Karen Remmer, and the tremendous graduate students at Duke University for hosting a conference on the topic of my research in 2005. During this project, I have been fortunate to work with very generous scholars at Ohio State University and Columbia University. One could not wish for better colleagues. I also recognize financial support from the Mershon Center at Ohio State University and the Harriman Institute at Columbia University.

I thank Mark Beissinger, Boyan Belev, Sarah Brooks, Nauro Campos, Dinissa Duvanova, Venelin Ganev, Scott Gehlbach, Lucy Goodhart, John Huber, Marcus Kurtz, Eddy Malesky, Isabela Mares, Vicki Murillo, Irfan Nooruddin, Pablo Pinto, Tom Remington, Graeme Robertson, Aleksandra Snajder, Dan Treisman, Joshua Tucker, and Milada Vachudova for reading all or parts of the manuscript. I also thank two anonymous reviewers for Cambridge University Press for providing especially detailed and insightful comments. I appreciate very much the time that everyone took from their busy schedules to give the manuscript a close read. Their comments greatly improved the work.

I am grateful to Lowell Barrington, Carles Boix, Rick Ericson, Anna Grzymala-Busse, Bob Kaufman, Pauline Jones Luong, Mike McFaul, Massimo

Morelli, Jonas Pontusson, Grigore Pop-Eleches, and Phil Roeder for providing invaluable comments on papers related to the manuscript. I also benefited greatly from long discussions of the work with Massimo Morelli and Roger Schoenmann.

Jan Box-Steffensmeier, Dave Darmofal, Luke Keel, Nealia Khan, Eduardo Leoni, and Lyndsey Stanfill gave invaluable methodological advice. Tim Colton and the Davis Center at Harvard University provided a congenial place to work during a sabbatical leave in 2007–2008.

While conducting field research, I benefited from the help of Roumen Avramov, Boyan Belev, Dina Beleva, Gano Ganchev, Henry Hale, Elena Iankova, and Vesselin Minchev. I received substantial research assistance on this project from Quentin Beazer, Israel Marques, and Richard McDowell, each of whom went beyond the call of duty. Thanks also go to Ron Meyer for proofreading the manuscript.

I also thank Lew Bateman and the staff at Cambridge University Press for shepherding the manuscript from submission to production and Brian Mac-Donald for his editorial assistance. Chapter 4 contains some ideas from an article published in *World Politics*. I am thankful to Johns Hopkins University Press for permission to use this material.[1]

Last, but far from least, I thank Kira, who made too many useful suggestions on the manuscript to count, but whose greatest contributions were the love, encouragement, and patience that made this project possible. I also thank my son, Vanya, whose birth made a compelling case for finally submitting the manuscript for review.

This book is dedicated to my parents, Dick and Betty Lou.

---

[1] Timothy M. Frye, "The Perils of Polarization: Economic Performance in the Postcommunist World," *World Politics* 54:3 (2002): 308–337. © The Johns Hopkins University Press. Reprinted with permission of The Johns Hopkins University Press.

Introduction

> The hardest part of the transformation, in fact, will not be the economics at all, but the politics.
>
> Jeffrey Sachs, 1993: 5

In the popular Soviet-era movie *An Irony of Fate*, a bout of drinking leads a Russian man to board a flight to St. Petersburg by mistake. Upon arrival, he hails a taxi and tells the driver to take him to his apartment on Construction Workers' Street. The ride takes him through a familiar landscape of seemingly identical apartment buildings, public service signs extolling socialism, and milk and bread shops with innovative names like "Milk" and "Bread." After reaching his address, he enters a nondescript building and takes the lift to an equally nondescript two-room apartment. He then goes to bed with no idea that he is in the wrong city.

Two decades into the transformation of the Eurasian space, this premise is implausible. If the watchword of the communist era was conformity, the watchword of the postcommunist world is diversity. The bustling streets of Prague are a far cry from the drab thoroughfares of Minsk, and the faux-rococo design of Moscow's Manezh Square has little in common with the staid old-European atmosphere of central Zagreb. The hardwiring of the planned economy cannot be easily replaced, but the scope of change across countries in a relatively brief period is remarkable.

Poland, the economic basket case of the 1980s, introduced a range of economic reforms that led to a robust market economy, while Moldova struggled to reform its economy and became the poorest country in Europe. The change in state institutions was no less dramatic. Estonia and Hungary reformed their state institutions to govern the market, while Russia and Bulgaria entered the new millennium with state regulatory institutions infested with corruption. It is hard to imagine that only a short while ago a single model of economic and political institutions dominated the region.

Effect of democracy

This variation in economic and institutional reform across countries raises fundamental questions for comparative politics and political economy that are the central concerns of this book. Does democracy promote the creation of market economies and robust state institutions? If so, how? Under what conditions do state building and market building work at cross-purposes and when are they mutually reinforcing? More generally, if economic and institutional reforms promise to leave the majority of citizens better off, then why are they so difficult to conduct? To explore why countries fail to capture the gains from economic and institutional reforms, observers invariably invoke politics. Some argue that the problem is too much democracy; for others it is too little democracy. Some stress the importance of partisan elites committed to reform; others suggest they are irrelevant. Some point to the benefits of concentrating power in the executive; others emphasize the value of dispersing political power. To add to the confusion, empirical studies of the roots of economic and institutional reforms have produced rather equivocal results.

These debates are part of a broader reevaluation of the role of states and markets in promoting economic development. In the 1960s and 1970s, scholars and policy makers argued that state agencies could serve as engines of development by accumulating capital and coordinating investment. In the 1980s and 1990s, the intellectual pendulum swung in favor of markets as many pushed a broad agenda of economic openness, price liberalization, and the privatization of state-owned assets. The first decade of the new millennium saw the pendulum moderate as policy-making and academic communities came to recognize the dynamism of markets but also to appreciate the importance of state institutions. Yet, the global financial crisis of 2008 shattered this consensus and compelled scholars to revisit their basic assumptions about how states and markets interact. The experience of the postcommunist countries offers an excellent opportunity to contribute to these debates, as we can observe the dual processes of the formation of markets and state regulatory institutions simultaneously in real time.

This book examines variation in two types of policies: *economic reforms*, including price liberalization, the privatization of state firms, and trade liberalization; and *institutional reforms*, including the creation of state bodies to protect property rights, oversee monopolies, and regulate markets. To begin, I explore why countries differ in the pace at which they conducted economic and institutional reforms. Some pursued both types of reforms at a rapid pace, whereas others favored more gradual reforms. Conceptually, I treat the "pace" of institutional and economic reform as the sum of all reforms across policies that liberalize the economy and strengthen state regulatory institutions.

But countries also diverge in the "consistency" of their reforms, that is, the relative speed at which they liberalize their economies and construct state regulatory institutions.[1] Countries may pursue "consistent" economic reforms in

---

[1] Murphy et al. (1992) and Hellman (1998) identify this pattern of "partial" reforms. Here I use the term "inconsistent" reforms. This problem is also apparent in reforms in Latin America (Schamis 1999; Murillo 2009).

TABLE I.1. *Predictions*

	Low Polarization		High Polarization
Democracy	Faster reform		Slower reform
	More consistent reform		Less consistent reform
	More generous transfers		Less generous transfers
Autocracy		Slower reform	
		Less consistent reform	
		Less generous transfers	

which economic liberalization and the creation of state regulatory institutions proceed at roughly the same pace. Here state institutions can buttress economic reform by constraining new owners from raiding their firms for personal profit. Alternatively countries may conduct "inconsistent" economic reforms in which economic liberalization proceeds very rapidly while the construction of state institutions lags. For example, the privatization of state firms may be fast, but the creation of corporate governance institutions may be slow. This sequence of reforms leaves new owners of former state enterprises well placed to strip assets for personal benefit rather than to use them for the good of all shareholders (cf. Stiglitz 2000; Roland 2000). One of the most important lessons of the postcommunist transformation is the significance of accounting for the relative speed of economic and institutional reform (Murphy et al. 1992; Hellman 1998).

To account for this variation in the pace and consistency of reform, this book develops an argument that relies on the interplay of political polarization and democracy. Political polarization is viewed as the policy distance on economic issues between the executive and the largest opposition faction in parliament.[2] In highly polarized political systems, the opposition has economic policy preferences far different from those of the executive so that should the opposition take power, policy is likely to change dramatically. *Polarization*

This book posits that the impact of democracy on economic and institutional reform is conditional on the level of political polarization. As indicated in Table I.1, democracy is positively related to more rapid and consistent reform when political polarization is low, but each increase in polarization dampens the beneficial impact of democracy on the pace and consistency of reform. Similarly, incumbents in low-polarization democracies provide much more generous

Impact of democracy ≷ polarization

[2] "Executive" refers to presidents in presidential systems and prime ministers in parliamentary systems. In highly polarized systems, right (old-left) executives face strong opposition from old-left (right) factions in the legislature. Examples of old-left elites and factions include the Socialist Party of Albania, the Bulgarian Socialist Party, and the National Salvation Front in Romania and personalist leaders like Islam Karimov in Uzbekistan and Heydar Aliev in Azerbaijan. The social democratic ex-communist parties in Poland, Hungary, Slovenia, and Lithuania that advocated market reforms do not fit this description and are treated as centrist parties. A brief list of right elites and factions includes the United Democratic Front in Bulgaria, FIDESZ in Hungary, Freedom Union in Poland, and nonparty right elites, such as Boris Yeltsin in Russia and Askar Akaev in Kyrgyzstan. See Appendix 2.1 in Chapter 2.

transfer payments than their counterparts in high-polarization democracies or in autocracies.

The argument assumes that for institutional and economic reforms to suc-ceed, citizens need to alter their behavior to take advantage of the new policy. Firm managers should create new products rather than wrest subsidies from the state. Workers should acquire new skills better suited to a market econ-omy rather than rely on skills developed for a command economy. Owners of capital should create new firms rather than ship their assets out of the country. However, because these forms of "investment" require up-front costs for the promise of future gains, these changes in behavior are unlikely if citizens expect policy to be reversed before they reap their gains.[3] Producers must believe that the policy is credible, that is, likely to be maintained over time, an outcome that is less likely as governments become more politically polarized or more autocratic.[4] Political polarization in a democracy increases the likelihood of a reversal in policy should the opposition come to power unexpectedly and thereby weakens the incentives of citizens to invest. Autocracy has a similar dampening effect on the response to reforms as the executive typically faces little cost for changing policy. Because politicians can anticipate the weak response of producers to economic and institutional reforms in the future, they have strong incentives to subvert reforms today. Thus, the pace and consistency of reform should be greater in less polarized democracies than in more polarized democracies or in autocracies. Pace + Consistency greater in less polarized democracies

I present the logic of the argument in greater detail in the next chapter, but for now consider policy making in a country with three groups: groups benefiting from rapid reform, or new-economy interests who are represented by right politicians; groups benefiting from gradual reforms, or old-economy interests who are represented by old-left politicians; and groups dependent on the state budget for income, including many bureaucrats, pensioners, and the unemployed, among others who are represented by centrist politicians.[5] To stay in power, governments pursue partisan policies that deliver benefits to their core supporters, but in a democracy they also must find revenue to buy political support from one other group as well. Their ability to do so, however, is constrained by the degree of political polarization and by the extent of democracy.

When polarization is low in a democracy, the policy distance between the largest factions is small. Here, executives introduce partisan policies, and pro-ducers can be confident that policies will not be reversed. Right executives

---

[3] Here "investment" is used broadly and refers to actions that require up-front costs for the promise of future benefits, including opening new firms, restructuring existing firms, exploring new markets, buying new equipment, and gaining new skills. Others use the term "adjustment" to describe this behavior (Berglof and Bolton 2002).

[4] "Producer" refers to the economically active part of the population and includes workers and managers.

[5] The term "old left" is admittedly cumbersome, but it reminds us that these parties favor economic policies that are typically more statist than left parties in other regions.

Low Polarization = Greater certainty of reform pace = more inv.

facing little opposition from old-left factions can introduce rapid economic and institutional reforms across a wide range of policies that provide benefits for new-economy interests, including younger and more highly skilled workers, the new private sector, competitive firms, and urban dwellers. Old-left executives facing little opposition from right factions can introduce more gradual economic and institutional reforms across a range of policies that aim to protect old-economy interests, including older, less skilled workers, firms in the state-owned sector, and rural dwellers. Centrist executives can introduce reforms at a moderate pace. As the government is unlikely to be replaced by a successor with very different preferences over policy, producers can invest with little concern that policy will be reversed. In turn, the government can tax this investment and use the revenue to buy political support from other groups, such as the dependent sector of the population. Here, the creation of markets and state regulatory institutions proceed hand in hand.

But as polarization increases in a democracy, executives have a much more difficult time conducting economic and institutional reform. Where the opposition in parliament is large and favors an economic strategy far different from that of the executive, uncertainty about the stability of future policy is likely to reign. Producers may reasonably expect challengers to take power, perhaps even before the government serves its full term. New-economy interests that would benefit from rapid reforms under a right government and old-economic interests that would benefit from gradual reforms under an old-left government will be reluctant to invest because they anticipate that current policies are likely to be reversed. This expected investment shortfall leaves incumbents with a smaller tax base and less revenue to pay social groups that are dependent on the state, such as pensioners, budget workers, and the unemployed.

With less revenue to buy political support, politicians in more polarized democracies have stronger incentives to subvert reform either by slowing economic and institutional reforms or by conducting inconsistent reforms that deliver benefits to producer groups at the expense of the dependent sector of the population. Inconsistent reforms, in the form of rapid privatization combined with weak state institutions, targeted tax breaks, and below-market privatizations generate rents for producers and allow incumbents to buy the votes of new- and old-economy interests even as they deliver few benefits to the dependent sector. In a democracy, the degree to which politicians subvert economic and institutional reforms depends on the extent of polarization as higher levels of polarization move policy away from the government's preferred policy of consistent reform. The distortions inherent in slower and less consistent reform provide political benefits in the short run but weaker economic performance in the long run when compared to more consistent reform. In this setting, state building and market building work at cross-purposes as politicians weaken state institutions to provide benefits to producers in the old and new economies.

Finally, consider policy making in an autocracy. Regardless of the level of polarization, autocrats have more difficulty generating a robust response to reforms from producers because executives face fewer institutional constraints on changing policy than do their democratic counterparts.[6] Once a producer invests in an autocracy, the incumbent government has stronger incentives to seize the investment by changing policy opportunistically. Anticipating this policy change, producers will be more reluctant to invest and government revenue will fall. In hopes of retaining office, right (old-left) incumbents in autocracies will tend to favor inconsistent rapid (gradual) reform strategies that deliver rents to producers at the expense of the dependent sector.

The interplay of democratic institutions and political polarization yields several propositions about policy making. We should find that, other things being equal:

1. Democracies conduct faster and more consistent economic and institutional reforms and have higher transfer payments when polarization is absent.
2. Polarization reduces the positive impact of democracy on the pace and consistency of economic and institutional reform and on the size of transfer payments.
3. Autocracies conduct slower and less consistent economic and institutional reforms and have lower transfer payments than democracies when polarization is low.

Take, for example, Russia in the early 1990s. A right president, the stridently anticommunist Boris Yeltsin held office in a relatively democratic and highly polarized environment. Here we find an inconsistent mix of rapid economic reforms in some policy areas, such as extensive privatization, but also weak state regulatory institutions, tax breaks for well-connected firms, and minimal transfers to the dependent sector.

Similarly, consider Bulgaria in 1995. The old-left Bulgarian Socialist Party held a plurality of seats in parliament but faced strong opposition from the right-wing Union of Democratic Forces. In this highly polarized and democratic setting with an old-left executive, we find inconsistent gradual reforms, including slow privatization, tax breaks for state-owned and privatized firms, weak state institutions, and low transfers to the dependent sector.

In contrast, where political polarization is low in a democracy, firms have stronger incentives to invest, which allows politicians to collect more tax revenue on this investment and buy political support from the dependent sector using transfers. Poland in the early 1990s illustrates this logic. A right government made policy under conditions of low polarization as the successor to the Communist Party in Poland had transformed itself into a social democratic party that favored a market economy with a generous welfare state (Ishiyama 1995; Kitschelt et al. 1999; Grzymala-Busse 2002). In this relatively

---

[6] The credibility of policy commitments varies in autocratic regimes (cf. Haber et al. 2003). Here the claim is that autocracies cannot rely on the same electoral dynamics as democratic incumbents to generate a credible commitment.

nonpolarized democracy led by a right executive, we find rapid and consistent economic and institutional reform, fewer tax breaks for state-owned and privatized firms, strong regulatory institutions, and generous transfer payments funded by a vibrant new private sector.

Finally, Uzbekistan began the transition led by an old-left executive in an autocratic environment. Here we observe an inconsistent mix of gradual economic reforms, tax breaks to state-owned firms, limited transfers to the dependent sector, and weak state regulatory institutions. In sum, elite partisanship, democracy, and political polarization have fairly predictable effects on policy choice. To assess these arguments, I use a variety of data from twenty-five postcommunist countries between 1990 and 2004, a survey of business elites in twenty-three countries conducted in 1999, and case studies from Bulgaria, Poland, Russia, and Uzbekistan.

One key concept in the argument is political polarization, which is measured by the distance on economic policy between the executive and the largest opposition party in parliament.[7] Where the largest opposition faction in parliament has many seats and holds economic policy preferences far different from the executive, polarization is deemed to be high. Political polarization may influence policy choice in at least two ways. It may impede reform by making it more difficult to create majorities in parliament in support of policy change (Haggard and Kaufman 1995; Murillo 2009). Indeed, political gridlock induced by polarization blocked policy change in several cases in this study, including Russia and Ukraine (Aslund and de Menil 2000). However, the evidence presented later in this book suggests that it is especially common for polarization to shape policy by heightening uncertainty over future policy in democracies. This problem is especially severe because democratic governments that serve their full term are the exceptions rather than the rule in the region.

Political polarization in the cases under study is associated with higher levels of income inequality, although it is difficult to identify whether political polarization is generating income inequality or vice versa. As we shall see, countries that experienced large increases in income inequality early in the 1990s remained highly polarized into the next millennium. This link between political polarization and economic inequality makes it tempting to argue, as others have, that economic inequality is the underlying source of policy instability (Alesina and Rodrik 1994; Boix 2003; Stasavage 2003; Acemoglu and Robinson 2006). This claim may have merit in the postcommunist cases, but it is difficult to document, given the scarcity of high-quality data on income inequality over time and across countries. Annual measures of political polarization are available for each country, but annual measures of income inequality

---

[7] Notice that political polarization refers to economic policy rather than polarization around other issues, such as ethnic relations, the structure of government, or regime type. Given that polarization is used in a variety of ways in the literature, I devote much of Chapter 2 to my use of the term.

are scarce. The argument focuses on political polarization as one determinant of policy choice, recognizing that income inequality may provide a social base for political polarization.

Explanations for policy choice that rely on political polarization and democracy face the common problems of endogeneity and reverse causation (cf. King et al. 1994; Persson and Tabellini 2005). That is, while political polarization and democracy may shape policy choices today, they also may be a reflection of past policy choices, which makes it difficult to identify relationships among democracy, polarization, and policy. This difficult problem is often swept under the rug. The cases under study have the fortunate feature that initial levels of political polarization and democracy are taken from the first postcommunist election that precedes the introduction of economic and institutional reform. The timing of elections in the postcommunist world ensures that at least initially polarization and democracy are driving choices of economic and institutional reform rather than vice versa. This is important given the possibility that economic reform choices may influence subsequent levels of political polarization – an issue I address in much more detail in Chapter 6.

Similarly, there are grounds to believe that the level of democracy is endogenous to the economic and institutional reforms under study (Acemoglu et al. 2001). Omitted variables, such as the quality of the decision-making process, may be correlated with both the level of democracy and the extent of institutional and economic reform. The main focus here, however, is on the conditional effects of democracy on economic and institutional reform. To the extent that the omitted variables and sources of endogeneity linking democracy and reform are at work in high-polarization and low-polarization environments, it should be possible to estimate the conditional impact of democracy on reform without bias (Denisova et al. 2009). In other words, while it is difficult to make strong claims about the direct impact of democracy on economic and institutional reform, we can be more confident in identifying whether the differences in reform outcomes between democracies with high and low levels of polarization are significant.[8]

Existing Explanations and the Broader Literature

This book builds upon but departs from existing literature in a number of ways. For example, it differs from many works by examining both economic and institutional reforms and their interplay with a single argument. Many studies have focused on a single economic or institutional reform, such as trade policy or regulatory policy. These studies have provided great insights into policy choice but may fail to capture how politicians make trade-offs

---

[8] In the long run, political polarization associated with high levels of income inequality may undermine democracy, which would raise additional endogeneity concerns. Here I am interested in shorter-run dynamics. Many countries have remained democratic with high levels of inequality or autocratic with low levels of inequality in the short run.

among these different types of reforms. Thus, they risk missing the central feature of postcommunist transformation: the simultaneous overhauling of economies and states. Those few studies that have examined the interplay of economic and institutional reform have tended to be normative and aimed at identifying the optimal sequence of reforms (cf. Mckinnon 1991).[9] In contrast, this study develops a positive argument that explores how politicians make choices over the absolute and relative speeds of economic and institutional reform. By reframing the object of study, this book aims to provide a more nuanced treatment of postcommunist transformation.

Democratic Institutions and Winners Take All

The argument aims to contribute to a number of debates on the sources of economic and institutional reform. To begin, it provides a slightly different take on the long-standing controversy over the relationship between democracy and reform. Reviewing economic reform efforts in Latin America in the 1970s and 1980s, some scholars pointed to the advantages of autocratic governments (Foxley 1983; Sheahan 1987: chap. 12). But others suggested that democracies and autocracies were simply too varied in their actual operation to have a systematic influence on policy outcomes (Haggard and Webb 1994; Haggard and Kaufman 1995). Entering the 1990s, few argued that authoritarian governments were better able to conduct reforms, but few also expressed confidence that democracies could do much better.

Indeed, early in the 1990s many scholars of postcommunism were pessimistic about the compatibility of democracy and economic reform. Offe (1991: 881) opined that "a market economy is set in motion only under predemocratic conditions. In order to promote it, democratic rights must be held back to allow for a healthy dose of original accumulation." Elster (1993) penned a chapter cheekily titled: "The Necessity and Impossibility of Simultaneous Political and Economic Reform." Jowitt (1992: 302–303) observed: "In Eastern Europe, the immediate political imperative is economic. Any successful response to this imperative is likely to take an authoritarian cast. Take a 'good case' for democratic capitalism, Czechoslovakia... It will take the type of liberal authoritarianism that existed in 19th century Western Europe" for reforms to succeed. Przeworski (1991) famously warned that rapid economic reforms under democratic conditions in Eastern Europe would lead to a pendulum swinging between populism and technocratic responses with each being equally ineffective.

The experience of the postcommunist world has led to a quite unexpected consensus that democracy has promoted economic and institutional reform (cf. EBRD 1999). Numerous works identify a positive correlation between democracy and reform, but scholars have had less success in identifying the

---

[9] Hellman (1998) and Schamis (1999) provide important exceptions that theorize trade-offs among institutional and economic reforms, while also providing evidence in support of their case.

mechanisms by which democracy contributes to this result. They have cited more frequent alternations in power, more competitive elections, more active civil society, and more robust political opposition as critical to economic and institutional reforms, but these scholars have reached little agreement (Hellman 1998; EBRD 1999; Frye and Mansfield 2004; Grzymala-Busse 2007; Hoff and Stiglitz 2008). Indeed, others raise the possibility that the correlation between democracy and economic reform is spurious and is driven by deeper causal factors (Kopstein and Reilly 2000; Darden and Grzymala-Busse 2007).

The most sophisticated argument on the relationship between democracy and reform in recent years comes from Hellman (1998), who observes that economic and institutional reforms not only produce short-term costs but also generate short-term gains to groups taking advantage of market imperfections generated during the transition. These short-term winners are well placed to use their political power to block further reform. It is the bankers cum mafiosi, enterprise managers, and corrupt bureaucrats whose gain in the short term jeopardizes economic reform in the longer term. These groups back some elements of economic and institutional reform that increase their access to rents, while opposing other elements of reform.[10] Often this policy mix includes support for rapid economic liberalization and privatization but opposition to institutional reforms that regulate the market and limit rents.

Hellman proposes the disciplining effects of coalition building and political competition as the key to constraining the short-term winners. Broad-based governing coalitions that include groups losing from reform provide a check on the winners and can prevent the latter from capturing the state. In addition, frequent, free, and fair elections can subject narrow interest groups of short-term winners to public scrutiny and compel them to take into account the interests of groups harmed by reform. Fragmented governments and robust democracy should be positively associated with economic and institutional reform.

Hellman's "winners take all" argument is one of the most important contributions of postcommunist studies to comparative political economy, but it offers little insight into why politicians introduce economic and institutional reforms. A lack of accountability may lead the short-term winners to exacerbate the inconsistency of reforms once policies are under way, but this argument does not tell us why politicians in some countries but not others introduce reforms in the first place. Absent an explanation for why politicians take the costly step of introducing reforms, the winners-take-all view becomes less compelling. The lack of an independent role for politicians in the theory suggests that this argument may be missing part of the story.

In addition, the winners-take-all account helps us understand why it is more difficult to capture the state in some settings rather than others, but it does not provide a positive argument about how reform proceeds when the state is not

---

[10] Sonin (2003) and Hoff and Stiglitz (2004) provide formal models that build on these insights. Bunce (1999b) also addresses these issues.

captured by short-term winners bent on distorting reforms. Initial reforms may not produce concentrated winners, but this does not mean that other groups will arise to advance painful reforms of economic and state institutions. More specifically, it is not clear what precisely is driving economic and institutional reform in the absence of state capture. The winners-take-all argument is better seen as an explanation for the dynamics of reform once introduced than an explanation for variation in the extent of reform.

These shortcomings appear to be related to the lack of attention in the argument to the preferences of political elites. The argument suggests that no matter the partisan hues of political elites, greater fragmentation of political power and political competition should lead to more durable constraints on political elites and more reform. However, whether the governing coalition is dominated by representatives of state-owned enterprises, labor, and agriculture or by manufacturers, exporters, and small businesses is likely to have considerable impact on the extent of economic and institutional reform.

More generally, arguments that trace policy choices to institutions alone, such as the level of democracy, generally make indeterminate predictions about policy outcomes. One can often surmise as many reasons why democracy would inhibit as promote economic and institutional reform. Democracy may foster reform because it increases accountability and transparency, but it may hinder reform by reducing the time horizons of political leaders or by requiring the agreement of narrow groups in the governing coalition whose preferences are at odds with economic and institutional reform. Without more precision, it is difficult to make unambiguous predictions about the relationship between democracy and reform.

This work suggests that the impact of democracy on economic and institutional reform is conditional on the extent of political polarization. When polarization is high in a more democratic setting, the likelihood of a swing in policy increases should the incumbent government cede power. This potential swing in policy tomorrow heightens incentives for incumbent politicians and firms to subvert economic reforms today. In contrast, executive turnover when political polarization is low is unlikely to produce swings in policy, given minimal differences in economic policy between rival factions. In this setting, producers can invest with confidence and incumbents can tax this investment to buy political support. In a nonpolarized democracy, the need to buy support from groups beyond the incumbent's core constituency can blunt incentives to change policy opportunistically. In sum, the argument aims to identify conditions under which democracy should have greater and lesser impacts on policy choice and thereby make more precise predictions about the relationship between democracy and reform.

States and Markets

This work also informs discussions of the interaction of state building and market building – a topic that has been a focus of comparative politics for decades and a special interest for scholars of postcommunism in recent years. Early in the transformation some argued that rapid economic reform would gut the state, leaving it too weak to protect property rights, provide public goods, and maintain generous transfers (Amsden et al. 1994; Przeworski et al. 1995). Ganev (2006: 14) vividly depicts this view: "At its core lies the contention that the problems afflicting post-communist states were caused by the policies of the newly empowered reformers . . . who proceeded to 'dismantle' the state in order to open room for 'markets.' . . . In sum, the state was weakened because this is what local neoliberal zealots and their international capitalist mentors wanted." According to this school of thought, rapid economic reforms were expected to weaken the state and to work at cross-purposes with state building.

Others, however, argued that this school had it backwards. It was precisely the absence of economic liberalization that posed the greatest threat to the integrity of postcommunist states (Sachs 1993; Aslund 1995, 2007a, b). Far from liberal economic politicians emasculating powerful state bureaucracies, it was the networks of officials with deep ties to the state and Communist Party bureaucracy who were most interested in a dysfunctional state. More generally, observers feared that entrenched economic bureaucracies, particularly industrial ministries and state planning agencies, would strangle markets in their infancy and therefore emphasized putting constraints on the "grabbing hand" of the state to prevent market failure (Lipton and Sachs 1990; Frye and Shleifer 1997; Shleifer and Vishny 1998). This body of work suggested that a strategic weakening of state economic bureaucracies was critical to building markets and suggested a tension between certain aspects of building states and markets.

But many quickly realized that for markets to flourish, reducing the role of the state economic bureaucracies on its own was insufficient. State institutions that provided minimal levels of public order, like courts, police, and central banks, needed to be strengthened. In addition, new institutions, such as anti-monopoly commissions and state bodies to regulate banks and stock markets, had to be created. The speed with which many state institutions failed (or were sabotaged) in some countries led to a concern that weak state institutions were incapable of underpinning markets and sparked a new stress on strengthening state regulatory institutions (cf. Sachs 1994b; Holmes 1996; Easter 2002, 2006). This view suggested that the processes of building states and markets were complementary.

This work identifies conditions under which politicians try to keep state institutions weak for political advantage and when they seek to strengthen state institutions to provide public goods, such as economic and institutional reform. State building and market building should go hand in hand when polarization is low and leaders are constrained by democracy. However, when polarization is high in democracies or in any autocracy, state building and market building work at cross-purposes. Weak state institutions are, in part, the result of conscious decisions by politicians and their supporters rather than solely a function of economic crisis, the policies of international financial institutions, or the desires of neoliberal politicians.

More generally, the argument attempts to endogenize "state capacity," at least as it relates to regulatory institutions. Many scholars cite weak state capacity as a source of various ills in the postcommunist region. In emphasizing the importance of dysfunctional states for economic and political outcomes, Holmes (1996: 50) observes: "The universal problem of postcommunism, which cuts across the enormous variety of countries involved, is the crisis of governability." This insight was especially helpful at the time as scholars' attention was focused elsewhere, but it is also easily taken too far. The weak state argument implies that state capacity is exogenous and beyond the ability of politicians to change. But not all states in the region are equally dysfunctional and not all politicians are powerless to change the capacity of state institutions. Some politicians and their constituencies have gutted the state for personal enrichment, while others have exerted considerable effort to bolster state capacity. What we need are arguments that identify the incentives facing politicians to strengthen and weaken state institutions.

Partisanship

In recent years, the impact of elite partisanship on the politics of reform has been a subject of increased attention. The conventional wisdom of the politics of reform suggests that the value of partisan elites committed to economic reform because of economic liberalization leads to large gains dispersed throughout society in the future but imposes social costs that are large, concentrated, and immediate (Przeworski 1991; Nelson 1993; Williamson 1994). To ride out the reaction of groups losing from reform in the short run requires elites with a strong partisan commitment to economic liberalization. Studies from Latin America produce rather mixed results on the extent to which partisanship shapes economic policy outcomes (cf. Stokes 1996, 2007; Remmer 2002; Murillo 2009). In the postcommunist world, Aslund et al. (1996) and Fish (1998) show that in countries where more liberal parties won the first postcommunist election, economic liberalization in the early to mid-1990s was faster. Pop-Eleches (2009) finds that government partisanship in the region influences macroeconomic policy, but not during economic crises, while Horowitz and Browne (2008) find that party systems dominated by ideologically moderate parties conduct extensive reform.

However, other arguments suggest that partisanship is likely to be a weak guide to policy in the cases at hand. Postcommunist politicians chose policies during a period of heightened globalization, which many believe diminishes the impact of partisanship on policy. The need to attract foreign investment and to satisfy international financial institutions compels governments of all partisan hues to pursue similar policies if only through a process of competitive emulation (Kurzer 1993; Simmons 1999; Weyland 2005). In addition, the complete collapse of the Soviet model of economic development only reinforced the hegemony of neoliberal economic ideas and made deviations from economic orthodoxy more difficult (Williamson 1994; Appel 2004). Others have suggested that when politics are dominated by patronage rather than partisanship, the power of patron-client relations will tend to override the ideological orientation of the government as a determinant of policy (Stokes 2007). This characterization appears to fit the postcommunist cases well (Hale 2006: 4–5). Most importantly, scholars have tended to downplay the impact of elite partisanship in policy choice because partisan identities are thought to be weak, malleable, and in flux.[11] Scholars regularly point to the rapid appearance and disappearance of parties that are little more than vehicles for individual elites (cf. Zielinski 2002). Yet arguments about the malleability of partisan identities may be too narrowly focused on individual parties rather than on broader groups of parties. Certainly, political elites changed parties often in many countries, but, as I argue later, they rarely move across three broad partisan camps, and their economic policies can be readily characterized as old left, centrist, or right.

One reason why scholars may underestimate the importance of the partisanship of the executive is that its impact is often mediated by power relations or by institutions. Incumbents of a similar partisan bent may choose different policies depending on the nature of the opposition or on the quality of democracy. If this is the case, then explanations relying solely on elite partisanship may be misleading.

Recognizing this possibility, this book places partisan elites at the center of the argument but also analyzes how institutions and power relations shape policy choice. The argument aims to add to the literature on the partisan politics of economic and institutional reform by making policy choices endogenous to the partisanship of the executive, levels of political polarization, and the extent of democracy. It builds on the insights of the literature on credible commitment and partisan politics (North and Weingast 1989; Persson and Tabellini 1994; Alesina and Rosenthal 1995; Weingast 1997) and clarifies the political trade-off between rewarding producer groups in the old and new economies and granting benefits to the dependent population. It suggests that inconsistent reforms, such as rapid privatization in combination with weak corporate governance institutions, are not the result of mistaken policies, corruption, or a lack of accountability. Instead, these policies are part and parcel of attempts to retain office in polarized democracies. Like all politicians, incumbents in postcommunist democracies trade economic benefits for political support, but they strike worse bargains than their counterparts in less polarized democracies.[12]

The argument can also help account for the puzzling coexistence of rapid reform and generous welfare states in the postcommunist region. Indeed, in democracies with little polarization, it is the rapid expansion of market forces

---

[11] See Hale (2006: 4–6) for a good discussion of this issue among observers of Russia.

[12] Rather than criticizing inconsistent reforms as inefficient, this view implies that inconsistent reforms can be seen as a "second-best" economic strategy induced by political considerations.

that allows politicians to pursue their preferred policies by decreasing their political reliance on groups bent on distorting economic reforms. Rather than cutting transfers to free up the market, it is the transfers to the dependent sector that allow politicians to introduce more extensive economic and institutional reforms. The argument leads to the intuition that burgeoning new private sectors and generous transfer payments to pensioners and unemployed should go hand in hand. These insights fit uneasily with neoliberal policy recommendations that emphasize cutting state spending in order to free up the market (Williamson 1994). It also departs from works in the Polanyian tradition that attribute generous transfers and vigorous markets to popular demand for social insurance against heightened economic volatility (Polanyi 1944; Rodrik 1998). Here it is strategic politicians rather than popular revolts that account for generous welfare states and rapid reform.

Initial Conditions, Increasing Returns, and the Lure of Europe

Scholars have also debated how initial structural conditions influence economic and institutional reform. Strong versions of the argument in the postcommunist countries suggest that events and policy choices after 1989 had only marginal impacts on reform outcomes. Scholars point to geography, the European Union, institutional legacies, and resource endowments as central to economic and institutional reform. Przeworski (1991: 190) observes: "The main reason to hope that Eastern Europe will escape the politics, economics, and culture of poor capitalism, and that it will soon join the West, is geography." One version of this argument claims that proximity to Western Europe strengthens norms of behavior that are conducive to reform (Kopstein and Reilly 2000). Another suggests that countries located near Western Europe have greater chances of joining the European Union (EU) (Roland 2000; Mattli and Plumper 2002; Vachudova 2005). Certainly, the EU has loomed large in policy making in the region, given the prospect of wealth transfers, policy advice, and the guarantee that political and economic reforms would be difficult to reverse (Vachudova 2005; Grzymala-Busse 2007). Thus, many argue that the prospect of EU accession pushed postcommunist countries to pursue economic and institutional reform.

Others, however, are more skeptical. One difficulty is identifying the direction of causation. Economies close to Brussels may have performed well for reasons having little to do with potential EU membership, and this good economic performance may have made them more attractive candidates to the EU.[13] EU member countries vigorously debated the merits of expansion until at least the mid-1990s. One senior commission official in the mid-1990s noted "the EU's current level of seriousness about enlargement is not minimal; it

---

[13] Imagine a hypothetical situation in which economic reform in Eastern Europe went awry early in the 1990s. Would the EU have been as welcoming had the economies of these countries been less robust in the mid-1990s?

simply does not exist" (Mattli and Plumper 2002: 551). Moreover, member countries disagreed about which countries would qualify as potential members, suggesting that it would be difficult for potential members to identify themselves. Mattli and Plumper (2002: 550–551) use the example of EU economic cooperation agreements with Ukraine, Russia, and Belarus to argue that "the boundaries of an enlarged EU were not clearly drawn in the minds of the EU leaders during the first half of the 1990s. It is thus difficult to argue that the submission of EU membership applications by some Central and Eastern European countries (CEECs) during those years were motivated primarily by a clear understanding of what countries the EU would deem acceptable. Further, even though the EU had signed various types of economic cooperation agreements with the CEEC's, it was careful not to encourage those countries to push for membership."

Similarly, in her study of regulatory reform in eleven East European democracies, Grzymala-Busse (2007: 89) notes that "while the EU demands were extensive and nonnegotiable, they do not account for the patterns of institutional adoption. The pressures exerted by the European Union came too late, and too inconsistently, to explain observed variation. The EU did little to influence developments directly prior to 1997." Surely, causality is running in both directions, and divining the relative importance of the "push" for EU membership from new members and the "pull" of support from old members is tricky. The role of the EU in shaping policy choices is certainly an important part of the transformation of the postcommunist world, but identifying the magnitude of its impact is difficult.[14]

Scholars have pointed to other initial conditions as well to account for reform outcomes. Here initial conditions are broadly conceived to include structural factors, including country wealth, resource endowments, geography, level of industrialization, and various distortions inherent in the command economy circa 1989.[15] Some argue that the countries of the former Soviet Union (FSU) were more autarkic, started their economic transitions later, and had far greater distortions in their economies and political systems than did their counterparts elsewhere in the region and therefore achieved less progress in economic and institutional reform (Hewett 1988; Kornai 1992; De Melo et al. 2001; Gaddy and Ickes 2002; Hoff and Stiglitz 2004; Gehlbach 2008). Others contend that natural resource riches inhibit reform by granting those who control access to these resources the political muscle to distort the economy to their own ends (Sachs and Warner 1995). Others posit that the level of poverty and inequality in the late 1980s depressed the level of economic and institutional reform in the 1990s (Jensen 2003). Still others link the paths of extrication of socialist regimes to their subsequent path of economic reform (Stark and Bruszt 1998).

[14] To use terminology from American football, the EU may be very helpful when countries are in the "red zone" near the goal line but is less important when teams are not in striking distance of the end zone.

[15] Like many others, I use the composite index created by De Melo et al. (1996) to measure initial conditions.

Finally, some argue that different experiences with state building in the interwar period shaped the economic prospects of countries in the postcommunist period (Kitschelt and Malesky 2000).

One question that has received less attention is whether the impact of initial conditions on reform outcomes increases or decreases over time. That is, should we view countries with bad initial conditions for conducting economic and institutional reform as suffering from a birth defect whose effects will persist? Or are these countries struck by a childhood disease that has a pronounced effect early in the transition, but whose impacts recede with time? If the former view is correct, then we should expect to find increasing divergence between countries with weak and strong initial conditions over time. This view suggests that a strong version of path dependence linking initial conditions to economic outcomes is at work in the cases under study. Alternatively, if the latter holds, then countries with bad initial conditions should lag at first but eventually come to look more like their initially better-endowed neighbors. This result suggests that path dependence is a rather weak constraint.

The impact of initial conditions on economic and institutional reform has potentially important implications for the study of institutional change and path dependence in comparative politics. Most prominently, theorists of the welfare state and economic development have devoted attention to whether institutional legacies have increasing or decreasing returns, but quantitative empirical tests of such claims are often difficult to conduct (cf. North 1990; Pierson 2004; Brooks 2008). In addition, others have suggested that positive feedback loops that indicate increasing returns are essential to the identification of "critical junctures" in political and economic development (Thelen 1999; Mahoney 2003). The view that initial structural conditions and initial policy choices have pushed countries onto different trajectories of reform is widely held in the literature on the postcommunist transformation, but the metaphor of path dependence is more often invoked than demonstrated (Page 2006). The postcommunist cases offer a good opportunity to assess broader claims about the relationship between initial conditions and institutional change, given that the transformation began at a roughly similar time across many countries and we have reasonable data to measure initial conditions and institutional outcomes.

Evidence on the impact of initial conditions over time is equivocal. Initial conditions, measured as a composite of structural features of each country at the start of the transformation, have a strong and direct impact on the pace and consistency of reform (De Melo et al. 2001). Countries with better initial conditions conducted more extensive and more consistent reform, but the impact of initial conditions on reform outcomes neither increases nor decreases over time. Thus, a simple form of path dependence in which initial conditions lead to divergence or convergence in reform outcomes across countries over time does not seem to be at work.

In contrast, there is evidence of decreasing returns to promising initial conditions on economic growth. Good initial conditions are associated with faster growth in the first year of transformation but are associated with slower growth rates over time. This result implies that strong versions of path dependence that lock countries into suboptimal paths of economic growth do not apply in the cases at hand. Moreover, it suggests a likely convergence in patterns of economic growth between countries with good and bad initial conditions. Certainly other forms of path dependence may be at play, but the importance of initial conditions as a constraint on economic growth appears to decline over time. By exploring how the impact of initial conditions varies over time, this book hopes to enrich our understanding of the influence of path dependence and history on policy outcomes. In addition, it offers a means to assess whether initial conditions shape policy outcomes over time in other countries and on other issues.

Causal Depth and Causal Mechanisms

Disentangling the impact of initial conditions on economic and institutional reforms has heightened interest in the role of causal depth and causal mechanisms in the postcommunist transformation and in theories of comparative politics more generally. On one hand, recent studies caution against attributing causation to temporally close factors that may be the result of deeper historical factors and suggest the value of exploring the origins of independent variables of interest to guard against simple forms of endogeneity (Kitschelt 2003; Darden and Grzymala-Busse 2007; Pop-Eleches 2007). On the other hand, others have emphasized the value of drawing tight causal links between independent and dependent variables and cited the danger of relying on historical causes that are loosely tethered to outcomes (cf. Elster 1983; Bates 1990).

This book takes these critiques seriously. Good explanations not only should have causal depth but should also draw tight links between variables of interest. Identifying the microfoundations of the argument is important because cross-national studies in comparative political economy typically rely on data collected at the national level, but theories often begin with assumptions about the behavior of individuals. The fit between the assumptions of behavior at the individual level and the data collected at the national level is rarely tested (Steenbergen and Jones 2002; Gelman and Hill 2007). Identifying a relationship between national-level variables, like political polarization, and national-level outcomes, like economic reform, is important but does not specify the causal mechanism between the two. To address this potential problem, I use survey data collected in 1999 from twenty-three postcommunist countries to show that businesspeople in highly polarized countries view policy as less stable; rate policy instability as a more severe obstacle for their business; and invest at lower rates than their counterparts in less polarized countries. This step shortens the causal chain between political polarization and economic outcomes by identifying a path by which polarization may influence economic reform.

Recognizing that polarization shapes policy leads one to ask, Why did some countries become polarized, while others did not? Answering this question could easily generate another book, and the argument here is speculative at best, but I begin by focusing on how nationalism is related to levels of polarization in the postcommunist period. More specifically, where ex-communist parties could claim a degree of sovereignty over foreign policy before 1989, they were better placed to use nationalism to rally popular support after 1989. In these settings, political polarization has been especially acute, as the ex-communist factions used nationalism to introduce a second dimension into politics and expand their base of support. Tracing the source of political polarization to institutional differences in the Soviet period increases the causal depth of the argument, but it also aims to allay concerns that economic reform may be driving political polarization rather than vice versa. To further examine the exogeneity of political polarization to economic and institutional reform, I turn to an instrumental variable analysis that uses the relation of the Communist Party to national sovereignty before 1989 to predict reform outcomes after 1989.

In addition, I use comparative case studies to examine the qualitative evidence in support of the argument. I focus on comparisons between countries that have much in common but vary in the political variables of interest. I trace how changes in political polarization, democracy, and executive partisanship in Bulgaria, Poland, Russia, and Uzbekistan influenced policy choices over time. By looking at a single country over time, I hold constant a range of factors that are commonly associated with variations in economic and institutional reform and isolate the impact of variables of interest. Bulgaria and Russia are especially informative because they vary considerably over time in their extent of polarization, partisanship, and democracy.

Data Issues

The theoretical and empirical issues raised thus far have been studied in a variety of settings from Latin America and Africa to East Asia and Europe, but the postcommunist cases provide a number of advantages for learning about the politics of reform. They have more diverse economic and political makeups than other regions. Governments range from highly democratic to highly authoritarian and span the ideological spectrum from staunch old-left politicians to Thatcherite economic liberals. In addition, economies range from the resource-rich petro-states of Turkmenistan and Azerbaijan to resource-poor states, like Armenia and Hungary. This range of variation permits insights into a number of debates that are difficult to assess in more-limited regional samples.

However, the region also controls for factors that often bedevil cross-national research. Because homogenization was a key ingredient of the Soviet rule, each country began the transition with relatively similar formal political and economic institutions. In addition, each country began the transition at roughly the same time. To be sure, significant differences existed across countries, and initial conditions shape policy choice. At the extreme, Kyrgyzstan circa 1990 was not Hungary circa 1990. Where these differences across countries are uncorrelated with the dependent variables of interest, they are not a cause for concern. Where they may be associated with the outcomes under study, the empirical tests try to take them into account.

The period under examination is relatively short. Studies of policy of Organisation for Economic Co-operation and Development (OECD) or Latin American countries can identify long-term trends and avoid being overly influenced by short-term factors. Observers of the postcommunist world have to make do with analyzing the experience of the past twenty years at most. Nonetheless, now is a good time to take stock. More than a half-dozen countries from the region joined the European Union (EU) in May 2004. Their membership in this exclusive club marks the end of one transformation and the beginning of another. Indeed, there are some advantages to focusing on just twenty-five countries over a relatively short period. The number of countries is sufficiently large to make comparisons but small enough to allow deep immersion in the secondary literature. A close reading of this scholarship can give greater confidence that concepts like political polarization, elite partisanship, and reform can be measured with more accuracy than is often the case in global datasets (Brady and Collier 2004).

This manuscript uses a variety of statistical tests but is designed to be accessible to readers with little knowledge of quantitative social science. Whenever possible, I begin with simple statistical tests that illustrate the results before moving on to slightly more sophisticated methods. With the goal of making the argument as accessible as possible, I present a broad range of evidence and tests. The use of multiple methods to assess the argument is particularly important. As is often the case in cross-national research, the problem of multicollinearity raises difficult issues of identification. Where two explanatory factors are highly correlated, it is often difficult to divine the relative importance of each. It is important to recognize that statistical analysis can help mitigate this problem but also faces real limits. Throughout the quantitative analysis, I point to instances where this type of collinearity might be problematic and how it may affect the results. In addition, statistical analysis is very good at identifying correlations between variables of interest, but it is also often less able to capture the process by which explanatory factors influence results. Here the case studies and survey evidence can complement the cross-national quantitative analyses by tracing how the variables of interest are related to policy outcomes. I draw the broad outlines of the argument in the cross-national statistical analyses and try to provide the fine details of the argument in the case studies.

1

The Political Logic of Economic and Institutional Reform

> The task I have set before the government is to make the reforms irreversible.
>
> President Boris Yeltsin, 1991, before the Russian Duma

> Finality is not the language of politics.
>
> Benjamin Disraeli, 1859, before the British House of Commons

Scholars often study the introduction of markets in the presence of functioning state institutions and frequently analyze the creation of state regulatory institutions in the presence of functioning markets, but the postcommunist cases offer the rare occasion to study the processes of creating markets and state regulatory institutions at the same time in real time. This chapter takes advantage of this opportunity and develops an argument that identifies how politicians make choices about economic and institutional reform. More specifically, it focuses on how partisan control of the government, the balance of partisan power, and the quality of democratic institutions affect the pace and consistency of economic and institutional reform. I begin by discussing the logic of the problem of credible commitment that underpins much of the analysis, before developing the argument.[1]

Credible commitment problems are inherent in economic and institutional reforms because they promise benefits in the future for changes in behavior today. Consider a government that announces a sweeping reduction on import tariffs. Given this change in policy, firms may want to enter the importing business. However, because the creation of a new business entails up-front costs and only the promise of future benefits, this decision creates risks. Should the businessperson invest the time and capital to create a new firm and policy change before the firm begins to generate revenue, she will suffer a loss.[2] The

---

[1] Here credibility refers to expectations about the future actions of strategic actors and expectations about future states of the world. See Deirmeier et al. (1997: 22–23).

[2] Workers also make decisions about the value of investing in new skills and likely take concerns about the credibility of government policy into consideration when making this decision.

critical issue for the businessperson is to calculate whether she believes that the government will continue current policy in the future.

More generally, businesspeople trying to evaluate the predictability of future policy have two concerns. First, they fear an "exogenous" policy reversal.[3] Consider a situation in which the incumbent favors low tariffs on imports but the largest opposition party does not. Should the opposition replace the current government, policy will swing sharply toward higher tariffs and businesspeople positioned to benefit from low tariffs will be reluctant to create a new firm in anticipation that policy will change dramatically in the future. These exogenous policy swings can occur for a variety of reasons: a negative shock to the economy such as a fall in international prices, the ill health of a leader, a foreign policy setback, or a government scandal. Where the primary challenger holds policy preferences that vary dramatically from that of the incumbent, it is reasonable to expect a sharp swing in policy should the government fall and the challenger take office. Governments in lower- and middle-income countries where political coalitions are often fragile and governments lack strong informal norms to resolve disputes among members are likely to be especially vulnerable to these swings in policy. This concern is certainly valid in the post-communist regions where democratic governments often fall before serving their full term. Moreover, even those governments that do serve a full term often face crises that put their survival in doubt and may lead producers to withhold investment.

Now consider an "endogenous" policy reversal, which is more insidious. The current government introduces a policy of low tariffs. In response, a producer decides whether or not to create a new firm that can turn a profit given the tariff policy promised by the government. After the firm has invested, however, it becomes vulnerable to a change in policy by the *current* government, which could increase the tariff rate to, say, 100 percent and essentially seize the new investment. If the producer expects the government to renege on its policy after it invests, it will be reluctant to create the new firm in the first place because the producer is better off not investing than losing its investment. The problem of credible commitment is not confined to tariff policy but is present in all policies that introduce immediate costs and only the promise of future gains for citizens and politicians, including privatization, price liberalization, and institutional reform.

Because governments are sovereign, they can change policy at any time. A revenue shortage, a change in political priorities, or simple opportunism by the leader can lead to a change in policy that effectively seizes private investment. But this flexibility comes at a cost. Absent confidence in the stability of policy over time, producers anticipate that the government policy will change and are reluctant to invest and engage in productive economic activity in the first

---

[3] Svensson (1998), Spiller and Tomassi (2003), Stasavage (2003), and others treat policy instability induced by polarization as exogenous and examine how polarization exacerbates the commitment problem.

place. This leaves the government with a smaller tax base and less revenue to provide public goods for society as a whole. The tragedy here is that even if the government is sincere in pursuing its policy of stable tariffs and producers can make an after-tax profit by creating a new firm, the latter will not invest if they do not expect the government to abide by its policy pledge.

This credibility problem leaves the producer vulnerable to ex post changes in policy but also leaves the incumbent government vulnerable because it receives less tax revenue from foregone investment. If incumbent politicians anticipate that producers are unlikely to invest and that they will have less tax revenue to buy the political support needed to stay in office, they may turn to other tools to buy political support, such as keeping regulatory institutions weak, providing tax breaks, or giving away state assets. These tools provide direct economic benefits to important political constituencies but do not require raising tax revenue. This is a common strategy in low- and middle-income countries but is an especially appealing course of action in the postcommunist world, given the exceedingly large state sectors bequeathed to incumbents and the weak institutional environment that marked the early years of the transition. Opportunities for diverting states' assets for partisan advantage were (arguably) far greater here than in other regions (Tarkowski 1989; Solnick 1998). In sum, integrating elite partisanship into the politics of reform highlights the dilemma of credible commitment.

Partisan Policies versus Convergence

It may seem obvious that politicians pursue policies that benefit their core constituents. However, scholars have made powerful claims that the logic of mobile capital so constrains politicians as to swamp any preferences for partisan policies. Extrapolating from Lindblom (1977), many argue that the logic of economic competition in a global market for capital induces politicians to converge on roughly similar policies that are friendly to the holders of mobile assets, particularly mobile capital (cf. Kurzer 1993). Should politicians stray too far from market-friendly policies by raising taxes on capital too high or by failing to provide public goods essential for markets, holders of mobile assets will "vote with their feet" by taking their capital abroad to the detriment of the local economy (Strange 1996). Facing the threat of the exit of capital and declining economic performance on their watch, politicians may avoid partisan politics and pursue similar promarket policies, regardless of their partisan convictions. These pressures may be especially strong in the postcommunist region where autarky ruled for the last half century, economies are price takers, and countries began the transformation woefully unprepared for global economic competition.[4]

---

[4] In her study of Latin American countries, Remmer (2002: 30) notes: "While it might be presumed that international economic constraints are more likely to overwhelm domestic political factors

A similar argument suggests that robust political competition encourages politicians of all partisan stripes to converge on policies that appeal to the median voter (Black 1958). In competitive political systems with free entry of parties and a normal distribution of voter preferences, politicians who stray from the median voter lose support. As most votes are found in the center of the voter distribution, politicians who play to partisan interests lose ground to more moderate rivals. Thus, in "first past the post" elections, candidates are likely to converge on similar policies that cater to the median voter.[5] This argument has been qualified as scholars have found that bargaining within coalitions, the presence of party activists, limits on the free entry of parties, and high uncertainty may lead politicians to favor partisan policies (Aldrich 1983; Alesina and Rosenthal 1995). In general, though, the logical power of the median voter theorem makes it a common assumption in theories of political economy.

In addition, others argue that the 1980s and 1990s were marked by a neoliberal convergence on economic policies (Williamson 1994; Appel 2004). In this view, the consensus among international financial organizations, technocrats, and policy advisers holds that an orthodox reform strategy of rapid liberalization, economic openness, and privatization further reduced the scope for policy differences among competing political groups. The leverage of this neoliberal othodoxy was thought to be particularly strong in the developing world and the countries in transition from a command economy (Stallings 1992; Amsden et al. 1994; Stone 2002).

Partisan Strategies in Transition Economies

Yet partisan concerns are likely to be especially potent in transition countries in part because the assumptions underlying convergence arguments are more tenuous in this setting. For example, the compressed time frame of transition politics makes partisan strategies especially attractive. Garrett (1998: 7) notes that "the short-term nature of democratic politics creates a bias in favor of distributional strategies. Governments cannot afford to do what is good for the economy if this immediately hurts their core constituencies." The same logic holds for autocratic regimes as well.[6] This seems particularly clear for the postcommunist cases, where the average time between elections for the executive is just two and a half years.[7] Upon taking his position in President

---

outside the North Atlantic Basin, the limitations of existing research make it difficult to offer definitive answers to such questions."

[5] To some extent, nondemocratic regimes in which elites face competition from rivals from other factions may face a similar dynamic (Frye and Mansfield 2003).

[6] If all politicians had sufficiently long time horizons, they would likely converge on efficient policies that promote growth. They would then redistribute enough of the surplus to their supporters to retain office, while reserving the rest for themselves. This luxury is unavailable in the transition economies where short-term politics dominate.

[7] Even if highly autocratic governments with Freedom House scores greater than 5 are excluded, this figure is largely unchanged (2.58 versus 2.47).

Yeltsin's cabinet in late 1991, economic adviser Yegor Gaidar deemed his cabinet a "kamikaze government." In a similar vein, Sachs (1994a: 503) deemed policy making in Poland in the year of shock therapy as "life in the economic emergency room."

Partisan politics are also likely to predominate because of the weak organization of political parties in the transition countries (Alesina and Rosenthal 1995). Credible promises to pursue convergence policies that benefit median voters upon assuming office depend on relatively strong party organizations that punish politicians for deviating from their preelection pledges. Members of well-organized parties have an incentive to police party elites and ensure they fulfill their campaign promises. Doing so helps to protect the party's brand name and to ensure donors that the party's promises are meaningful. In contrast, a politician who is a member of an organizationally weak party whose members are unconcerned about the party's long-term reputation have little incentive to punish candidates for pursuing policies that provide short-term benefits to partisans but tarnish the long-term image of the party as economic managers.[8] Thus, voters depend on strong parties to police their members from straying too far from efficient policies. Alesina and Rosenthal (1995: 18) note "the lack of credibility of campaign promises greatly reinforces the tendency to diverge in a two-party election."

In transition economies, political parties have generally been too weak as organizations to discipline politicians who promote partisan politics. While citizen attachments to broad groups of party families have been relatively high and voters have tended to cast their ballots for similar types of parties, these ties have not translated into strong party organizations (Kitschelt et al. 1999; Fidrmuc 2000, 2003; Colton 2000; Brader and Tucker 2001; Tucker 2006; Hale 2006). With the exception of the ex-communists in some countries, parties in the region have had difficulty generating a reputation that compels individual party officials to sacrifice in defense of the party's collective brand name. As parties can rarely credibly threaten to punish individual elites who favor partisan over convergent policies, voters will expect politicians to favor partisan strategies.[9]

Finally, partisan politics are likely to predominate where the effects of policy are uncertain. Incumbent politicians who are unclear about the consequences of economic policy are likely to favor policies that coincide with their partisan bent. Take an old-left politician whose base lies in the agricultural and import-competing sectors – groups likely to lose from a rapid expansion of market forces. Given conflicting advice about whether a gradual or rapid reform will provide the greatest boost to the economy as a whole, he will likely choose the option that provides greater partisan advantage. Again, this description fits the postcommunist cases, particularly in the early 1990s where the most efficient

---

[8] See Deirmeier et al. (1997) for details.
[9] Wernke (2001) provides evidence that policy switches in the postcommunist world have been rare.

path from a command economy was hotly debated. Roland (2000: 12) notes that "even if there is a clear goal of transition, there is no accepted theory of how to get there." Lacking clear guidelines about which policies will produce the greatest collective benefits, the lure of partisan politics is likely to be strong. In sum, the conditions supporting convergence in policy between competing factions appear less powerful in the postcommunist setting than elsewhere.

In certain respects it should not be too surprising to find that partisan effects dominate pressures to converge to the median voter in the cases at hand. Partisan effects on different policies have been found in a wide variety of geographic and institutional settings from the United States (Alesina and Rosenthal 1995; Bartels 2008) to Latin America (Remmer 2002; Murillo 2009) to Europe (Boix 1998; Garrett 1998; Bearce 2007). Moreover, the transition environment may heighten the impact of elite partisanship. Politicians everywhere must balance efficiency and partisan concerns, but the latter are likely to be especially attractive in a transition economy.

Previewing the Argument

To preview the argument, I assume that politicians and citizens exchange transfers and rents for political support.[10] To pay for transfers, which take the form of cash payments, politicians must raise tax revenue. To generate rents, politicians use inconsistent reforms that typically do not require raising tax revenue. The terms of the exchange between politicians and citizens, however, vary depending on executive partisanship, political polarization, and the quality of democracy. To be more precise, other things being equal, we should find not only that democracies conduct more rapid and consistent reforms when polarization is absent but also that each increment of polarization reduces the positive impact of democracy on reform and also reduces transfer payments to the dependent sector of the population.

Assume a polity of three groups. First are old-economy interests that will be harmed by market-oriented reforms, including rural residents, unskilled workers, managers and workers in uncompetitive economic sectors, and state bureaucrats in planning agencies and ministries responsible for economic production. They are represented by old-left factions. Second are new-economy groups that will gain from economic and institutional reforms. They include urban residents, skilled workers, managers and workers in competitive sectors, and the young and are represented by a right faction. Finally, the dependent sector of the population includes the unemployed, pensioners, and state bureaucrats outside planning agencies and ministries responsible for

---

[10] Here I build on the work of Kapstein and Milanovic (2000), who identify a trade-off facing incumbents between providing benefits via privatization to managers and workers and providing cash transfers to pensioners and budget-sector workers. I add to their model by introducing time-inconsistency and partisan effects.

production. Because they live solely off transfer payments from the state,[11] members of this group are indifferent toward economic strategy as long as it provides sufficient revenue to deliver generous transfer payments. The dependent population is represented by centrist factions.

Policy making proceeds in the following fashion. Nature chooses a government, which in turn chooses a reform strategy, which determines the pace and consistency of institutional and economic reform. New- and old-economy interests decide whether to risk their capital and effort by making an investment specific to the reform strategy. With some exogenously determined probability, the government falls and is replaced in the next stage by the largest challenger faction in parliament. If the government stays in power, it decides whether to reverse policy by seizing the investment or to respect its initial reform strategy. If the government respects its policy, the producers reap their investment, and the dependent sector receives its transfer. After the commitment game is played in an autocracy, no votes are held. But in a democracy, the three groups vote, and the incumbent is returned to power if he receives the votes of two groups.[12] No group by itself constitutes a majority, but any combination of two of the three groups does so.[13]

Preferences and Policy Making under Democracy

First, consider the preferences over outcomes of policy makers, producers, and the dependent sector. The argument begins with the assumption that executives seek to maximize revenue for themselves and their supporters, contingent on remaining in office. Ideally, incumbent executives would like to entice producers to invest and then change policy opportunistically to seize this investment, but absent a credible commitment that policy will not change in the future, executives will be unable to generate investment in the first place. As a second best, executives prefer a consistent reform in line with their partisan interests that benefits their core constituents but raises sufficient revenue to buy political support from the dependent sector.[14] Under consistent reform, partisan executives pursue economic policies that are in line with the interests of

---

[11] State bureaucrats in planning and production ministries under the command economy are treated as old-economy interests because their positions will be dramatically reduced in a market economy, whereas state bureaucrats in other sectors, including the police, military, welfare agencies, and courts, are treated as the dependent sector.

[12] Later in the chapter I consider the effects of holding elections before the delivery of the transfer.

[13] Kapstein and Milanovic (2000: 4) suggest the plausibility of this distribution of preferences. They note that "pensioners represent 20–25 percent of the population in transition economies; employees in the budget sphere represent another 10 percent. Workers and managers in nonagricultural state-owned enterprises are, at the beginning of the transition, 30–40 percent of the population."

[14] One could easily add that incumbents and their producers share revenues obtained above the level needed to satisfy the dependent sector.

their core constituencies. Right executives favor policies of rapid economic and institutional reform that promise greater benefits to new-economy interests; old-left executives favor gradual economic and institutional reforms that favor old-economy interests. Centrist executives pursue both types of reform at a moderate rate.

If incumbents are unable to seize investment, or promote a consistent reform that reflects their supporters' interests, a third-best outcome is inconsistent reform that provides rents to producers in their core constituency and to producers in the challenger camp. Here inconsistent reforms include rapid privatization with weak governing institutions, targeted tax breaks, and below-market price privatizations. This strategy gains the support of old- and new-economy producers in the short run but at the expense of support for the dependent sector. Politicians prefer a consistent to an inconsistent reform, as the former raises more investment and tax revenue for the state than the latter. Moreover, inconsistent reform provides weaker incentives for producers to invest, and with less investment, economic performance suffers, which over time will reduce support for the incumbent. In the short run, however, inconsistent reforms can help buy political support on the cheap without having to raise tax revenue.

Finally, the worst outcome for the incumbent is to take the risky step of pursuing consistent economic and institutional reforms but to receive little investment from their core producers (and hence revenue to buy support from the dependent sector). Without votes from either the dependent sector or the challenger producers, the incumbent risks losing office. Thus, the incumbent prefers, in descending order, seizing investment, consistent reform,[15] inconsistent reform, and no investment.

In contrast, the first preference of producers is to receive rents in the form of inconsistent reforms, including privatization under weak corporate governance, selected tax breaks, and below-market privatizations. Inconsistent reforms allow producers in the old and new economies to gain revenue without having to assume the risks associated with investment. As a second-best outcome, producers prefer that executives pursue consistent reform policies in line with their interests that allow them to gain a return on their investment. New-economy producers prefer rapid and consistent institutional and economic reforms that allow them to take full advantage of their skills and assets, while old-economy producers prefer more gradual and consistent economic and institutional reforms that cushion the transition to a market economy. A third-best outcome for the producer is to be in the opposition because the incumbent government will propose a strategy that offers much lower returns on investment. New-economy producers will invest less under a gradual and consistent economic reform, whereas old-economy interests will invest less under a rapid and consistent economic and institutional reform. Finally, producers prefer not

---

[15] That is, consistent reform in line with his partisan preferences. So a right executive would prefer a rapid consistent reform, an old-left executive would pursue a gradual consistent reform, and a centrist executive would pursue a moderate consistent reform.

investing to the worst outcome of risking their capital and effort, only to lose this investment because of a swing in policy. Thus, producers favor, in descending order, inconsistent reform, consistent reform,[16] no investment, and seizing investment.

The dependent sector, including state workers outside the economic and planning ministries, pensioners, and the unemployed are indifferent as to whether reform is gradual or rapid because it relies solely on transfers from the state. The dependent sector prefers a consistent economic and institutional reform that generates more tax revenue and larger transfers to an inconsistent reform that provides much lower transfers.[17] Thus, recipients of transfers favor consistent reform over inconsistent reform, seizing investment, or no investment.

To retain office in a democracy, incumbents must find political support from their core supporters and one other group: either the dependent sector or "challenger" producer interests. To gain the political support of the dependent sector, executives must find revenue to pay for transfers, and they do so by taxing the economically active sections of the population, including new- and old-economy interests.[18] When polarization is low, incumbents can pursue a consistent economic and institutional reform confident that the producers will respond vigorously and generate tax revenue to provide transfers to the dependent sector.

Incumbents in a polarized democracy and autocracies face a much more difficult task. A consistent economic and institutional reform will produce only a weak response from producers who fear that a swing in policy before the election will threaten their investment. With less investment from firms, incumbents will lack the revenue to pay for transfers to the dependent sector of the population. They can, however, try to stay in power by using slower and less consistent reforms to deliver rents to their core constituents and to challenge producer

[16] The producer prefers a consistent reform in line with its partisan interest over a consistent reform not in line with its partisan interest.

[17] The size of the transfer needed for the dependent sector to vote for the incumbent can be determined in several ways. Here I simply assume that if one producer group invests in a consistent reform, the tax revenue generated by this investment produces sufficient revenue to buy the support of the dependent sector, and the after-tax profits to the producer from investing remain positive. In the model in the Appendix 1.1, one could relax the assumption that each group is a unitary actor, which would allow one to assume that support for the incumbent from the dependent sector is increasing in the number of investors in the old and new economies. In both cases, transfers are increasing in the size of investment and decreasing in the level of polarization.

[18] This work does not address tax policy directly. For excellent works on this issue from the postcommunist region, see Easter (2002, 2006) and Gehlbach (2008). Gehlbach tackles a different type of credible commitment problem. He argues that firms and the state face a commitment problem in their exchange of tax revenue for political support and it is the inability of firms that can hide taxes easily to convince state actors that they are paying their share that undermines commitment. In his argument firms that can hide taxes easily receive fewer public goods. This result dovetails nicely with the argument made here in which core producers pay taxes and receive favorable policies.

interests at the expense of the dependent sector of the population.[19] This inconsistent reform strategy trades off political benefits today for better economic performance in the future. Incumbents use inconsistent reform to gain the support of old- and new-economy interests, but this strategy provides weak incentives to engage in the types of activity that promote longer-term economic growth. This strategy may be especially attractive in a postcommunist setting, given the size of the rents available to incumbent politicians at the start of the transformation.

Policy Making in a Democracy with Low Polarization

In a democratic political system in which polarization is low, the likelihood of a far-reaching swing in policy is negligible, because all major political factions have roughly similar preferences over policy. Right governments can pursue a consistent liberal strategy of rapid economic and institutional reforms and new- and old-economy producers can invest their time and effort to take full advantage of the reform policy. The government can then tax this economic activity and use the revenue to buy enough political support from the dependent sector of the population to increase its chances of staying in office.

When polarization is low, right executives can rely on revenue from investments by new- and old-economy interests to support dependent populations and thereby avoid having to use inconsistent reforms to buy political support. Somewhat surprisingly, this strategy generates generous payments to the dependent sector because of a robust new private sector. As depicted in the upper-left panel of Table 1.1, the strategy yields policy that benefits a coalition of interests from the new economy with support from the dependent sector at the expense of old-economy interests.

Similarly, old-left governments in a low-polarization democracy can pursue a consistent strategy of gradual economic and institutional reform policies as depicted in the lower-left panel of Table 1.1. Old- and new-economy producers can choose an investment profile specific to a gradual reform, confident that reforms will not be reversed. The government can expect to earn greater revenue from firms that depend on a predictable investment environment. By conducting a gradual reform that gains the support of old-economy interests and by keeping transfers high enough to win the support of the dependent population, old-left incumbents in a nonpolarized democracy can increase their hopes of retaining power.[20]

---

[19] Here I assume that the preference of a centrist government is to support the dependent sector and ally with the new private sector to promote a moderate pace of economic and institutional reform. This can be justified theoretically as rapid economic and institutional reform may bring greater benefits than more gradual reform, given its higher powered incentives for producers. When faced with high polarization, however, centrist governments will use inconsistent reforms to stay in power, even as this strategy undercuts the dependent sector.

[20] Old-left governments that are highly democratic and have little polarization are very rare in the sample. Of the twenty-seven old-left democracies in the sample, only five have polarization scores of zero.

TABLE I.I. *Economic and Institutional Reform in a Democracy*

	Low Polarization	High Polarization
Right executive	Consistent liberalism • Rapid economic and institutional reform • Consistent economic and institutional reform • High transfers New economy/dependent sector coalition	Inconsistent liberalism • Rapid economic and institutional reform • Inconsistent economic and institutional reform • Low transfers New economy/old economy coalition
Centrist executive	Consistent social market • Moderate economic and institutional reform • Consistent economic and institutional reform • High transfers New economy/dependent sector coalition	Inconsistent social market • Moderate economic and institutional reform • Inconsistent economic and institutional reform • Low transfers New economy/old economy coalition
Old-left executive	Consistent gradualism • Gradual economic and institutional reform • Consistent economic and institutional reform • High transfers Old economy/dependent sector sector coalition	Inconsistent gradualism • Gradual economic and institutional reform • Inconsistent economic and institutional reform • Low transfers Old economy/new economy coalition

This logic is similar for a centrist incumbent in a democracy when polarization is low as depicted in the middle-left panel of Table 1.1. Centrist executives likely face little polarization, given their policy preferences of relatively liberal markets combined with generous social welfare policies. Indeed, given their past association with the ex-Communist Party in some cases, they may have even stronger incentives to signal their reformist credentials by pursuing extensive economic and institutional reforms. Thus, we should expect consistent economic and institutional reforms across a broad range of policies proceeding at a moderate pace, a predictable policy environment that encourages economic activity, and a generous social welfare policy. Here a coalition of new-economy interests with support from the dependent sector of the population makes policy that can help return a centrist executive to power.

Most importantly, when polarization is low and incumbents make policy in a democratic setting, the processes of state building and market building reinforce each other. Incumbents have little incentive to buy political support from producer interests by granting tax breaks, conducting below-market privatizations, or weakening state regulatory institutions, because doing so will only reduce the revenue needed to buy the support of the dependent sector. By pursuing a consistent economic reform that reflects their partisan interests but also builds state institutions, incumbents can increase their chances of retaining power without jeopardizing economic performance. In this setting, the process of building states and markets goes hand in hand.

Policy Making in a Democracy with High Polarization

In contrast, consider a right executive in a democratic setting facing high levels of polarization. The government decides whether to pursue a rapid and consistent reform across all dimensions or to pursue an inconsistent reform that includes rapid privatization but slow institutional reform. Because polarization is high, new- and old-economy producers consider it likely that current policy will change dramatically in the near future and will be reluctant to risk the time, effort, and capital needed to invest. Incumbent executives anticipate this lack of investment, and hence tax revenue, to buy the political support of the dependent sector of the population. If the government cannot raise sufficient revenue to buy the support of the dependent sector, it risks losing power.

Old-left incumbents in a polarized democracy face a similar dynamic. They would like to conduct a consistent gradual reform strategy that rewards supporters in the old economy and generates tax revenue to pay for transfers to the dependent sector, but absent confidence that policy will be maintained over time, old- and new-economy interests will invest at rates too low to generate the tax revenue needed to buy the support of the dependent sector.[21] To try to make up for lost tax revenue and for the subsequent decline in the ability to buy political support from the dependent sector, incumbents in a polarized democracy have strong incentives to use reform to deliver rents to producer groups. Because postcommunist politicians inherited massive bureaucracies, large state-owned sectors that can be sold at below-market prices, and weak legal environments, they have many opportunities to raise rents without having to collect taxes.

Where a right executive heads the government in a highly polarized democracy as depicted in the upper-right panel of Table 1.1, economic and institutional reforms are likely to be slower and less consistent than those achieved by their right counterparts in a less polarized setting. We would expect right incumbents to pursue an inconsistent mix of rapid economic reform, slow institutional reform, and low transfer payments to the dependent sector. Here we find new-economy interests with support from old-economy interests benefiting at the expense of the dependent sector of the population. Similarly, centrist incumbents will likely favor a moderate pace of institutional and economic reform that benefits old- and new-economy interests at the cost of gaining revenue for the dependent sector of the population as depicted in the middle-right panel.[22]

---

[21] New-economy producers prefer a more rapid reform as a consistent gradual-reform strategy prevents them from using their skills and assets to their full potential.

[22] Centrist governments are unlikely to be highly polarized as the policy distance to the largest opposition is likely to be small.

When polarization is high in a democracy and an old-left executive holds power as depicted in the lower-right panel of Table 1.1, incumbents face a similar commitment problem. One might expect an inconsistent gradual policy of slow economic reform to gain the support of old-economy interests and slower institutional reform to gain the support of new-economy interests. The coalition benefiting from this set of policies is dominated by old-economy interests with support from new-economy interests at the expense of the dependent sector.

This mix of policies can help incumbents try to retain office in the short run but produces a less vigorous response from economic agents than would more consistent policies and, therefore, less robust economic performance and ultimately less tax revenue. Thus, incumbents face a trade-off between pursuing consistent policies in line with their partisan interests that encourage investment but risk lower political support and pursuing inconsistent reforms that yield less investment but increase their chances of retaining office in the short run. In sum, each increase in polarization under a democracy makes it more difficult for incumbent executives to pursue a consistent reform in line with their partisan preferences.[23]

These hypotheses have implications for building states and markets as the incentives of staying in power in a polarized democracy lead incumbents to favor slower and less consistent institutional reforms that make state building and market building work at cross-purposes. To retain office, incumbents weaken state institutions to give producer interests greater benefits. By distorting the process of state building, incumbents can increase their likelihood of retaining power today but at the cost of economic performance tomorrow.

Policy Making under Autocracy

In an autocratic setting, no vote will be held after playing the commitment game so the incumbent does not need to gain support of two of the three groups in the polity. By satisfying some subset of their core constituents, autocratic leaders can retain office.[24] Regardless of the level of polarization, reforms are likely to be inconsistent because of the threat of an endogenous policy reversal.[25] After the producers invest, an autocratic government faces no binding election and

[23] These policies do not guarantee a return to office for the incumbent as elections often turn on events not under the control of a politician. The claim is only that politicians will choose certain policies under certain political conditions with an eye toward returning to office.

[24] Because autocracies require revenue to pay for the costs of repressing the opposition, one could argue that some subsets of producers on whom the government relies for the revenue needed to repress the opposition may have greater confidence that their investment will not be seized.

[25] Other commitment mechanisms may be available to autocratic regimes. Gehlbach and Keefer (2008) note that autocratic regimes may build political parties to help reduce the commitment problem. In a global sample, they find little difference in the ability of democratic and autocratic regimes to attract foreign investment. Haber et al. (2003) identify conditions under which autocratic government in Mexico respected investments in certain sectors. The minimal claim

TABLE 1.2. *Economic and Institutional Reform in an Autocracy*

	Low Polarization or High Polarization
Right executive	Inconsistent liberalism • Moderate economic and institutional reform • Inconsistent economic and institutional reform • Low transfers New economy/old economy coalition
Centrist executive	Inconsistent social market • Moderate economic and institutional reform • Inconsistent economic and institutional reform • Moderate transfers New economy/old economy coalition
Old-left executive	Inconsistent gradualism • Gradual economic and institutional reform • Inconsistent economic and institutional reform • Low transfers Old economy/new economy coalition

is therefore less dependent on raising revenue through taxation in order to buy political support. Because autocratic governments can change policy with few constraints, they can effectively seize the investments from the productive sector of the economy by changing policy ex post (Olson 1993; Deirmeier et al. 1997; Wintrobe 1998; but see Gehlbach and Keefer 2008). If producers expect the government to change policy strategically, then they will be reluctant to invest in the first place. Indeed, because concerns over the credibility of policy may prevent autocrats from pursuing consistent reforms that induce high levels of investment from producers, they will prefer inconsistent reforms that produce low levels of investment to the prospect of proposing consistent reforms that produce no investment from producers who fear a change in policy ex post.

Thus, under autocracy right autocrats will tend to favor inconsistent liberal policies of rapid economic reform with weak regulatory institutions, targeted tax breaks, and giveaway privatizations. Similarly, old-left autocrats will find inconsistent gradual economic reform, selective privatizations, and generous tax breaks attractive. Centrist autocrats will tend to pursue an inconsistent liberal mix of moderately paced economic reforms and slow institutional reforms (Table 1.2).[26] The logic here suggests that in autocracies state building and market building work at cross-purposes because executives are unable to generate investment from producers and therefore weaken the state to gain political support.

made here is that more autocratic governments face more severe credibility problems than more democratic governments.

[26] Only six cases have centrist governments under autocratic rule.

Assumptions

The argument relies on several assumptions that should be made explicit. First, investments are specific to reform strategies. There is a cost to producers of changing investment strategies if the government changes policy. If firms could switch investment strategies without cost, then they would bear little political risk in investing, and there would be little relation between political polarization and investment. In addition, investments are made shortly after policy is announced but take time to be realized. Producers make their investment decisions well before elections and, therefore, in the face of uncertainty over whether the current government will even survive its term. This uncertainty forces producers to base their investment strategy on the probability that the current government will fall during its term and be replaced by a successor who favors a different strategy.[27]

Second, politicians in a democracy face a cost for "policy switching" – that is, making policies that do not cater to their core constituency (Stokes 2001b). One could entertain the possibility that a right executive introduces rapid and consistent reform, producers invest and pay taxes, and the government seizes the investment and taxes to redistribute to the dependent sector and to old-economy interests. However, this strategy is unlikely to be appealing. If incumbent producers can punish their executives in future elections for reneging on their policy promise, they can be deterred from changing policy after the investment is made.[28] In addition, the logic of signaling suggests that incumbents would have to transfer even more to opponents across the partisan divide than they would to their own supporters to gain their support (Rodrik 1989).

Third, the argument assumes that the dependent sector votes for the incumbent after receiving its transfer. One might ask why dependent-sector voters do not take the transfer but vote for the opposition.[29] After all, strategic opposition parties can promise transfers equal in size to those delivered by the incumbent. The argument made here implicitly builds in an incumbency advantage because the dependent sector can measure the actions of the incumbent only against the promises of the opposition. This assumption can be defended in the cases at hand by noting that few opposition parties have strong track records of performance in office. Because the dependent sector attaches greater uncertainty

---

[27] One irony is that because investment takes time to be realized, if producers are mistaken in their belief that the government will fall during its term, they cannot invest just before elections, pay taxes, and allow incumbents to buy the support of the dependent sector. If the incumbent producer knew that the government would make it to the next election, it would invest, pay taxes, and ensure that the incumbent is returned and current policies continued. However, the producer makes its decision without full knowledge of the staying power of the current government.

[28] This repeat-play logic is not captured in the model, but see Kreps (1990) and Deirmeier et al. (1997).

[29] This is the familiar "last mover" problem in commitment models that is common to all models of politicians exchanging benefits for support.

to the policy promises of the opposition, it is likely to vote for incumbents over challengers if both parties promise equal transfers.

Fourth, the argument does not depend on the notion that a rapid economic reform or gradual economic reform provides stronger incentives to invest, and hence greater tax revenue to the state. The assumption here is that if rapid economic reform and gradual economic reform are pursued consistently, they provide sufficient tax revenue to the state to buy the support of the dependent sector. This assumption thus does not bias the argument in favor of either old-left, centrist, or right political factions.

Extensions

To keep complexity at bay, I have tried to present the argument as starkly as possible. Doing so brings the logic to the foreground while pushing some potentially interesting roads of inquiry to the background. In the future, the argument could be extended in several ways. First, the model could be extended to make elections occur before the investment is realized and transfers are delivered as in Besley (2006). Here I have treated the sequence of play so that producers reap their investment gain, incumbents obtain their taxes, and those in the dependent sector receive their transfers all before elections. However, one could assume that in a democracy the three groups vote before investors realize their investment and transfers are made. This "elections first" version of the argument would begin with the incumbent executive choosing a reform strategy, and then, in response, the producer would decide whether to invest. One could assume that these investments are private information or at least difficult for the dependent sector to verify, perhaps because they are realized after the election. The three groups would then vote, and the investment would be realized and the transfer be made after the election only if the incumbent is returned to power.

Changing the order of play in this way is likely to produce similar predictions. The key decision in the "elections first" setup depends on whether the dependent sector believes that the producer has invested. If so, on the basis of the expectation that the government will provide the transfer, it will vote for the incumbent. If the dependent sector believes that the producer has not invested, however, it will not expect the government to deliver the transfer and consequently will vote against the incumbent. To the extent that the dependent sector of the population takes its cue on whether the producer has invested from the same signal as the producers do when they invest, the predictions of the model should be the same. As polarization increases in a democracy, the dependent sector is less likely to back incumbents because it will expect producers to withhold their investment. Anticipating this possibility, the incumbent executive will pursue inconsistent reforms that benefit old- and new-economy interests.

In addition, for the predictions to be consistent between the two models, the incumbent executive would have to convince the dependent sector that he would actually deliver the transfer after he has been returned to office. In the "elections first" argument under consideration, the dependent sector worries about whether the incumbent will deliver the transfer after the dependent sector votes. The logic is akin to the concern of the incumbent in the "transfers first" argument presented earlier in this chapter that the dependent sector would not deliver its vote after receiving the transfer. In a low-polarization democracy, an incumbent can be deterred from withholding the transfer, if he is sufficiently concerned about his reputation in future elections (Kreps 1990). Punishment strategies inflicted by core producers on "their" representatives could minimize this type of reneging. Moreover, the incumbent may resist withholding the transfer because of the fear of being replaced by another politician within his own camp (Deirmeier et al. 1997). Thus, polarization may mute reform even if elections occur before transfers are made.

Second, the direct macroeconomic consequences of policy choices could be incorporated into the argument. Here I have focused on the distributional effects of policy and not considered consumption generated by a growing economy as part of the utility function of the producers or the executive (Grossman and Helpman 1994). The delivery of large rents to producers via inconsistent reform impairs economic growth, and thereby reduces consumption from a growing economy for producers and revenue for the state. In other words, incumbent politicians cannot pursue inconsistent reform indefinitely without slowing economic growth and reducing the consumption of producers. If we assume that producer interests take the state of the economy into account in their vote choices, then at some point the distortions introduced by inconsistent reform will hurt the economy and erode support for the incumbent.[30]

Indeed, as producers' rents and consumption fall because of deteriorating economic performance, the risk of investing may become more palatable. Producers will prefer consistent reform to inconsistent reform when the gains from rents and slower growth fall below the potential gains from investing and faster growth, taking into account the probability of a swing in policy. Similarly, as rents decline because of impaired economic performance, incumbent politicians may be more willing to risk pursuing more consistent reforms (Rodrik 1996). Adding the macroeconomic consequences of policy will likely retain the logic of the argument but put a lower bound on the extent to which incumbents can retain office using slower and less consistent reforms.

Third, the argument has generally taken polarization as exogenous and static, and there are some good reasons to do so. Initial levels of polarization can be taken from the first postcommunist election in each country, and these elections precede choices over economic and institutional reform. In addition, as argued in Chapter 6, some of the sources of polarization can be found in the nature of rule in the Soviet period. Thus, it is plausible to assume the exogeneity of polarization as a starting point. However, one could imagine

---

[30] There is some empirical basis for this assumption as high levels of inconsistent reform led to macroeconomic crises in Bulgaria in 1996, Romania in 1996, Albania in 1997, and Russia in 1998 that ultimately contributed to changes in the political environment that fed back into policy choices.

several ways that polarization could be made endogenous to the argument and dynamic over time. Inconsistent reform may exacerbate economic inequality and thereby heighten political polarization in the future. This could lead to a "revenue trap" in which the government is no longer able to generate sufficient revenue to pay for rents.[31] Alternatively, early rounds of reform could change the distribution of the population among new-economy interests, old-economy interests, and the dependent sector. For simplicity's sake, I have treated these groups as roughly equal in size, but one could allow this to vary. For example, rapid reforms that impose costs on the old-economy sector could increase the size of the dependent sector in future elections, reduce the power of the old-economy interests, and thereby lower polarization.

Finally, the reservation transfer of the dependent sector – the amount that it requires to vote for the incumbent – can be determined in several ways. Here I take the simplest approach and assume that if one producer group invests under consistent reform, the tax revenue generated on this investment is sufficient to buy the support of the dependent sector and the after-tax profits to the producer are still positive. Another approach would treat the dependent sector as a median voter and link the reservation transfer to the preelection promises of the opposition and to the value of inconsistent reform to an incumbent producer. Borrowing from the logic of Boix (2003) and Acemoglu and Robinson (2006), the median voter would demand a reservation transfer greater than the transfer that an opposition could credibly promise but lower than the benefits of inconsistent reform to an incumbent producer. If the reservation transfer (and therefore the tax rate) on the incumbent producer was too high, then the incumbent producer would choose to ally with an opposition producer and pursue an inconsistent reform. If the reservation transfer was too low, then the opposition could promise a more generous transfer than the incumbent and the latter would lose office. As in other works, the greater distance between the preferred policy of the median voter and that of other powerful economic groups, the greater the distortions in policy (Boix 2003; Acemoglu and Robinson 2006). In the argument made here, it is helpful to note that polarization both reduces the credibility of the opposition's promise to increase transfers because it has farther to move to the center and increases the value of inconsistent reform to the incumbent producer by making investment less attractive. Thus, in both the proposed extension and approach adopted here, the size of transfers and the consistency of reform are both declining in polarization. These four extensions to the argument hardly exhaust interesting possibilities for future work but are best left for another day.

Scope Conditions

The theoretical argument is cast in rather general terms, but it may have less bite in some settings than in others. The argument is less likely to hold where

[31] See Gehlbach (2008) for a related argument.

existing institutions share power and provide strong institutional checks on policy reversals. Countries with strong federalism, powerful bicameralism, divided governments, or strong regulatory institutions may lower the likelihood of a policy reversal and thereby blunt incentives in favor of inconsistent reform (Holmes 1995; Tsebelis 1995; Stasavage 2003; McCarty et al. 2006). In contrast, political regimes in the postcommunist region tend to have strong "majoritarian" qualities that may exacerbate the impact of polarization on policy instability. Most regimes in the sample are parliamentary, with the implication that any election could produce a one-party majority that faces few checks and balances on policy making (Sartori 1976; Tsebelis 1995; Cox 2001). Among parliamentary systems, elections produced a single party with a majority of seats in ten of thirteen countries. Thus, the threat of single-party rule in a parliamentary system is eminently plausible.

Policy making in the presidential regimes in the region greatly favors the executive through extensive powers of executive decree, high thresholds for overturning a presidential veto, and vast influence over government formation and dismissal (Frye 1997b). Informal norms of policy making further strengthen the executive in many presidential regimes (Holmes 1996; Taras 1997; Breslauer 2002; Jones Luong 2002; Collins 2006). The types of "checks and balances" and power-sharing arrangements that distinguish presidential from parliamentary regimes in more long-standing democracies like the United States are largely absent in the region.[32] In addition, most presidential regimes in the sample are autocratic, which suggests that introducing policy changes will not be especially difficult. Thus, on balance, the majoritarian nature of policy making in the region heightens the threat of policy reversal compared to countries with stronger checks and balances (McCarty et al. 2006).[33]

The logic of the argument may also be weaker where incumbents have less access to state-generated rents. Incumbents in the postcommunist region inherited overstaffed states and economies dominated by state-owned enterprises that offered vast opportunities for distributing rents. This inheritance may make it possible for incumbents to pursue inconsistent reform for a longer

---

[32] Possible exceptions include the mixed presidential-parliamentary regimes of Poland, Lithuania, and Romania, and, in some years, Moldova, which have directly elected but not especially powerful presidents. In these cases parliaments and prime ministers have much more authority over economic policy.

[33] It is perhaps therefore not surprising that, if anything, more institutional and partisan veto points in the policy-making process are associated with greater increases in economic reform, particularly early in the transformation (Hellman 1998; Gehlbach and Malesky 2008). The positive correlation between veto points and reform is due in part to the concentration of political power and extremely "statist" economic status quo at the start of the transition. In countries that did not experience a turnover in government early in the transition, we find a coincidence of old-left executives and autocratic governments with few veto points in countries that pursue little reform. By contrast, each group that entered the political arena was likely to have partisan preferences that were typically less statist than the incumbents who held power before 1989 (Frye and Mansfield 2003).

period in the cases at hand than in other settings. The argument may travel less well to settings where fewer rents are available.

Related Literature

This work is far from the first to link political polarization to dysfunctional economic and political outcomes. Scholars have argued that polarization may influence economic policy by making governments slow to respond to an economic crisis. Most prominently, Alesina and Drazen (1991) argue that polarization, combined with imperfect knowledge about the costs that parties are willing to bear, can increase incentives for parties to delay compromises on policies that provide collective benefits. Thus, the greater the policy distance between parties and the higher the uncertainty about the resolve of the other group, the greater are the gains to delaying an agreement to change policy from the status quo. Exogenous shocks that reduce uncertainty about the other group or change the balance of power lead to large swings in policy because policy makers cannot agree on how to compensate the party who loses.

Others emphasize that polarization can increase policy instability. Svensson (1998) argues that polarization-induced instability over future policy may lead governments to provide fewer institutional reforms. He assumes that an incumbent party and the opposition disagree over the size of spending on reform. In a two-period model, the incumbent chooses the level of institutional reform in the first period, and more institutional reform leads to higher revenue for the government but only in the second period. As in this work, the catch is that the incumbent faces an exogenously determined probability of not being reelected and being replaced by a challenger with different policy preferences. The greater the possibility of losing office and the larger the policy distance between the incumbent and the challenger, the weaker are the incentives of the incumbent to invest in institutional reforms that will provide revenue for the government only after she has left office. Thus, the greater the political polarization, the lower is spending on institutional reform in the first period. Similarly, Keefer and Knack (2002) find that polarization as proxied by income inequality is associated with slower growth. Moreover, they trace this slow growth to policy instability induced by large income differentials between the rich and the poor.

I am also interested in the impact of political polarization on policy making and link policy instability to polarization and economic inequality, but, whereas these works study the direct effect of different types of polarization on economic outcomes, I explore the conditional impact of polarization within democracies. In addition, these studies assume that social indicators of political polarization translate easily into policies, whereas I begin to explore whether the social roots of polarization are actually translated into the political arena. Finally, the argument made here adds a selection process to policy making by considering how politicians use policy to build coalitions in hopes of staying in power.

This work also differs from several important works that examine various aspects of economic and institutional reform in the postcommunist region. Among others, Hellman (1998) and Grzymala-Busse (2002) explore the relationship between democracy and policy choice over economic and institutional reforms, but whereas they argue that the impact of democracy on reform is direct, I argue that it is conditional on the level of polarization. O'Dwyer (2006) links economic reforms to government partisanship and weakly institutionalized parties but examines only democracies in Eastern Europe. Aslund et al. (1996), Fish (1998), Stone (2002), and Horowitz and Browne (2008) argue that executive partisanship is directly related to economic reform outcomes. I replicate this result but also find that partisanship of the opposition is a determinant of economic and institutional reforms. Pop-Eleches (2009) argues that the impact of partisanship on macroeconomic policy is conditional on economic crisis, but here I focus on economic and institutional reforms rather than macroeconomic policy. In exploring variations in tax policy and public good provision across countries, Gehlbach (2008) examines the credibility of the exchange between producers and politicians. Here I examine the credibility of policy promises over time between current and future governments.

Conclusion

The argument developed in this chapter differs from much existing literature by integrating partisanship, political power, and democratic institutions into an explanation for economic and institutional policy choices. Autocratic rule and high polarization in democracies induce policy makers to subvert reforms. Slow and inconsistent reforms are less the direct result of weak political competition, "bad" policy choices, incompetence, or corruption per se than the logic of raising revenue in a particular political environment.

In addition, the argument suggests that the effects of democracy on economic policy choices are conditional on the level of political polarization. Political institutions shape economic policy by influencing policy instability. When the main opposition faction has policy preferences far different from the incumbent in a democracy, producers invest less, and the government has less revenue to buy political support. Therefore, incumbents have strong incentives to subvert economic and institutional reform to reward producer groups and stay in power in polarized democracies. In contrast to much existing literature that suggests a direct relationship between democracy and reform, this argument suggests that the impact of democracy on economic and institutional reform is conditional on the level of polarization.

Finally, the argument places the partisanship of political elites and the social groups that they represent at the center of the analysis. Existing cross-national literature on the politics of economic reform has tended to underplay elite partisanship by treating political elites as motivated by concerns for economic efficiency or by emphasizing the homogenizing effects of the international economy on policy choice. In either case, elite partisanship takes a back seat. In this analysis, political elites and their constituents behave strategically in response to the partisanship of the executive, the strength of their political rivals across the partisan divide, and the quality of democracy.

Appendix 1.1

Consider a polity of three groups: old-economy interests that seek to maximize revenue, including rents, and are represented by old-left politicians (O); new-economy interests that seek to maximize revenue, including rents, and are represented by right politicians (N); and the dependent sector of the population that seeks to maximize transfers and is represented by centrist politicians (D).

The voting population consists of O, N, and D, and each group may differ in size. O and N seek to maximize capital gains (g) generated by privatization and rents (e) generated by the quality of state regulatory institutions. Capital gains, g, equals $\pi(K^* - K)$, where K^* equals the market price of state assets, K equals the price actually paid for the asset, and π equals the share of state assets that have been privatized. K represents a below-market price for a formerly state asset sold via privatization. The progress of reforming institutions is modeled as a tax on producers on the notion that strong regulatory institutions constrain producers from obtaining rents, while weak institutions generate rents for firms. Thus, tax exemptions (e) generated by institution quality equals ($t^* - t$), where t^* equals strong institutions (hence a high tax rate) and t equals weaker institutions (lower tax rate). Total tax exemptions in the economy equals b:

$$b = \pi Y_N(t^* - t) + \pi Y_O(t^* - t), \tag{1}$$

where Y_N = total income among new-economy interests, Y_O equals total income among the old-economy interests, and π equals the privatized part of the economy.[34]

Electoral support, E, provided by O and N is an increasing function of g and b:

$$E_N, E_O = \alpha(g + b), \tag{2}$$

where $\alpha > 0$ and ranges from 0 to 1. Old- and new-economy interests seek to maximize g and b. If the executive transfers all state assets to old- and new-economy interests for free and imposes no taxes, α is maximized.

Transfer recipients seek to maximize transfers, p, and their electoral support, E_D, is an increasing function of p. Again, β translates transfers into votes and ranges from 0 to 1. Here, β for the dependent sector is akin to α for producers:

$$E_D = \beta(p). \tag{3}$$

The incumbent executive seeks to return to office and to provide benefits to their supporters. In a democracy, he must receive the votes of more than

[34] It is important to note that privatization can be directed toward old- or new-economy interests. Old- and new-economy producers benefit when they buy state assets at below-market prices.

50 percent of the population. To return the executive to office, equation (4) must be satisfied, where S is the share of the population in each group:

$$\alpha S_O + \alpha S_N + \beta S_D > .5. \tag{4}$$

To gain the support of the dependent sector, the incumbent must raise tax revenue. Whereas the support of the O and N can be bought with policy benefits, including capital gains via privatization and weak institutions, the dependent sector of the population needs cash raised by taxes. Thus, total expenditures, Pp, must equal tax revenues from old- and new-economy interests in the privatized and state-owned economy as is indicated in equation (5):

$$Pp = [\pi t_N Y + \pi t_O Y] + (1 - \pi)Y_N(t^*) + (1 - \pi)Y_O(t^*). \tag{5}$$

That is, total transfers equal the taxes actually paid by new-economy interests and old-economy interests. If we take income, the number of pensioners, and the statutory tax rate as given, equation (5) indicates that once the government identifies the transfers needed to return to office, this determines the value of tax exemptions for the private and the state sector. That is, $Pp = [t^* - e\pi]Y$.

Thus far, the model hews very closely to the notation and logic of Kapstein and Milanovic (2000). The key to the model is that there is a link between taxation and transfers, and politicians must choose between the two. The next section builds on their model by incorporating the policy choices of politicians and the decision of firms to invest under the constraint of varying levels of polarization.

Figure A1.1 presents the moves of a simple commitment game. To simplify the notation, here I represent the producing sectors of the economy by a median producer whose skills and assets place it midway in the distribution between old- and new-economy producers. We can consider that under a right government, producers to the right of the median producer who have skills better suited to a market will invest more, whereas producers to the left of the median producer will invest at lower rates if they believe that policy will be stable over time.[35]

Incumbent politicians trade rents and transfers for political support and face a budget constraint that transfers and rents should not exceed tax revenue plus privatization revenue as in equation (5).

The sequence of moves in the commitment game is in the following five stages:

1. Nature chooses an old-left, centrist, or a right politician to head the executive.
2. The incumbent government chooses π, which represents the capital gains generated by the pace of privatization, and e, the size of tax exemptions, which are modeled here as the pace of institutional reform. Again, the

---

35 For clarity's sake, here I do not depict the moves by a centrist government, but the logic is the same as with old-left and right governments. The only difference is that centrist governments pursue moderate rates of economic and institutional reform. With the continuous measure of polarization, centrist governments are not polarized by construction.

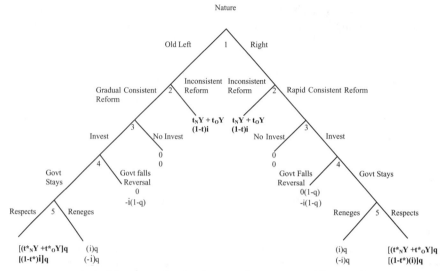

FIGURE A1.1. A decision tree of a simple commitment game. The top figure represents the payoff for the government and the lower figure represents the payoff for the median producer. Equilibria are in bold.

progress of reforming institutions is modeled as a tax on producers on the basis of the notion that strong regulatory institutions constrain producers from obtaining rents, while weak institutions generate rents for firms. Consider strong institutions as t^*, a statutory tax rate, and weak institutions as t, a lower tax rate that provides rents to producers.

3. The producers in the core constituency and in the opposition decide to invest their capital by making an investment that is specific to the reform strategy chosen by the government and takes time to be realized.

4. The government experiences an exogenous shock sometime during its term. To simplify, the government stays in power with a probability of (q) and is replaced by a challenger from across the partisan divide in the next stage with a probability of $(1 - q)$. Thus, q is a proxy for polarization.

5. The government in power decides whether to reverse or respect its previous policy in the next stage of the game.

After the game is played in a democracy, the old-economy interest, the new-economy interest, and the dependent sector of the population vote. In an autocracy no votes are cast.

Consider the preference orderings over outcomes of the government, the producers, and the dependent sector of the population. The government is best off if it reneges on its promise and seizes the investment made by the producer. Its second-best option is to conduct a consistent reform by respecting its policy promise and receive, $t^*_N Y + t^*_O Y$, that is, the revenue generated by investment at the statutory tax rate for all new-economy and old-economy interests. Its third-best preference is to pursue an inconsistent reform that delivers rents to the old- and new-economy interests in the form of weak institutions and receive $t_N Y + t_O Y$. If the investor does not invest or the government falls from power, it receives o.

Thus, for the government,

$$i > t^*_N Y + t^*_O Y > t_N Y + t_O Y > o.$$

Now consider the producer's preferences. She prefers inconsistent reform that delivers rents in the form of lower taxes, t, and that will give her $(1 - t)i$. Her second preference is to invest and pay taxes at the politician's preferred (statutory) rate $(1 - t^*)(i)$. Her next best option is not to invest and receive o. If policy swings endogenously through the fall of the government in a polarized setting, or if the government reneges on its policy, the producer receives $-i$, which is her worst option.

Thus, for the producer,

$$(1 - t)i > (1 - t^*)(i) > o > i.$$

The dependent sector of the population has no capital to invest, but it does have the power to vote in a democracy. It votes for the incumbent, if it receives a sufficiently large transfer payment, otherwise it votes against the incumbent. The incumbent raises this revenue by taxing producer interests in the old and new economies.[36]

Democracy Low Polarization

Suppose that the target level of transfers, Pp, needed to return the executive to office requires a consistent reform strategy that imposes taxes at the statutory rate t^* on the entire economy. Thus, strong institutions must be imposed on the entire economy $(t^*_N Y + t^*_O Y)$.

Consider policy making in a nonpolarized democracy headed by a right government.[37] Because polarization is low, (q), the probability that policy will be maintained into the future equals 1. Start with the last stage of the commitment game. Here the incumbent decides whether to respect or renege on his policy promise. If the incumbent respects his policy promise, he receives $(t^*_N Y + t^*_O Y)$ and can use this revenue to buy the vote of the dependent sector. Moreover, a right incumbent will receive the vote of the new-economy interest by

---

[36] Alternatively one could fix the reservation transfer wage at a given level and allow the incumbent government to retain any revenue obtained above the reservation transfer.

[37] The logic here is similar under an old-left or center government. The executive introduces a gradual reform and producers invest, confident that the government will respect its policy choice. The government taxes the investment to buy support from the dependent sector of the population. Old-economy interests vote for the incumbent because of the gradual reform, the dependent sector votes for the incumbent because of the transfer payments, and the incumbent is returned to office. The same logic holds for a center government that relies on new-economy producers for investment.

pursuing a rapid economic and institutional reform policy. Thus, by respecting his policy promise, a right incumbent can stay in power with the votes of the dependent sector and the new-economy interest and an old-left incumbent can stay in power with the votes of the old-economy interest and the dependent sector. If the incumbent reneges and seizes the investment, he receives i. Reneging, though, loses him the vote of new-economy interests in future elections, which will turn to other parties within the right camp. This threat of replacement from within the right camp will lead the incumbent to respect his policy promise.[38] In stage 4, a right government stays in power.[39] In stage 3, the producer prefers to invest and pay taxes at the statutory rate rather than to not invest because she is confident that the incumbent will not renege on his policy promise, $(1 - t^*)i > 0$. In stage 1, a right incumbent will therefore pursue a rapid and consistent rather than an inconsistent reform because $(t^*_N Y + t^*_O Y) > (t_N Y + t_O Y)$.[40] Thus, the need to build an electoral coalition can lead an incumbent government to respect rather than to renege on its policy promises.

Democracy High Polarization
Now consider policy making in a polarized democracy. Because polarization is high, the probability (q) that policy will be maintained in the future equals 0. As before, we begin with stage 5; here the government prefers to respect its policy promise rather than renege as in the nonpolarized example. However, in stage 4 there is an exogenous shock which causes a swing in policy. In stage 3, the producer anticipates this swing in policy and does not invest as she prefers not investing to losing her investment, $0 > -i$, after the turnover in government. In stage 2, the government anticipates that the producer will not invest, which leaves it with a smaller tax base to generate revenue to pay for transfers to the dependent sector of the population.

To make up for this shortfall, the incumbent can weaken institutions, and effectively lower t, which will benefit producers; increase g, by reducing the price at which state assets are sold; or increase π, the speed of privatization, to benefit producer interests.

Each of these moves increases the level of inconsistent reforms. With increasing polarization, the incumbent chooses an inconsistent reform that increases rents and capital gains to old- and new-economy interests but offers fewer transfers for the dependent sector of the population. The old- and new-economy interests provide increasing support for the incumbent who has delivered them inconsistent reform and thereby increases the likelihood of keeping the government in power. The threat of an exogenous policy reversal undermines the

---

[38] The punishment strategy here is not modeled, but it has long been known that repeat play and costly punishments for reneging can promote cooperation (cf. Kreps 1990).

[39] One could argue that the current government stays or that it falls but is replaced by a party with similar preferences. The important point is that producers and the dependent sector expect policy to remain unchanged when they make their investment decision.

[40] Similarly, an old-left incumbent will pursue a gradual and consistent rather than an inconsistent reform.

credibility of a government pursuing a consistent reform. This leads to the prediction that increased polarization should be associated with less consistent reform under democracy.

Autocracy

Consider a policy-making process in an autocracy headed by a right government. Under an autocracy, no vote will be held. Thus, the executive does not need to raise revenue to buy the support of the dependent sector. Start with the last stage of the commitment game, stage 5. The executive prefers reneging on its policy promise and receiving (i) to respecting its policy promise and receiving ($t^*_N Y + t^*_O Y$). In stage 4, the government stays in power. In stage 3, the investor anticipates that the government will renege and prefers not to invest and receive (o) rather than to invest and receive ($-i$). If the producer does not invest, the government receives (o). To avoid this outcome, the government conducts a rapid and inconsistent reform in stage 2 that includes a lower tax rate, which provides the government with ($t_N Y + t_O Y$), which is greater than (o). The producer receives ($1 - t$)(i). As this is the producer's first choice, she has no incentive to deviate. If nature has chosen a right executive in an autocracy, we should expect to find a mix of inconsistent rapid reform that delivers rents to new- and old-economy interests at the expense of the dependent sector of the population. The logic is the same if the executive is headed by an old-left government. The old-left government introduces a gradual reform; old-economy interests expect the government to renege, and the government pursues inconsistent reforms that reward both old- and new-economy interests. Similarly, in a centrist autocracy, we would find an inconsistent reform policy albeit with a more moderate pace of reform than in a right autocracy.

2

Political Polarization and Economic Inequality

Measure what is measurable, and make measurable what is not so.

Galileo Galilei

The previous chapter emphasized how executive partisanship and political polarization influence economic policy making but did not define or describe these terms with much rigor. This chapter seeks to do so. It begins by discussing the measurement of partisanship and political polarization before presenting data on levels of political polarization. Clarifying these concepts is important, given that scholars use the terms in different ways. Moreover, the peculiarities of the postcommunist cases present special challenges for measuring partisanship and polarization. At the start of the transformation, parties and factions did not have long histories of policy making that could serve as reliable guides to partisanship. In addition, the postcommunist cases include presidential and parliamentary regimes as well as democracies and autocracies, a variability that makes defining these terms especially challenging.

In addition, this chapter identifies economic inequality as a potential social base for political polarization. Increases in economic inequality early in the transformation map well onto levels of polarization, although it is difficult to make claims about the direction of causality. Countries that experienced large increases in income inequality in the early years of the transformation have significantly more polarized political systems later in the transformation. Large gaps in income between rich and poor are a feature of polarized political systems, suggesting that income inequality may provide a social base for political polarization. Establishing that political polarization has deeper roots in society suggests that it may be more than epiphenomenal. Investigating this relationship is important because, while scholars often use social indicators as measures of political polarization, not all social cleavages are reflected in politics (cf. Posner 2004).

Classifying Political Factions

Classifying political factions into broad groups is necessary to evaluate the claim that the partisan divide between old-left and right camps affects economic policy.[1] I am interested in three types of partisan factions: old left, centrist, and right. To place political factions into these three categories, I borrow heavily from the Comparative Political Data-Set II created by Armingeon and Careja (2004) and updated by Armingeon et al. (2008). For each of the countries in the sample, the authors placed each party into one of eleven families. I discuss coding issues in more detail in Appendix 2.1, but for now I call factions "old left" if they were coded as postcommunist, left-communist, or communist by the Comparative Political Data-Set II.[2] I also place executives who held power continuously from the Soviet period in the old-left category. They are often, but not always, members of communist successor factions that retained the assets of their predecessors, for better and for worse. Their constituent base typically includes groups threatened by economic liberalization, including those with skills specific to the command economy that offer less return in a market environment, such as bureaucrats in planning and economic ministries, managers and workers in loss-making factories, rural residents, and older workers. A second potential source of support comes from those dependent on policy commitments emanating from the old regime, including pensioners and veterans. Old-left executives are also likely influenced by their previous ideological training in the state or party apparatus to be skeptical of liberal reforms. Classic examples of old-left political factions include the Albanian Social Democratic Party, the Bulgarian Socialist Party, the National Salvation Front in Romania, and personalist old-left leaders like Islam Karimov in Uzbekistan and Heydar Aliev in Azerbaijan.

Old-left factions differ from their communist-era predecessors. No longer do they have cells in the workplace, issue obligatory paeans to Marx and Lenin,

---

[1] I use "faction" as a broad term to include political parties and movements organized around individuals. It includes political parties whose candidates run on a party ticket and have a degree of organization, such as the SLD in Poland. It also includes political movements headed by individuals who hold high office but are not backed by cohesive parties. This usage of the term faction is somewhat akin to that of Richard Rose, who refers to a faction as a "self-consciously organized body with a measure of cohesion" (see Sartori 1976: 72–73). I am primarily interested in the behavior of these factions in the legislative arena rather than in their ties to societies, which are often weak.

[2] Before finding the Armingeon and Careja data, I coded all parties and leaders. Old-left parties were led by politicians who held a high position in the Communist Party or state before 1989; were backed by communist successor party; and advocated a dominant role for the state in the economy. Right parties were all others (Frye 2002a). The codings are similar to those of the Comparative Political Data-Set (CPDS II), compiled by Klaus Armingeon and Romana Careja at the University of Bern. They code parties and factions on the classificatory scheme developed by Lane et al. (1997) who divide parties into eleven types. For simplicity and transparency's sake, I use the CPDS II codings when possible. The small changes that I have made to their codings are described in detail in Appendix 2.1.

or express hope for the proletarian revolution.[3] In some cases, they play by democratic rules and have made important contributions to the building of democracy. However, old-left factions have constituencies, policies, and ties to the old regime that make their economic policies distinct from those of their more liberal rivals. Old-left leaders hold the executive in 36 percent of the cases in the sample.

In contrast, right political factions are generally headed by elites who did not hold high office in the party or state apparatus in 1989, ran for office without the backing of the communist successor party after 1989, or advocate a dominant role for the private sector. More specifically, factions coded as conservative, liberal, or right nationalist in the Comparative Political Data-Set II are treated as right factions in this analysis. A brief list of right elites and factions includes the United Democratic Front in Bulgaria, FIDESZ in Hungary, Freedom Union in Poland, and nonparty right elites, such as Presidents Boris Yeltsin in Russia and Askar Akaev in Kyrgyzstan. These categorizations are largely consistent with existing literature (Ishiyama 1995, 1997; Kitschelt et al. 1999; Grzymala-Busse 2002; Stone 2002; Bugajski 2002).

The partisanship of right executives emanates from two sources as well. Their policy preferences are rooted in social groups expecting to benefit from reform, including the young, city dwellers, the educated, and those in export-oriented sectors, as well as economic interests in the new private sector, including services, finance, and retail. There is considerable evidence that such groups vote for right parties and that right politicians expect them to do so (Warner 2001; Jackson et al. 2005; Frye 2003; Tucker 2006).

In addition, politicians in the right camp appear to come to their support for economic liberalism via an abiding anticommunism. Particularly in the early stages of the transformation, the factions that fall into the right camp were united as much by their anticommunism as by their support for economic and institutional reform. Indeed, in certain respects, anticommunism has an affinity for liberal reform. At the start of the transformation, the remnants of the communist regime had a base of power within the state. Because economic and institutional reform is designed to take decision-making power from state bodies, it is a short jump from an anticommunist political stance to advocating rapid reforms. For example, trade and price liberalization undercuts the political power of planning ministries. Similarly, postcommunist privatization is thought to weaken political opponents within the state apparatus (Boycko et al. 1995). The process of conducting economic reform itself often entails the strengthening of some state bureaucracies, but on balance it weakens old state structures populated by appointees of the outgoing regime.

It is difficult to demonstrate empirically the link between anticommunism and right economic preferences without a more extensive treatment of individual politicians and their policy preferences, but there is evidence that right

---

[3] In a sign of the times, the Bulgarian Socialist Party traded in the hammer and sickle for the red rose of socialism. See also Bulgarian Socialist Party (1994).

politicians and their advisers understand this logic.[4] In advising the government in Poland, Sachs (1993) justified rapid economic reform in part on the grounds that it would take away power from state bureaucrats appointed by the old regime.[5] Anticommunist executives need not understand the fine points of economic theory to recognize that promarket reforms can take resources away from their opponents within the state. Right leaders control the executive in 49 percent of the cases under study.

Twelve percent of the cases involved nationalist factions, such as the Estonian National Independence Party, Franjo Tudjman's Croatian Democratic Union, and Vladimir Meciar's Movement for a Democratic Slovakia. These cases are difficult to categorize. The economic policies pursued by these parties are often vaguely populist, which may place them in the centrist category, but the anticommunism espoused by many nationalist politicians often inclines them against the heavy-handed statism of their old-left rivals and in some cases in favor of liberal policies. The "noise" in this measure is likely to make statistical estimates of the impact of their partisanship on reform less precise. I begin by treating them as right factions, as does the Comparative Politics Data-Set in its OECD coding of parties, which has only left, center, and right categories (Armingeon et al. 2008). Placing all nationalist parties in a single category makes it easier to identify the direction of potential bias in the coding. In addition, however, I explore the results by placing each nationalist party in the analysis in its own category based on my readings of its economic platform and also by dropping them from the analysis.[6] As I discuss later, either of those modifications to the coding rules makes little difference to the results.

A third type of faction, the centrist faction, includes parties coded as socialist or agrarian by the Comparative Political Data-Set. They include the social democratic ex-communist parties of Poland, Hungary, Lithuania, Slovenia, and eventually Slovakia that have advocated market reforms and faced competition from parties to their left. These "centrist" parties do not fit the description of old-left parties. (To paraphrase Stalin, the term old left fits the Polish Alliance of Left Democrats like a saddle fits a cow.)[7] They also include social democratic and agrarian parties, such as the Social Democratic Party of the Czech

---

[4] Of course, politicians are more likely to frame their arguments in support of policy as promoting general social welfare rather than particularistic political interests.

[5] In recounting his advice to the first postcommunist government in Poland, Sachs (1993: 43) noted: "I stressed that the idea of radical reform was not just an economic strategy, but also a political strategy to overcome Solidarity's lack of personnel and control in the ministries. . . . The point was simple: if the reformers do not control the ministry of foreign economic relations, all the more reason to let the foreign exchange market allocate foreign exchange!"

[6] For example, in the revised coding I treat the Movement for a Democratic Slovakia as centrist and the Estonian National Independence Party as a right party.

[7] There is a dispute whether Stalin compared Poland's fitness for communism to a cow, an ox, or a pig, but it any case, the fit is poor.

Republic, the Social Democratic Party of Croatia, and the Agrarian Party of Moldova, that are not linked organizationally to the communist successor parties (Crowther 1997). Their policies are more market-friendly than old-left parties, but they do not fit easily in the right camp as they also favor far more generous social welfare policies and more support for the dependent sector than do their right-wing rivals. In many cases, these parties benefit from weak competition among old-left parties as the outgoing communist parties were widely seen as discredited. The weakness of the old left helps it not only to draw from constituencies dependent on generous social welfare policies but also to gain support from some groups benefiting from liberal policies. These cross-class bases of support set centrist parties apart from old-left and right rivals (Bozoki 2002; Grzymala-Busse 2002). Centrist parties control the executive in 15 percent of the cases.

This is not to neglect differences in the policy preferences of factions and elites within each camp. While agreeing on the core direction of economic policy, factions within each camp often differed on the scope and speed of particular policies. Within-camp differences were typically greater in the right political camp, but were hardly absent in the old-left camp (Kitschelt et al. 1999). The claim here is that policy differences within camps were less pronounced than the policy differences across camps.

It is important to note that voters recognize these distinctions among parties and support parties that promote their individual economic interests. On the basis of mass surveys before parliamentary elections in Russia in 1995, Colton (2000: 94–95) finds that concerns for the performance of the national economy are especially important, but also that "pocketbook assessments and personal traumas do have measurable, independent effects on voting outcomes." Summing up results from his nine-country study of public opinion in the mid-1990s, Evans (2006: 260) finds "high levels of class identification, perceived relative deprivation between classes and links between class position and economic expectations. These aspects of class formation are in turn accompanied by the endorsement of divergent political programs by social classes." Reviewing studies of public opinion across postcommunist countries more generally, Evans (2006: 257) adds that "even at this early point in the postcommunist era (1993–1994) there was evidence of social bases to party support across the region, with social class, age and education providing inequalities of support for pro- versus anti-market political groupings." Pacek (1994) and Tucker (2006) find that gainers from economic transformation tend to back right parties, while losers tend to support old-left parties. Fidrmuc (2000) provides evidence of economic voting in electoral results from four Central European countries in the mid-1990s. Frye (2003) notes that managers of firms created after 1989 that never had any state ownership were especially likely to vote for reform-oriented parties in parliamentary elections in Russia in 1999. Jackson et al. (2005) demonstrate that the creation of new private firms is associated with larger vote shares for right parties at the district level in parliamentary elections in postcommunist Poland in 1993 and 1997. Finally, Lewis (2000: 56) notes that the "established left-right party differentiation is indeed valid and has widespread meaning" in the postcommunist region.

It is often difficult to gauge partisanship in different regional and political contexts, but the policy distance across factions in these cases appears to be large in comparative perspective. The visions of the economy put forward by rightist and old-left political factions in the postcommunist world differ to a greater extent than the alternatives put forward by the Democratic and Republican parties even during the high levels of polarization found in the contemporary United States (McCarty et al. 2006). Similarly, the centrist parties in the sample would fit well within the social democratic family of parties in Europe or Latin America. In contrast, the economic policies of the old-left parties in the postcommunist cases have few analogues among major parties in Latin America, Europe, or the United States, save perhaps for Hugo Chavez's Fifth Republic Movement in Venezuela and Evo Morales' Movement toward Socialism in Bolivia. The policy distance between major factions in the polarized cases at hand appears to be large, especially early in the transformation.

It is also helpful to note that partisanship changes over time only when a political party merges with another party. For executives who are treated as independents by Armingeon and Careja, I code them on the basis of their economic platform during their first run for office and hold this coding constant throughout the transformation. Certainly some long-serving executives changed their economic policy over the course of the transition, but it is difficult to determine whether these changes are due to changes in the partisan preferences of the executive or to other constraints and opportunities. By keeping partisanship constant over time, I guard against the possibility of categorizing the partisanship of the executive on the basis of his behavior in office, which can easily lead to tautology. Keeping partisanship constant over time should make it more difficult to find a relationship between partisanship and reform outcomes.

Measuring Political Polarization

The seat share and policy platform of the largest opposition party relative to the executive determines the extent of political polarization. The executive here refers to a president in a presidential system and the prime minister in a parliamentary system. Where one camp dominates the political arena, polarization is low, and where neither dominates, polarization is high. To gain a more exact measure of polarization, I create a three-category measure of polarization based on the partisanship of the executive and the partisanship of the largest opposition party, provided it has at least 20 percent of the seats in parliament. I code old-left executives as 0; centrist executives as 1; and right executives as 2. I then code the partisanship of the largest opposition faction if it has more than 20 percent of the seats. I subtract the latter from the former and create a polarization measure that takes the value of 0, 1, or 2. For example, in Hungary in 1994 a centrist executive held power and the right opposition had more than 20 percent of the seats, yielding a polarization score of 1. In Albania in 1994, a right party controlled the prime minister and the old-left Albanian Socialist Party had 27 percent of parliamentary seats. In this year, Albania's polarization score was 2. The logic of this coding scheme borrows from the World Bank's Data-Base of Political Institutions, which also uses a tripartite category of polarization based on right, left, and centrist parties (Beck et al. 2001, 2004).

In addition, I create a continuous measure of polarization by counting the percentage of seats held by the largest right faction when an old-left executive is in office and the largest old-left faction when a right faction holds the executive.[8] In cases where a centrist party controls the executive, polarization is scored as 0. For example, in Bulgaria in December 1994 the old-left Bulgarian Socialist Party won a slight majority of seats and Zhan Videnov, a former high official in the Bulgarian young communists' association, became prime minister. The largest right party, the Union of Democratic Forces, won 29 percent of the seats in parliament. Bulgaria's polarization score on the continuous measure of polarization for 1995 was 29. This measure of polarization aims to capture the relative strengths and the differences in the policy positions of the two camps. The average polarization score for the region is just under 10 percent, but 25 percent of the observations in the sample have polarization scores greater than 20, which typically means that the two largest factions in parliament are in the old-left and right camps. Given the large number of independents in many parliaments and the great electoral volatility in the region, holding 20 percent of the seats in parliament typically makes one a potential threat to hold office in the next election (Zielinski 2002; O'Dwyer 2006: 204; Epperly 2008).

The categorical and the continuous measures are correlated at .79, but have somewhat different strengths. The continuous measure offers greater range, but the categorical measure has the advantage of allowing greater discrimination between old-left and centrist executives. Table 2.1 reports the average annual level of polarization for the countries in the sample.

This measure focuses on the electoral strength of the opposition across the partisan divide relative to the president in a presidential system or the prime minister's party in a parliamentary system. Making such comparisons across presidential and parliamentary systems is a challenge. Studies from Latin America avoid the problem as all regimes are presidential. Studies from OECD countries have only to focus on Finland, the United States, and Fifth Republic France as presidential regimes. It is also a challenge to develop measures of partisanship and polarization relevant to democracies and nondemocracies alike. Note that I am not trying to assess the ability of parties from across the partisan divide to block legislation, although I address this issue empirically in subsequent chapters. Instead, I seek a rough measure of the risk that the executive will cede power to the opposite camp in the next election.

---

[8] See Appendix 2.1.

TABLE 2.1. *Average Annual Polarization Score,*
1990–2004

	Continuous	Categorical
Albania	24.3	1.29
Armenia	6.3	0.0
Azerbaijan	11.8	0.08
Belarus	7.2	0.46
Bulgaria	29.3	2.0
Croatia	6.8	0.67
Czech Republic	8.2	0.0
Estonia	2.1	0.15
FYR Macedonia	19.1	1.47
Georgia	2.0	0.15
Hungary	0.0	0.73
Kazakhstan	1.6	0.0
Kyrgyzstan	18.7	1.38
Latvia	5.6	0.15
Lithuania	1.0	0.61
Moldova	15.1	1.08
Poland	0.0	0.27
Romania	21.9	1.60
Russia	20.2	1.23
Slovakia	6.2	0.0
Slovenia	0.0	0.0
Tajikistan	1	0.0
Turkmenistan	0.0	0.0
Ukraine	22.2	1.53
Uzbekistan	2.0	0.0
Sample mean	9.4	0.60
(standard deviation)	(12.3)	(0.86)

In the cases at hand, there is little difference in the average levels of polarization in parliamentary and presidential systems (9.8 and 8.4, $t = 1.0$). Polarization is not consistently related to regime type. The correlation between the continuous measure of democracy and the continuous measure of polarization is only .03. Using a Freedom House democracy score of 3 as a cutoff, polarization averages 10.3 in democracies and 8.0 in autocracies ($t = 1.7$). Polarization is roughly equally distributed between old-left and right governments, 11.5 and 10.5, respectively ($t = 0.57$).

One alternative means of measuring polarization is to subtract the seat share of the party associated with the executive from the seat share of the largest party across the partisan divide. In a postcommunist setting, such measures are not very helpful because executives in presidential systems are often only weakly, if at all, affiliated with particular parties in the legislature. In relatively competitive presidential systems like Armenia, Georgia, Russia under Boris

Yeltsin, Ukraine, and Kyrgyzstan before 1996, and in many less competitive presidential regimes, like Azerbaijan, Kazakhstan, and Uzbekistan, executives had only tenuous ties to political parties in parliament. Indeed, in some settings, presidents are constitutionally barred from being members of political parties. Measuring polarization by focusing on the seat share of the executive's party would understate polarization where the executive is not directly affiliated with a party.[9]

Alternatively, one can measure the threat of reversal of policy by the frequency of turnovers in government between the two camps.[10] However, this strategy fails to take into account near misses of government replacement where economic and political agents change their behavior because of the expectation of turnover. In the run-up to presidential elections in Russia in 1996, many investors anticipated great changes in policy should the incumbent President Yeltsin lose to his communist rival Gennady Zyuganov. Expecting a change in policy, many investors pulled out of Russia, driving down the bond and equities markets (Kiewiet and Myagkov 1998; Frye 2000). Calculating the threat of electoral reversals by the replacement rate would treat Russia as a paragon of stability, but this seems at odds with the case. It is helpful to have a measure that considers these near misses given the powerful impact of "hindsight" bias, which leads us to subsequently discount the possibility of events that were considered likely at the time but did not happen (Gilbert 2007: 78–81). After the fact, it is easy to convince ourselves that we "knew all along" that President Yeltsin would win, even if we harbored great doubts about this outcome before the election.[11]

By counting the share of seats held by the largest party across the partisan divide, this measure captures the relative electoral strength of the two camps.[12] Opposition parties that claim many seats will be well placed to challenge an incumbent from a different political camp. By measuring the relative strength of the largest party across camps, this measure also takes into account

---

[9] Moreover, in many presidential regimes a large number of deputies were unaffiliated with any party.

[10] With a longer time period, one could generate a relatively reliable hazard rate that would predict the probability that an executive from one camp would cede power to an executive from another camp. Franzese (2002) creates a measure of polarization across governments in two steps. Relying on the actual duration of the incumbent, he generates a hazard rate that predicts the probability that a government will fall in a given year. He then multiplies this rate by the standard deviation of the center of gravity across governments.

[11] The classic text is Fischhoff (1975). See Bryant and Guilbault (2002) for a discussion of this bias in the Clinton impeachment hearings.

[12] This measure may inflate the relative power of a prime minister in a fragmented government by assuming that voters who support the government coalition would be more willing to cast ballots for an executive from another party within the coalition than for a candidate across the partisan divide. This seems to be a reasonable assumption given the great differences in policy preferences between the two camps, but it depends on the heterogeneity of the incumbent's camp.

the ideological distance between camps. Moreover, this measure can be calculated reliably from election returns.[13]

One potential concern is that by focusing on the seat share of the largest party across the partisan divide the measure may understate the threat posed by a large but fragmented opposition. Measuring the seat share of all opposition parties across the partisan divide, however, raises the risk of overstating the electoral prospects of a fragmented opposition by suggesting that all voters who went to the polls for any party within the camp would be willing to do the same for any candidate within the camp in the future.

Fortunately, in practice, these trade-offs are less pressing than they seem at first glance.[14] The old-left camp is typically quite unified around a single party or individual. When an old-left faction is in the opposition, their seat share is a good measure of the threat of a policy reversal generated by a turnover in government. Almost two-thirds of the observations based on country-years (221 of 345) from the sample of twenty-five countries from 1990 to 2004 fall into this category.

The risk of misstating the strength of the polarized opposition is greater when an old-left politician controls the executive and faces right opposition that is large but dispersed across a number of parties. Of the 124 observations where an old-left executive holds power, the right camp controls no seats in 42. These are highly autocratic political systems in which open opposition within the parliament is difficult to discern. In another 36 of these 124 cases, the right opposition has less than 10 percent of the seats. In the remaining 46 cases, when an old-left executive faces a right opposition that has at least 10 percent of the seats, the right opposition is almost always represented by a single party. For example, save for a few unaffiliated deputies, and a handful of small parties, a single party represented the right opposition when an old-left faction controlled the executive in Albania in 1991 and 1997–2002, Azerbaijan in 1992–1995, Bulgaria in 1990–1991 and 1993–1996, Moldova in 1990–1994 and 2000–2002, Macedonia in 1990–1999, and Ukraine in 1990–1994. It is appropriate to focus on the seat share of the largest party across the partisan divide in these cases.[15]

Political polarization resembles divided government in that it takes partisan positions held by political factions as important (Alesina and Rosenthal 1995;

---

[13] The correlation between vote share and seat share in the cases at hand is over .95.

[14] Counting all seats in the opposition camp, rather than just the largest party, produces similar results.

[15] Placing factions or elites into three broad camps is common in settings where precise estimates of partisan preferences of elites are difficult to come by. For example, in studies from Latin America, executives and parties are often categorized as labor based or business oriented (Remmer 2002); popular or not popular (Kaufman and Seguro-Ubiergo 2001); welfare oriented or efficiency oriented (Stokes 2001b); conservative or populist (Murillo 2001; 2009). Studies from OECD countries often categorize parties as left, center, and right (Woldendorp et al. 1998). Similarly, the World Bank Data-Base of Political Institutions uses a tripartite categorization of parties.

Fiorina 1996). Yet it differs by focusing on political competition between particular types of factions that have highly divergent preferences over policy. Under divided government, one party holds the executive, while another party controls the assembly. In this study, political polarization focuses only on competition between political camps. Where a right party controls the executive and a center party controls the assembly, this may be considered a case of divided government, but an example of only moderate political polarization. Moreover, the measure of political polarization used here does not require that the opposition have a majority in the assembly.

My treatment of political polarization is similar to that of Haggard and Kaufman (1995: 167), who use antisystem parties, which they describe as "left and populist parties that have historically mobilized around anti-capitalist or antioligarchic protests," as indicators of polarization. This depiction rings true for old-left parties that remain committed to dominant state sectors and high levels of protection, and generally oppose private property in land (Ishiyama 1995; 1997). Having discussed coding issues in detail, I examine whether economic inequality serves as the social basis for political polarization in the cases at hand.

Economic Inequality and Political Polarization

Identifying the social basis for partisanship not only provides greater insights into political polarization; it can also help determine whether differences in political polarization are likely to be enduring. One measurement issue related to polarization is worth noting. Scholars frequently use social indicators, such as income inequality or the extent of religious and ethnic fractionalization, to measure political polarization (Alesina and Drazen 1991; Esteban and Ray 1994; Rodrik 1999; Keefer and Knack 2002). However, this approach assumes that these social indicators are translated into politics on a one-to-one basis, which is not always the case. High levels of inequality or ethnic fractionalization may not map directly onto political representation for a variety of reasons: other issues may be more salient, electoral rules may offset social inequities, or social cleavages may be crosscutting rather than overlapping. Indeed, a number of scholars have argued for measuring "politically relevant" societal cleavages rather than all social cleavages precisely because not all social cleavages are expressed in politics (cf. Posner 2004). Thus, it is important to distinguish analytically and empirically between political polarization and its social sources. Second, because scholars have identified a number of potential social cleavages that may be translated into political polarization, including ethnicity, regionalism, and religion, it is important to identify which of these factors is at work. In sum, this work measures political polarization using expressly political indicators while also seeking to determine the social roots that underpin political polarization.

It begins by focusing on the relationship between income inequality and political polarization. One difficulty in establishing this relationship is divining the direction of causation. High levels of income inequality may lead politicians and voters to eschew the middle ground and take more extreme positions on the ideological spectrum. If more voters are gathered at the high and low ends of the income distribution, and if they vote on the basis of their position in the economy, we should expect to find high levels of income inequality leading to greater political polarization.

Alternatively, political polarization may lead to stark increases in income inequality. Executives facing a polarized opposition have difficulty earning revenue from businesses that are reluctant to invest because of policy uncertainty. Therefore, they have heightened incentives to buy political support from producer interests using fire-sale privatizations, tax breaks, and other distortions in the reform process. In addition, politicians in polarized settings may have weaker incentives to build state institutions that are costly in the short run but provide benefits in the long run (Svensson 1998). These subversions of the reform process may generate large gains to concentrated interest groups and dispersed losses to the dependent sector of the population, which should be evident in heightened levels of income inequality (Hellman 1998).

Distinguishing between these two positions is a challenge because inequality and polarization often change slowly over time and comparable data on income inequality across countries and over time are scarce. Even with copious data on inequality and good measures of polarization at the individual level over time, scholars are often reluctant to make strong claims of causality (McCarty et al. 2006). In the case at hand, data concerns are especially relevant because the most reliable and comprehensive source for cross-national income inequality in the region has data from eighteen countries at two points in time: 1987–1988 and 1993–1994 (Milanovic 1998). Because we have comparable and relatively high-quality data from only two points and must rely on cross-sectional analysis using averages over time, strong claims about the direction of causation between income inequality and political polarization are unwarranted. However, it is valuable to assess whether there is any relationship between income inequality and political polarization to help identify a possible social base of political polarization.

Data on any aspect of income inequality require a variety of caveats, and these are no exception. I use figures from the World Bank that have been compiled by Branko Milanovic (1998). The data are taken from household budget surveys conducted during the last years of the command economy and the early years of transition. Milanovic (1998: 143) discusses the potential biases of comparing data from the pre- and post-1989 period at some length and notes that "the bottom line of these systematic changes – assuming an unchanged survey design – is that incomes are more underestimated than they were in the past (and that increases in poverty will thereby be biased upwards); the effect of these changes on income inequality is less clear. In the past, surveys underestimated inequality by not taking into account the many fringe benefits received by the elite and, in the Soviet case, by systematically excluding the poor. Today they might underestimate inequality by not covering those with high incomes who refuse to participate." Milanovic (1998: 146–155) estimates that the bias against including the poor in household budget surveys ranged from around −0.5 in the 1988 and 1994 samples in the Czech Republic to around −0.3 in the 1988 and 1994 samples in Kyrgyzstan.

Nonetheless, these data are useful because they begin before the transition and provide a baseline for measuring change over time. Moreover, the differences across countries in the size of increases in inequality are greater than is likely to be accounted for by measurement error. These data have also been widely cited (Hellman 1998; Stiglitz 2000).

Most countries began the transition at relatively moderate levels of income inequality. Average levels of income inequality as measured by the gini coefficient in 1987–1988 were around .24. Indeed, the narrow range of variation in income inequality in these countries before 1989 is remarkable. However, in the next half-dozen years some countries experienced epic increases in income inequality, while others experienced smaller gains. Income inequality in Russia and Moldova doubled, while inequality increased by "only" 10 percent in Poland and 18 percent in Uzbekistan during this period. These are very large increases in a short period of time. One of the most interesting cases is Slovakia, which experienced almost no change in its level of inequality between 1988 and 1994 and, by most measures, had fairly low levels of inequality compared to its peers (Milanovic 1998). Table 2.2 places countries for which data are available into groups with polarization scores higher or lower than average for the period 1987–1994.

Countries with polarization scores higher than average between 1987 and 1994 experienced about a 66 percent increase in income inequality, while countries with polarization scores lower than average experienced only a 29 percent jump. The latter figure is large given the short time period of the analysis but is much smaller than the former. Thus, there appears to be a relationship between the size of the increase in income inequality and the extent of political polarization during the early years of the transformation.

Multivariate analysis provides a slightly more rigorous approach. The dependent variable in the first model in Table 2.3 is the average level of polarization for each country between 1990 and 1994. The variable *Gini 1993–1994* is the country's level of income inequality in 1993–1994 as measured by Milanovic (1998). I add a variable for the level of income inequality in 1987–1988 for each country and a variable that measures the extent of ethnolinguistic fractionalization (ELF) as measured by Campos and Kizuyev (2007). This variable helps to control (albeit quite imperfectly) for the possibility that ethnic cleavages within society are responsible for the extent of political polarization in the early years of the transformation.[16] I then repeat the analysis but add the size of the change in income inequality between 1987–1988 and 1993–1994 as an independent variable.

---

[16] The ethnolinguistic fractionalization is widely used but has been subject to much criticism (cf. Posner 2004).

TABLE 2.2. *Polarization and Income Inequality, 1987–1988 to 1993–1994*

	Gini Coefficient Income Inequality, 1987–1988	Gini Coefficient Income Inequality, 1993–1994	Percent Change in Gini Coefficient
Countries with lower-than-average polarization scores			
Poland	26	28	8
Czech Republic	19	27	42
Hungary	21	23	10
Slovakia	20	19	−5
Slovenia	22	25	14
Estonia	23	35	52
Latvia	23	31	35
Lithuania	23	37	61
Kazakhstan	26	33	27
Turkmenistan	26	36	38
Uzbekistan	28	33	18
AVERAGE			29
Countries with higher-than-average polarization scores			
Bulgaria	23	34	48
Romania	23	29	26
Belarus	23	38	65
Moldova	24	48	100
Russia	24	47	96
Ukraine	23	39	70
Kyrgyzstan	26	55	112
AVERAGE			66

Caution is appropriate in interpreting the results reported in Table 2.3, given the small number of cases and the measurement error associated with income inequality data, but the results are intriguing. In Model 2.1, the positive and significant coefficient on *Gini 1993–1994* suggests that income inequality in 1993–1994 is associated with the average level of political polarization between 1990 and 1994. A ten-point-higher level of income inequality in 1993–1994 is associated with about an eleven-point-higher average political polarization score. Income inequality at the start of the transformation is negatively associated with political polarization between 1990 and 1994. The index of ethnolinguistic fractionalization is unrelated to polarization.

In Model 2.2, I examine whether the change in income inequality between 1987–1988 and 1993–1994 is associated with levels of political polarization during this period. This turns out to be the case. Greater increases in income inequality are positively and significantly related to higher average polarization scores during 1990–1994. A one-standard-deviation (.42) increase in the gini coefficient between 1987–1988 and 1993–1994 is associated with an average level of political polarization that is 12 points higher between 1990 and 1994.

TABLE 2.3. *Accounting for Polarization and Income Inequality*

	Model		
	2.1	2.2	2.3
Level of gini 1993–94	1.08*** (.22)	–	1.30*** (.29)
Change in gini 1987–94	–	25.53*** (5.97)	–
Level of gini 1987–88	−2.27*** (.65)	−.27 (.58)	−2.49*** (.64)
Ethnolinguistic fractionalization, 1989–94	−8.14 (12.37)	−7.35 (12.47)	−.71 (9.59)
Constant	32.49** (13.61)	26.26* (13.70)	27.19** (11.99)
Dependent variable	Average polarization 1990–94	Average polarization 1990–94	Average polarization 1994–2004
Observations	18	18	18
R^2	.43	.42	.65

Note: The results of OLS regression with robust standard errors are in parentheses. $*p < .10$, $**p < .05$, $***p < .01$.

To assess the robustness of the results, I added in succession other variables, including GDP per capita in 1989, dummy variables for countries experiencing war, membership in the former Soviet Union, and the presence of natural resource wealth. These variables were not significantly related to the level of polarization and did not significantly change the relationship between income inequality and political polarization. Again, because this analysis relies on cross-sectional data using averages over time, it is inappropriate to make claims about the direction of causation, but there is evidence that in the early period of the transformation there is a positive relationship between income inequality and political polarization.

Data constraints make it difficult to judge the relationship between economic inequality and political polarization cross-nationally in subsequent years. Data on economic inequality in the region are available for some countries at different points in the transition and often rely on different methodologies. However, available data suggest that the large increases in economic inequality that marked the early years of the transition were largely a one-off event and were followed by incremental annual changes thereafter.[17]

In Model 2.3, I examine whether the level of income inequality in 1993 is associated with average levels of political polarization between 1994 and

[17] See the World Bank's World Development Indicators 2005 at http://web.worldbank.org/ WBSITE/EXTERNAL/DATASTATISTICS/0,,menuPK:232599~pagePK:64133170~ piPK:64133498~theSitePK:239419,00.html and UNICEF's Transmonee Data-Base 2004 at http://www.unicef-irc.org/article.php?id_article=94.

2004. Indeed, controlling for initial levels of income inequality and the extent of ethnolinguistic fractionalization, the level of income inequality in 1993–1994 is positively and significantly associated with political polarization in the subsequent decade. A ten-point-higher income inequality score in 1993–1994 is associated with a thirteen-point-higher average level of polarization between 1994 and 2004. After the early years of transition, high levels of income inequality appear to be linked to political polarization.

In sum, there is evidence of a relationship between economic inequality and political polarization at the national level, although it is difficult to make strong claims about the direction of causality. This finding helps to root political polarization in the large gaps in economic inequality that emerged at the start of the postcommunist transformation. In addition, that polarization and inequality seem to go hand in hand suggests that there is a social basis for differences in political representation across countries.

Appendix 2.1: Categorizing Factions

Coding rules are based, for the most part, on the Comparative Political Data-Set II (CPDS II) of twenty-eight postcommunist countries compiled by Klaus Armingeon and Romana Careja at the University of Bern. I have recoded some personalist parties according to the rules used in Frye (2002a) that are described here. (For examples of some partisan factions, see Table A2.1.)

Old-left factions are coded as Left-Socialist, Communist, and Postcommunist by CPDS II. Parties coded as personalist by the CPDS II that are headed by a leader who held a ministerial or Central Committee appointment within the Communist Party at the regional or all-union level before 1989, advocated a dominant state sector in the economy, and campaigned with support from the ex-communist party or a renamed version of the ex-communist party are coded as old-left factions.

Center factions are coded as Agrarian or Socialist by CPDS II. Socialist parties include ex-communist parties that advocate a broad role for the market, such as the Alliance for Democratic Left in Poland, the Hungarian Socialist Party, and the Lithuanian Right Democratic Party. Agrarian parties, such as the Agrarian Party of Moldova, are in this category as are social democratic parties, such as the Social Democratic Party of the Czech Republic.

Right factions are coded as Conservative, Liberal, or Right-Wing-Nationalist by CPDS II. Parties coded by the CPDS II as personalist that are headed by leaders who either left or never held high positions in the state or Communist Party apparatus before 1989, or ran for office against the largest ex-communist party or renamed version thereof, or advocated a dominant role for the private sector in the economy are treated as right factions. Parties coded by the CPDS II as nationalist such as the Estonian National Independence Party, Meciar's HZDS in Slovakia, IMRO in Macedonia, and Franjo Tudjman's CDU are treated as right parties, but the results are largely unchanged if they are dropped from the sample, or if they are coded according to their individual economic platforms.

TABLE A2.1. *Examples of Partisan Factions*

	Examples of Old-Left Factions	Examples of Centrist Factions	Examples of Right Factions
Albania	Socialist Party of Albania		Democratic Party of Albania
Armenia	Armenian Communist Party		Republic Bloc, Armenian National Movement
Azerbaijan	Aliev's New Azerbaijan Party (P)		Azerbaijan Popular Front (N)
Belarus	Party of Communists of Belarus		Belarusian Popular Front
Bulgaria	Bulgarian Socialist Party, Coalition for Bulgaria		Union of Democratic Forces, Coalition of Simeon II (P)
Croatia	League of Communists of Croatia	Social Democratic Party of Croatia	Croatian Democratic Union (N)
Czech Republic	CP of Bohemia and Moravia (Czech Republic)	Czech Social Democratic Party	Civic Democratic Party
Estonia	Justice Party	Rural Union	Homeland, Moderates
(FYR) Macedonia	League of Communists of Macedonia		Internal Macedonian Revolutionary Organization (IMRO) (N)
Georgia	Communist Party of Georgia, Socialist Party of Georgia		Shevardnadze's For New Georgia (P)
Hungary	Hungarian Socialist Workers Party	Hungarian Socialist Party	FIDESZ
Kazakhstan	Nazarbaev's Peoples' United Party (P)		Azamat
Kyrgyzstan	Party of Communists of Kyrgyzstan		Akaev's Ata-Meken (P)
Latvia	Latvian Socialist Party, Latvia's Unity Party		Latvia's Way
Lithuania		Lithuanian Democratic Labor Party	Homeland Union
Moldova	Party of Communists of Moldova, Socialist Unity Party	Agrarian Party of Moldova	Democratic Party of Moldova
Poland		Democratic Left Alliance Peasant Party	Freedom Union, PiS

Romania	NSF/Social Democratic Party of Romania		Democratic Convention of Romania
Russia	Communist Party of the Russian Federation	Putin, United Russia	Democratic Choice, Union of Right Forces
Slovakia	Association of Slovak Workers, Party of the Democratic Left[a]	Party of the Democratic Left	Democratic Coalition of Slovakia, Movement for a Democratic Slovakia (N)
Slovenia	Party of Democratic Renewal (Slovenia)	Social Democratic Party of Slovenia	Right Democracy of Slovenia
Tajikistan	Rakhimov's Communist Party of Tajikistan (P)		People's Democratic Party of Tajikistan (P)
Turkmenistan	Niyazov's Democratic Party (P) (Turkmenistan)		None
Ukraine	Communist Party of Ukraine, Socialist Party of Ukraine		Rukh (N)
Uzbekistan	Karimov's People's Democratic Party (P) (Uzbekistan)		Erk, Birlik (both banned)

Note: P = personalist, N = nationalist.
[a] The Party of the Democratic Left in Slovakia forms an electoral alliance with a right party in 1994 and is considered an old-left party only for 1990–1993.

Independent deputies are excluded. If the government is a nonparty or care-taker government, I trace the partisanship of the prime minister to the largest party in parliament that backs the candidate. Elections that take place after July 1 are reported in the following year.

Note three exceptions to the CPDS II. I code the Lithuanian Democratic Labor Party as a socialist rather than a postcommunist party (Ishiyama 1999; Janusauskiene 2002). This makes sense as Algirdas Brzauskas's party that evolves from the LDLP is coded as a social democratic party. I code the National Salvation Front in Romania and its offshoots as an old-left party, not a socialist party. Most observers view it as further left than the ex-communist parties of Hungary, Poland, Slovenia, and Lithuania (Ishiyama 1995, 1997; Kitschelt et al. 1999; Bugajski 2002). I code the Party of the Democratic Left in Slovakia after 1994 as a socialist-democratic party, not a left socialist party. See Grzymala-Busse (2002) for a discussion of the economic policy of the Party of the Democratic Left. These codings seem closer to the secondary literature. In addition, they better capture the economic policies that are the focus of the analysis.

Old-Left Parties

The Bulgarian Socialist Party (BSP) offers a good example of an old-left party. It inherited the assets of its predecessor, the Bulgarian Communist Party (BCP), and its leaders have tended to be former high-level officials within the BCP or its youth organization. The Communist Party of Ukraine (CPU) presents another example of an old-left faction. Its leaders emerged from the remnants of the Ukrainian Communist Party, and it advocated a large role for the state in the economy, and, in particular was a vocal opponent of the privatization of land (Rakhmanin and Mostovaya 2002). Like many old-left parties, it draws much of its support from the rural sector and other groups threatened by economic liberalization (Aslund and de Menil 2000; Aslund 2002). One judgment call involves the Party of the Democratic Left in Slovakia. I classify it as an old-left party before 1994, when it joined the Common Electoral List with other anti-HZDS parties. At this point, I classify it as a center party.

Some old-left political factions are organized along more personal lines. In Uzbekistan, Islam Karimov became first secretary of the Uzbek Communist Party in 1989 and has fended off all post-Soviet challengers. Jones Luong (2002: 130) notes: "Karimov and his supporters successfully assimilated the organiza-tional and numerical strength of the former Communist Party of Uzbekistan in a new government party apparatus and eliminated opposition to its monopoly on political power." Similarly, before 1989 Heidar Aliev headed the Commu-nist Party of Azerbaijan and was a member of the Politburo of the CPSU in the Gorbachev era. Aliev took power in a coup in 1993, following almost two years of political instability due to clashes between the nationalist Popular Front of Azerbaijan and a bloc of former communists (Alstadt 1997). Aliev created the New Azerbaijan Party, drawing largely on elites from his native Nakhichevan and former members of the Azerbaijan CP who were loyal to Aliev during his long years as first secretary.[18] As Pribylovsky (2003: 9) notes, "The backbone of the founders of the [New Azerbaijan] Party were old Soviet party-economic nomenklatura." Aliev's son assumed his position upon his father's death in 2003.

One difficult case is Nursultan Nazarbaev in Kazakhstan, who spent his adult career within the party organization and became the first secretary of the Kazakh CP in 1989. Olcott (1995: 171) describes his career within the Kazakh CP under Soviet rule as that of a "loyal functionary" and notes that the guardian of CPSU ideology, Mikhail Suslov, viewed Nazarbaev as his "protégé." Olcott (1997: 127) notes that "as an economic reformer Nazarbaev was equally cautious. In the first year after independence he showed a fundamental distrust of the private sector. His own training as a Soviet-era manager inclined him to regard management of the most important industrial and agricultural enterprises as a government responsibility. But by degrees, Nazarbaev expanded his understanding of the advantages of a market, and he announced an ambitious privatization program in 1993." Following the first dissolution of parliament in 1993 (another followed in 1995), Nazarbaev backed the creation of the United People's Party, which was heavily populated by state functionaries. Given Nazarbaev's occupational past and his constituency within the party and state apparatus, it is best to categorize Nazarbaev as old left.

Centrist Parties

Not all ex-communist parties fall into the old-left category. Ishiyama (1995, 1997), Kitschelt (2003), Grzymala-Busse (2002), and others have argued that the Hungarian, Polish, Lithuanian, and Slovenian ex-communist parties are far more committed to market-oriented reforms than are other ex-communist parties in the region. These parties differ from their old-left counterparts in several respects. Party leaders often held much-lower-level posts in the Communist Party or state apparatus before 1989. They adopted economic platforms that were roughly akin to European social-democratic parties and called for relinquishing control of the commanding heights of the economy (Mencinger 1993; Sachs and Pleskovic 1993). Indeed, they have obtained a fair degree of support from private capital. Bozoki (2002: 90) refers to the Hungarian Socialist Party as a "managerial capitalist party," while Grzymala-Busse (2002: 166) notes that by 1991, the ex-communists in Poland "supported a free market with some government intervention to protect the interests of working people." Finally, these parties often faced competition from more left-wing ex-communist factions. Centrist parties also include social democratic and agrarian parties, such

---

[18] Aliev took steps to distance himself from the Azerbaijani Communist Party following its poor showing in presidential elections in 1992, but he used his power bases within the Nakhichevan party apparatus and the republic's KGB to consolidate his power (Alstadt 1997).

as the Social Democratic Party of the Czech Republic, the Social Democratic Party of Croatia, and the Agrarian Party of Moldova.

Right Factions

The Civic Democratic Party in the Czech Republic provides a classic example of a right party. Led by Vaclav Klaus, a former academic who never held high position in the Communist Party, this party was formed on the remnants of the anticommunist Civic Forum movement, advocated a rapid transition to a market, and was sharply critical of the role of the Communist Party (Orenstein 2001: 62–63; Tworzecki 2003: 68–69). Other right factions in the region included the Union of Democratic Forces in Bulgaria, the Democratic Convention of Romania, the Freedom Union in Poland, the Liberal Democratic Party in Slovenia, Latvia's Way, FIDESZ and Hungarian Democratic Forum in Hungary, and the Democratic Party of Albania.

Other factions within the right camp are rooted more in individual members than in parties. In Russia, President Yeltsin fits better in the right than the old-left camp but lacked a clear attachment to any party. Yeltsin was a career Communist Party apparatchik but was expelled from the CPSU in 1988 and later ran for office against its successor, the Communist Party of the Russian Federation. Indeed, anticommunism was the defining feature of his political platform after 1988 (Aron 2000; McFaul 2001). He also strongly backed a market economy. Similarly, in Kyrgyzstan, Askar Akaev is classified as a right politician because he was an academic rather than a high member of the party or state apparatus during the Soviet era. In 1990 he became president by winning an election within the Kyrgyz parliament against a candidate backed by the Communist Party of Kyrgyzstan. His margin of victory was slightly more than 50 percent of the vote, indicating a high degree of polarization (Collins 1999: 46–47). President Kuchma is a right politician given his training as a manager rather than a party or state bureaucrat; in the Soviet period, he ran against the candidate of the Ukrainian Communist Party or Ukrainian Socialist Party in his presidential races. In addition, in his first term he advocated rapid reforms. Birch (2000: 95) places Kuchma in the camp of economic reformers. Thames (2005) finds significant party effects in the voting behavior of deputies in the Rada, suggesting that even in the personalized politics of Ukraine party affiliation is meaningful.

Nationalist parties are placed in the right camp. IMRO in Macedonia and Kocharyan's supporters in Armenia are nationalist parties that are coded as right. In Macedonia, the main opposition party, IMRO, boycotted the 1994 parliamentary election. This boycott artificially dampened the measure of political polarization. In Slovakia, the HZDS is coded as right as in Lewis (2000: 56, 166), but the results are unchanged if it is coded as a centrist party as in Haughton (2001) or is dropped from the analysis. In general, Slovakia is a difficult case given the shifting position of the PDL and the HZDS and Meciar's penchant for populism and personal attacks (Butora and Butorova

1999). However, because income inequality is remarkably low throughout the period in Slovakia, the distance between factions on economic policy may matter less than in other settings. Indeed, much of the polarization in Slovakia under Meciar was rooted in nationalism, concern for corruption, and personal rivalries.

3

The Pace and Consistency of Reform

> We hoped for the best, but it turned out as usual.
>
> Russian prime minister Viktor Chernomyrdin, 1999

The great diversity of economic and institutional outcomes in the postcommunist world over the past twenty years invites explanation. In this chapter, I test the argument developed in the previous chapter using data from twenty-five postcommunist countries between 1990 and 2004, and three results emerge from the analyses. First, the effects of democracy on the pace and consistency of economic and institutional reform are conditional on the level of political polarization. While democracies exhibit faster and more consistent reform when polarization is absent, each increase in polarization reduces the positive impact of democracy. In addition, autocracies conduct slower and less consistent reforms than nonpolarized democracies.

Second, a similar dynamic is at work in transfer payments. Democracies with low polarization provide generous transfers, while democracies with high polarization and autocracies are much stingier. These results are not only consistent with the argument developed in the preceding chapter; they also shed light on the puzzling coexistence of rapid reforms and generous transfer payments in the postcommunist cases.

Third, while countries with better initial conditions experienced more rapid and consistent economic and institutional reform, there is little evidence that the impact of initial conditions exhibits increasing or decreasing returns. This suggests that a simple form of path dependence is not at work in reform outcomes in the cases at hand. I begin the chapter by describing patterns in the data related to democracy, political polarization, and economic and institutional reform using simple correlations before turning to multivariate statistical analysis. I then examine the determinants of the pace and consistency of economic and institutional reform and the size of transfer payments.

The Data

Before considering the progress of economic and institutional reform in post-communist countries since 1989, it is useful to remember their starting point. For all its perversities, the command economy was an equilibrium outcome for much of its existence (Ericson 1991, 1992; Kornai 1992). Each participant in the system responded rationally to the socially perverse incentives provided by the command economy. Given the rules of the system, no individual participant had an incentive to deviate from this strategy. State planners rather than market forces set prices and output targets. For the most part, property was held nominally by the state rather than by private agents. Indeed, in most command economies the state sector produced more than 90 percent of GDP. Firms experienced soft rather than hard budget constraints, and managers were rewarded on the basis of their ability to fulfill preset (but oft-changed) targets with little consideration for social or private costs.[1] The "all thumbs" Soviet economy could direct resources to specified ends but lacked the nimbleness of information-rich market economies (Lindblom 1959).

Firms in the planned economy differed from their nominal counterparts in market economies in other ways as well. They often provided considerable social benefits for their workers and often for the community as well. Moreover, they were integrated to varying degrees into a web of economic relations at the republic, national, and international levels. Managers typically had little freedom to choose buyers and sellers. Of course, the ideal type command economy never existed. Relations between managers and state agencies were characterized by bargaining as much as by planning. Managers often misrepresented the true capacity of their firms and labor forces to convince planners to choose lower targets (Rutland 1985; Hewett 1988; Kornai 1992). Moreover, plan targets were subject to frequent renegotiation.

By the early 1980s, the high growth of the postwar years was a memory and decline had long taken hold. By 1989 many countries had begun to introduce some elements of market competition, but even the most reformed command economies began the transition missing the basic institutions of a market economy, including free prices, private property, and competitive markets.[2] To retain proper perspective of the scope of the changes over the past decade, it helps to remember that the starting point for most countries in the region was bleak.

Despite these difficult starting conditions, some postcommunist countries moved quickly to introduce a market economy. Poland, Hungary, and Estonia

---

[1] The boldest reform programs of the communist era were tame compared to even the more moderate economic reform programs in the postcommunist era.

[2] Perhaps Yugoslavia had the most market-oriented economy, but it began the 1990s with a very fragile macroeconomic position.

made great progress in building states and markets, while others such as Russia, Belarus, and Bulgaria struggled. The European Bank for Reconstruction and Development (EBRD) has created a reasonable set of measures of different types of economic and institutional reforms that permit comparisons across countries and over time.[3] Each year experts from the EBRD rate each country's progress in eight different policy areas: large privatization, small privatization, corporate governance, trade and foreign currency liberalization, price liberalization, competition policy, bank reform, and securities market reform. Experts rate each dimension of reform along a scale of 1 to 4.3, with the highest measure roughly equivalent to the level found in a developed market economy. For example, the highest score on the measure of trade liberalization is "standards and performance norms of advanced industrial economies: removal of most tariff barriers; membership in the WTO" (EBRD 2003: 17).

The coding scheme gives countries a fairly wide berth to choose how they liberalize, privatize, and regulate the economy and can easily accommodate different varieties of capitalism (Esping-Andersen 1990). The highest levels do not necessarily represent a fixed endpoint on which all countries in the region will converge as, for the most part, these measures represent performance targets rather than strict definitions of institutions. For example, Estonia's "variety of capitalism" is different from Hungary's, but each country scores at the high end of the EBRD reform index (Bohle and Greskovits 2006). Each measure aims to capture a country's performance in a single dimension of economic reform. Taken together, they provide a way to assess economic and institutional reform across countries.

Like all data, the EBRD reform scores have strengths and weaknesses. Because of their limited range, they are not as fine grained as one might like.[4] They are based on expert evaluations rather than solely on "hard" data, such as inflation or tariff rates, and thereby introduce an element of subjectivity into the measures. Experts may be unduly influenced by the expected reactions of their peers, by recent events, or by hearsay, producing an echo chamber effect among observers of a country.[5] They also do not make great distinctions in liberalization across all sectors of the economy.

On the positive side, these reform scores cover a range of different policies, are collected annually, and are highly correlated with other measures of economic reform, such as the World Bank's Annual Liberalization Index.[6] The

---

[3] For all coding rules, see http://www.ebrd.com/country/sector/econo/stats/index.htm.

[4] These measures can take values of 1, 1.3, 1.7, 2, 2.3, 2.7, 3, 3.3, 3.7, 4, and 4.3.

[5] A more subtle form of institutional bias may exist. Because the EBRD is governed by a board consisting of representatives from the postcommunist countries, experts may be reluctant to note reversals of economic reform.

[6] For the first seven years of the transition, country experts at the World Bank created their own measures of reform (De Melo et al. 2001). These measures are highly correlated with the EBRD measures.

TABLE 3.1. *Dimensions of Economic and Institutional Reform, 1990–2004*

	Average[a]	Minimum	Maximum
Small privatization	3.35 (.99)	1	4.3
Foreign trade and currency liberalization	3.31 (1.13)	1	4.3
Price liberalization	2.95 (.67)	1	3.3
Large privatization	2.57 (.95)	1	4
Bank reform	2.26 (.88)	1	4
Corporate governance	2.06 (.73)	1	3.3
Competition	1.99 (.64)	1	3
Securities market	1.92 (.73)	1	3.7

[a] Average annual reform scores across all countries, 1990–2004, with standard deviation in parentheses. $N = 334$.
Source: EBRD.

coding rules are also fairly explicit.[7] These data capture a range of different economic and institutional reforms and permit comparisons across countries over time using a standardized measure. As a result, they have been widely used. Most importantly, they include measures of economic reform, such as privatization and trade liberalization, as well as institutional reform, such as competition policy and corporate governance reform. This makes it possible to analyze the dual transformation of the state and the market in the postcommunist context. It is important to recognize their limitations, but these data are the most comprehensive available for the postcommunist world.[8]

Table 3.1, which reports the average annual reform score in each of eight dimensions of reform in the countries under study, indicates that progress has varied considerably across the type of reform. Most countries have made great strides in opening their economies to foreign trade, in conducting small privatization, and in liberalizing domestic prices. Other dimensions of reform have seen slower progress.

---

[7] To increase consistency in the measures across countries, these scores are circulated to country experts at the World Bank for comments before being returned to the EBRD, where they undergo further revision.
[8] See Campos and Horvath (2007) for a trenchant critique of using the EBRD measures to predict growth.

In the analyses that follow, I examine economic and institutional reform in two ways. I begin by examining the *pace* of economic and institutional reform as an index that captures the sum total of economic and institutional reform. I also explore the *consistency* of economic and institutional reform by measuring the relative speeds of different types of reform, such as the privatization of industrial enterprises and the quality of state regulatory institutions. This two-pronged approach gives a more complete picture of the process of building states and markets in the region.

To begin, I consider economic and institutional reform in a single dimension. If different types of reforms proceed at different paces, then to speak of "reform" as a single process may mislead. Various types of economic and institutional reforms in the postcommunist world are, however, highly correlated. All bivariate correlations of the eight dimensions of reform are positive and significant at the .01 level or better. The lowest level of bivariate correlation is .53 between reform in competition policy and reform in price liberalization. The average correlation among different types of reforms is .72.[9] Principal component analysis indicates that almost all factors of reform load on a single dimension (Dunteman 1989). Taken together, this single dimension explains almost 80 percent of the variation among different types of reforms. Thus, there is good reason to treat reform in a single dimension. Table 3.2 reports progress in economic and institutional reform using the index from principal components analysis. The scores on this reform index are generally consistent with the received wisdom. Poland, Estonia, Hungary, and Slovenia receive the highest scores, while Belarus and Turkmenistan receive the lowest.

Data and Methods

As a first cut at the relationship between the partisanship of the executive and the level of reform, I divide the sample into countries headed by old-left, centrist, and right executives. If an old-left, centrist, and right executive heads the government, the reform index averages 5.8, 8.7, and 7.9, respectively.

As argued previously, polarization may also influence the level of economic and institutional reform. I compare the average score on the reform index in a given year under polarized and nonpolarized political systems. For simplicity's sake, polarized political systems are those in which the largest old-left (right) party has at least 20 percent of the seats in the assembly and a right (old-left) leader holds the executive in a given year.[10] The 20 percent threshold is arbitrary, but given the high levels of party fragmentation in the postcommunist

---

[9] The Cronbach's Alpha for these eight dimensions of reform is .74 with a standardized mean and .62 without one. See Appendix Table A3.1 for details. See Appendix Table A3.2 for a full description of the variables.

[10] As centrist executives receive a polarization score of 0, they are categorized as nonpolarized using this continuous measure. Using the three-category measure, which allows centrist executives to take a nonzero value, produces similar results.

TABLE 3.2. *Reform Index, 1990–2004*

	Annual Average Level of the Reform Index[a]
Albania	6.67
Armenia	6.76
Azerbaijan	5.73
Belarus	4.48
Bulgaria	7.28
Croatia	7.96
Czech Republic	8.96
Estonia	9.42
FYR Macedonia	7.37
Georgia	6.85
Hungary	9.33
Kazakhstan	6.90
Kyrgyzstan	7.63
Latvia	8.45
Lithuania	8.64
Moldova	7.13
Poland	9.06
Romania	6.94
Russia	7.43
Slovakia	8.66
Slovenia	8.32
Tajikistan	5.39
Turkmenistan	3.44
Ukraine	6.32
Uzbekistan	5.53
Sample mean (standard deviation)	7.27 (2.12)

[a] Results from a principal components analysis of eight dimensions of economic and institutional reform from 1990 to 2004.
Source: EBRD.

world, controlling one-fifth of the seats in parliament typically indicates the presence of a major party. More importantly, it may indicate that the opposition from across the partisan divide has a good hope of controlling the executive in the future.[11]

Table 3.3 suggests that on average polarized countries have made less progress on a variety of dimensions of reform. Countries with polarized political systems have an average score on the EBRD rating of large privatization of 2.35, while countries with nonpolarized political systems have an average

[11] Haggard and Kaufman (1995) use a 15 percent threshold for polarization.

TABLE 3.3. *Polarization and Reform*

	Polarized Political System	Nonpolarized Political System	T-stat (*p*-value)
Reform index (all eight dimensions)	6.75	7.47	2.80 (.00)
Large privatization	2.35	2.65	2.54 (.00)
Small privatization	3.10	3.45	2.89 (.00)
Corporate governance	1.76	2.17	4.73 (.00)
Foreign trade and currency reform	3.32	3.32	.02 (.55)
Price liberalization	2.87	2.99	1.42 (.34)
Competition	1.76	2.07	4.00 (.00)
Bank reform	1.99	2.36	3.39 (.00)
Securities market reform	1.65	2.02	4.18 (.00)

Notes: Average economic and institutional reform scores for country-years in which polarization scores are (>20) and (≤20). $N = 344$.

score of 2.64, a difference that is significant at the .01 level.[12] In addition, the reform index reported in row 1 in Table 3.3, which measures the main underlying dimension of various types of reform as captured by a principal components index, indicates a statistically significant difference between countries with polarized and nonpolarized political systems. The average rating on the reform index is 6.75 for a country in a year in which the political system is polarized and 7.47 when it is not.

Table 3.4 permits a preliminary examination of the conditional effects of democracy and polarization on reform. I divide the observations into four groups depending on whether the country is a democracy or an autocracy and whether the political system was polarized in a given year.[13] I then take the average score on the index of economic and institutional reform for each country for each year. The top row reports the average scores on the reform index for countries with a democratic government in nonpolarized and polarized settings, 8.81 and 7.22, respectively. Thus, political polarization is associated with lower levels of economic and institutional reform in democracies. The bottom

[12] The correlation between the economic reform score and the continuous polarization measure is .23 and is significant at the .01 level.

[13] Polarized countries have polarization scores in a given year of 20 or higher. Democracies have scores on the Freedom House score for political rights of 3 or less.

TABLE 3.4. *Average Scores on the Reform Index*

	Nonpolarized	Polarized
Democracy	8.81	7.22
	(1.62)	(1.47)
	$n = 127$	$n = 52$
Autocracy	6.16	6.13
	(1.85)	(2.02)
	$n = 130$	$n = 32$

Note: Standard deviation in parentheses; n = number of observations in the relevant categories. Polarized countries have polarization scores in a given year of 20 or higher. Democracies have Freedom House scores for political rights of 3 or less. $N = 341$.

row repeats the exercise for autocratic governments. The average reform score for autocratic governments is 6.16 in a nonpolarized political system and 6.13 in a polarized system.

These results point to a systematic difference in the level of economic and institutional reform between countries based on the type of political regime and the extent of political polarization. However, these analyses do not control for other factors that may be associated with progress in reform. Neglecting these factors is likely to produce misleading results if they are systematically related to the variables of interest.

Multivariate Analysis

This section begins by estimating a series of ordinary least squares (OLS) regressions to identify the effects of a range of variables on the extent of economic and institutional reform. Scholars have reached only a modest consensus on how to measure, model, and analyze different aspects of the transformation of command economies. Given the disparate views, I present a variety of approaches that attempt to address different methodological concerns.

The data are gathered over time (years) and across units (countries). Time-series cross-section data have several advantages over cross-sectional analyses that average data across a single time period (Beck et al. 2001; Beck and Katz 2004; Hsiao 2003; Wawro 2003). They provide more observations and hence more information. They also permit the analysis of change over time, an important consideration given vociferous debates about the proper "speed" of reform.

I report results using an error-correction model to account for temporal dependence in the data (Greene 1993; Achen 2000; Beck 2001; Franzese 2002; De Boef and Keele 2008). The dependent variable, in this case the index of economic and institutional reform, is measured in first differences and the independent variables are measured in first differences and in lagged levels.

Because year-to-year changes in the various reform indices are generally less highly correlated with changes in the preceding year, these analyses are less subject to concerns about temporal dependence. Independent variables measured in annual changes aim to capture the short-term or transitory effects on the dependent variable. The independent variables measured in lagged levels seek to identify long-term effects on the dependent variable and capture the underlying relationship between the independent and dependent variables in equilibrium.[14] The magnitude of the effect of the lagged independent variable depends on its coefficient and on the coefficient of the lagged dependent variable.[15] The error-correction model is conservative because it is much less restrictive than other time-series models and mitigates integration problems (De Boef and Keele 2008). In addition, it not only accounts for temporal dependence in the data but also permits the identification of short- and longer-term factors that may be influencing the results. This is important because the impact of polarization and democracy may shape expectations into the future. All models include panel-corrected standard errors to adjust for potential problems of heteroskedasticity in the data (Beck and Katz 1995).[16]

The direct relationship of democracy to reform is likely to be endogenous and difficult to disentangle, but here the focus is on the effect of democracy conditional on the level of polarization. The estimation relies on the assumption that the omitted variables and sources of endogeneity associated with democracy and reform are at play in low-polarization and high-polarization settings alike. To the extent this assumption holds, it should be easier to estimate the model without this particular form of endogeneity bias (Denisova et al. 2009).

In Model 3.1, I examine the impact of democracy on the index of economic and institutional reform under varying levels of polarization.[17] The dependent variable in the first two analyses is the year-on-year change in the index of economic and institutional reform described previously. *Polarization* is a categorical variable ranging from 0 to 2, based on the ideological distance between the executive and the largest opposition, provided the latter has at least 20 percent of seats in parliament. *Democracy* measures the extent of political rights in a given country in a given year and is based on the annual measure

---

[14] For an introduction to error-correction models in a political science setting, see the essays in Freeman (1994). More specifically, I estimate: $\Delta Y_{it} = Y_{i(t-1)}.\beta + \Delta X_{(t-1)}.\beta = X_{(t-1)}.\beta + \varepsilon_{it}.$ where ΔY_{it} is the index of reform in country i in year t and $Y_{i(t-1)}$ is the lagged level of the index; $\Delta X_{i(t-1)}$ is the first difference of the independent variables; $X_{i(t-1)}$ is the lagged level of the independent variables; and ε_{it} is the error term.

[15] I use a number of different methods to account for temporal dependence in the data, including alternative specifications using a panel-specific first-order autocorrelation, a lagged dependent variable, and a variable that captures a time trend in the data by creating a variable that equals 1 for the first year in the sample and increases by 1 for each year.

[16] See Appendix Table A3.3 for a correlation matrix of the values of interest.

[17] Creating a triple interaction term using partisanship, polarization, and democracy as the components is problematic given the small number of cases. In particular, the small number of observations of old-left, polarized democracies makes it very difficult to estimate the model.

of political rights created by country experts at Freedom House.[18] The dummy variable equals 1 for countries that score 3 or lower on the Freedom House scale.[19] I create an interaction term *Democracy*Polarization* by multiplying the dummy variable measure of democracy by the categorical measure of polarization.[20] The coefficient on this interaction term examines the impact of democracy under varying degrees of polarization, while the coefficient on *Polarization* reveals the effects of polarization in a nondemocracy and the coefficient on *Democracy* indicates the impact of democracy when polarization equals zero.

Partisanship is also a categorical variable ranging from 0 to 2 and equals 0, 1, and 2 when an old-left, a centrist, and a right executive hold office, respectively. I include a dummy variable for each year that a country was involved in a foreign or domestic conflict. At a minimum, war is likely to hamper reform.[21] Because economic crises may spur economic and institutional reform, I included the logged value of the annual rate of inflation (Rodrik 1996). I add two variables to capture the initial conditions. *Oil* is a dummy variable for the four economies that are largely dependent on oil or gas, including Azerbaijan, Kazakhstan, Russia, and Turkmenistan.[22] I include *Initial Conditions*, a variable based on an index created by De Melo et al. (2001) that has been widely used in cross-national statistical analyses.[23] This initial-conditions variable is

[18] I use the political rights measure from Freedom House because the civil rights measure includes elements of economic liberalization (Kono 2008). The POLITY IV measure includes a number of curious coding decisions. Russia under Putin is highly democratic (9) – even more democratic than under Yeltsin (7) – and as democratic as Poland in 2002. Estonia is less democratic than Russia or Poland throughout the period under study. In addition, Belarus in the first half of the 1990s receives a score of 7, which places it well in the democratic camp.

[19] I use the three-point cutoff for democracy, because the number of old-left-led countries with scores of 2 or less on the Freedom House scale in the sample is twelve, but when the cutoff is 3 the same figure is thirty-three. The results are somewhat weaker using this more restrictive measure of democracy. The results are also consistent using Freedom House scores of 4 or less as a cutoff. This is theoretically justified as the argument is less concerned with procedural aspects of democracy than with the possibility that an election will produce a turnover in government. "Partially free" governments should be prone to the effects of polarization.

[20] See Kam and Franzese (2007) on interpreting the component elements of interaction terms.

[21] Countries involved in war are Albania, Armenia, Azerbaijan, Georgia, Moldova, and Tajikistan. Most conflicts took place early in the 1990s. Only 6 percent of the observations in the regression analysis are coded as war years.

[22] A dummy variable is appropriate for these cases as countries either have relatively high (40 percent or more) or negligible levels of fuel exports as a share of total exports. Multiplying the dummy variables by the price of a barrel of oil in a given year produces similar results.

[23] The measure of initial conditions is based on a principal components analysis of eleven different factors facing postcommunist governments (De Melo et al. 2001). The underlying factors include GDP per capita in 1989; pretransition growth rates; trade dependence on the Council of Mutual Economic Assistance (CMEA); the degree of overindustrialization; the urbanization rate; a natural resources dummy; the number of years under central planning; a dummy for pretransition existence of a sovereign state; repressed inflation; and the black market premium. The variable is normalized so that the mean equals zero. Higher scores indicate more propitious initial conditions.

correlated with a dummy variable for the former republics of the USSR at .93; a variable measuring miles from Vienna to the capital city in each country at .84; and the average level of GDP per capita at purchasing power parity at .74. Thus, it provides a plausible control for a number of important structural factors inherited by each country, including membership in the USSR, the lure of the European Union, and country wealth.

Results from Table 3.5 are roughly consistent with the argument.[24] Democratic governments when polarization equals zero have significantly higher reform scores as indicated by the positive and significant coefficients on *Democracy*. These effects are present in both the long and short term. Increases in polarization under democracy are associated with lower levels of reform in the long run, as indicated by the coefficient on $Democracy_{i(t-1)}*Polarization_{i(t-1)}$. The coefficients on $\Delta Polarization$ and $Polarization_{i(t-1)}$ indicate that polarization does not have a statistically significant impact on the reform index when democracy equals zero but is significantly and positively related to reform over time. The latter result is surprising, but there are very few cases in the sample when democracy is at its lowest value and the level of polarization exceeds single digits, so we should not read too much into it.

Model 3.2 uses a continuous measure of democracy and a continuous measure of polarization, and the results for the main variables of interest are quite consistent.[25] Democracy is associated with more robust reform, whereas heightened polarization mutes this effect.[26]

Calculating the size of these effects is somewhat complicated. The reform index is a latent variable distilled from eight different types of reform, which complicates interpretation of the coefficients. Because the analysis does not predict the extent of any particular type of reform, the size of these coefficients should be treated as suggestive. In addition, the coefficients on the lagged independent variables must be interpreted in conjunction with the lagged dependent variable. Error-correction models recognize that the total impact of the lagged independent variables may be dispersed over several years. Determining the total impact of the independent variables requires calculating the long-run multiplier (LRM) by dividing the coefficients on the lagged independent variables by the coefficient on the lagged dependent variable. The LRMs are larger than the coefficients in the original model because they include the immediate and lagged effects. To calculate the standard errors of the LRM, I use the

---

[24] Using a similar analysis but dropping the interaction term, I find that the direct effect of polarization on the reform index is negative and significant while the direct effect of democracy on the reform index is positive and significant controlling for other factors. Moving from o to 2 on the polarization index is associated with a 0.48 decrease in the reform index, while a one-unit increase in democracy is associated with a 0.38 increase in the reform index.

[25] When employing the continuous measure of polarization, I drop the highest value, 78, from Azerbaijan in 1992 as a significant outlier.

[26] Here the coefficient on *Polarization*, which indicates the impact of polarization when democracy equals zero, is significant. Only twelve cases have democracy scores of zero and nonzero polarization scores, and nine of these cases come from Tajikistan and Uzbekistan.

TABLE 3.5. *Polarization, Democracy, and Reform*

	Model					
	3.1	3.2	3.3	3.4	3.5	3.6
ΔPolarization	-.017	-.005	—	—	—	—
	(.049)	(.003)				
Polarization$_{i(t-1)}$	.071*	.010**	.023***	.010**	-.044***	.009**
	(.043)	(.005)	(.008)	(.004)	(.009)	(.004)
ΔDemocracy	.340***	.127***	—	—	—	—
	(.072)	(.023)				
Democracy$_{i(t-1)}$	.363***	.180***	.511***	.136***	.482***	.121***
	(.082)	(.033)	(.027)	(.033)	(.048)	(.039)
ΔDemocracy*ΔPolarization	.082	.005	—	—	—	—
	(.107)	(.005)				
Democracy$_{i(t-1)}$*Polarization$_{i(t-1)}$	-.208***	-.004***	-.011***	-.004***	—	-.003***
	(.062)	(.001)	(.002)	(.001)		(.001)
ΔPartisanship	.144**	.082*	—	.104*	—	.089
	(.056)	(.049)		(.054)		(.054)
Partisanship$_{i(t-1)}$	.171***	.146***	.140*	.173***	.189**	.152***
	(.034)	(.030)	(.051)	(.032)	(.083)	(.033)
ΔWar	-.469***	-.469***	—	-.526***	—	-.533***
	(.162)	(.151)		(.145)		(.148)
War$_{i(t-1)}$	-.562***	-.527***	-.738***	-.659***	-1.306***	-.636
	(.144)	(.135)	(.175)	(.120)	(.222)	(.120)
ΔInflation	-.059**	-.079***	—	-.043	—	-.049*
	(.026)	(.025)		(.029)		(.030)
Inflation$_{i(t-1)}$	.001	-.012	-.266***	-.005	-.323***	-.023
	(.023)	(.023)	(.036)	(.024)	(.027)	(.019)
Initial Conditions$_{it}$	.057***	.036**	.139***	.049***	-.107*	.059**
	(.016)	(.017)	(.028)	(.015)	(.064)	(.029)

(continued)

TABLE 3.5 *(continued)*

	Model					
	3.1	3.2	3.3	3.4	3.5	3.6
Oil_{it}	-.003	.055	.101	.032	.021	.027
	(.074)	(.084)	(.103)	(.071)	(.434)	(.072)
$\text{Reform}_{i(t-1)}$	-.223***	-.249***	—	-.236***	—	-.211**
	(.030)	(.032)		(.030)		(.041)
TimeTrend_{it}						-.022
						(.033)
$\text{InitialConditions}_{it}$ *TimeTrend_{it}						-.001
						(.33)
Constant	1.033***	.913***	3.96***	.836***	4.387***	1.035***
	(.180)	(.157)	(.137)	(.147)	(.244)	(.202)
Dependent variable	ΔReform Index	ΔReform Index	Reform Index	ΔReform Index	Reform Index	ΔReform Index
Polarization	Categorical	Continuous	Categorical	Continuous initial level	Continuous	Continuous initial level
Democracy	Dummy	Continuous	Dummy	Continuous initial level	Continuous	Continuous initial level
Groups	25	25	25	25	25	25
Observations	331	330	304	331	330	330
R^2	.46	.48	.85	.45	.76	.45
Prob > χ^2	.0000	.0000	.0000	.0000	.0000	.0000
First-stage f-stat					103.22	

Notes: ***p < .01, **p < .05, *p < .10. Panel-corrected standard errors in parentheses. Models 3.1, 3.2, 3.4, and 3.6 use error-correction models, while Models 3.3 and 3.5 use fixed-effect vector decomposition (XTFEVD) and instrumental variable regression (XTIVREG), respectively. Model 3.4 uses an ar1 correction. Model 3.6 includes a time-trend variable to account for temporal dependence in the data.

TABLE 3.6. *The Marginal Effect of a One-Unit Increase in Democracy on the Reform Index Conditional on Polarization*

Polarization	Marginal Effect (standard error)
0	.48 (.02)
5	.43 (.02)
10	.37 (.02)
15	.32 (.02)
20	.27 (.03)
25	.22 (.03)
30	.17 (.04)
35	.12 (.05)

Bewley transformation (Bewley 1979; De Boef and Keele 2008; Kono 2008). Appendix Table A3.5 reports the LRMs and standard errors for the variables of interest.

To assess the substantive impact of democracy on economic reform under varying degrees of political polarization, I begin by presenting the marginal effects and standard errors based on the coefficients from Model 3.2, which uses continuous measures of polarization and democracy. I calculate the long-run multiplier to capture the full effect of democracy and polarization and report the results in Table 3.6. Doing so reveals that, when polarization is absent, each one-unit increase in democracy is associated with a .48 increase in the index of economic reform; however, when polarization equals .25, the marginal effect of a one-unit increase in democracy is only .22.

To present the substantive impact of democracy on economic reform under varying degrees of political polarization in a different format, I compare the results of an increase in polarization in democracies and nondemocracies using the coefficients from Model 3.1, and again calculating the long-run multiplier. Figure 3.1 presents a simulation in which independent variables are kept at their mean values for each year, and the categorical measure of polarization is set at 0, increases to 2 for the years from 1997 to 2001, and then returns to 0. I run the simulation for democracies and nondemocracies using dummy variables for each. The results indicate that democracies experience higher levels of reform

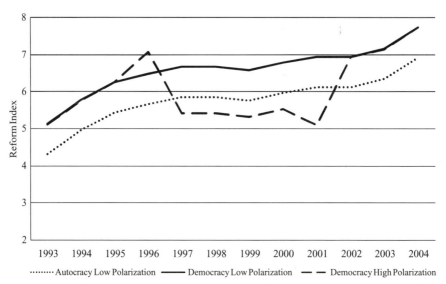

FIGURE 3.1. Polarization, democracy, and reform: The impact of an increase in polarization on the pace of reform in a democracy and a nondemocracy.

when polarization is absent as indicated by the solid line, but in the years when polarization equals 2, the index of reform declines sharply, as indicated by the dashed line. Indeed, differences in the level of economic and institutional reform between polarized democracies and autocracies are small, as indicated by the dashed and dotted lines.[27]

The next three analyses examine the robustness of the results. Model 3.3 explores whether the results are vulnerable to the inclusion of country fixed-effect dummy variables for each country. Ideally one would like to include dummy variables for each of the twenty-five countries in the sample to control for historical experiences, institutional legacies, personal characteristics of leaders, and factors specific to a country that are not captured by other variables (Greene et al. 2001; King 2001). Excluding fixed-effect dummy variables risks overstating the impact of political polarization, partisanship, and other explanatory variables.

Unfortunately, fixed-effect dummy variables have the well-known shortcoming of masking the effects of variables that change slowly over time (Beck and Katz 2001). In this case, polarization and democracy do vary over time but at rather slow rates, because these measures are taken from elections held on average every 2.5 years.[28] These slow-moving independent variables may be correlated with omitted country fixed effects, inducing bias. In other words, the inclusion of fixed-effect dummy variables is less informative than one might

[27] The impact of polarization on nondemocracy is minimal and is not shown in the graph.

[28] The correlation between polarization this year and polarization in the preceding year is .81. Similarly, the correlation between democracy and its value lagged by one year is .83.

desire in the cases at hand as they may understate the importance of variables that change slowly over time.

To address this concern, I report a fixed-effect vector decomposition model that uses a multistage estimation to parse the impact of slow-moving independent variables and unit-level fixed effects (Plumper and Troeger 2007; Kurtz and Brooks 2008). As suggested by Plumper and Troeger, I use OLS regression with a first-order serial correlation to account for temporal dependence in the data and panel-corrected standard errors.[29] Again, the results are in line with the argument, suggesting that the results are not unduly biased by the absence of fixed-effect variables for countries.

Models 3.4 and 3.5 begin to examine the possibility that economic reform may be endogenous to levels of political polarization. OLS regression assumes that the explanatory variables do not strongly influence each other. That is, the impact of each explanatory variable is assumed to be independent of others in the model. For example, if initial conditions in a country influence the extent of polarization and both initial conditions and the level of polarization influence the level of reform, then the estimates in an OLS model will be biased. A related problem is the possibility of reverse causation. That is, in the cases at hand economic outcomes may be driving political polarization rather than vice versa.[30] In previous models, I used an error-correction model that lags the value of political polarization by one year (De Boef and Keele 2008). In effect, this construction of the variable builds a lag into polarization between elections and thereby makes a simple form of reverse causation less likely. I also explored other lag structures, but these have little impact on the results. This is perhaps not surprising, as the polarization measure is constant between elections. To probe this issue further, I take advantage of the sequencing of political and economic reform in the region. In all countries, the first elections after 1989 were held before the introduction of economic and institutional reform, which allows us to use the scores for polarization and democracy after the first election to predict subsequent levels of economic and institutional reform. Because the measures of polarization and democracy precede the introduction of reforms, it is unlikely that the latter is related to the former. More specifically, in Model 3.4 I regress scores on the index for economic and institutional reform on the levels of polarization and democracy after the first election, and their interactions and the results are again reassuring. The coefficients on *Democracy* and *Democracy*Polarization* retain their signs and levels of significance.

In Model 3.5, I use an instrumental variables regression and employ a lagged value of polarization as an instrument for polarization. This test is not especially demanding given the lag structure of polarization, and does not test for an

---

[29] The slow-moving and time-invariant models include *Polarization, Democracy, Democracy* Polarization, Initial Conditions, War*, and *Oil*.

[30] I deal with this issue in greater detail in Chapter 6 by exploring the sources of political polarization and by using an instrumental variable approach to examine the relationship between polarization and various types of reform.

interactive effect, but the results hold up well. Again, we see that the impact of democracy on reform is conditional on the level of political polarization.

These results are also robust to the use of a dummy variable for democracy taken from the World Bank's Data-Base of Political Institutions (Beck et al. 2001, 2004). This is encouraging in part because the Beck et al. measure of democracy is based on the observed level of competitiveness, whereas the Freedom House measure is based on a mixture of procedural rules and subjective judgments. In addition, the inclusion of a variable for the price of oil (whether interacting with *Oil* or not) and a time-trend variable that increases by one year for each year of the transformation has little impact on the variables of interest. The results are robust to a slightly more complex measure of polarization that equals the seat share of the largest opposition party multiplied by the ideological distance on a three-point scale between the camp of the executive and the largest opposition party. That the results hold using the different measures of democracy and polarization suggests that they are not driven by any particular quirks of coding.[31]

In sum, these results indicate that the impact of democracy is conditional on the level of polarization. When polarization is low, democracy is associated with higher levels of economic and institutional reform, but each increment of polarization reduces the positive impact of democracy on reform. In addition, the partisanship of the executive is consistently associated with reform outcomes, whereas inflation is generally associated with less reform, although the estimates are not always precise.

Initial Conditions

One robust finding throughout these analyses is that countries with better initial conditions as measured by the De Melo et al. (2001) index experienced more rapid economic and institutional reform. That is, on average, initial conditions are associated with higher reform scores. In Model 3.6, I explore whether the impact of initial conditions on the reform index is increasing or decreasing over time. Doing so not only helps clarify the trajectories of reform but also speaks to debates on whether institutional legacies exhibit increasing (decreasing) returns, which will lead to greater divergence (convergence) among countries over time in their extent of economic and institutional reform.

To test the argument, I considered how the measure of initial conditions interacts with *TimeTrend*, a variable that equals zero in the first year of a country's transformation and increases by one for each year thereafter. The results, however, reveal little evidence of a relationship between the influence of initial conditions and this linear-time trend. The coefficient on *InitialConditions* is positive and significant, which indicates that in the first year of the transformation, having good initial conditions is associated with higher reform

---

[31] The results appear to hold for both old-left and right leaders, although it is difficult to make strong claims given the small sample size.

scores, but the coefficient on the interaction is not significant. That the impact of initial conditions does not increase or decrease over time, at least not in the simple fashion examined here, implies that politicians are not completely beholden to the structural conditions that they inherit and that strong versions of path dependence are not likely to be at play in the cases at hand.

The Consistency of Reforms

Accounting for the pace of economic and institutional reform in a single dimension is an important task, but scholars have also expressed interest in understanding the interplay of economic and institutional reform. Most prominently, scholars have been concerned about the rapid privatization of industrial assets in combination with the slow construction of state regulatory institutions to protect property (Hellman 1998; Stiglitz 2000; Zinnes et al. 2001). This type of inconsistent reform transfers property to enterprise insiders when state regulatory institutions are ineffectual. As such, it gives right holders weaker incentives to use these assets productively than when state regulatory institutions are strong.

Debates about the consistency of reforms across dimensions focus on two issues. Scholars have discussed whether, as an empirical matter, economic and institutional reforms move in lockstep or proceed at different paces. In addition, scholars have debated the economic consequences of reforms that proceed at different paces.

Many have recognized that economic and institutional reforms have different time horizons and therefore should proceed at different rates (Rodrik 1996; Hellman 1998; EBRD 1999). As Balcerowicz (1994: 82) notes, "Different processes of economic reform have different maximum speeds." With the stroke of a pen, ministers can open markets to foreign competition or remove price controls. Other reforms, such as large privatization or institutional reforms, take time. Even Russia's breakneck voucher privatization of large enterprises in the early 1990s took more than thirty months to conduct. One should expect different reforms to proceed at different paces. That different reforms proceed at different speeds should not be a cause for concern.

Other observers take a less sanguine view (Murphy et al. 1992). Most prominently, Hellman (1998) argues that social groups gaining from economic reform along one dimension may seek to slow progress in reform along another dimension to maximize the benefits that they gain from distortions in the transition economy. A firm manager may support an industrial privatization program that gives her control over an enterprise, but oppose the creation of institutions to regulate markets. This strategy gives the manager control over the enterprise without subjecting her to the disciplining effects of strong corporate governance. What Hellman terms "partial reform" is thought to impede the creation of market economies (Hellman 1998; Sonin 2003; Hoff and Stiglitz 2004).

Others expect reforms to be inconsistent, but argue that this should make reforms easier to conduct. Dewatripont and Roland (1995) and Roland (2000) posit that governments can use reforms to reward pivotal interest groups early in the transition in order to build support for other more politically costly types of reform later in the transition. By implementing different reforms at different speeds, governments can minimize the political costs associated with a "big bang" reform. These types of "inconsistent" reforms should be common and associated with more extensive economic reform.

Still others argue that progress in one area of reform should deepen reform in other areas (Fischer et al. 1996). For example, governments may liberalize prices and trade simultaneously to allow international market forces to shape domestic prices. Similarly, improving the quality of banking institutions may promote corporate governance by preventing incumbent managers from using corrupt banks to shield profits from shareholders. Inconsistent reform should be rare and, on balance, reforms should complement each other. Advocates of shock therapy relied on this logic to make the case for the introduction of rapid reform across a variety of policies.

Measuring the Consistency of Economic and Institutional Reforms

Measuring the relative speed of economic and institutional reform is a challenge. Following Hellman (1998), one may measure the interplay of different reforms by taking the standard deviation of each reform from the average level of reform across all dimensions in a given country in a given year and then adding them into an index. For example, one can measure the extent to which the level of trade liberalization in a given country in a given year differs from the average level of all other types of reform in that country in that year. However, this measure is not very informative because it is difficult to determine a priori the economic consequences of a high or low score. High scores that involve building institutions and then liberalizing markets could be associated with robust economic performance (Dewatripont and Roland 1995; Roland 2000). Similarly, high scores that are driven by rapid privatization and slow institution building may impede economic performance. Thus, the economic impact of the relative speed of different types of reforms depends on the type of reform.

To take a slightly different cut at the issue, I focus on the relative speed of the privatization of large firms and the quality of state regulatory institutions. Countries that privatize their industrial assets quickly without improving the quality of institutions to regulate markets provide perhaps the best illustration of the potential negative impacts of inconsistent reform (Hellman 1998; Zinnes et al. 2001; Stiglitz 2000; Hoff and Stiglitz 2004). To calculate this more narrow measure, I take the average annual score for the four measures of institutional quality created by the EBRD – corporate governance, securities market reform, bank reform, and competition reform – and then subtract this score from the extent of large privatization in each country for each year.

If a country has privatized its industrial assets extensively without improving the quality of regulatory institutions, then the score on the index of inconsistent

TABLE 3.7. *Inconsistent Reforms, 1990–2004*

	Annual Average Industrial Privatization	Annual Average Index of Institutional Reform	Annual Average Inconsistent Reform Index
Albania	1.89	1.62	0.27
Armenia	2.53	1.70	0.83
Azerbaijan	1.57	1.70	−0.13
Belarus	1.16	1.56	−0.40
Bulgaria	2.63	2.04	0.59
Croatia	2.57	2.16	0.41
Czech Republic	3.47	2.76	0.71
Estonia	3.54	2.86	0.68
FYR Macedonia	2.42	1.72	0.70
Georgia	2.65	1.68	0.97
Hungary	3.47	2.94	0.52
Kazakhstan	2.61	1.88	0.73
Kyrgyzstan	2.90	1.88	1.02
Latvia	2.82	2.51	0.31
Lithuania	3.10	2.50	0.61
Moldova	2.69	1.92	0.77
Poland	2.81	2.83	−0.02
Romania	2.54	1.86	0.68
Russia	3.11	1.99	1.12
Slovakia	3.20	2.57	0.63
Slovenia	2.45	2.42	0.03
Tajikistan	1.97	1.32	0.59
Turkmenistan	1.24	1.04	0.20
Ukraine	2.20	1.93	0.27
Uzbekistan	2.43	1.72	0.70
Sample mean[a]	2.57	2.06	0.51
	(0.95)	(0.68)	(0.53)

[a] Standard deviation in parentheses.
Source: EBRD.

reforms will be high. If the two processes proceed at the same pace, then the score will be zero. Note that this is a scale of the *in*consistency of reforms and higher scores indicate greater distortion (see Table 3.7). The mean score on the index of inconsistent reforms is 0.51 for all countries, which indicates that on average large privatization scores have outpaced the quality of institution scores.[32] The rankings make intuitive sense. Countries with relatively rapid privatization and weak institutions, like the Czech Republic and Kyrgyzstan, score high on this index, whereas countries in which privatization and corporate governance proceeded at a similar pace, like Poland and Slovenia, score below the mean. The lowest average score (−0.13 and −0.40) comes from

[32] The maximum of the Inconsistent Reform Index is 1.625 and minimum is −.75.

Azerbaijan and Belarus, whose weak corporate governance scores exceeded even their very limited privatization. The highest average score (1.12) comes from Russia, where large privatization proceeded quickly, while institutional reforms did not. This is a noisy measure, but captures the underlying concept of what I have called the inconsistency of reform. Most importantly, it permits an analysis of one aspect of the dual transformations of states and markets in the postcommunist region.

The estimation strategy is similar to the preceding analysis. I use an error-correction model and examine the effects of democracy on the index of inconsistent reforms conditional on the level of political polarization. I begin by using a categorical measure of *Polarization* and a dummy variable measure of *Democracy* and create an interaction term by multiplying *Polarization*Democracy*.[33] In this analysis, I also include a variable for economic and institutional reform, as some scholars argue that inconsistent reform depends on the level of other reforms (Hellman 1998). I report the results in Model 3.7 in Table 3.8. The positive and significant coefficients on $\Delta Democracy_{it}$ and $Democracy_{i(t-1)}$ reveal that when polarization is absent, democracies experience more consistent reform in both the short and long run. In contrast, the coefficient on $Democracy_{i(t-1)}*Polarization_{i(t-1)}$ indicates that polarization in a democracy is significantly associated with more inconsistent reform over time. These results support the main contentions of the argument: the impact of democracy on the consistency of reform depends on the level of polarization; and polarization reduces the positive impact of democracy on the consistency of reform.

The coefficients on $\Delta Polarization$ and $Polarization_{i(t-1)}$ indicate that polarization in a nondemocracy is not significantly related to the inconsistency of reform in the long run but is significantly associated with more inconsistent reform scores in the short run.

Model 3.8 introduces a continuous measure of polarization and democracy, and the results tell a similar story. The level of polarization is associated with significantly more inconsistent reform in democracies, and where polarization is absent, democratic governments are associated with more consistent reform. Model 3.9 uses a fixed-effect vector decomposition model to analyze whether the results are biased because of the absence of country-level fixed effects. As before, democracy is correlated with more consistent reform when polarization equals zero and the coefficient on $Democracy_{i(t-1)}*Polarization_{i(t-1)}$ is negative and significant. This suggests that the results are not unduly biased by the

---

[33] I also explored the direct effects of the variables of interest. Polarization is significantly and directly correlated with increases in inconsistent reform in the short term and higher levels of inconsistent reform over time as indicated by the coefficient on $\Delta Polarization$ and $Polarization_{(t-1)}$. Democracy by contrast is associated with lower inconsistent reform scores in the short and long run over time. Calculating the long-run multiplier (LRM) for each of these variables indicates that moving from a polarization score of 0 to 2 is associated with a 0.44 increase in the inconsistent reform index, while a one-unit increase in democracy yields about a 0.16 decline.

TABLE 3.8. *Polarization, Democracy, and Inconsistent Reform*

	Model					
	3.7	3.8	3.9	3.10	3.11	3.12
ΔPolarization$_{it}$	.118***	.007**	—	—	—	—
	(.037)	(.003)				
Polarization$_{i(t-1)}$	-.001	-.004	-.001	-.009*	.013***	-.009*
	(.029)	(.004)	(.004)	(.005)	(.004)	(.005)
ΔDemocracy	-.176***	-.066***	—	—	—	—
	(.060)	(.025)				
Democracy$_{i(t-1)}$	-.274***	-.076***	-.071***	-.099***	-.048**	-.104***
	(.061)	(.018)	(.012)	(.022)	(.024)	(.023)
ΔDemocracy* ΔPolarization	-.144	-.003	—	—	—	—
	(.134)	(.003)				
Democracy$_{i(t-1)}$* Polarization$_{i(t-1)}$	.118***	.003***	.002**	.004***		.004***
	(.040)	(.001)	(.001)	(.001)		(.001)
ΔPartisanship	-.045	-.011	—	-.005	—	-.009
	(.045)	(.045)		(.049)		(.046)
Partisanship$_{i(t-1)}$	.024	.027	-.014	.025	.008	.018
	(.020)	(.023)	(.039)	(.022)	(.036)	(.022)
ΔWar$_{it}$	-.172	-.170	—	-.185	—	-.202
	(.113)	(.118)		(.127)		(.125)
War$_{i(t-1)}$	-.086	-.068	-.024	-.036	-.178*	-.047
	(.068)	(.091)	(.088)	(.085)	(.094)	(.087)
ΔInflation	.022	.028*	—	.023	—	.016
	(.017)	(.017)		(.017)		(.017)
Inflation$_{i(t-1)}$	.018	.025**	.005	.026**	.010	.012
	(.012)	(.012)	(.011)	(.012)	(.014)	(.014)
InitialConditions$_{it}$	-.030***	-.027***	-.060***	-.028**	-.063**	-.039
	(.011)	(.010)	(.008)	(.012)	(.032)	(.018)

(continued)

TABLE 3.8 *(continued)*

	Model					
	3.7	3.8	3.9	3.10	3.11	3.12
Oil_{it}	−.040	−.076	−.081	.085	−.113	−.089
	(.069)	(.052)	(.061)	(.068)	(.223)	(.068)
ΔReform	.164***	.178***	—	.156***	—	.150***
	(.033)	(.033)		(.032)		(.032)
$Reform_{i(t-1)}$	.071***	.110***	.168***	.097***	.162***	.103***
	(.020)	(.020)	(.022)	(.018)	(.021)	(.019)
Inconsistent Reform$_{i(t-1)}$	−.294***	−.331***	—	−.348***	—	−.039**
	(.068)	(.064)		(.070)		(.018)
TimeTrend$_{it}$						.012*
						(.006)
InconsistentReform$_{it}$ *Time Trend$_{it}$						.001
						(.002)
Constant	−.192***	−.218**	−.079	.080***	−.151	.052
	(.094)	(.094)	(.059)	(.111)	(.134)	(.132)
Dependent variable	ΔInconsistent Reform Index	ΔInconsistent Reform Index	Inconsistent Reform Index	ΔInconsistent Reform Index	Inconsistent Reform Index	ΔInconsistent Reform Index
Polarization	Categorical	Continuous	Continuous	Continuous initial level	Continuous	Continuous initial level
Democracy	Dummy	Continuous	Continuous	Continuous initial level	Continuous	Continuous initial level
Groups	25	25	25	25	25	25
Observations	331	330	304	331	330	331
R^2	.25	.25	.64	.22	.30	.23
χ^2	.0000	.0000	.0000	.0000	.0000	.000
First stage f-stat					21.74	

Notes: ***$p < .01$, **$p < .05$, *$p < .10$. Panel-corrected standard errors are in parentheses. Models 3.7, 3.8, 3.10, and 3.12 use error-correction models, while Models 3.9 and 3.11 use fixed-effect vector decomposition (XTFEVD) and instrumental variables (XTIVREG), respectively.

TABLE 3.9. *The Marginal Effect of a One-Unit Increase in Democracy on the Inconsistent Reform Index Conditional on Polarization*

Polarization	Marginal Effect (standard error)
0	−.21 (.02)
5	−.18 (.02)
10	−.15 (.02)
15	−.12 (.02)
20	−.09 (.02)
25	−.06 (.03)
30	−.03 (.03)

absence of country-level fixed effects. Model 3.10 includes the initial values of polarization and democracy taken after the first election (and before economic and institutional reforms were introduced) to assess possible reverse causation between these variables and inconsistent reform. The results are encouraging. Initial levels of polarization and democracy and their interaction predict the inconsistency of reform in subsequent years. Model 3.11 uses the lagged values of polarization as an instrument for current levels of polarization and the results comport well with the argument.

To determine the full impact of the coefficients of interest on the inconsistent reform index requires a calculation of the long-run multiplier (LRM) using coefficients from Model 3.8. Table 3.9 indicates that when polarization is absent each one-unit increase in the democracy score is associated with a .21 decline in the inconsistent reform index, but only a .09 decline when polarization equals 20. Thus, democracy is a less potent influence on inconsistent reform when polarization is high. These changes are substantively important, as the mean of the inconsistent reform index is .51.

Figure 3.2 reports the results of a simulation using the coefficients from Model 3.7 transformed using the Bewley technique. Here I keep continuous independent variables at their mean and independent dummy variables at their modal values and manipulate the level of polarization and the regime type. Polarization equals 0 from 1990 to 1996, increases to 2 from 1997 to 2001, then falls to 0 in subsequent years. The solid line indicates that, when polarization is absent, democracies conduct relatively consistent reform, but when

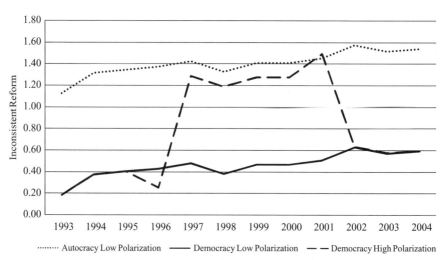

FIGURE 3.2. Polarization, democracy, and inconsistent reform: The impact of an increase in polarization on the inconsistency of reform in a democracy and a non-democracy.

polarization is increased to two, democracies experience large increases in the inconsistency of reform, as indicated by the dashed line. Indeed, polarized democracies report reforms that are almost as inconsistent as those found in autocracies when polarization is absent, as indicated by the dotted line. The results also imply that, other things being equal, autocracies conduct less consistent reforms.

It is interesting to note that the effects of polarization and democracy on the inconsistency of reform are especially pronounced early in the transformation when the looting of state assets was arguably at its peak (Solnick 1998; Ganev 1998, 2006). In results not reported here, the impact of democracy and polarization on the inconsistency of reform is especially strong when the sample is restricted to the period 1990–1996. Despite the smaller sample, the coefficients on the variables of interest are large and retain their levels of significance.

Taken together, these results suggest that in autocracies and polarized democracies, state building and market building work at cross-purposes, as politicians have incentives to weaken state institutions to provide benefits to powerful economic actors. However, when polarization is low in a democratic setting, the strengthening of state institutions and markets goes hand in hand.

These results are robust to a number of specifications. For example, using dummy variables to measure partisanship or polarization rather than the categorical measure produces largely similar findings. The results are unchanged if we drop cases in which the government is headed by a nationalist executive. The results are also robust to the inclusion of a dummy variable for the especially tumultuous year of 1992 and the use of the POLITY IV measure of democracy. They are also largely unaffected by the inclusion of a time-trend variable.

Initial Conditions and Increasing Returns

Finally, Model 3.12 assesses whether the impact of initial conditions on the inconsistency of reform is increasing or decreasing over time. There is little evidence that this is the case. The coefficient on the interaction term $InitialConditions_{it}*TimeTrend_{it}$ is insignificant, which casts doubt on the view that initial conditions induce a simple form of path dependence on the consistency of reforms.

Presidents and Parliaments

The preceding analysis of the pace and inconsistency of reforms has not explored institutional differences across countries beyond regime type, but other institutional differences may be in play. To this end, I examined whether the results reported in Tables 3.5 and 3.8 are affected by whether a country has a presidential or a parliamentary system. This analysis is difficult given the extent of collinearity between parliamentary government and democracy. The continuous measure of democracy is correlated with parliamentary government at .74, and a t-test indicates significant differences in the level of democracy between presidential and parliamentary regimes ($t = 20.7$). As a first cut at this relationship, I split the sample into presidential and parliamentary regimes and reestimated Model 3.2, which examines the impact of the variables of interest on the economic and institutional reform index. I then repeated this technique using the inconsistent reform index as the dependent variable. The results, which are reported in Appendix 3.4, show no clear pattern across parliamentary and presidential regimes. In the case of the index of economic and institutional reform, the lagged values of *Polarization* and *Democracy* are significantly associated with the reform index in parliamentary regimes, whereas the lagged values of *Polarization*, *Democracy*, and their cross terms are significantly related to reform in presidential regimes. In the case of the inconsistency of reform, the cross terms for *Democracy* and *Polarization* are both positive and significant in presidential and parliamentary regimes, whereas the lagged value of *Democracy* is significant in parliamentary regimes. Thus, although the small number of observations and split-panel analysis suggest some caution when interpreting these results, the impact of presidential or parliamentary government across these four results does not appear to be systematic.

Transfer Payments

The argument also suggests that, other things being equal, democracies when political polarization is absent should provide more generous transfer payments to the dependent sector of the population, but that this generosity should decline as polarization increases.[34] Incumbents in a highly polarized democracy (or in any type of autocracy) are likely to face a fiscal crunch because of the difficulty of inducing investment from producers who fear sharp swings in policy. Faced with the choice of preserving transfer payments or rewarding producer groups at minimum expense through inconsistent reform, politicians in a polarized setting have strong incentives to choose the latter course.

Data on many types of transfer payments across countries and over time are difficult to obtain (Ringold 1999). For example, comparable data on health spending, pensions, or aid to the poor across countries and over time are generally too few to conduct the types of statistical analysis conducted earlier in the chapter (Milanovic 1998). I use health spending per capita and pension spending divided by GDP as a rough proxy for transfer payments to the dependent sector. The data do not imply that all spending on health reaches its desired targets or has any discernible effect on health outcomes. Rather, they represent choices made by politicians under various constraints. In Table 3.10, I report the average annual level of pension and health spending as a percentage of GDP, and the level of health spending per capita across the twenty-three countries for which data are available.[35]

As a first cut, I divide the sample into countries with above- and below-average polarization scores and compare levels of transfer payments. In each case, countries with below-average polarization provide more transfers than countries with above-average polarization. In the former, pension spending as a share of GDP and health spending per capita are 7.7 percent and $143, and in the latter they are 7.3 percent and $79. These figures are suggestive, but may be misleading because factors other than polarization may be driving these relationships. In addition, because pension spending as a share of GDP is a ratio, changes in the numerator (GDP) may be influencing the results. A country may appear to be devoting more to health care only because the economy is shrinking. Thus, it is useful to introduce some variables to control for these concerns.

Data on transfer payments are much scarcer than data on economic and institutional reform, which makes using the statistical techniques described previously problematic. As a result, I average the measures of the variables of interest for each country for as many years as data are available and estimate an OLS model in a simple cross section. I include the categorical measure of polarization, the dummy variable measure of democracy, and an interaction term for polarization and democracy.[36] In addition, I include measures for

---

[34] For studies that address some aspect of transfer payments in the region, see Muller (1999), Cook (2007), Haggard and Kaufman (2008), and Inglot (2008).

[35] Data from Milanovic (1998) indicate that other forms of transfers, such as social cash transfers, may be lower in polarized countries but are too sparse to allow stronger claims.

[36] The results are less robust when the continuous measure of polarization is used. The coefficient on *Democracy* remains positive and significant, and the coefficient on *Democracy*Polarization* has the correct sign but falls short of significance in most estimations. The difference in the impact between *Democracy* and *Democracy*Polarization* remains statistically significant.

TABLE 3.10. *Transfers*

	Pension Spending/GDP	Health Spending Per Capita (in constant 1995 $)
Albania	5.6	25.6
Armenia	2.7	34.3
Azerbaijan	3.8	6.1
Belarus	7.0	70.8
Bulgaria	8.9	60.0
Croatia	8.7	392.0
Czech Republic	7.8	348.6
Estonia	6.7	183.8
FYR Macedonia	11.5	121.0
Georgia	–	39.7
Hungary	10.5	307.2
Kazakhstan	5.4	62.0
Kyrgyzstan	7.0	n/a
Latvia	9.3	115.6
Lithuania	5.8	112.8
Moldova	7.4	58.9
Poland	14	188.9
Romania	7.4	58.9
Russia	5.6	107.0
Slovakia	8.6	219.5
Slovenia	12.5	835.2
Tajikistan	4.7	n/a
Turkmenistan	–	30.7
Ukraine	8.0	38.1
Uzbekistan	7.2	38.3
Sample mean	7.7	143.0
(standard deviation)	(2.7)	(183.0)

Source: World Bank (2000, 2003).

economic growth and GDP per capita at purchasing power parity in 1989 as controls. This approach fails to capture temporal dynamics in the data, but does permit the introduction of some basic controls. Given the much smaller number of observations and fewer degrees of freedom, the analysis here is more tentative than the preceding analyses.

The first column in Table 3.11 explores the determinants of pension spending. Model 3.13 finds that when polarization equals zero, democracy is positively and strongly associated with pension spending as indicated by the coefficient on *Democracy*, but each increase in polarization reduces the positive impact of democracy on pension spending as revealed by the coefficient on *Democracy*Polarization*. This coefficient on the interaction term is significant at .11, which lies just beyond normal levels of significance. Model 3.14

TABLE 3.11. *Polarization and Transfers*

	Model		
	3.13	3.14	3.15
Polarization	1.72	53.46	28.27
	(1.32)	(46.32)	(33.77)
Democracy	5.89***	241.49**	150.20***
	(2.53)	(104.57)	(50.53)
Polarization*Democracy	−3.21^	−199.76*	−102.49*
	(1.89)	(111.92)	(53.01)
GDP per capita (,000)	.02	.02*	.02**
	(.01)	(.01)	(.01)
Growth	−.04**	–	–
	(.235)		
Constant	6.03***	−77.94	−28.09
	(1.82)	(63.17)	(31.34)
Dependent variable	Pension spending/ GDP	Health spending per capita	Health spending per capita
Polarization	Categorical	Categorical	Categorical
Democracy	Dummy	Dummy	Dummy
With Slovenia	Yes	Yes	No
Observations	23	24	23
R^2	.38	.46	.44
Model fit Prob > F	.09	.13	.01
Test significance of interaction terms	.03	.04	.01

Notes: $^\wedge p = .11$, $^* p < .10$, $^{**} p < .05$, $^{***} p < .01$. This table reports results of an OLS regression with robust standard errors in parentheses. Independent and dependent variables measured using annual averages for as many years as data are available.

examines health spending per capita and produces a similar result, although the model fit is not especially good. Again, when polarization is at its minimum value, democracy is associated with higher levels of health spending, but each increase in polarization in a democracy is associated with lower levels of spending on health. In Model 3.15, I drop the outlier case of Slovenia and repeat the analysis. Doing so changes the magnitude but not the significance of the coefficient on *Polarization* and improves the model fit.

Other variables also provide insight into transfer payments. Countries that began the transition with more wealth per capita generally spend more per capita on health. Economic growth is not related to the size of transfer payments, but it is important to include this variable as the dependent variable in Model 3.13 is a ratio. Taken together these results indicate that when polarization is negligible in democracies, spending on transfers is higher, but also that increases in polarization reduce the impact of democracy on spending.

The extent of political polarization not only influences policy choices over economic and institutional reform; it also shapes transfer spending. Here I have focused on health and pension spending as rough proxies for transfer payments and make no claims about other forms of transfer payments. Again, caution is appropriate, given the small number of observations in the analysis, and these results should be treated as suggestive.

Conclusion

This chapter used a variety of quantitative techniques to explore how partisan power and democracy shaped economic and institutional reform in the post-communist world. Results from these analyses have largely been compatible with the theoretical claims developed in previous chapters. No single statistical test should be taken as conclusive, given the lack of consensus on proper ways to model cross-national data such as these. But there is a range of evidence that political polarization and the extent of democracy influence policy choices. In this analysis, the impact of democracy on the pace of economic and institutional reform is positive when polarization is absent, but higher levels of political polarization in democracies are associated with slower and less consistent economic and institutional reform. This suggests that when polarization is low in a democracy the processes of state building and market building go hand in hand, but that in high-polarization democracies and in autocracies, the two processes work at cross-purposes.

In addition, more limited evidence implies that nonpolarized democracies spend more generously on transfers than do polarized democracies or autocracies. These results suggest that the pressure to retain office in a polarized democracy heightens incentives for executives to subvert economic and institutional reform and to reduce transfer payments. More generally, they help account for the somewhat puzzling coexistence of extensive reforms and generous transfer payments in the low-polarization democracies in the sample.

Appendix Tables A3.1–5

TABLE A3.1. *Correlation Matrix of Economic and Institutional Reforms*

	1	2	3	4	5	6	7	8
1. Large privatization	1.00							
2. Small privatization	0.81	1.00						
3. Corporate governance	0.83	0.78	1.00					
4. Securities reform	0.73	0.67	0.79	1.00				
5. Bank reform	0.83	0.80	0.90	0.79	1.00			
6. Competition	0.76	0.64	0.79	0.81	0.74	1.00		
7. Trade liberalization	0.75	0.84	0.77	0.60	0.81	0.60	1.00	
8. Price liberalization	0.67	0.70	0.64	0.53	0.67	0.56	0.73	1.00

Note: All correlations are significant at .01.
Source: EBRD.

TABLE A3.2. *Descriptive Statistics*

Variables	Mean (sd)	Min/Max	Source and Notes
Reform Index	4.53 (2.11)	0/8.06	European Bank for Reconstruction and Development; principal components index of 8 types of economic and institutional reform (minimum set to zero)
Inconsistent Reform Index	.51 (.53)	−.75/1.625	European Bank for Reconstruction and Development; large privatization score minus average score on 4 institutional reforms
Polarization (continuous)	9.36 (12.4)	0/78	Armingeon and Careja (2004) plus author calculations
Democracy (continuous)	3.48 (1.98)	0/6	Freedom House; minimum set to 0
Partisanship	1.13 (.91)	0/2	Armingeon and Careja (2004) plus author calculations
Oil	.15 (.36)	0/1	Dummy variable for Russia, Kazakhstan, Azerbaijan, Turkmenistan
Index of Initial Conditions	.08 (2.30)	−3.43/3.53	De Melo et al. (1996, 2001); principal components index of 11 factors; normalized mean = 0; low scores mean worse conditions
Inflation (log)	3.21 (2.06)	.01/9.65	European Bank for Reconstruction and Development
War	.06 (.23)	0/1	Author calculation

TABLE A3.3. *Correlation Matrix of Variables of Interest*

	1	2	3	4	5	6	7	8	9	10	11	12	13
1. Reform Index	1.0												
2. Inconsistent Reform Index	.45	1.0											
3. Polarization (categorical)	-.07	.05	1.0										
4. Polarization (continuous)	.23	.01	.78	1.0									
5. Democracy (continuous)	.68	.10	.12	.02	1.0								
6. Democracy dummy	.55	.03	.14	.06	.87	1.0							
7. Partisanship	.42	.12	.09	.10	.56	.41	1.0						
8. Oil	-.28	-.02	.13	.02	-.43	-.31	-.32	1.0					
9. Initial conditions	.51	.01	.13	.07	.70	.56	.44	-.49	1.0				
10. Inflation, log	-.69	-.32	.19	.24	-.31	-.20	-.18	.12	.29	1.0			
11. War	-.37	-.24	-.04	.05	-.14	-.15	-.03	.01	.14	.36	1.0		
12. Miles from Vienna	.42	.13	-.19	-.11	-.73	-.60	-.42	.45	-.85	.24	.11	1.0	
13. FSU	-.39	.05	-.13	-.10	-.49	-.40	-.26	.36	-.92	.24	.11	.67	1.0

Notes: Based on annual measures of each independent variable used in the analysis. FSU = member of the former Soviet Union.

Appendix 3.4: Presidentialism and Parliamentarism

Identifying the impact of parliamentary and presidential regimes is difficult, given constraints on the data. Parliamentarism is associated with the continuous measure of democracy at .74 and the dummy variable measure of democracy at .67. Thus, it is problematic to include it in the model either directly or by interacting it with polarization. Indeed, there are no presidential regimes that are in the "free" category, that is, earning a score of 1 or 2 according to the Freedom House index in the sample. Similarly, only 6 of 189 observations among parliamentary governments fall in the not free range of Freedom House scores of 6 or 7. In addition, parliamentary and presidential regimes change very rarely. Only two countries in the sample switch between presidential and parliamentary regimes. Thus, estimating the impact of these variables is difficult in a time-series cross-section analysis.

As a first cut, I split the sample of countries into presidential and parliamentary regimes and estimated Model 3.2, which examines the impact of *Democracy* and *Democracy*Polarization* on the index of economic and institutional reform, and report the results in columns 1 and 2 of Table A3.4. I then repeated this exercise using the index of inconsistent reform as the dependent variable and report the results in columns 3 and 4 of Table A3.4.

TABLE A3.4. *Reform in Presidential and Parliamentary Regimes*

	Parliament	President	Parliament	President
ΔPolarization	−.017	−.073	.140***	.052
	(.063)	(.080)	(.045)	(.058)
Polarization$_{i(t-1)}$	−.139	.410***	−.290***	.089
	(.101)	(.139)	(.098)	(.085)
ΔDemocracy	.112**	.256***	−.109**	−.044
	(.043)	(.060)	(.037)	(.038)
Democracy$_{i(t-1)}$	.121***	.150***	−.121***	−.059*
	(.043)	(.047)	(.032)	(.033)
ΔDemocracy* ΔPolarization	−.021	.191**	−.105	−.002
	(.092)	(.088)	(.068)	(.072)
Democracy$_{i(t-1)}$* Polarization$_{i(t-1)}$	.009	−.165***	.072***	.045*
	(.024)	(.042)	(.022)	(.027)
Constant	1.475***	.063***	.487**	−.212
	(.197)	(.256)	(.210)	(.160)
Dependent variable	ΔReform Index	ΔReform Index	ΔInconsistent Reform Index	ΔInconsistent Reform Index
Observations	178	151	178	151
R^2	.66	.42	.32	.31

Notes: Control variables for war, initial conditions, inflation, and oil included, but not reported. $^*p < .10$, $^{**}p < .05$, $^{***}p < .01$. Model reports the results of regressions using error-correction models with panel-corrected standard errors in parentheses dividing the sample into parliamentary and presidential systems. Polarization is measured using a categorical variable (0–2) and democracy is measured using a continuous variable (0–6) described in the text.

The results should be treated with caution given the smaller sample sizes. Presidential regimes have 151 observations; parliamentary regimes have 178. Moreover, while the average number of observations per case is sufficient, in one country that switches between parliamentary and presidential regimes, the minimal number of observations is less than 3. The results do not seem to be affected by splitting the sample. *Democracy* and *Polarization* have greater leverage on the pace of economic and institutional reform in presidential regimes as indicated in columns 1 and 2, but are associated with significantly higher scores on the inconsistent reform index in both parliamentary and presidential regimes as demonstrated in columns 3 and 4. This cannot rule out the possibility that parliamentary and presidential regimes have a systematic impact on reform but does give some confidence that the results are not driven solely by presidential or parliamentary regimes.

TABLE A3.5. *Interpreting the Impact of Polarization and Democracy*

	Model			
	3.2A	3.3A	3.5A	3.6A
Polarization$_{i(t-1)}$	.128*	.027***	.071*	−.003
	(.066)	(.007)	(.037)	(.005)
Democracy$_{i(t-1)}$	1.19***	.478***	−.450***	−.208***
	(.105)	(.019)	(.062)	(.020)
Democracy$_{i(t-1)}$*	−.503***	−.010**	.224***	.006***
Polarization$_{i(t-1)}$	(.100)	(.002)	(.050)	(.001)
Partisanship$_{i(t-1)}$	.766***	.562***	.056**	.079***
	(.052)	(.033)	(.027)	(.024)
War$_{i(t-1)}$	−2.314***	−2.081***	−.309***	−.192*
	(.129)	(.117)	(.083)	(.098)
Inflation$_{i(t-1)}$	−.073**	0.077	.056***	.074**
	(.033)	(.024)	(.013)	(.013)
Initial	.248***	.139***	−.100***	−.081***
conditions$_{it}$	(.017)	(.016)	(.009)	(.010)
Oil$_{it}$	−.130	.140	−.119	−.219***
	(.123)	(.124)	(.073)	(.068)
Constant	7.584***	3.841***	.607***	−.681***
	(.123)	(.123)	(.100)	(.101)
Dependent variable	Reform Index	Reform Index	Inconsistent Reform Index	Inconsistent Reform Index
Polarization	Categorical	Continuous	Categorical	Continuous
Democracy	Dummy	Continuous	Dummy	Continuous
Observations	331	330	331	330

Notes: *$p < .10$, **$p < .05$, ***$p < .01$. Results using error-correction model with panel-corrected standard errors in parentheses. Coefficients calculated using the Bewley transformation that estimates the full effect of a one-unit change in the variables of interest. R^2 and lagged dependent variable are not reported in the Bewley transformation.

4

Political Polarization and Economic Growth

Previous chapters demonstrated a link between political polarization, democracy, and policy choices. Extensive political polarization in democracies and autocratic rule more generally impedes the development of state regulatory institutions and slows economic reforms. But so far the analysis has not examined economic performance. Is political polarization associated with slower economic growth? If so, how does it work? In addition, how do initial conditions shape economic performance? This chapter finds that political polarization is correlated with slower economic growth. In addition, there is some evidence that polarization impedes growth by slowing economic and institutional reform. Finally, initial conditions have a profound impact on economic growth, but these effects decline significantly over time.

I begin by developing an argument linking political polarization to economic performance on the basis of insights generated in Chapter 1 before presenting arguments linking economic reform and initial condition to economic growth. I then assess these arguments by examining variations in growth rates across the postcommunist world from 1990 to 2004. Given disagreements about the proper way to analyze economic growth, particularly over periods as short as those examined here, the empirical results should be seen as suggestive rather than definitive.[1]

I focus on economic growth rather than investment, in part, because of data constraints. Perhaps the best data on investment at the national level come from the EBRD, but its measure includes investment by both the state and the private sector.[2] Because much of the investment by the state is a legacy

---

[1] See Appendix Table A4.1 for a table reviewing the methods used to study economic growth in the postcommunist world. A more complete model would account explicitly for the potential endogeneity between economic reform and other variables, but this one-step model is common in the literature and places less stringent demands on a small dataset. See Rodrik (2005) for a critique of the large literature on how policy affects economic growth.

[2] The EBRD notes: "Gross domestic investment consists of additional outlays to the economy's fixed assets, plus net changes in inventory levels. Fixed assets include: land improvements (fences,

of the inefficient command economy or is directed to constituents for political benefits, there are good reasons to avoid this measure in a model of economic growth. The bivariate correlation between this measure of investment and the rate of economic growth is $-.09$, and some countries enter the dataset with investment rates of more than 50 percent of GDP. This is probably why few analyses of economic growth in the region use this measure. In the next chapter, I take up the link between polarization and investment using firm-level data.

Political Polarization and Economic Growth

Insights developed in Chapter 1 yield several propositions about the relationship between political polarization and economic growth. Political polarization should have both direct and indirect effects on economic performance. By shaping the level of economic and institutional reform, political polarization should influence economic performance indirectly. Working from the assumption that higher levels of economic and institutional reform produce stronger incentives to produce and faster rates of growth, polarization may slow growth by inhibiting progress in economic reform. As in Svensson (1998) and Keefer and Knack (2002), this work examines whether political polarization influences economic growth via economic policy.

Even controlling for the level of economic reform, however, we might expect political polarization to have a direct impact on economic performance by weakening the incentive to take advantage of policy change. Economic reform is intended to motivate producers to put their assets to good use. Yet, because economic and institutional reforms typically impose short-term adjustment costs before generating benefits, businesspeople consider the likelihood that policy will be reversed, a much greater possibility in highly polarized political systems. Political polarization may therefore influence economic performance by blunting incentives to invest in response to changes in policy. Adjusting to specific reforms typically requires short-term costs for the promise of future economic gain. Facing a higher probability of a policy reversal should a government from the other camp come to power, businesses in highly polarized political environments are likely to respond to economic reforms with far less gusto than in more predictable settings. Rather than adjusting to new policies, they may prefer to reduce investment or park their funds abroad until the uncertainty over policy diminishes.[3] Those investments that are made when

---

ditches, drains, etc.); plant, machinery and equipment purchases; and the construction of roads, railways, schools, offices, hospitals, private residential dwellings, commercial and industrial buildings, etc. Inventories are stocks of goods held by firms to meet temporary or unexpected fluctuations in production or sales and 'work in progress.' Net acquisitions of valuables are also considered capital formation."

[3] One might expect to find different types of investment in the two settings. In more polarized settings investors may favor shorter-term and less-capital-intensive investments. To the extent that longer-term, capital-intensive investments are larger than less-capital-intensive investments, we should find a high correlation between the type and size of investment.

polarization is high are more likely to be short term or in the informal economy. Thus, political polarization may impede economic performance directly by blunting incentives to adjust to new policies and indirectly by reducing incentives to implement economic and institutional reforms.

Economic Growth and Economic Strategy

Perhaps the most rancorous debate in postcommunist studies is how the speed of economic reform influences economic growth (Roland 2000). Rapid reform advocates argue that fast liberalization and privatization on a wide front offer the best hope for spurring growth. Four claims support this argument. Rapid reforms allow governments to introduce efficiency-enhancing policies during their honeymoon period and thereby increase the chances that the reforms will take root. Fast liberalization is more likely to bring rewards before the next round of elections, thus ensuring that the transition from a command economy would not be reversed (Lipton and Sachs 1990). This strategy also reduces opportunities for rent seeking when compared to the distortions inherent in maintaining the status quo of partially reformed economies (Boycko et al. 1995). Finally, rapid reform signals to domestic and foreign audiences that the government is willing to initiate reforms that will be costly in the short run but beneficial in the long run (Rodrik 1989). Advocates of this view tend to see the economic situation of the postcommunist countries at the start of the 1990s as spiraling out of control and requiring drastic remedial efforts (Aslund 2002). Moreover, they generally have little faith in the capacity of the state to oversee and manage economic reform. In other words, market failures were likely to produce less damage than government failures.[4]

In contrast, gradualists advocate a slower pace of transformation. Some supporters of this position encourage politicians to sequence reforms to their advantage. First-stage reforms may produce rewards for some groups and allow politicians to build coalitions that can provide a strong social base for second-stage reforms (Aghion and Blanchard 1994; Roland 2000). Others argue that gradual economic reforms allow greater opportunities for "learning by doing" (Murrell 1992; Kornai 1990). The great uncertainty of the transformation may heighten the benefits of experimentation – a strategy that is possible with a gradual reform that does not lock the country into policies that appear optimal ex ante but are not ex post (Murrell 1992; Stiglitz 2000). Gradualists tend to view the condition of the economy in the early years of the transition as dire but hardly justifying rapid liberalization (Stiglitz 2000). Instead, they focus on the relatively high levels of economic development, well-educated populaces, and low levels of inequality in the region as essential tools for economic growth. They also tend to see the costs of state failure as greater than the costs of market failures.[5]

---

[4] For a critique, see Murrell (1992).

[5] Some, but not all, gradualists invoked China as an example of successful gradual transition, but this comparison is not without problems (Mau 2000).

The debate over the impact of economic reforms on performance has gen- erated more heat than light, and many issues remain controversial given the complexity of the task and the bluntness of the tools available to study the issue (Aslund et al. 1996; Fischer et al. 1996; De Melo et al. 2001; Berg et al. 1999; Heybey and Murrell 1999; Falcetti et al. 2002).[6]

Initial Conditions: Birth Defect or Childhood Disease?

In addition to economic reform, scholars have debated the extent to which initial conditions shape economic performance. Some argue that initial condi- tions, such as membership in the former Soviet Union, levels of wealth, indus- trial composition, extent of overindustrialization, and other structural factors have a pronounced effect on economic performance – one that is greater than that of economic policy choices (Krueger and Ciolko 1998; Popov 2000). For example, De Melo et al. (2001) create an initial conditions index based on eleven different structural features of the economy in each country at the start of the transition and argue that initial conditions are associated with slower growth. In this view, the institutional legacies of the command economy leave a deep imprint on future economic performance.

In some respects, studies of the impacts of initial conditions mirror a broader discussion in political science on the nature of institutional and economic change. Scholars have examined how initial conditions and institutional lega- cies have influenced a variety of outcomes. To cite just a few examples, Treis- man (2000) explores whether former British or French colonials experience higher levels of corruption after independence, while Geddes (2003) analyzes how previous regime type influences prospects for democracy. Indeed, many scholars have linked various aspects of the legacy of communist rule to politi- cal and economic outcomes (cf. Hanson 1995; Geddes 1995; Linz and Stepan 1996; Stark and Bruszt 1998; Kitschelt 2003).

One interesting question that has begun to receive more attention in recent years is whether the impact of initial conditions and institutional legacies increase or decrease over time (North 1990; Pierson 2004; Brooks 2008). If initial conditions and institutional legacies exhibit increasing returns, then we should find greater divergence between countries that began the transition with different starting points and legacies. This suggests the creation of a great divide between countries with more promising and less promising initial conditions.

---

[6] A number of authors have pointed out that much of the debate on the impact of economic reforms confuses the *level* of economic reform with the *speed* of economic reform (Heybey and Murrell 1999; Berg et al. 1999; Staehr 2005). While countries that achieve high levels of economic reform may experience better performance, the wrenching process of instituting economic reforms may increase uncertainty, raise transaction costs, and heighten "disorganization" within the economy and produce lower rates of growth in the interim (Blanchard 1997). Alternatively, the rapid removal of distortions in the economy may provoke a quick response from the private sector, leading to high rates of growth in the short term. The error-correction model accounts for short- and long-term effects of liberalization on economic growth.

If, however, these initial conditions and institutional legacies exhibit decreasing returns, then countries should overcome their initial difficulties with time. In sum, the outcome of this debate has implications for the future economic trajectory of countries in the region, but can also inform broader debates in comparative politics about the impact of institutional legacies.

The Data

Most observers begin their analysis of the transformation in 1989, and this one does so as well, but it is useful to remember that the countries of the region began the 1990s on the heels of a long economic decline (Kotkin 2000). Campos and Corricelli (2002) note that average annual growth rates among the economies of the former Soviet Union were just 1.5 percent between 1981 and 1990. Total factor productivity (TFP) growth in this period was 0. Looking across eight East European countries, they find that average annual growth rates and TFP growth were only 0.5 and 0.8 in this same period. Governments coming to power amid the rubble of the command economy ruled countries mired in long-term economic stagnation.

If we turn to the postcommunist era, economic performance reveals great variation across countries and over time. Some countries did much better than expected. It is rarely recalled today, but economic performance in Poland in the 1970s and 1980s was dismal. Saddled with a large per capita foreign debt, a militant labor movement, an inefficient agricultural sector, and a declining industrial base, Poland's economic prospects looked bleak. However, Poland became a regional economic power in the 1990s. After an initial decline in 1990 and 1991, growth rates in Poland averaged more than 5 percent per year from 1992 to 2000.

Another surprising case comes from Central Asia. Among the former republics of the Soviet Union, Uzbekistan had the highest growth rate in the 1990s. By 2000 the average annual growth rate in Uzbekistan was slightly negative (-0.01). Given the highly authoritarian government of Uzbekistan, one might doubt the veracity of these data, but electricity usage, which is harder to hide, fell only slightly in Uzbekistan during the 1990s.[7] Even the International Monetary Fund, which has been very critical of Uzbek economic policy, published an article in the *IMF Staff Papers* entitled "The Uzbek Growth Puzzle" (Zettelmeyer 1999). By other indicators, Uzbekistan's performance was less impressive. Inflation and budget deficits were about par for the region, while growth slowed relative to the region after 2000. Yet, the growth path of this landlocked, poor, and largely agricultural economy merits explanation.

Other economies underperformed expectations. Ukraine's well-educated populace, proximity to Europe, balance of agriculture and industry, and social homogeneity led Deutsche Bank to predict that it would be the fastest-growing

---

[7] Uzbekistan's level of industrial development was relatively low, a factor that may have contributed to its small drop in electricity usage in the postcommunist period.

former Soviet republic, but growth averaged −2.8 percent per year, far below the benchmark for the region (Schroeder 1998).

Data on economic performance from the postcommunist region suffer from a variety of well-known shortcomings. In many countries, much economic activity takes place off the books, and while state statistical agencies have tried to incorporate estimates of the unofficial economy, the success of these efforts likely varies across countries (Johnson et al. 1997).[8] As Table 4.1 indicates, economic growth has generally been weak across the region. The average annual rate of economic growth from 1990 to 2004 is just under one-half of 1 percent. Even adjusting rates of economic growth for the size of the informal economy suggests that growth has been marginally positive.

While economic growth in the postcommunist world has been dire, claims that the economic contraction was unprecedented are perhaps too strong. Much of the economic decline was concentrated in the first half of the 1990s, when average annual growth rates were −.5 percent. Growth rates rebounded after 1994 and averaged 4.2 percent over the next decade. In retrospect, the sharp declines early in the transformation are unsurprising as countries in the region inherited economic, political, and social structures poorly adapted for a market economy. Moreover, civil wars dotted the region and impaired economic growth. Somewhat more surprising are the impressive rates of growth across the region beginning in 1999.

Focusing on average annual rates of economic growth, however, masks considerable diversity across countries and over time. Increases in the price of natural gas helped the petro-state of Turkmenistan grow by 18 percent in 2000. In contrast, GDP fell by 42 percent in Armenia in 1992, dragged down by civil war and the trade shock of the collapse of the Soviet Union. Growth rates have also varied greatly within countries over time. For example, Russia saw a 15 percent drop in GDP in 1992 and an 8 percent increase in 2000.

Statistical Analysis

Selecting the variables to include in statistical models of economic growth is a challenge (Islam 1995). After reviewing several decades of studies of economic growth from around the globe, two economists from the World Bank noted laconically: "There does not exist a consensus theoretical framework to guide

---

[8] Estimates of economic growth rely on state statistical agencies that began the transition possessing neither the human nor organizational capital to gather data in a market economy. While many state statistical agencies began cooperation with international agencies to improve the quality of their data in the early 1990s, they remain underfunded and understaffed in many countries (Aslund 2002; Herrera 2008). Scholars have developed means to address this problem. Some use rules of thumb to increase the size of output in countries with large unofficial economies, while others rely on estimates of electricity usage (Selowsky and Martin 1997; Dobozi and Pohl 1995). In the quantitative analysis, I find that the results do not depend significantly on the measures for growth.

TABLE 4.1. *Economic Growth in the
Postcommunist World, 1990–2004*

	Average Annual Rates of Economic Growth
Albania	2.5
Armenia	2.6
Azerbaijan	−0.5
Belarus	1.5
Bulgaria	−0.6
Croatia	−0.3
Czech Republic	1.0
Estonia	2.8
Macedonia	−0.8
Georgia	−1.6
Hungary	1.3
Kazakhstan	1.7
Kyrgyzstan	−1.0
Latvia	0.7
Lithuania	0.5
Moldova	−3.8
Poland	2.5
Romania	0.2
Russia	−0.5
Slovakia	1.4
Slovenia	1.9
Tajikistan	−1.4
Turkmenistan	1.8
Ukraine	−2.8
Uzbekistan	1.1
Mean (standard deviation)	0.44 (9.29)

Source: EBRD.

empirical work on growth, and existing models do not completely specify the variables that should be held constant while conducting statistical inference on the relationship between growth and variables of primary interest" (Levine and Renelt 1992: 242). Their review indicated that more than "50 variables have been found to be significantly correlated with growth in at least one regression" (Levine and Renelt 1992: 242). Many of these variables are not particularly relevant for growth over the short or medium term studied here, but this review points to the lack of consensus on the variables to be included in a model of economic growth.

These concerns are also apparent in the growing literature on macroeconomic outcomes in the postcommunist countries, but most studies have adopted a fairly similar framework.[9] To date, analyses of economic growth have rarely relied on standard Solow-style growth models, which may be better at analyzing long-term economic growth than the short and medium terms analyzed here. Instead, they have focused on two sets of variables. First, scholars have argued that the initial conditions in each country at the start of a transition, such as membership in the former Soviet Union, the level of wealth, the extent of industrialization, and the structure of the economy, shape economic growth (De Melo et al. 2001; Popov 1999; Krueger and Ciolko 1998). Second, scholars have devoted particular attention to how various types of reform influence economic growth (Fischer et al. 1996; Aslund et al. 1996; Berg et al. 1999; Heybey and Murrell 1999; Havrylyshyn and van Rooden 2003; Staehr 2005). As such, they tend to include measures of economic policy, such as the extent of privatization, commercial openness, price liberalization, or the exchange rate regime in analyses of economic growth.[10]

One difficulty of examining the effect of individual economic policies on performance is that different policies are highly correlated, which may create problems of multicollinearity when each dimension is added individually. This makes it difficult to identify which factors are actually driving the results. To address this problem, I use the index of economic and institutional reform from preceding chapters (Havrylyshyn and van Rooden 2003; Staehr 2005).

Identifying the impact of reform on economic growth is also complicated by a difficult measurement problem. Rodrik (2005) argues that measures of economic reform often fail to distinguish between two distinct components: policy effort exerted by the government and reform outcomes. That is, governments more committed to reform may devote more effort and also may achieve higher levels of economic growth, but measures rarely decompose the impact of economic reforms into these two different elements. Thus, measures of economic reform that are weighted heavily toward policy outcomes should be especially likely to be associated with economic growth. As Campos and Horvath (2007: 4) point out, the EBRD measures combine "policy inputs as well as outcomes (for instance, for external liberalization, one can find tariff levels as well as trade openness)." Because the EBRD measures include policy outcomes, they may be capturing economic performance as well as policy change. This insight suggests that regressing economic growth on reform is an easy test of the

---

[9] I do not use a Cobb-Douglass production function, due in part to difficulties gaining data but also to the difficulty sustaining some of the underlying assumptions in this approach. The problem of economic growth in the postcommunist world is less the accumulation of capital than in using the existing capital more efficiently. Most authors have been skeptical of this technique for analyzing economic growth in transition. The standard Barro-style growth regressions are better at capturing long-run growth trends (Barro 1991).

[10] This literature generally takes policy change as exogenous to other variables. A more complete approach would take into account the determinants of policy choice and try to model how these factors influence growth directly rather than solely through their impact on policy change. Berg et al. (1999) offers a three-step model to account for the impact of input and policy choice on economic performance using a general to specific approach.

argument that economic reform is associated with faster growth. Therefore, the point estimates of the direct impact of economic reform on economic growth may be inflated.

Over the first decade of transformation, scholars produced a substantial literature on economic growth, and Havrylyshyn (2001: 60) sums up the initial findings: "To wit, standard factors inputs are not important; stabilization is necessary for growth; liberalization and structural reform strongly affect growth performance, and unfavorable initial conditions can hinder growth," and he adds that "these results are not dramatically altered in those studies with a large observation set and much more sophisticated econometrics." Havrylyshyn (2001: 79–81) adds that there is continuing debate on the timing and sequencing of institutional reforms, the speed of reforms, whether initial conditions affect performance directly or through policy choices, and the nature of the effects of privatization. Campos and Horvath (2007: 4) report less consensus in their analysis of thirty-six studies of the impacts of economic reform on growth in transition economies. They find that roughly one-third of the coefficients on economic reform were positive and statistically significant, roughly one-third were negative and significant, and roughly one-third were not significantly different from zero.

The Model

The analysis in Table 4.2 employs econometric methods commonly found in studies of economic growth in transition economies. I begin by using ordinary least squares (OLS) regression with panel-corrected standard errors, and an error-correction model to account for temporal dependence in the data before using alternative specifications (Beck and Katz 1995, 2001; Franzese 2002). The measure of economic performance is the annual rate of economic growth in a given country in a given year (EBRD 1999, 2005). I add a categorical variable for political polarization that ranges from 0 to 2 based on the ideological distance between the executive and the largest opposition party in parliament, provided the former has at least 20 percent of the seats.[11] I create a variable for reform based on the index of economic and institutional reform used in previous chapters. I add *War*, which is a dummy variable that equals 1 for countries involved in civil conflict. Consistent with existing literature, I include a variable for the logged value of inflation and fixed-effect dummy variables for each country to control for factors specific to each country, such as geography, leadership, natural resource endowments, initial conditions, and historical legacies.

Results from Model 4.1 reveal that political polarization is correlated with slower economic growth in the short and long run, as indicated by the negative and significant coefficients on both measures of *Polarization*. *Reform*$_{i(t-1)}$

---

[11] The results are largely unchanged using a continuous measure of polarization. Note that I am examining the direct – not the conditional – effect of polarization on growth. Including both reform and democracy as explanatory variables would exacerbate endogeneity concerns, given the results from Chapter 3.

TABLE 4.2. *Accounting for Growth*

	Model					
	4.1	4.2	4.3	4.4	4.5	4.6
ΔPolarization	−1.50**	−1.19*	—	—	—	—
	(.71)	(.71)				
Polarization$_{i(t-1)}$	−2.72***	−2.49***	−.03**	−2.06**	−2.38***	−.02*
	(.55)	(.54)	(.01)	(.97)	(.84)	(.01)
ΔReform	.39	−.17	−1.47**	—	—	−2.06**
	(.71)	(.79)	(.61)			(.58)
Reform$_{i(t-1)}$	2.06***	.97	−0.32	.86	—	.45
	(.48)	(.64)	(.26)	(.72)		(.34)
ΔInflation	−1.45***	−1.60***	−1.70***	—	—	−1.54***
	(.42)	(.40)	(.37)			(.34)
Inflation$_{i(t-1)}$	−.94*	−1.52***	−1.47***	−.78	−.87	−.47
	(.37)	(.37)	(.33)	(.65)	(.63)	(.32)
ΔWar	−11.82***	−11.66***	−10.86***	—	—	−10.44***
	(1.71)	(1.86)	(2.08)			(2.08)
War$_{i(t-1)}$	−8.53***	−7.79***	−7.90***	−8.34**	−9.78***	−8.37***
	(1.71)	(1.77)	(2.00)	(3.38)	(3.32)	(1.8)
Growth$_{i(t-1)}$	−.84***	−.81***	−.71***	.33***	—	−.78**
	(.09)	(.09)	(.09)	(.08)		(.08)
Initial Conditions$_{it}$	—	—	—	—	—	1.18***
						(.36)
TimeTrend$_{it}$	—	—	—	—	—	.60***
						(.16)
Initial Conditions$^*_{it}$	—	—	—	—	—	−.19***
Time						(.05)
Trend$_{it}$						

(continued)

TABLE 4.2 *(continued)*

	Model					
	4.1	4.2	4.3	4.4	4.5	4.6
Constant	2.73 (3.08)	9.11** (4.14)	10.28*** (2.06)	.18 (.17)	.41** (.19)	−2.49 (2.44)
Dependent variable	Annual rate of change of GDP	Annual rate of change of GDP	Annual rate of change of GDP	Annual rate of change of GDP	Annual rate of change of GDP	Annual rate of change of GDP
Polarization	Categorical	Categorical	Continuous initial level	Categorical	Categorical	Continuous initial level
Fixed effects	Country	Country and year	Year	Country	Country	–
Observations	332	330	332	332	332	332
R^2 /Wald χ^2	.58	.58	.54	182.56	120.85	.53

Notes: $*p < .10$, $**p < .05$, $***p < .01$. Results estimated using error-correction models in Models 4.1, 4.2, 4.3, and 4.6 and Arellano-Bond Estimates (XTABOND) in Models 4.4 and 4.5. The XTABOND models used lagged values of the independent variables as instruments to predict rates of economic growth.

is positively and significantly associated with economic growth over time, whereas *Inflation* and *War* are negatively and significantly related to economic growth in both the short and long run. These results comport well with the conventional wisdom on growth in the region as well as the argument made in the preceding chapters.

In Model 4.2, I repeat the analysis, using fixed-effect dummy variables for countries and for years. These estimates are conservative as the dummy variables for country and year account for a host of unobserved and time-invariant variables related to the countries and time period under study. In this estimation, both measures of *Polarization* retain their sign and significance as do *Inflation* and *War*. The lagged level of reform is still positively associated with growth but is less precisely estimated $(p = .13)$. The dummy variables for each year reduce the significance of the impact of economic reform, which suggests that there is an important temporal dimension to the relationship between the reform index and economic growth. Model 4.3 uses a continuous measure of the initial value of polarization, and the results are largely unchanged. I also repeated the analysis using the General Method of Moments (GMM) and the Arellano-Bond correction that differences the regression equation and uses lagged values of the level variables as instruments. This model helps to reduce concerns about potential endogeneity between polarization and growth. Model 4.4 reports these results, which include fixed effects for countries.[12] The coefficient on $Polarization_{i(t-1)}$ is still negative and significant. Thus, the results tell a similar story across models.

The substantive effects of polarization on growth are worth noting. After using the Bewley technique (1979) to transform the coefficient on polarization in Model 4.2, I find that a one-unit increase in polarization is associated with a drop of about 2.8 percent in growth. The results are somewhat smaller using the Arellano-Bond technique reported in Model 4.3.

Model 4.5 examines whether polarization influences economic growth by dampening the level of economic and institutional reform. One simple way to assess this possibility is to drop the variable for the reform index from the regression and examine how the coefficient on polarization changes. Svensson (1998) and Keefer and Knack (2002) pursue a similar strategy. This model suffers from omitted variable bias in the estimates because reform is not included, but it sheds some light on relationships among polarization, reform, and growth. When the variable for economic and institutional reform is dropped, the coefficient on polarization decreases from −2.06 to −2.38 percent. This suggests that polarization is influencing economic growth in part by dampening economic reform, but polarization also may be having a direct effect on economic growth. Indeed, holding other variables at their means indicates that a two-unit increase in the categorical measure of polarization is associated with about a 4 percent drop in the growth rate.

---

[12] This is a powerful tool, but it has been shown to perform no better than OLS in samples with few time units (Judson and Owen 1999).

Initial Conditions

Finally, Model 4.6 examines the impact of initial conditions on economic growth. To explore whether these initial conditions exhibit increasing or decreasing returns in their impact on economic growth, I created an interaction term between initial conditions and a time-trend variable that increases by one unit for each year in the dataset. I have recoded *TimeTrend* so that 0 equals the first year of the transformation. Because the initial conditions do not change over time, I drop the fixed-effect dummy variables for each country.

The results suggest that *InitialConditions* are associated with significantly slower economic growth in the first year in transition, as indicated by the coefficient on initial conditions. Over time, however, initial conditions appear to become significantly less important, as indicated by the coefficient on *InitialConditions*TimeTrend*. A one-unit increase in the index of *Initial Conditions* is associated with a 1.2 percent drop in economic growth in the first year of transition; however, each year reduces the size of this drop in growth by about 0.2 percent. Thus, the impact of the institutional legacies of communism on economic growth appears to exhibit decreasing returns. Countries with poor initial conditions are thus not doomed to slower growth but overcome these initial barriers more rapidly than many observers contend.

Polarization and Growth: A Different Take

Because there is considerable debate about the merits of analyzing year-on-year changes in growth, I also use an alternative specification.[13] In studies of economic growth in longer time periods, scholars often smooth the data by grouping growth rates in five-year periods. This approach reduces the impact of atypical short-term fluctuations in the data and is best for studying long-run economic growth. In the cases at hand, this method is more difficult given the short time period, but in Table 4.3, I divide the data into three five-year periods by taking the average of the variables of interest during the period and report the results.[14] In Models 4.7 and 4.8, I include controls for initial levels of GDP per capita in each country, a dummy variable for energy-rich states, the average number of years that each country was at war in each period, and period averages for the logged value of *Inflation* and the categorical measure of *Polarization*. The log value of inflation is highly correlated (.80) with the level of reform in this shorter version of the dataset, and the latter is initially dropped from the analysis. I include *Reform* (and drop *Inflation*) in Models 4.9 and 4.10. In Models 4.8 and 4.10, I add dummy variables for the first two four-year periods in the data, and the results are consistent with the argument.

[13] See Pritchett (1998) for a skeptic's view of year-on-year growth regressions.
[14] The three periods are 1990–1994, 1995–1999, and 2000–2004.

TABLE 4.3. *A Different Take on Economic Growth*

	Model			
	4.7	4.8	4.9	4.10
Polarization	−1.77**	−1.86**	−2.85**	−2.01**
	(.99)	(.80)	(1.04)	(.84)
Inflation	−2.91***	−1.27***	–	–
	(.52)	(.57)		
Reform	–	–	2.29***	−.08
			(.79)	(.45)
War	−7.26*	−8.09**	−12.23**	−10.04**
	(4.18)	(3.63)	(5.02)	(3.84)
Oil	1.75	2.25	2.06	.48
	(1.67)	(1.55)	(1.96)	(1.53)
Wealth	−.2.00	−2.13*	−4.33**	1.30
	(1.20)	(1.21)	(1.61)	(1.67)
Constant	12.40***	12.38***	−5.10	7.20**
	(1.20)	(1.36)	(4.31)	(2.19)
Dependent variable	Economic growth (5-year averages)	Economic growth (5-year averages)	Economic growth (5-year averages)	Economic growth (5-year averages)
Polarization	Categorical	Categorical	Categorical	Categorical
N	75	75	75	75
R^2	.69	.75	.52	.75
Time dummies	No	Yes	No	Yes

Notes: $*p < .10$, $**p < .05$, $***p < .01$. Reports the results of a regression using OLS and robust standard errors with clustering on country. The dependent and independent variables are measured in four-year averages to reduce the impact of year-to-year fluctuations.

Again, *Polarization* is negatively and significantly related to economic growth, as are *Inflation* and *War*. *Reform* is significantly and positively associated with economic growth in Model 4.9, but the estimate is less precise in Model 4.10, when the dummy variables for time periods are included. The substantive effects of polarization on the annual rate of GDP growth in these four models range from a 1.7 percent decrease in Model 4.7 to a 2.8 percent decrease in Model 4.9. Thus, the estimates in Models 4.1–4.10 are relatively consistent across specifications, particularly given the large variation in annual growth in the region.

Statistical information on the macroeconomy in the postcommunist world suffers from measurement error, and scholars have expressed particular concern about the quality of data on economic growth. Some charge that the official data overstate the fall of output by, among other things, including estimates of the informal economy that are too small and by overstating output before 1990, while others argue that the fall in GDP was larger than reported, given the extensive use of barter between firms in some countries (Aslund 2002; Gaddy and Ickes 2002).

Scholars have adopted a number of means to address this issue. I estimated Model 4.2 using two other dependent variables as proxies for economic growth: a measure for the annual growth rate adjusted by estimates of the size of the informal economy developed by Selowsky and Martin (1997) and a measure of growth based on the annual rate of change in electricity usage (Dobozi 1995; Dobozi and Pohl 1995).[15] Polarization and economic reform retain their signs and levels of significance when the dependent variable is the growth rate adjusted for the size of the informal economy. The results are also consistent when electricity usage is used as a proxy for economic growth, although the data are more scarce. That polarization is associated with various measures of economic growth gives good grounds to believe that the relationship between polarization and economic growth is not an artifact of measurement error.

Might it be that economic performance is driving the degree of polarization rather than vice versa? One could imagine a spiral in which bad economic performance encourages old-left and right parties to take more extreme positions on the economy to court voters seeking an end to the economic downturn. I examined whether the lagged value of growth is associated with the level of polarization in the current year. I estimated Model 4.1 but include the change in polarization as the dependent variable and growth as an independent variable. The coefficients on the first difference and the lagged level of economic growth do not approach statistical significance. This suggests that current levels of political polarization are not driven by the level of economic growth in the preceding year and provides a reason to believe that the results are not due to a simple form of reverse causation. This result is perhaps not surprising as the measure of political polarization is taken from the first year of an election and then remains unchanged until the next election. Moreover, in a transition environment voters may be more willing to forgive bad economic performance, particularly early on (Stokes 1996, 2001a). More sophisticated forms of endogeneity that are difficult to detect may be present.

These analyses cover a relatively small number of years in an extraordinary period of world history. They have not uncovered the determinants of long-term economic growth. Nor have they made claims of generality beyond the cases at hand. Moreover, the results should be seen within the context of the ongoing debates on the best way to model economic growth.

These initial analyses point to several areas for future research. Scholars could pay greater attention to the potential interaction among explanatory variables. The analysis in this chapter has taken economic reform as exogenous. This is a useful and common assumption for the analysis at hand, but is clearly a simplification. For example, one might examine the extent to which policy

---

[15] The electric energy consumption and informal economy adjusted measures of economic growth are correlated with the formal measures of economic growth at the .40 and .95 levels, respectively.

choices are endogenous to initial conditions. Second, scholars may develop more sophisticated two-stage analyses to get a better handle on causation. Finding instrumental variables associated with economic reform, but not with economic growth, is a challenge.

Conclusion

This chapter examined the determinants of economic growth in the postcommunist world between 1990 and 2004. Most importantly, the evidence is consistent with the argument that political polarization is negatively associated with economic growth. Moreover, there is some evidence that political polarization shapes economic growth in part by dampening the level of economic and institutional reform.

In addition, the initial conditions inherited by each country at the start of transition are strongly associated with economic performance. Countries that began the transition with particularly inauspicious conditions exhibit slower growth in the first year of transition; however, the impact of these initial conditions appears to decline over time. In the cases at hand, initial conditions exhibit decreasing returns over time. Rather than being doomed by their inheritance at the start of transition, countries can overcome institutional legacies with time.

No single analysis can be definitive, and it is critical to expose hypotheses to a variety of statistical techniques and tests. That the results are fairly consistent across these analyses increases confidence in the findings, but given the bluntness of our statistical tools, and disagreements about how to model economic growth in a transition setting, these results are tentative. This analysis has examined what might be called the deep background conditions that influence macroeconomic outcomes over the medium term in the postcommunist world. The next chapter goes deeper to examine one mechanism by which political polarization may influence economic outcomes.

Appendix Table A4.1

TABLE A4.1. *Quantitative Studies of Economic Growth in the Postcommunist World at a Glance*

	Method	Initial Condition Variables	Liberalization Variables	Other Variables	Main Findings
De Melo, et al. 1996	Cross-section, 1989–1995	Income, War	World Bank Index	Inflation	Liberalization +*
Sachs 1996	Cross-section, 1989–1995		EBRD index		Liberalization +*
Selowsky and Martin 1997	Panel, 1989–1995, one-stage	FSU, War	World Bank Index	Inflation	Liberalization +*
Aslund et al. 1996	Cross-section, 1989–1995	FSU, War		Inflation	FSU −* War −*
Fischer et al. 1996	Panel, 1992–1994, fixed effects, one-stage	Initial income, 1992 dummy		Fiscal deficit, fixed exchange rate	All variables*
De Melo et al. 1997	Panel, 1990–1996, three-stage	Initial conditions cluster	World Bank Index	Political freedom	Initial conditions −* Liberalization +*
Havrylyshyn et al. 1998	Panel, 1990–1997, fixed effects one-stage	Initial conditions cluster	EBRD legal reform	Investment share, export growth	Fixed effects* Liberalization +*
Campos 1999	Cross-section and panel, 1990–1997	Initial income, FSU		Investment, schooling, population growth	FSU −*, Income*, but not if FSU included
Heybey and Murrell 1999	Cross-section, three-stage	Exports to CMEA, growth in 1988–1989	Rate and level of liberalization		Growth affects liberalization

(continued)

120

Zinnes et al. 2001	Panel, 1990–1997	Many initial conditions	Price liberalization, capital markets, tax reform, land reform	EBRD legal reform, hard budget constraint	Privatization +* only with good supporting institutions
Fischer and Sahay 2000	Panel, 1990–1998, one-stage	Initial conditions cluster introduced separately	EBRD reform scores	Inflation, fiscal balance	Stabilization +* Structural reform +*
Falcetti et al. 2002	Panel, 1990–1998, three-stage	Latent variable	Reform index Reform index lagged	Fiscal balance	Reform −* Reform lagged +*
Staehr 2005	Panel 1990–2000, one-stage	War	EBRD index using principal components	Time trend	Reform +*
Havrylyshyn and Van Rooden, 2003	Panel 1990–1998, one-stage		EBRD reform scores in index	Inflation Institutions Index	Institutions +* Liberalization +*

Notes: *indicates statistically significant at the .05 level; + and − indicate positive and negative effects. FSU = Former Soviet Union; CMEA = Council of Mutual Economic Assistance.

5

Political Polarization and Policy Instability

The View from the Firm

To explain is to provide a mechanism.

Jon Elster, 1983

Previous chapters have used cross-country analyses to establish that political polarization is associated with distortions in various types of economic and institutional reform and with slower economic growth. However, these cross-national tests have only examined data collected at the national level and have not explored whether the individuals depicted in the theory behave as predicted. The theory suggests that businesspeople in less polarized democracies should view policy as more predictable and engage in more productive economic activity than their counterparts in more polarized democracies and in autocracies. Identifying the link between individual behavior and economic outcomes is important because high levels of political polarization and bad economic outcomes may "go together" for reasons other than those depicted in the argument. For example, polarization may induce gridlock, which, in turn, blunts efforts to conduct economic and institutional reforms (McCarty et al. 2006).[1] Alternatively, polarization may shape levels of uncertainty and thereby influence policy choices.

This chapter examines the relationship between political polarization and reform outcomes in two ways. I begin by analyzing the determinants of reversals of the reform index used in previous chapters on the notion that reversal should be significantly more likely in more polarized democracies than in less polarized democracies or in autocracies. I then turn to an analysis of the perceptions of policy instability and investment as recorded in a survey of businesspeople in twenty-three postcommunist countries conducted in 1999. Each of these analyses helps to identify the path by which polarization shapes policy

---

[1] McCarty et al. (2006: 165–181) discuss a variety of ways that political polarization may influence policy.

outcomes. In addition, the survey evidence focuses on the behavior of individuals and thereby helps to identify policy instability as a causal mechanism linking polarization and reform outcomes. By identifying relationships among political polarization, policy instability, and investment at the level of the individual, this chapter offers additional tests of the argument and provides microfoundations for the claims made in previous chapters.

Polarization-Induced Policy Instability or Gridlock?

The logic of the argument in previous chapters relied on concerns about the predictability of policy induced by political polarization. However, polarization may influence policy outcomes via other channels. For example, it may exacerbate policy gridlock between competing factions by reducing the potential for compromise between groups with vastly different political agendas (Alesina and Drazen 1991). Thus, polarization may produce gridlock that inhibits reform (McCarty et al. 2006: 176–179). It also may make "strategic disagreement" more likely as incumbents try to shift blame for failure to pass legislation to their opponents (Groseclose and McCarty 2000).

This polarization-induced gridlock argument has considerable appeal for the cases at hand, as some observers have attributed the tortured economic reforms of Russia and Ukraine in the 1990s to the difficulty of passing legislation when the executive and large groups in parliament had very different policy preferences (Aslund 1995; Remington 2001a, 2006; Frye 2006; Cook 2007; for Ukraine, Aslund and de Menil 2000; de Menil 2000). In these cases, polarization appears to have hindered compromise between major political factions. However, there is also evidence in these cases that perceptions of policy instability were quite high (Frye 1997a, 2000: 199). Distinguishing between these two logics of polarization in the broader sample of cases is difficult, but two types of analyses may shed light on the issue.[2]

First, we can examine reversals of economic reform. The polarization-induced policy instability argument suggests that the probability of a reversal of reform is more likely in polarized democracies and in autocracies than in nonpolarized democracies. In contrast, the polarization-induced gridlock argument suggests that reversals should be unlikely in polarized settings because of the difficulty of reaching agreement on a change in policy. Second, we can examine perceptions of the predictability of policy. If businesspeople view policy as less predictable when polarization is high, this would support the polarization-induced uncertainty argument. If, however, businesspeople view policy as more predictable when polarization is high, then this would be evidence in favor of

---

[2] In some sense the distinction here is artificial because policy instability may influence incentives for competing factions to reach agreement. With low polarization, successful reforms may ease agreement by increasing the size of side payments. With high levels of polarization, factions may be more likely to resort to strategic disagreement. These results hardly undermine the argument that polarization leads to policy gridlock more generally.

the polarization-induced gridlock argument. I begin by examining reversals of economic and institutional reform.

Reversals of economic reform, measured initially by any year-on-year decrease in the index of economic and institutional reform, are more frequent than is commonly appreciated. Reversals of the reform index occur in about one-quarter of the years in the sample and take place in at least one country in every year between 1992 and 2004, except for 2003. In 1998, the year of the financial crash in Russia, about half of the countries in the sample experienced backsliding, but reversals are common in other years as well.[3] The nature of the coding scheme may suggest a slight bias against reversals. The EBRD, which rates each country on progress in economic and institutional reform, is run by a board of the member countries. As a reversal indicates backsliding in progress toward a market economy, it may be objected to by the country representative on the board of executives. Thus, even small reversals are worth examining.[4] In addition, I analyze "major" reversals in which the reform index declines by at least 0.10 points, which occurs in 6 percent of the cases.

As a first cut, consider that reversals and major reversals are much less likely to occur in democracies than in autocracies. Indeed, reversals of the reform index occur in 18 percent of cases in democracies versus 33 percent of cases in autocracies, while major reversals take place in democracies in 3 percent of cases compared to 8 percent in autocracies.[5] In addition, reversals and major reversals are less likely in democracies when polarization is low than when it is high. When the categorical measure of polarization equals 0, reversals and major reversals occur in 14 percent and 2 percent of observations, but these figures rise to 17 percent and 8 percent, when polarization equals 2.

To explore the relationship between polarization and the likelihood of a reversal of reform, I estimate a probit model using a dependent variable that is coded 1, for any year in which the level of the reform index is lower than in the preceding year and 0 otherwise. The argument suggests that reversals of the index of economic and institutional reform are especially likely in polarized democracies and less likely in democracies when polarization is absent. Thus, I include the categorical measure of polarization, the continuous measure of democracy, and their product, *Polarization*Democracy*. I include the level of the reform index and its squared term in the model, as we might expect reversals to be especially unlikely at very low levels of reform because little reform has been achieved and at high levels where interest groups defending their gains are likely to make reversals less likely. I include a variable for initial conditions and a dummy variable for countries at war. I also add the annual rate of inflation as dire economic circumstances may also make backsliding in reform more likely. Alternatively, economic crises provoked by inflation may lead to

[3] Including a dummy variable for 1998 in the regression analyses reported later has little effect on the results.

[4] I thank Eddy Malesky for this point.

[5] Here democracy equals 3 or less on the Freedom House scale.

further liberalization and make backsliding less likely (Rodrik 1996).[6] I report the results below in Table 5.1.

The results from Model 5.1 are consistent with the claim that polarization undermines reform by promoting policy instability. The coefficient on *Democracy* indicates that when polarization equals zero in a democracy reversals of economic and institutional reform are especially unlikely. In contrast, polarization in a democratic setting is associated with a greater likelihood of a reversal as indicated by the coefficient on *Polarization*Democracy*. Reversals are also less likely at lower and at higher levels of economic reform as indicated by the joint impact of the coefficients on *Reform Index* and *ReformIndexSquared*. Higher levels of inflation are correlated with a lower likelihood of a reversal in reform.

In Model 5.2, I repeat the analysis using "major" reversals as a dependent variable, and the results are less consistent but still encouraging, given the small number of major reversals. Major reversals are no more likely in democracies when polarization is absent, as indicated by the coefficient on *Democracy*. But we still find that the polarization in a democratic setting is associated with a greater likelihood of a major reversal of the reform index. Finally, in Model 5.3, I repeat the analysis, but drop the squared term on the reform index. Doing so improves the model fit, and the results on the main variables of interest are largely unchanged. Policy reversals are especially likely in polarized democracies. In addition, there is weaker evidence that policy reversals are less likely in democracies when polarization is absent.

These results are substantively large. Model 5.1 suggests that when democracy is relatively high (3 in the Freedom House scale), moving from a polarization score of 0 to 2 increases the probability of a reversal from .18 to .28.[7] However, when democracy is low (5 in the Freedom House scale), the likelihood of a reversal is .31 whether polarization equals 0 or 2. More broadly, these analyses support the view that on average polarization shapes policy outcomes primarily through the channel of policy instability rather than gridlock.

This outcome may be attributed in part to the frequency of majoritarian policy-making institutions in the region. The polarization-induced gridlock argument was developed for "shared power" political systems, like the United States, rather than for the more majoritarian systems in this study. Federalism

---

[6] The model does not include a measure of veto points because one common measure of veto points used in the postcommunist cases is fairly highly correlated with the measure of democracy. The measure of veto points used in Hellman (1998) and Frye and Mansfield (2003) is highly correlated with democracy in the full sample at .70. Moreover, the measure of democracy captures, albeit somewhat imperfectly, the greater difficulty of changing policy in democracies compared to autocracies. Adding this veto point measure does not change the results. I also do not use the Henisz (2004) measure of political concentration as it takes into account the ideological dispersion within parliament in a way that is already captured in the polarization measure.

[7] The confidence intervals at the 90th percentile for the predicted probabilities are .18, [.14–.22] and .27 [.22–.34].

TABLE 5.1. *Polarization and Reversals of Reform*

	Model		
	5.1: Probability of Reversal	5.2: Probability of Major Reversal	5.3: Probability of Major Reversal
Polarization	−.19	−.38	−.36
	(.19)	(.33)	(.33)
Democracy	−.23**	−.11	−.16
	(.07)	(.12)	(.13)
Polarization*Democracy	.09**	.14*	.15**
	(.04)	(.07)	(.07)
Reform Index	−.39*	.10	−.19**
	(.21)	(.21)	(.10)
Reform Index Squared	.05**	−.04	−
	(.02)	(03)	
Initial Conditions	−.04	−.02	.03
	(.05)	(.09)	(.09)
War	.23	−	−
	(.35)		
Inflation (log)	−.11*	−.21**	−.20**
	(.06)	(.08)	(.08)
Constant	1.02	.099	.32
	(.62)	(.63)	(.55)
Dependent Variable (0,1)	Any reform reversal	Major reform reversal	Major reform reversal
Polarization	Categorical	Categorical	Categorical
Democracy	Continuous	Continuous	Continuous
Observations	334	334	334
Wald chi	28.60	15.06	18.70
Prob > χ^2	.0004	.0353	.0047
Pseudo-R^2	.08	.14	.13

Notes: *p < .10, **p < .05, ***p < .01. Results from a probit model with robust standard errors. Reform reversals are measured as any year-on-year decline in the index of economic and institutional reform. Major reversals indicate a year-on-year decline of 10 percent in the index of economic and institutional reform.

and "shared power" systems, such as strong bicameralism, make polarization-induced gridlock more likely by giving more political factions the opportunity to block reversals of policy and by giving voters the chance to moderate policy by splitting their tickets (Alesina and Rosenthal 1995). Moreover, polarization is especially likely to lead to gridlock under divided government in presidential systems (McCarty et al. 2006).

In the postcommunist world, however, various forms of majoritarian systems predominate. Most countries have parliamentary regimes in which the possibility that a single party may win a majority in the next election and govern largely unconstrained is always a possibility.[8] During the period under study, ten of thirteen countries in the sample with parliamentary systems had elections that produced a single party with enough seats to govern as a majority government on its own. Given the potential for the concentration of power in a single party in a parliamentary system, the threat of a reversal in policy is quite high should the opposition replace the current government.

A similar but more pronounced dynamic prevails in the presidential regimes in the region. They typically have very strong presidents who can make policy with little input from parliament (McGregor 1994; Frye 1997b). Further, most presidential regimes are autocracies and offer the executive great leeway to make policy. Only twenty-two observations in the sample are pure presidential regimes that are also relatively competitive (Freedom House score of 4 or less); Ukraine and Russia comprise fifteen of these cases. Presidents in both Russia and Ukraine faced polarized oppositions in parliament that at times impeded the implementation of their preferred policies, but these cases are the exception rather than the rule.[9] Thus, the types of majoritarian political systems found in the postcommunist world may exacerbate the threat of policy reversals. More generally, evidence from this initial analysis suggests that on average political polarization shapes economic and institutional reform primarily via policy instability.

The Importance of Microfoundations

As noted, the polarization-induced instability and polarization-induced gridlock arguments make different predictions about the perceived stability of policy. The former suggests that polarization is associated with greater instability, while the latter suggests the opposite. Before examining these two versions of the argument using data from a survey of businesspeople in twenty-three countries, I present a brief discussion of the importance of identifying the microfoundations of the argument.

Like many theories in comparative political economy, the argument presented in previous chapters identifies how a national-level variable (political polarization) influences a national-level outcome (economic policy choice). Whether linking economic openness to state spending, electoral rules to party fragmentation, or democratic governments to fighting wars, theories that link national-level variables to national-level outcomes are staples of comparative political economy (Cameron 1978; Cox 2001; Doyle 1986). They have the attractive feature of being sufficiently precise to make generalizations beyond specific cases without being so abstract as to be impervious to empirical scrutiny. They are, however, often vulnerable to criticism on two fronts. First,

---

[8] Poland, Romania, and Lithuania have mixed presidential-parliamentary systems in which both the president and a prime minister elected by parliament must approve economic policy.

[9] Russia is the only country in the region with a true federal system for most of the years under study.

the causal chain between national-level variables and national-level outcomes often goes underspecified. For example, democracies may be less likely to go to war with other democracies, but without knowing which causal mechanisms underpin this relationship, we may risk conflating correlation with causation (Rosato 2003).[10]

Elster (1983: 24) makes the case for causal mechanisms most forcefully. He argues for viewing mechanisms as "intentional chains from a goal to an action as well as causal chains from an event to its effect" and adds that "the role of mechanisms is twofold. First, they enable us to go from the larger to the smaller: from molecules to atoms, from societies to individuals. Secondly, and more fundamentally, they reduce the time lag between *explanans* and *explanandum*. A mechanism provides a continuous and contiguous chain of causal or intentional links." Finding the linkages between macrolevel variables tightens the casual chain and reveals how one variable influences another. For Elster (1983, 1998), one of the goals of explanation is to break down the causal chain into shorter and shorter ties.[11] On some level, explanations absent causal mechanisms are unsatisfying (Hedstrom and Swedborg 1998).

Many theories in comparative political economy face a second and related problem: a mismatch between theory and data. Analyses of economic outcomes across countries often rely on data aggregated at the national level but start with predictions about the behavior of individuals. They identify correlations between national-level factors that reflect their assumptions about individual-level behavior but rarely examine the behavior of individuals directly.[12] The analyses that follow assess whether individuals facing greater political polarization view policy as less predictable and invest at lower rates.

The BEEPS Dataset

One difficulty in testing cross-national arguments using individual-level evidence is the scarcity of data. National statistical agencies typically provide little information about the traits of specific firms, and even when such data are collected, they are rarely comparable across countries. Fortunately, the EBRD and the World Bank conducted a survey of more than four thousand businesspeople in twenty-three postcommunist countries in the summer of 1999 that permits analysis of the argument presented in preceding chapters at the level of the individual businessperson. The Business Environment and Economic Performance Survey (BEEPS) includes a battery of questions on the characteristics of the firm

---

[10] Much of the recent literature on the democratic peace is devoted precisely to uncovering these mechanisms.

[11] See Elster (1983), Bates (1990), Hedstrom and Swedborg (1998), and Katznelson (2003) for thoughtful discussions of microfoundations and causal mechanisms.

[12] I relied on this strategy of cross-national data analysis in preceding chapters when I argued that political polarization leads individuals to expect policies to be less predictable and invest at lower rates. At the national level, the results of these investment decisions were evident in less extensive and more inconsistent reform as well as in slower growth in highly polarized countries.

and managers' perceptions of policy and the business environment. In addition, interviewers asked respondents a variety of questions about the behavior of their firm. The sample included at least 125 respondents from each country.[13]

The sampling strategy aimed to include firms in a variety of categories to conduct statistical analysis.[14] Firms were drawn randomly from eleven economic sectors and from different geographic settings within each country, including rural towns and small and large cities.[15] Eighty-five percent of firms were private, with many created from scratch. Just under half had less than 50 employees; 29 percent had between 50 and 200 employees; 14 percent had between 200 and 500 employees; and 8 percent had more than 500 employees. The sample is not representative of all firms in each country because the information needed to weight the sample was unavailable in some cases. The survey used quotas to ensure variation across sector, number of employees, property type, and size of exports (Hellman et al. 2000: 7–10). Surveys were conducted in the native language at the respondent's place of work.

The opacity of the business environment in the postcommunist region presents special challenges for researchers hoping to gain honest answers from businesspeople. Asking direct questions about the volume of sales, turnover, profit margins, and tax payments tends to provoke hostile reactions and is counterproductive.[16] Fortunately, most of the questions used in this analysis are innocuous and provide few incentives to dissemble.

The BEEPS survey provides a unique window on the business environment but is not without shortcomings.[17] Like all surveys, it provides only a snapshot at one point in time. Moreover, gaining equivalency in meaning of concepts across countries is difficult. The survey was conducted in the summer of 1999, a year after the financial crash in Russia in August 1998, but traces of this event may still influence responses. In addition, the more abstract questions may suffer from anchoring problems common in cross-national surveys (Malesky 2003).[18]

---

[13] Russia, Poland, and Ukraine had more firms in the sample (552, 246, and 247, respectively), which is perhaps justified given the far larger populations of these countries. Results hold after dropping Russia from the analysis. I also report the results using a balanced sample.

[14] For a description of the BEEPS dataset, see Hellman et al. (2000).

[15] Because the EBRD and the World Bank are especially interested in foreign investment, the sample included slightly more firms with foreign ownership than is typically found in most countries in the sample. At least 10 percent of the firms in each country had some level of foreign ownership.

[16] Two surveys of small businesses in Russia found that firms that revealed their wealth by renovating their place of business were more likely to be inspected by state bureaucrats and to be contacted by racketeers (Frye and Zhuravskaya 2000; Frye 2002b).

[17] For a review of firm-level surveys in the postcommunist region, see Djankov and Murrell (2002), Frye and Shleifer (1997), Hendley et al. (1997), Hendley et al. (2000, 2001), McMillan and Woodruff (2002), Frye and Zhuravskaya (2000), Frye (2002b), and Hellman et al. (2003).

[18] The authors of the BEEPS assess the equivalence of the perceptions of the respondents with reasonable proxies for objective indicators (Hellman et al. 2000: 8–9). They find that perceptions of exchange rate variability and telephone infrastructure problems correspond with the actual

Like most surveys of businesspeople, the BEEPS data may suffer from "survivor bias" because firms that do not survive are not included in the sample. This problem is more severe for samples that focus on small firms that are especially unlikely to survive and should be less of a problem in a broad cross section of firms. In the case at hand, this bias should make it more difficult to find a relationship between polarization and policy uncertainty because only firms that have managed to find ways to handle high levels of policy uncertainty remain in the sample. In addition, it would have been helpful if the survey had been conducted earlier in the transition. In a sense, this should also make it more difficult to find results as the overall policy uncertainty was likely higher earlier in the transition.

Despite these shortcomings, the BEEPS dataset has clear strengths. Respondents in each country were asked identical questions, which permits comparisons across countries. The survey was conducted at roughly the same point in time in each country so the international context is roughly similar. In recent years many scholars have used the BEEPS data (cf. Hellman et al. 2000; Hellman et al. 2003; Gehlbach 2008; Jensen 2003).

The survey included several questions that tap respondents' perceptions of the predictability of policy. Interviewers asked: "How predictable are changes in the government's economic and financial policies which materially affect your business?" Responses ranged from 1 (completely predictable) to 6 (completely unpredictable). On average, firm managers rated such policies as 4.2 on this scale, indicating that most managers viewed policy as fairly unpredictable.[19] Dividing the sample into countries whose polarization scores for the years 1996–1999 are low (less than 1), medium (between 1 and 2), and high (equal to 2) reveals the differences across these groups. Businesspeople in countries with low, moderate, and high levels of polarization rate policy unpredictability as 4.02, 4.21, and 4.56, respectively.[20] For the responses, see Table 5.2.

Later in the survey, respondents were asked: "Can you tell me how problematic are these different factors for the operation and growth of your business?" Interviewers then read a list of eleven problems, including "policy instability or uncertainty." Table 5.3 presents the responses.

Of these eleven problems, policy instability/uncertainty ranks fourth, behind only taxes and regulations and inflation and just below financing. On a scale

---

rate of change in the exchange rate and the level of telephones per population. This provides some confidence that the results are not driven solely by perceptual biases.

[19] See Appendix Table A5.1. Interviewers asked: "How predictable are changes in rules, laws, or regulations, which materially affect your business?" Respondents used the same scale as in the previous question, and the average response was 4.18.

[20] See Appendix Table A5.2 for country scores. While anchoring issues are often problematic in cross-national survey research, here averages across countries for ratings of policy predictability appear fairly consistent with received wisdom. Policy is fairly predictable in lightly polarized Uzbekistan, Azerbaijan, Poland, and Slovenia and fairly unpredictable in highly polarized Russia, Ukraine, Romania, and Moldova.

TABLE 5.2. *Polarization and Perceptions of Policy Unpredictability*

	Policy Unpredictability[a]
Low polarization	4.02
	(1.29)
	$n = 2,216$
Medium polarization	4.21
	(1.21)
	$n = 410$
High polarization	4.56
	(1.31)
	$n = 1,030$

Notes: Standard deviation in parentheses. $N = 3,656$. Averages taken using country years in which low polarization = 0; medium polarization = 1; high polarization = 2.
[a] On a scale of 1–6.

TABLE 5.3. *Obstacles Faced by Business*

	Perception of Obstacles[a]
Taxes and regulations	3.25
	(.89)
Inflation	3.01
	(1.02)
Financing	2.99
	(1.09)
Policy instability	2.98
	(1.06)
Exchange rates	2.66
	(1.18)
Corruption	2.46
	(1.15)
Theft/street crime/disorder	2.40
	(1.13)
Anticompetitive practices by government or private business	2.39 (1.12)
Mafia	2.26
	(1.21)
Functioning of the judiciary	2.12
	(1.05)
Infrastructure (e.g., telephone, land, roads, water, electricity)	2.05 (1.09)

Notes: $N = 3,635$. Mean responses with standard deviation in parentheses.
[a] 1 = not an obstacle, 4 = major obstacle.

TABLE 5.4. *Polarization and Policy Instability*

	Policy Instability as an Obstacle[a]
Low polarization	2.71
	(1.09)
	$n = 2,188$
Medium polarization	3.14
	(1.01)
	$n = 414$
High polarization	3.32
	(.90)
	$n = 1,041$

Notes: Standard deviation in parentheses. $N = 3,643$. Averages taken using country years in which low polarization $= 0$; medium polarization $= 1$; high polarization $= 2$.
[a] On a scale of 1–4.

where 1 means not an obstacle and 4 means a major obstacle, policy instability or uncertainty rated a 2.98, or just below 3, a moderate obstacle. Other factors that have received far more attention in the policy-making literature are perceived to be less problematic by businesses.

In Table 5.4, I compare the extent to which policy instability is perceived to be a problem in countries with varying degrees of polarization scores for the years 1996–1999. Firm managers in countries with low, moderate, and high levels of polarization rated policy instability as an obstacle at 2.71, 3.14, and 3.32, respectively. Comparing the averages across these three groups reveals sharp differences in the perceived severity of policy instability as an obstacle to business development.

As in preceding chapters, I use multivariate statistical analysis to examine the impact of political polarization. To do so, I integrate national-level variables, including political polarization, the level of democracy, membership in the former Soviet Union, and country wealth, into the BEEPS data. When combining national-level political variables and the firm-level BEEPS data, it is important to recognize that the data are "nested."[21] Observations are taken from firms that operate in countries. Factors at each level of analysis – firm and country – might be influencing the outcome. Policy stability may vary because of firm-level factors, such as the sector in which a firm is located, and with national-level factors, such as the level of wealth in a given country. Combining data from different levels of analysis in a single-level model without recognizing that the data are nested raises difficulties for statistical analysis (Snijders and Bosker 1999; Steenbergen and Jones 2002: 218).[22] First, including data from individual and national levels in a single-level model assumes

[21] See Gelman and Hill (2007) for an excellent treatment of multilevel models.
[22] Scholars may introduce dummy variables to account for higher-level variables, but this tells us little about which factors specific to the higher level are influencing the outcome.

that all individual-level observations are independent of each other, but this is often not the case. In the case at hand, for example, simple pooling of the data from the national and firm levels would assume that firms are not influenced by being in the same country.[23] This assumption may lead to overconfidence in the precision of the estimates, a pernicious problem because it is likely to lead to a false positive – the identification of a relationship between two variables when one may not exist.

Second, combining data in a single-level model overlooks the possibility that intercepts may be variable across countries, which could lead to overestimation of the effects of higher-level variables (Anderson and Tverdova 2003: 98). For example, the variable for polarization may be capturing the effects of polarization on policy instability as well as other country-specific effects. This is likely to lead one to believe that polarization is a more powerful predictor of policy instability than it is in reality.

To address these potential concerns, I estimate a hierarchical model that takes into account factors specific to the firm, such as its size, property type, and sector, and factors specific to the country, such as its level of polarization, extent of democracy, membership in the former Soviet Union, and wealth, to explain variation in perceptions of policy unpredictability (Steenbergen and Jones 2002). Each of these factors operating at different levels of analysis may influence perceptions of policy stability, and this type of statistical model estimates the impact of factors at both levels of analysis. More specifically, I use a generalized linear latent and mixed model (using Stata's GLLAMM command) and an ordered logit model. I estimate the following model using maximum likelihood.[24]

$$Policy\ Unpredictability_{ij} = \beta_{oj} + \beta_{1j}Private_{ij} + \beta_{2j}Lobby_{ij}$$
$$+ \beta_{3j}Employees_{ij} + \beta_{4j}Export_{ij} + \beta_{5j}\Sigma Sector_{ij} + r_{ij} \qquad \text{(level 1)}$$

$$\beta_{oj} = \gamma_{oo} + \gamma_{o1}Polarization_j + \gamma_{o2}Wealth_j$$
$$+ \gamma_{o3}Democracy_j + \gamma_{o4}FSU_j + U_j \qquad \text{(level 2)}$$

The dependent variable is the extent to which policy is perceived to be unpredictable in *firm_i* in *country_j* with 1 being very predictable and 6 being very unpredictable. At the level of the firm (level 1), I include *Employees*, a categorical variable that ranges from 1 to 7 depending on the number of employees in the firm. Larger firms may have more resources to cope with policy instability. I add *Private*, a dummy variable for private-sector firms, as they may

---

[23] This "duplication" of observations is a violation of the assumption that they are independent (Steenbergen and Jones 2002: 220).

[24] I also split the sample into democracies and nondemocracies. Polarization significantly increases policy unpredictability in both subsamples, so I report only the full sample. Reporting results using the full sample allows me to have twenty-three observations at the second level. Here data constraints prevent me from testing for an interactive effect between democracy and polarization on policy unpredictability and investment.

be less likely to use ties with state officials to learn of unforeseen changes in policy. The excluded category is state-owned firms. I also include *Lobby*, a variable that measures the firm's reported ability to lobby different branches of government.[25] If a firm lobbies successfully at any level of government, it is coded as 1, and 0 otherwise. Twenty-seven percent of firms are in this category. Firms that are better able to lobby the government are more likely to view policy as predictable, as they are likely to be better informed and better able to withstand changes in policy. I include a variable, *Export*, that measures whether the firm exports its product to other countries, as dependence on foreign markets may also influence perceptions of policy stability. I also include *DateFounded*, a dummy variable for firms created after 1989, to capture some elements of the firm's history. I add dummy variables for eight economic sectors (the excluded category is manufacturing firms) because policy stability may vary across sectors.[26] The term r_{ij} represents the error term for variables operating at the firm level.

I then turn to cross-national factors, which are depicted as second-level variables. In the model, polarization captures the ideological distance between the executive and the largest opposition party, provided that the latter has greater than 20 percent of the seats in parliament and ranges from 0 to 2. Firms in wealthy countries may be less likely to experience high levels of policy instability, so I included the GDP per capita at the start of the transition, *Wealth*. I include *Democracy*, which is the country's average level of democracy as measured by Freedom House from 1996 to 1999 and ranges from 1 to 7.[27] Finally, I include a dummy variable (FSU) for countries that are former members of the Soviet Union. The term U_j captures effects of error operating in the second-level variables.[28] Models 5.4 and 5.6 use data from the original sample, which was designed to include more respondents from Russia, Ukraine, and Poland. Models 5.5 and 5.7 use a more balanced sample of firms with roughly equal numbers of firms per country.[29] I report the results in Table 5.5.

First, I assess the impact of variables at the national level in Model 5.4. Higher levels of political polarization are associated with perceptions of greater policy unpredictability as indicated by the coefficient on *Polarization*. Businesspeople in more democratic countries perceive policy as more predictable,

[25] The question reads: "When a new law, rule, regulation, or decree is being discussed that could have a substantial impact on your business, how much influence does your firm typically have at the national level of government to try to influence the content of that law, rule, regulation or decree?" Answers range from 1 (never influential) to 6 (very frequently influential).

[26] Sectors include forestry/fishing/farming/mining/quarrying; building/construction; wholesale trading; retail trading; transport; financial services/personal services/business services; and manufacturing.

[27] This measure inverts the Freedom House scores so higher scores mean more democratic.

[28] Using a somewhat different dataset, Kenyon and Naoi (2007) find that hybrid regimes have higher levels of policy uncertainty than do either highly autocratic or highly democratic regimes.

[29] I created the balanced sample by including every fifth firm in the original sample from Russia and every other firm from Ukraine and Poland. In the balanced sample, the minimum number of observations per country was 125 and the maximum number of observations was 183.

TABLE 5.5. *Accounting for Perceptions of Policy Unpredictability*

	Model			
	5.4	5.5	5.6	5.7
Polarization	.22***	.15***	.59***	.31***
	(.05)	(.06)	(.04)	(.04)
Democracy	−.10**	−.13***	.02	.04
	(.05)	(.05)	(.04)	(.05)
Wealth (in	.09***	.07***	−.06***	−.12***
thousands)	(.02)	(.02)	(.01)	(.02)
FSU	.75**	.52***	−.05	−.09
	(.10)	(.13)	(.09)	(.07)
Employees	−.09***	−.09***	−.02	.01
	(.02)	(.03)	(.02)	(.03)
Lobby	−.43***	−.39**	−.09	.09
	(.08)	(.09)	(.09)	(.10)
Private	.19*	.17**	.08	.09
	(.08)	(.08)	(.12)	(.13)
Export	−.08	−.07	−.11	−.11
	(.08)	(.09)	(.11)	(.10)
Date Founded	.17**	.16	.09	.09
	(.09)	(.09)	(.08)	(.09)
Cut points	−2.3, −1.3, .39, 1.8, 2.7	−2.5, −1.5, .22, 1.6, 2.6	−1.9, −.66, .66	−2.4, −1.1, .20
Dependent variable	Policy unpredictability	Policy unpredictability	Policy instability as obstacle	Policy instability as obstacle
Polarization	Categorical	Categorical	Categorical	Categorical
Firm level "*n*"	3,401	2,914	3,401	2,891
National level "*n*"	23	23	23	23
Sample	Original	Balanced	Original	Balanced
Variance and	.22***	.23***	.48***	.36***
covariance of random effects	(.02)	(.04)	(.06)	(.03)
Log likelihood	−5,191.79	−4,507.85	−4,073.39	−3,538.66

Notes: *p < .10, **p < .05, ***p < .01. Estimates from a hierarchical model using GLLAMM and ordered logit. Sectoral dummy variables included, but not reported.

whereas managers of companies in countries that were former members of the Soviet Union view policy as less predictable. Country wealth produces an anomalous result, as businesspeople in richer countries perceive policy as less predictable. This result holds even if *Democracy* and/or *FSU* is dropped from the estimation, which suggests that this is not a result of collinearity between democracy and wealth.

Firm-level variables also shape perceptions of policy predictability. Managers of firms with more employees and those with greater lobbying power view policy as more predictable. Managers of private-sector firms rate policy as less predictable than their counterparts in state-owned firms. Managers of firms in construction, wholesale trade, transportation, and the service sector view policy as significantly more predictable than managers in manufacturing. The results are quite similar using a balanced sample as indicated in Model 5.5.

The results are also largely unchanged if a measure of the intensity of policy instability as an obstacle for doing business is employed. Repeating the analyses using responses to a question about the extent to which policy instability was perceived to be a problem for their firm produced similar results for *Polarization*, as demonstrated in Models 5.6 and 5.7. The results are also similar when respondents rated the unpredictability of laws and regulations rather than the unpredictability of policy.[30] Across these different measures, political polarization is consistently associated with less predictability, even when controlling for other firm-level and national-level factors. In addition, the results are largely unchanged if we include the level of economic reform in the model. I exclude this variable because it is collinear with the level of democracy.

The impact of political polarization on policy unpredictability is pronounced. For example, taking the continuous variables at the means and the dummy variables at the modal category, the predicted probability that a businessperson believes that policy is highly unpredictable (a 5 or 6 on the 1–6 scale) is .45 when polarization equals 0 and .57 when polarization equals 2.

To guard against the possibility that these results are driven by biases in the responses, I tried to control for the unobserved tendency of businesspeople to complain. For example, to the extent that the tendency to express complaints varies by country and this tendency is correlated with polarization, the results may be spurious. That is, rather than estimating the impact of polarization on policy instability, we are capturing the impact of the tendency to complain about policy instability. I included a variable which is the average rating of five other obstacles to doing business in the analyses. This variable attempts to isolate the respondents' views of policy instability from their views of other obstacles to doing business. Adding this variable does not dramatically change the impact of the direct effect of polarization on perceptions of policy instability. The results are also robust to the use of the continuous measure of polarization described in previous chapters.[31]

Political Polarization and Investment

The argument made in previous chapters also suggests that political polarization should be associated with weaker incentives to produce, such as expanding operations, constructing new buildings, or buying new capital equipment.

[30] These analyses are available from the author.
[31] Results from a two-step hierarchical model are in Appendix Table A5.3 (Huber et al. 2005).

Because these types of investments typically require up-front costs for the promise of future gain, managers may be unwilling to invest if they believe that policy may change unexpectedly in the near term. These types of investment are critical for economic performance (Aghion and Howitt 1998).

The BEEPS survey asked respondents about changes in the level of their investment in the firm using the following series of questions: "Has your company's investment changed in real terms over the last three years?" Respondents could answer "Changed" or "Not Changed." If they responded that their levels of investment had changed, they were asked by how much did it increase or decrease? Almost half of the respondents noted that their levels of investment in the past three years had not changed.[32] Responses ranged from a 100 percent decrease to a 900 percent increase, but on average respondents reported an increase of about 14 percent.

This measure has the drawback of not capturing the speed with which businesses expect to recoup their investment and is therefore a somewhat imprecise measure of confidence in the stability of policy. To the extent that larger, more capital-intensive investments are correlated with the reported increase in investment, this measure should be appropriate; however, this is difficult to verify with the existing data. To identify the determinants of investment change for firms in the BEEPS sample, I use a hierarchical model that measures the impacts of variables at the firm level and the national level. The dependent variable is the log value of the reported rate of change in investment over the past three years. Taking the logarithm of this figure helps to reduce the influence of outliers because the rate of change in investment is highly skewed.[33]

I begin with cross-national factors that may influence the level of investment. Because greater political polarization may be associated with less investment, I include the average polarization score for each country for the years 1996–1999 using the categorical measure. I add a variable for the gross domestic product per capita in the years 1996–1999, as the wealth of a country may influence the level of investment, *Wealth*; and a variable that captures the average level of democracy during the same years, *Democracy*. I also include a dummy variable for membership in the former Soviet Union.[34]

Factors specific to the firm may also shape investment. As in the preceding analysis, I include the number of employees, sector, lobbying strength, founding

---

[32] Respondents may regard information about the level of investment as sensitive. Knowing how much a firm invested in recent years allows one to deduce the size of the respondent's tax liabilities. Asking about changes in investment over time, however, mitigates this problem to a great extent.

[33] To take the log, I transform the data to ensure that all figures are positive and nonzero. I do that by adding 100.001 to each observation. As −100 is the smallest observation in the untransformed data, this operation turns all observations in the transformed data positive and nonzero.

[34] I have also included perceptions of policy instability as a predictor in Model 5.8. Its coefficient is negative and significant and the coefficient on polarization retains its sign and level of significance.

date, and property type of the firm. In the postcommunist world, firms finance much of their investment through retained earnings, but they are often reluctant to give precise figures about their finances. As a second-best measure, I include a dummy variable for firms that increased their sales in the past two years, *Sales*. Firms with more sales may have higher investment rates.[35] I also include variables *Finance as Obstacle* and *Competition as Obstacle*, which measure the extent to which respondents believed that a lack of finance and intense competition were problems to their business on a scale of 1–4. I report the results in Table 5.6.

The results from Model 5.8 in Table 5.6 reveal that high levels of polarization are associated with smaller increases in investment as indicated by the negative and significant coefficient on *Polarization*. This result lies just within the bounds of conventional levels of statistical significance ($p = .08$). Using the more balanced sample in Model 5.9, the impact of polarization on investment is estimated with greater precision ($p < .05$).

Firm-level variables are associated with investment patterns. Firms that increase their sales in the two years before the survey invested at generous rates. Private-sector firms invest at higher rates than do state-owned firms, as do firms that can lobby the state. Firm size does not appear to be related to investment. In contrast, firms that faced more intense competition and more difficulty obtaining financing report less investment. Managers of manufacturing firms invest at higher rates than managers of the extractive industries of farming/fishing/forestry or mining, while managers of wholesale trade firms invest at higher rates.

These results are consistent with the argument, but it may be that responses from the most authoritarian countries are biasing the results. Some highly authoritarian countries have low polarization scores, and respondents may be afraid to voice the true extent of policy instability or the extent of policy instability as a problem. If this is true, then the results of the relationship between polarization and investment reported previously may be due to these biased responses rather than the actual relationship between polarization and investment. However, dropping the two most authoritarian countries from the sample – Belarus and Uzbekistan – produces few changes in the results.[36] This gives some confidence that the results are not strongly influenced by the fear of respondents in highly authoritarian countries.

Conclusion

Identifying the impact of national-level variables on national-level outcomes is challenging but is only a first step. Understanding how national-level variables influence individual behavior provides an even sterner test of the argument.

---

[35] Of course, heightened investment could lead to more sales. This variable is included as a control, and I make no claims about the direction of causality.

[36] Turkmenistan and Tajikistan are not in the sample.

TABLE 5.6. *Accounting for Investment*

	Model	
	5.8	5.9
Polarization	−.046*	−.053**
	(.026)	(.027)
Wealth (in thousands)	.043	.039
	(.092)	(.093)
Democracy	.010	.01
	(.020)	(.02)
FSU	−.022	−.03
	(.048)	(.05)
Employee	.014	.017*
	(.009)	(.010)
Private	.092**	.09**
	(.037)	(.04)
Lobby	.063**	.081**
	(.028)	(.030)
Competition as Obstacle	−.042**	−.041**
	(.019)	(.021)
Urban	−.011	−.015**
	(.007)	(.008)
Change in Sales	.021***	.020***
	(.008)	(.008)
Trade with State	.004	−.010
	(.024)	(.027)
Finance as Obstacle	−.040***	−.038***
	(.011)	(.011)
Exports	.024	.007
	(.029)	(.031)
Constant	4.64***	4.681***
	(.167)	(.172)
Dependent variable	ΔInvestment (logged)	ΔInvestment (logged)
Polarization	Categorical	Categorical
Firm-level *n*	3,401	2,922
National-level *n*	23	23
Sample	Original	Balanced
Random effects parameter	.075	.073
	(.021)	(.021)
Wald χ^2	82.88	81.43
Prob > χ^2	.0000	.0000
LR test vs. linear regression	10.81, chibar2 = .0005	9.60, chibar2 = .0010

Notes: *p < .10, **p < .05, ***p < .01. Hierarchical model using XTMIXED. The dependent variable is the log value of the size of the change in the reported level of investment from 1996 to 1999. Sectoral dummy variables included but not reported.

Indeed, in many cases theories developed about individual behavior do not test the predictions of the argument at the level of the individual. This is an important shortcoming because the relationship between two national-level variables may be spurious, absent evidence at the level of the individual. Moreover, we can often identify several paths by which a national-level variable is associated with another national-level variable. This chapter sought to address this problem by identifying the microfoundations of the argument linking polarization to economic policy choices. The evidence is consistent with the view that polarization shapes economic policy choice via policy instability.

Having identified some determinants of reversals of economic reform, the chapter turned to survey evidence. Analyses of the BEEPS data find that businesspeople in countries with increased political polarization tend to view economic policy as less predictable and to invest at lower rates. By using a survey of businesspeople to show that polarization is associated with greater perceived policy instability and less investment, this chapter establishes a tighter empirical link between political polarization and individual behavior.

Taken together, Chapters 3–5 provide evidence at the national level and individual level linking political polarization to greater policy instability, weaker economic reform, and slower economic growth. They have, however, only raised another question: why did some countries experience high levels of political polarization, while others do not? The next chapter begins to take up this question.

Appendix Tables A5.1–3

TABLE A5.1. *Variable Definitions from BEEPS Data and Descriptive Statistics*

Variables	Mean (sd)	Min/Max	Source and Notes
Percent change in investment	14.67 (59.84)	−100/900	Has your company's investment changed in real terms over the last three years? By how much did it increase or decrease? BEEPS
Policy unpredictability	4.2 (1.31)	1/6	How predictable are changes in the government's economic and financial policies which materially affect your business? 1 (completely predictable) to 6 (completely unpredictable). BEEPS
Policy instability as problem	2.94 (1.07)	1/4	Can you tell me how problematic is policy instability for the operation and growth of your business? 1 (no obstacle) to 4 (a major obstacle). BEEPS
Polarization	10.4 (10.90)	0/35	Average polarization score for years 1996–1999
Democracy	3.10 (1.72)	1/7	Freedom House
Country wealth	6,266 (3,233)	882/15,285	Country wealth per capita income at purchasing power parity from World Bank Development Indicators, 1996–1999.
Private	.85 (.35)	0/1	Dummy variable for all private or privatized firms. BEEPS
Finance as problem	2.99 (1.09)	1/4	Can you tell me how problematic are these different factors for the operation and growth of your business? 1 (no obstacle) to 4 (a major obstacle). BEEPS
Employees	3.92 (1.66)	1/7	Number of fulltime employees. 1 = 0 (as a screener question); 2 = 1–9 employees; 3 = 10–49; 4 = 50–99; 5 = 100–199; 6 = 200–499; 7 = 500 or more. BEEPS

TABLE A5.2. *Average Responses by Country*

	Policy Unpredictability[a]	Policy Instability as Obstacle[b]	Percent Change in Investment, 1996–1999
Albania	3.7 (1.1)	3.4 (.76)	13.4 (39)
Armenia	4.0 (1.7)	2.9 (1.0)	−6.2 (48)
Azerbaijan	2.9 (1.4)	2.3 (1.2)	−4.2 (18)
Belarus	4.5 (1.2)	2.9 (1.0)	17 (122)
Bulgaria	3.7 (1.5)	3.0 (1.0)	24.4 (71)
Croatia	4.0 (1.1)	3.1 (.91)	21.3 (80)
Czech Republic	4.0 (1.0)	2.8 (1.0)	5.6 (30)
Estonia	4.0 (1.2)	2.6 (1.1)	36.9 (94)
FYR of Macedonia	4.1 (1.2)	3.3 (.96)	4.25 (34)
Georgia	4.3 (1.5)	3.1 (.99)	10.1 (40)
Hungary	4.2 (1.2)	2.6 (1.1)	20.7 (50)
Kazakhstan	4.8 (1.2)	2.7 (1.1)	9.0 (57)
Kyrgyzstan	4.2 (1.1)	3.4 (.96)	−2.9 (26)
Latvia	4.1 (1.2)	2.8 (.97)	36.8 (127)
Lithuania	4.4 (1.4)	2.5 (1.1)	23.7 (75)
Moldova	4.4 (1.2)	3.6 (.69)	−4.5 (46)
Poland	4.0 (1.2)	2.7 (.99)	30.9 (71)
Romania	4.7 (1.3)	3.4 (.94)	13.4 (82)
Russia	4.8 (1.2)	3.4 (.83)	11.3 (72)
Slovakia	4.1 (1.2)	1.5 (.90)	11.0 (53)
Slovenia	3.7 (1.0)	2.5 (.94)	32.9 (66)
Ukraine	4.5 (1.2)	3.2 (.94)	4.9 (42)
Uzbekistan	3.6 (1.2)	2.0 (1.1)	29.9 (100)
Mean (standard error)	4.2 (1.3)	2.9 (1.07)	14.7 (70)

[a] 1 = completely predictable, 6 = completely unpredictable.
[b] 1 = not an obstacle, 4 = severe obstacle.

TABLE A5.3. *Two-Step Analysis: Polarization, Policy Instability, and Investment*

	1	2	3	4
Polarization	.020***	.022***	−.003^	−.003*
	(.005)	(.005)	(.002)	(.002)
FSU	−.110	.016	−.014	−.029
	(.165)	(.187)	(.051)	(.042)
Wealth	−.04	–	.07	–
	(.02)		(.06)	
Democracy	–	−.027	–	−.012
		(.072)		(.013)
Constant	2.96***	2.53***	4.57	4.67
	(.25)	(.242)	(.069)	(.038)
Dependent variable	Policy unpredictability	Policy unpredictability	% increase in investment	% increase in investment
Polarization	Continuous	Continuous	Continuous	Continuous
Observations in second stage	23	23	23	23
R^2	.28	.22	.19	.17
Prob > f	.0009	.0003	.0847	.1279

Notes: $*p < .10$, $**p < .05$, $***p < .01$, $^p = .105$. Here I use a two-step model as suggested by Huber et al. (2005). In the first stage I use OLS regression on the level-one variables reported in Models 5.4 and 5.8 with fixed effects for each country. I then take the coefficients from the fixed effects for each country and use these as the dependent variable in an OLS regression in the second stage. I report the results using these level-two variables as the predictors in the second-stage regression. I use the continuous measure of *Polarization*. Models 1 and 2 use policy instability as an obstacle as the dependent variable, and models 3 and 4 use the log of investment as the dependent variable.

6

Nationalism and Endogenous Polarization

> Nationalism is the last stage of Communism.
>
> Adam Michnik[1]

Recognizing the centrality of political polarization for policy outcomes leads one to ask, Why does it vary so much across countries? A fully satisfying answer could easily generate another book, but here I pose the question for two reasons. First, I aim to begin to address concerns about reverse causation.[2] If economic and institutional reforms are driving political polarization – rather than vice versa – then the argument made in preceding chapters is subject to challenge. To this end, I explore the sources of polarization across countries. Tracing the direction of causation in cross-national research is difficult, but the postcommunist cases are well positioned to explore this issue. In each country, initial levels of political polarization were determined by the first election after communism and therefore preceded the introduction of economic and institutional reform. That polarization predated policy choices indicates that at least initially the latter was driving the former. Whether this pattern continued later in the transformation is harder to divine.

Second, the chapter aims to add causal depth to the argument by exploring the determinants of political polarization. Satisfying explanations not only provide correlations between independent and dependent variables and identify causal mechanisms between them but also have causal depth. Independent variables should be at some temporal and conceptual distance from the dependent variable so as to avoid tautology. While recognizing that convincing accounts should rely on tight causal chains based on human agency, Kitschelt (2003) argues forcefully for explanations that also identify the sources of variation in

---

[1] Cited in Vujacic (1996: 152).
[2] In Chapters 3 and 4, I employed a number of statistical techniques to try to reduce concerns for simple types of reverse causation and endogeneity by using lagged dependent variables and by taking measures of partisanship and polarization from the first postcommunist election.

the institutions and structures that shape those choices. He (2003: 16) urges scholars to navigate between "an uncompromising structuralism that has a penchant toward excessively deep explanations without human action, on the one hand, and purely conjunctural theories that favor only the shallowest, most proximate of intertemporal social mechanisms, on the other." In reference to the cases at hand, Kitschelt (2003: 16) notes that "causal analysis in the comparative study of post-communist politicians should not be so shallow as to blur the distinction between *explanans* and *explanandum*, but it should also not be so deep as to evaporate any causal mechanism that could operate through human action, identified by preferences, skills, and expectation." Debates about proper causal depth are more epistemological than empirical. There is no objectively appropriate causal depth for an explanation, but accounts in which the cause and effect are so tightly linked as to be inseparable or are so far apart as to appear untethered should give pause.

In searching for the sources of political polarization, it may be beneficial to go back in time. Because political polarization emerged to varying degrees immediately after the first election in each postcommunist country, some of the variation in political polarization likely lies in events before 1989. The institutional legacy of the Soviet system distributed normative and material resources unevenly across political actors. In particular, it shaped the ability of outgoing communist parties to maintain their organizational integrity and ideological orientation while remaining politically competitive. This legacy also influenced the resources available to the political opposition (Zielinski 2002; Wittenberg 2006; Darden and Grzymala-Busse 2007).

National Identity, the Soviet Bloc, and Political Polarization

The next section develops an argument linking political polarization to the timing of the creation of national identity and the ability of old-left parties to play the nationalist card after 1989. It argues that the presence of two conditions promotes political polarization: where both national identity predated the arrival of communist rule and communist parties before 1989 exercised relative autonomy in foreign policy, political polarization is especially pronounced. In these cases the ex-communist parties could more easily use nationalist appeals after 1989 and thereby create a second dimension to politics and expand their base of support. By pointing to their defense of national sovereignty from foreign encroachment in the Soviet era, they were better positioned to rally support in the postcommunist era. The argument identifies three general patterns of relations between communist parties and national sovereignty before 1989 that begin to shed light on the sources of political polarization in the postcommunist period. In some countries, like Uzbekistan and Azerbaijan, national identity was created only after the arrival of communist power. This gave communist-era leaders considerable leverage after 1989 and made it difficult for right and centrist opposition parties to mobilize around nationalist themes. The result was low levels of political polarization as old-left ex-communist elites dominated the political scene and faced a weak and divided opposition.

In contrast, in countries like Poland and Estonia, national identity predated communist power and the local Communist Party played a subordinate role in the communist bloc. In this setting, hard-line communist leaders had great difficulty escaping their past complicity with a "foreign" power and communist parties tended to transform themselves into social democratic parties (cf. Poland, Lithuania, Slovenia) or to collapse (cf. Estonia, Georgia, Armenia).[3] Perhaps more importantly, right and centrist groups were well placed to play the nationalist card to undercut ex-communist elites. In these cases, the traditional wings of the Communist Party crumbled and allowed centrist and right parties to dominate the political scene after 1989.

In other countries, like Russia and Romania, national identity predated communist power, but the Communist Party played a relatively autonomous role within the communist bloc, which allowed communist successor parties after 1989 to credibly claim to have made policy without being subservient to a "foreign" power. In these cases, the Communist Party had greater credibility than its counterparts elsewhere in the region and could seek credit for some of the achievements of the communist period, while downplaying its worst features. These themes played well with some sectors of society but not with others and led to a pattern of polarized politics between a right and an old-left camp.

Many scholars have studied the impact of features of the old regime on political and economic outcomes in the postcommunist era. Volumes edited by Ishiyama (1999) and Bozoki and Ishiyama (2002) provide excellent case studies of how the legacies of the antecedent regime influenced the organization and programs of ex-communist parties. Grzymala-Busse (2002) develops an elegant treatment of how ex-communist parties in Poland, Hungary, the Czech Republic, and Slovakia adapted to competitive politics. To account for features of the party system in the postcommunist period, Kitschelt et al. (1999) create three ideal types of Communist Party rule: bureaucratic-authoritarian, national accommodative communism, and patrimonial communism. Laitin (1998) identifies three patterns by which peripheral ethnic groups were incorporated into the USSR and lays out how these patterns influenced identity formation. Abdelal (2001) links initial choices over foreign economic policy to the content of national identity, particularly its relationship to Russia. These arguments shed light on party systems, ethnic identity change, and foreign economic policy, respectively. I borrow and merge various aspects of these approaches to begin to identify the sources of political polarization. The argument here is closest in spirit to Darden and Grzymala-Busse (2007), who contend that the timing and content of mass education shaped national identity in ways that were reflected in the first postcommunist election. Countries in which national literacy

---

[3] "Foreign" is used in quotation marks here as central authorities in Moscow and Yugoslavia were de facto rather than de jure foreign by the late 1980s.

predated communism and the curriculum was infused with nationalist content exhibited more support for noncommunist parties at the start of the transition. Their work is a good example of a deep argument that traces a causal mechanism from the past to the present.[4]

Nationalism, Communism, and the Two Tiers of the Communist Bloc

To put my argument in its proper context, I begin with a discussion of sovereignty, nationalism, and the layers of the Communist "family" of nations.[5] It is helpful to consider the two layers of the communist bloc that emanated from Moscow but ranged from Vladivostok to Berlin. In the outer layer, the countries of the communist bloc were led by domestic communist parties but were also bound together by the military ties of the Warsaw Pact and the trade links of COMECON. While the leverage of the USSR over the member countries of these organizations waxed and waned during the postwar period, the former were always subservient to Moscow. At various points, reform movements in Hungary, Czechoslovakia, and Poland tested the boundaries of autonomy from the USSR, but each attempt ended with a reassertion of control by Moscow. Because militaries in the region were ultimately subordinate to the Warsaw Pact, and hence Moscow, domestic elites had little chance for military success. Until Gorbachev's "New Thinking" in foreign policy in 1987–1988, the ability of Warsaw Pact and COMECON members to pursue economic and security policies independent from Moscow was tightly circumscribed.

But not all countries in the communist bloc were so closely tied to the Warsaw Pact and COMECON. By dint of geography, history, and leadership style, Yugoslavia, Romania, and Albania demonstrated far greater autonomy from Moscow than other countries in the sample. Bunce (1999a: 70) pithily observes that Albania was outside the bloc, Yugoslavia was associated with the bloc but not a full member, and Romania was a member in bad standing. The relatively autonomous positions of these countries vis-à-vis Moscow had important implications for politics in the postcommunist period.

Moving to the inner layer of the bloc, we find the USSR an "unbreakable Union of free republics," if the Soviet national anthem is to be believed. The fifteen national republics of the USSR were organized on the principle of nationality, and titular national elites held formal authority at the republic level, but political power flowed from Moscow to the republics – not the reverse. The

---

[4] One drawback to the Darden and Grzymala-Busse argument for my purpose is that the timing of mass literacy may be directly associated with economic and institutional outcomes and is less useful as an instrumental variable.

[5] For a review of the complex history of nationality policy within the Soviet Union and the countries of Eastern Europe, see Pipes (1954), Motyl (1988, 1989), Nahaylo and Swoboda (1990), Roeder (1991), and Martin (2001). Suny (1993), Bunce (1999a), and Beissinger (2002: 48–57) provide especially concise and measured discussions of nationalities policy in the USSR. For a discussion of relations between Moscow and the countries of the Soviet bloc, see Marese and Vanous (1983), Bunce (1984–1985), and Stone (1996).

USSR recognized national diversity at the republic level and created opportunities for national elites to manage the republic, but it insisted on the political loyalty of the indigenous national elites to central authorities in Moscow. The two layers of the communist bloc revolved around Moscow's relations with the countries of Eastern Europe through the Warsaw Pact and COMECON and with the republics of the USSR through the national federal institutions of the Communist Party of the Soviet Union.

Despite the professed desire of communist parties in the region to elevate class over nationality, the institutional arrangements of both layers of the communist bloc helped to strengthen national identity. In multiethnic federations like the USSR and Yugoslavia, a scholarly consensus has emerged in recent years that the structure of political institutions reinforced titular national identities where they already existed and created titular national identities where they did not.[6] Central governments in Moscow and Belgrade devoted considerable funds for mass education and the teaching of national languages. In addition, they promoted the development of indigenous national elites and gave them considerable resources to manage the national-federal unit. Over time, central government policy gave national elites many of the building blocks to create a modern state should central power wane. Suny (1993: 24–25) captures this sentiment: "One of the central ironies of Soviet history is that a regime dedicated to effacing nationality and to creating a supra-ethnic community and a party that posited class rather than nationality as the key determinant of the social structure have presided over a process in which modern nations have been formed within the union they governed." More recently, Beissinger's (2002: 116) sophisticated statistical analysis reveals that "the Soviet regime's effort to modernize, silently and contrary to their manifest purpose, helped to foster the very conditions that eventually undermined control by creating urban national intelligentsias capable of providing leadership." Hirsch (2005) extends this line of reasoning by arguing that the Bolsheviks viewed nationalism as a stage of history that the ethnically constituted republics of the USSR had to pass through before reaching socialism.

A somewhat similar dynamic operated in the outer layer of the communist bloc as Moscow's dominant position helped to reinforce nationalism by providing a common target for blame. Similar to the national federal system of the USSR, the communist bloc recognized national diversity, while it simultaneously promoted the political dominance of communist parties that were ultimately dependent on Moscow to stay in power. The dual strategy of recognizing national diversity while also creating institutions to enhance the position

---

[6] See especially Roeder (1991), Suny (1993), Brubaker (1996), and Bunce (1999a). Brubaker (1996: 37) notes: "The repression of political nationalism was compatible with the pervasive institutionalization of nationhood and nationality as fundamental social categories. . . . the regime had no policy of nation-destroying. It might have abolished national republics; it might have abolished the legal category of personal nationality; it might have ruthlessly Russified the Soviet educational system; it might have forcibly uprooted peripheral elites, and prevented them from making careers in 'their own' republics. It did none of the above."

of a local communist party dependent on Moscow generated a similar logic of rule in the USSR and the communist bloc. Bunce (1999a: 39) notes that the national federation of the USSR and the communist bloc were "surprisingly similar in their design and their internal dynamics," before adding that the "very structure of the bloc and the federation put into place the necessary conditions for the rise of nations and nationalist movements in the peripheral units. With the collapse of the [Soviet] regime, this translated into the formation of newly sovereign states, as Eastern Europe was liberated from Soviet domination and as the republics within the federation were 'liberated' from the state." The decline of the Communist Party of the USSR therefore emboldened the member states of the communist bloc and the federal units of the USSR to reassert their national identity, but the manner in which states did so varied dramatically with important consequences for the balance of partisan politics. This analogy should not be pushed too far because the countries of the outer layer of the communist bloc had greater autonomy from Moscow than did the constituent republics of the USSR and were internationally recognized as states. Nonetheless, the logic of rule in each layer of the communist bloc shared some important common features that helped to bring national identity issues to the fore.[7]

Late National Model

In countries that followed a "late national" model of rule, the creation of a national identity occurred only after the arrival of communist power.[8] In Central Asia, national identity was weak in the 1920s when the Bolshevik Party and the Red Army took power. The nominal citizens of the new state attached far greater allegiance to tribal or clan interests than to any national identity. Huskey (1994: 399) notes that in the 1920s "the loyalties of the Kyrgyz, like those of other Central Asians, most notably the Kazakhs, lay first with family, clan, and tribe" rather than with the nation. In this region, representatives of Soviet power confronted local leaders of families and clans living a nomadic or seminomadic lifestyle and imposed a set of political and economic institutions upon them. The early years of Soviet power saw the first attempts to mold these disparate local identities into national identities attached to a republic within the Soviet Union. The establishment of republican governments, ruled ostensibly by titular ethnic groups, was the first step toward this end. In the years that followed, Soviet policies of indigenization sought to bolster national identities and cultures by introducing mass schooling, reforming the written language, and establishing cultural practices consistent with the new national identity (Suny 1993: 87). Carlisle (1991: 24) captures this sentiment nicely: "The history of Soviet Central Asia should be read as an attempt to create modern nations... where previously there were only ethnic groups."

---

[7] Bunce (1999a: 38–55) provides a more complete treatment of this analogy.

[8] Here a nation is understood as a community of people deserving political self-determination (and frequently its own state) primarily on the basis of its own claims to constitute a community.

Soviet efforts to create new nations where none existed were far from perfect. Regional identities persisted as did attachments to tribe and clan (Jones Luong 2002; Collins 2006). But socialization into national groups did leave an imprint on the polities of Central Asia. This claim fits well with Smith et al.'s (1998: 7) characterization of Soviet nationality policy:

Not only did such a form of institutionalized nation-building facilitate the preservation and reproduction of established niches for incumbents drawn from the indigenous cultures, it also enabled nationality divisions to remain an integral part and reference point of native public life and an organisational basis for reinforcing local national identities. Indeed, in some instances, notably in Central Asia, federalising ethnic homelands into ethnorepublics, the Soviet state actually created nations whose sense of nationness had previously barely existed.

This late national pattern of incorporation into the Soviet bloc gave local Communist Party elites a strong hand to play after 1989. With the weakening of central power in Moscow, local Communist Party leaders quickly grabbed the mantle of defenders of the nation and used the powers of the state apparatus to reinforce this claim. Communist leaders were still vulnerable to the charge of doing Moscow's bidding but far less so than in other countries in the region where communist power arrived only after the creation of a national identity. Moreover, they could continue to use the resources of the state, which had been less tarnished by association with the suppression of nationalism in the Soviet era, to their own advantage. Political elites could rely on long-standing patron-client relations based on regional or ethnic ties that were especially strong in these countries and were tightly fused to the state apparatus (Willerton 1992).[9]

Perhaps as important, opposition leaders in these settings were poorly placed to use nationalism to rally opposition to the former communist-led regime. Mass publics in these late national countries had not experienced nationhood independent of the Soviet experience, which made it difficult for opposition leaders to mobilize on the basis of appeals to nationalism. To the extent that national identity existed, Communist Party leaders could play the nationalism card as well or better than local opposition groups.

Identifying the timing of a nation's creation is an exercise fraught with imprecision.[10] However, there is little evidence of the popular expression of national identity before the arrival of communist power in seven countries in the sample: Azerbaijan, Belarus, Kazakhstan, Kyrgyzstan, Tajikistan, Turkmenistan, and Uzbekistan. In each of these late national cases, outgoing leaders from the communist era have relied on the state and party apparatus to retain office well into the postcommunist era. For example, Hunter (1993: 231) argues that the "Azerbaijan Communist Party remained influential after 1989 first aided by Soviet troops, then by acquiring a nationalist garb." Using similar language, Suny (1993: 156) describes the situation in the late 1980s: "In

---

[9] Willerton (1992) provides evidence on this score for Azerbaijan and Lithuania.
[10] See Connor's (1990) appropriately titled article: "When Is a Nation?"

Uzbekistan, Tajikistan, Turkmenistan, and Azerbaijan the old elites dressed up in nationalist garb to preserve their dominion and suppress democratic politics." Beissinger (2002: 37) points out the irony that "once loyal Soviet nomenklatura like Heydar Aliev, Mintimer Shamiev, and Saparmurad Niiazov could become the 'fathers' of their respective nations." In these late national cases, we generally find low levels of political polarization as outgoing communist-era leaders dominated the political scene, leaving little room for right opponents.[11]

Uzbekistan provides a clear example of a late national model of rule in which ex-communist leaders retained great power after 1989 and political polarization has been low. Uzbek national identity was largely created in the Soviet period. Before the arrival of Soviet power, much of the area currently known as Uzbekistan was part of tsarist Russia and was organized into two major khanates in Tashkent and Khiva, but with little sense of overarching national identity.[12] Carlisle (1994: 206) observes that the "configuration of national units like Uzbekistan was artificial, concocted only in the 1920s and stifled during the succeeding years as they became subordinate provinces of the Soviet empire." Gleason (1994: 335) notes: "The national identity of members of Uzbekistan's groups often continued to be quite weak. In the European borderland regions of the USSR, many national groups have a cohesive national identity based on a common language, common traditions, and a common historical experience.... By way of comparison, Uzbekistan's national groups are much less clearly defined, cohesive, or even self-conscious." During the Soviet period, Communist Party leaders devoted considerable resources to developing an Uzbek national identity from the various tribal, clan, and regional identities that predominated. These efforts aimed to create an Uzbek identity that was culturally salient but politically impotent, as Soviet officials kept the reins tight to ensure that these identities did not become politicized. However, after 1989, ex–Communist Party leader Islam Karimov played on themes of national independence to retain office and extend his power into the postcommunist era. Moreover, opposition groups had difficulty mobilizing a public that often identifies more strongly with clan or regional interests (Easter 1997; Jones Luong 2002; Collins 2006). This has led to a political system largely dominated by President Karimov and his protégés, many of whom had deep roots in the Soviet system. As a result, political polarization has been minimal in Uzbekistan.

Dependent National Model

By contrast, in the "dependent national" model of rule, the creation of a national identity predated the arrival of communist power and the local Communist Party played a subordinate role in the communist bloc. Many of these countries had a previous experience of independent statehood, which

---

[11] See Nissman (1993: 384) on Turkmenistan; Huskey (1994) on Kyrgyzstan; and Carlisle (1994: 205) on Tajikistan.

[12] On the incorporation of the two main local khanates, Tashkent and Khiva, see Pipes (1954: 12–14, 174–184).

allowed a period of intense nation building prior to communist rule. Communist Party elites before 1989 faced the difficult task of satisfying "foreign" masters while governing a public with a refined sense of national identity. By virtue of their subservience to Moscow or Belgrade, the outgoing Communist Party was vulnerable to the charge of not having defended national sovereignty before 1989. For example, some communist parties represented a marginal national group in the multinational federations of the USSR and Yugoslavia. In such a setting, long-time Communist Party leaders who ruled ethnorepublics were poorly placed to compete with opposition movements arguing in favor of greater national sovereignty after 1989. In Armenia, Georgia, Moldova, Latvia, Lithuania, and Estonia, local communist parties faced severe limits on their access to the highest institutions of state power in the Soviet period. Only two voting members of the Politburo between 1966 and 1980 were Georgian, and only one was Armenian. No Lithuanian, Estonian, or Moldovan served on the Politburo in this period (Lane and Ross 1999). In addition, titular elites ruling at the republic level were given little incentive to defend republic interests, and the rules for advancement rewarded ethnic elites who were loyal to Moscow rather than to the prior ethnic republic (Nahaylo and Swoboda 1990).

Moreover, political elites could rely on a sense of national identity that predated communism. Suny (1995: 148) captures this sentiment in Armenia and Georgia: "Armenians both in Karabakh and Armenia proper could refer to a clear sense of nationhood with a textual tradition of continuous existence and past statehood." Similarly, he observes (1993: 155) that "the discourse of the nation, with its inherent anti-Communist and anti-Russian overtones, was appropriated so completely by the extraparty intellectuals that communism and communist rule were easily constructed as alien to Georgianness." The Baltic states could point to the interwar years as a period of intense nation building prior to communism (Lieven 1993; Pettai and Kreuzer 1999).

In Yugoslavia, these relations took a similar, if less extreme, form. Yugoslavia had a much more decentralized version of rule, particularly after the adoption of a new constitution in 1974, but also had a hierarchy among the ethnic republics. Macedonia, Slovenia, and to a lesser extent Croatia played subordinate roles to Serbia in this multiethnic federation. Serbian elites were especially well represented in the military and security forces compared to the Croats and Slovenes – an important consideration in a period of transition. Rothschild (1989: 189) notes that the Serbs were "the most numerous and central ethnonation in the Yugoslav federation." Petersen (2002: 217–230, 225) provides much evidence that Croatian Party leaders chafed under Serb-dominated rule in Yugoslavia and notes more bluntly that, "first and foremost, Croatians have always had a problem with Serbian authority."[13]

---

[13] Bunce (1999a: 115–119) argues that Serbs perceived that they were underrepresented in other Yugoslav political bodies. In her view the Serbian political elite felt slighted by the 1974 constitution, which vastly increased political and economic equality in formal offices among

The dependence of Communist Party elites was most apparent in countries outside of the USSR that allowed foreign troops to repress demands for autonomy from Moscow in the communist period. Having allied with foreign troops to quell popular demands for political and economic reform before 1989, conservative Communist Party elites in Hungary, the Czech Republic, and Slovakia were especially poorly positioned to compete for office in the postcommunist period. In these cases, Communist Party elites exited power tarred with the charge of having failed to defend national sovereignty in the communist era.

Perhaps more importantly, anticommunist opposition groups in the center and on the right in countries having experienced a dependent national model of rule could use nationalism as a mobilization tactic to undermine local communist parties. Mass demonstrations called for the ousting of Communist Party elites and national sovereignty became "an ordinary part of the Soviet political landscape" in many republics in the Soviet Union in 1988 and 1989 (Beissinger 2002: 89). Similarly, the mass mobilizations that brought the end of communist power in Eastern Europe were movements in support of national autonomy at least as much as they were movements in support of democracy or economic reform (Garton-Ash 1993; Stokes 1993; Bunce 1999a). Facing mass mobilization around nationalist themes, the more traditional wings of these national communist parties were largely discredited in the eyes of the public and collapsed early in the transformation. In some cases, like Hungary, Poland, and Lithuania, ex-communist parties transformed themselves into social democratic parties by shedding their old-left elements and promoting their skills as technocrats (Ishiyama 1995; Grzymala-Busse 2002). In others, like Latvia and Georgia, communist parties fell apart quickly and remained largely absent from the political scene (Beissinger 2002: 99–102). In the postcommunist period, countries having experienced a dependent national model of rule had relatively low levels of political polarization as old-left factions were swept aside and opposition forces used nationalism to mobilize popular support against old-regime rulers.

Sovereign National Model

In countries ruled according to a sovereign national model, national identities preceded the arrival of communist power, but ex-communist parties could claim to have made policy without being subservient to a "foreign" power before 1989. For example, in the multiethnic states of the Soviet Union and Yugoslavia, sovereign national communist parties ruled in the name of national groups occupying positions of primacy within the political system.[14] In the

---

republics, and this perception of inequity fueled the desire of elites in Belgrade to expand their role by either re-creating a more centralized Yugoslavia or by creating a greater Serbia.

[14] Serbia would fit this role in Yugoslavia with some modifications. Serbia is not included in the sample because of lack of data on other dimensions. Czechoslovakia can also be categorized as a multinational federation, but given that both the Czech and Slovak republics were subservient to Moscow, they fit better in the dependent national category.

USSR, this was clearly Russia. This mixture of great-power nationalism and opportunities for upward mobility for Russians was a key element of the Soviet political system. Bialer (1982: 208) identified "great power nationalism" as the "most potent, unifying, and systemic force within the Soviet society, which accounts primarily for the political stability of the Soviet state in the last thirty years as opposed to the instability of the East European communist regimes." Russian elites dominated the governing bodies of the USSR. Members of the Politburo of the Communist Party of the Soviet Union came overwhelmingly from Russia and less frequently from Ukraine, with only token representatives from other ethnic republics (Rigby 1990: 260; Lane and Ross 1999: 35). Throughout much of the 1970s and 1980s, more than 85 percent of the Politburo of the Communist Party and Council of Ministers were Russian, Ukrainian, or Belorussian (Rigby 1990: 260).[15] In addition, elites from republics outside of Russia and Ukraine had extremely limited access to other high posts in the all-union party or state bureaucracy. In 1980 only three non-Slavs served in the top 150 positions in the central party apparatus, and the same number of non-Slavs held posts in the 97 offices of the Council of Ministers (Bialer 1982: 219–220). With the exception of Ukrainians, "the road to the central establishment... is closed to non-Russian elites" (Bialer 1982: 219). Ex–Communist Party leaders in this model could point to the achievements of the Soviet Union – particularly its influence on global affairs and its opportunities for upward mobility for Russians and Ukrainians – to assert their nationalist credentials.[16] To a great extent, the achievements of the Soviet Union were easily translated into the achievements of Russia.

Communist-era leaders in Romania and Albania can also be depicted as examples of the sovereign national model of rule. Both exercised significant autonomy from Moscow and were less vulnerable to the charge of having done the bidding of a foreign country while in power. Unlike Poland, Hungary, Czechoslovakia, or Bulgaria, Romania had no Soviet military troops on its soil after 1962. Romania refused to join other "friendly" countries in the invasion of Czechoslovakia in 1968 and resisted attempts at closer integration with the Warsaw Pact and COMECON. Moreover, Bunce (1999a: 169) notes that Romania pursued "a distinctive road to socialism that involved among other things... an independent foreign policy stressing Romanian nationalism." Rothschild (1989: 165) agrees, arguing that "for all their excrescences,

---

[15] In 1952 only 64 percent of the Politburo of the USSR were from the three Slavic Republics (Rigby 1990: 260).

[16] The Russian Federation was the only republic without a Communist Party of its own. Given the dominant position of the Russian Federation in the USSR, this structure may have been redundant. Brubaker (1996: 42) notes: "The high degree of overlap between the RSFSR and the Union – the fact that the great majority of key facilities were located on Russian territory (if not formally subject to Russian jurisdiction), and the fact that Soviet elites, in their great majority, were either Russian by nationality, or long standing residents of the RSFSR, or both – made it relatively easy for central Soviet military and bureaucratic elites to reorient themselves to the RSFSR at pivotal moments, especially during and immediately after the coup attempts."

distortions, repressions, and blunders, they [the Ceausescus] remained committed to the goal of protecting Romanian autonomy and sovereignty *vis-à-vis* the Soviet Union within the Soviet orbit."

In similar fashion, Albanian leaders assumed an independent stance toward Moscow after Khrushchev's denunciation of Stalin in the Secret Speech of 1956, and Albania was ultimately expelled from Soviet-led military and trade alliances. Albanian leader Enver Hoxha sided with China in the Sino-Soviet split, but relations with Peking soured, leaving Albania without a great-power ally.[17] Indeed, by the 1970s Albania became increasingly isolated from the outside world and took self-reliance to extremes (Biberaj 1998, 2000). In this sovereign national model of rule, the communist parties represented one of the dominant national groups in the country and could reasonably avoid the charge of subservience to a foreign power.

Ukraine is the most difficult case to categorize using these criteria. The largely Russified eastern and southern areas of Ukraine served as a bastion of Soviet power before 1989 and fit rather well in the sovereign national category. Western Ukraine, particularly areas incorporated after World War II, fits far better under the dependent nation model. Given these cleavages, a plausible case could be made for treating Ukraine as having been ruled according to either a dependent national or sovereign national model in the Soviet period. Despite the suppression of nationalist movements in the western regions of Ukraine, it is perhaps appropriate to view it as an example of the sovereign national model, given its privileged position within the governing structures of the Soviet Union and the overlapping development of Russia and Ukraine in the Soviet period. Ukrainian political elites generally had access to federation-wide governing bodies that were unavailable to other titular national elites. Bialer (1982: 222–223) discusses the unique position held by Ukrainian elites within the Soviet federal system:

The key to the national question on the all-union scale, though not the guarantee of its containment, rests with the Slavic republics and particularly with Ukraine.... It is not surprising that the treatment of the Ukrainian managerial and technical intelligentsia and especially the political and administrative elite differs from that in all other republics. In one crucial respect it goes beyond that of even the other self-administered republics. Ukrainians are afforded the opportunity to advance in significant numbers into the central elite and to serve in important positions, both as representatives of the central authorities in the non-Slav republics and as officials of all-union central functional bureaucracies.

Bialer then provides an impressive list of high positions in the central government, the KGB, and the military held by Ukrainians. No other titular ethnic group was even remotely represented in such numbers at the all-union level. Ukrainian elites also held a privileged position in social standing. Laitin (1998: 60) treats the Ukrainians as "most-favored lords" in the Soviet multiethnic

---

[17] On Albanian sovereignty from Moscow, see Rothschild (1989: 174–176).

federation because they "had rights and privileges equal to those of the elites of similar status and education in the political center (Russians)."

This is not to deny tensions between Russian and Ukrainian elites within political institutions in the Soviet period or to overlook the suppression of movements for greater national sovereignty in western Ukraine (Motyl 1988). The hierarchy within the USSR gave pride of place to Russians. But it is helpful to recognize that Ukraine's relatively privileged position in the USSR and political cleavages within Ukraine make it a difficult fit for any one conceptual category. Abdelal (2001: 122) recognizes this duality by characterizing Ukraine's national identity as "contested." In their empirical analysis, Darden and Grzymala-Busse (2007) divide Ukraine in two for this reason. In any case, none of the results are appreciably altered if Ukraine is dropped from the analysis.

In countries having followed a sovereign national model, both old-left ex–Communist Party elites and anticommunist opposition forces on the center and right could contest claims over the role of the Communist Party in relation to national sovereignty before 1989. Ex–Communist Party elites could point to policy successes in the Soviet period that were important to the dominant national group, particularly in maintaining political stability, increasing standards of living, and providing paths of promotion before 1989 to back their case. The anticommunist opposition could charge that the Communist Party had not done enough to protect national sovereignty, but these charges had less traction than in the dependent national model. This confrontation over national sovereignty between groups defending and opposing the outgoing regime contributed to bipolar competition between ex-communist elites and their anticommunist opponents and helped promote high levels of political polarization in the postcommunist period.

The sovereign national model of rule helps shed light on the puzzle of why ex-communist parties in some countries have relied heavily on nationalism to bolster their position in the postcommunist period.[18] Scholars have repeatedly noted that ex-communist parties in the countries that I place in the sovereign national category have resorted to political appeals rooted in nationalism. Bozoki and Ishiyama (2002: 8) argue that the Albanian, Russian, Serbian, Bulgarian, and Romanian ex-communist parties have used a "national-patriotic" strategy that "seeks to associate the party with nationalism, a modern ideological alternative to communism which in Eastern Europe is also historically anti-capitalist and anti-West." Chotiner (1999) argues that Communist Party leaders in Russia have consciously appealed to "national patriotic" themes

---

[18] The argument made here is in some respects close to that of Abdelal (2001), who traces differences in foreign economic policy to the content of different national identities. Here the content of national identity is not central. Rather it is the ability to make claims of defending national sovereignty that allows these communist parties to stay competitive in the political system, and their economic policies are derivative. See also Darden (2009) for the role of ideas in foreign economic policy making.

to improve their electoral chances. Bozoki and Ishiyama (2002: 6) observe that the Communist Party of the Russian Federation (CPRF) "identifies itself with the so-called patriotic elements within the old CPSU – the party of Soviet heroes, the cosmonaut Yuri Gagarin, Marshal Georgii Zhiukov.... Further this party claims that socialism is fully compatible with the primordial collectivist sentiments of the Russian people, and the promotion of socialism necessarily involves the defense of Russian culture and tradition." Flikke (1999: 275) identifies the orientation of the CPRF in the mid-1990s as "patriotic left-centrism" that aims to create "a popular identity as a party of patriots or dedicated defenders of Russian statehood and national identity in relentless opposition to the president and a government of 'traitors and fifth columnists.'" March (2002: 270) notes that for the CPRF "the unifying idea is 'state patriotism.'"[19]

Similarly, in the early years of the transformation the successor to the Romanian Communist Party, the Democratic National Salvation Front (DNSF) followed Ceausescu's tradition of "mixing nationalism with leftist etatism" (Murer 1999: 221).[20] Verdery (1993: 187) echoes this view by referring to the "moderate nationalism" of the DNSF before recounting that "President Iliescu celebrated Romania's national holiday in 1991 by sharing a toast with extreme national stalwarts, all of them apparatchiks of yore." The Ukrainian Communist Party has avoided calls to mobilize supporters on the basis of appeals to an ethnic form of nationalism but has relied heavily on great-power nationalism of the Soviet period to rally the faithful (Haran 2001).[21] Similarly, Biberaj (1998) reports that in the parliamentary elections in 1991 the Socialist Party of Albania "resorted to the old Communist tactic of putting heightened emphasis on nationalist themes and linking the SPA and socialism with the preservation of the country's independence." In general, scholars have suggested that the combination of nationalism and communism makes for ideologically uncomfortable bedfellows, but this strategy of ex-communist parties using nationalism to rally the faithful makes sense in the cases at hand in light of the arguments presented in this chapter.[22]

All broad classifications such as these simplify a complex reality, and some cases are more easily categorized than others. Painting with a broad brush allows one to cover more ground in hopes of uncovering relationships that are

[19] Indeed, many authors have noted that the Russian Communist Party relies heavily on a mixture of reformed Marxism and "patriotic statism" as its main ideological currents (cf. Sakwa 1998; March 2002).

[20] Horowitz (1985) notes that parties with an internationalist ideology are likely to fare poorly when nationalism comes to the fore.

[21] The Communist Party of Ukraine and the Socialist Party of Ukraine differ from the Communist Party of the Russian Federation in that the former does not rely on Ukrainian ethnicity to mobilize supporters. Instead it stands for a "Slavic idea" and an emphasis on "territorial patriotism" rather than "ethnic patriotism" (Haran 2001).

[22] This is not to argue that ex-communist parties are the only parties that play the nationalist card. It is only to make the case that some ex-communist parties are better positioned than others to play it.

TABLE 6.1. *The Roots of Political Polarization*

		Average Polarization Score	
		Continuous	Categorical
Late national rule	Azerbaijan	12	.08
	Belarus	7	.46
	Kazakhstan	2	0
	Kyrgyzstan	19	1.38
	Tajikistan	1	0
	Turkmenistan	0	0
	Uzbekistan	2	0
	Mean	6.0	.27
	N = 91	(11.5)	(.68)
Dependent national rule	Armenia	6	0
	Bulgaria	29	2
	Czech Republic	8	0
	Croatia	7	.67
	Estonia	2	.15
	Georgia	2	.15
	Hungary	0	.73
	Latvia	6	.15
	Lithuania	1	.61
	Macedonia	19	1.47
	Moldova	15	1.08
	Poland	0	.27
	Slovakia	6.2	0
	Slovenia	0	0
	Mean	7.3	.53
	N = 198	(10.9)	(.79)
Borderline case	Ukraine	22	1.53
Sovereign national rule	Albania	24	1.29
	Romania	22	1.60
	Russia	20	1.23
	Mean[a]	22.2	1.42
	N = 55	(10.2)	(.87)

Notes: Standard deviation in parentheses. N = number of observations in relevant categories.
[a] These totals include Ukraine, but excluding this case has little effect.

less apparent in smaller samples but at the price of overlooking the subtleties of individual cases. The goal here is to begin to identify a general pattern of relationships between a specific feature of communist rule and the partisan balance of power in the postcommunist era in hopes that the benefits of making broad comparisons outweigh the costs. As a first cut, I assess the plausibility of the argument by placing each country in one of the three categories and examining the average level of polarization in the years under study and report the results in Table 6.1.

At best, the results can only be suggestive, given the small number of countries in the sample and the crudity of the measures, but they do hint at some observable patterns that are consistent with the argument. Countries with late and dependent national modes of rule had low average polarization scores, 6.0 and 7.3, respectively. The latter score would be much lower save for the anomalous case of Kyrgyzstan in the first half of the 1990s. Countries following a sovereign national rule experienced the highest average level of political polarization, 22.2.

One outlier merits attention. Bulgaria is more polarized than might be expected, given its dependent national model of rule before 1989. Bulgaria's relations with Moscow, however, were more cordial than that of other countries experiencing dependent national rule, which may have made it harder for opponents of the ex-communist Bulgarian Socialist Party to play the nationalist card.[23] Unlike Hungary and Czechoslovakia, Bulgaria avoided intervention by Warsaw Pact forces and was widely regarded as having especially close relations with Moscow. Rothschild (1989: 211) observes: "Bulgaria was the only communist-ruled country in East Central Europe that never succumbed to the temptation to challenge Soviet hegemony, to deviate from Soviet directives or even to test Soviet tolerances in any policy dimension." The historically good relations between Bulgaria and Russia meant that charges that ex-communist elites of the Bulgarian Socialist Party were subservient to Moscow were perhaps less powerful in Bulgaria than in other countries experiencing a dependent national model of rule. This may have strengthened the hand of the Bulgarian Socialist Party and contributed to higher levels of political polarization. Upon closer inspection, the Bulgarian case appears to deviate from the argument because of factors consistent with the argument.

Multivariate Analysis

The next analysis assesses whether the relationship of the ex–Communist Party to national sovereignty is related to the extent of political polarization in the postcommunist period. In addition, it aims to quell concerns that political polarization itself is largely driven by economic reform or economic growth. That is, one may rightfully wonder whether high levels of economic reform or anemic growth rates are driving political polarization rather than vice versa. This analysis tests for a simple type of reverse causation and cannot exclude the possibility that economic factors may be influencing political polarization in more complex ways.

To begin to assess this possibility, I turn to a multivariate analysis that aims to assess the determinants of political polarization in the cases at hand. In

---

[23] Rothschild (1989: 211) attributes "Bulgaria's sustained allegiance to the Soviet Union" to a "real complementarity of economic interests and development strategies" rather than to "cultural servility or historically ordained sentimentality." Bulgarians also saw Russia as a bulwark against its traditional foe – the Ottoman Empire. See also Rothschild (1974).

Model 6.1 in Table 6.2, I include the change in political polarization in a given country in a given year as the dependent variable. To test the argument that the relationship between the Communist Party and national sovereignty influences political polarization, I add a dummy variable that equals 1 for countries having a sovereign national model of rule before 1989 and 0 otherwise. This analysis examines whether the level of political polarization in countries with a sovereign national model of rule differs significantly from the other types of rule.

Because slow growth may strengthen the appeal of extreme political parties and exacerbate political polarization, I include *Growth*, which measures the annual rate of economic growth. Similarly, because many expected rapid economic and institutional reforms to heighten social tensions, I add *Reform*, which is based on the index of economic and institutional reform used in previous chapters. I control for *InitialConditions*, using the De Melo et al. (2001) index of initial conditions. I add a dummy variable, *War*, for each year that a country was involved in a civil conflict; and *Oil*, a dummy variable for countries with resource-rich economies. I include the average score on the ethnolinguistic fractionalization for each country for the period 1990–2002, as ethnic divisions may be associated with political polarization (Campos and Kizuyev 2007). In subsequent models, I include a dummy variable for *Parliamentary* regimes to guard against the possibility that the results are driven by political institutions (Cox 2001). Because *Parliamentary* and *InitialConditions* are highly correlated (.78), I include them in separate models. I estimate an error-correction model to account for temporal dependence in the data and employ panel-corrected standard errors to account for heteroskedasticity. This analysis is only a weak test of a simple form of reverse causation that economic variables lagged by one year do not predict levels of political polarization in subsequent years, and it does not rule out more complex forms of reverse causation.

Results from Table 6.2 lend credence to the argument. The positive and significant coefficient on *SovereignNational* in Model 6.1 indicates that countries in which national identity preceded the arrival of communist power and the Communist Party could claim to have developed policy with some autonomy from foreign rule before 1989 experienced higher levels of polarization. Controlling for other factors, countries having a sovereign national model of rule had about a 5.94 point higher polarization score. Model 6.2 drops the dummy variable for sovereign national rule and adds dummy variables for countries with dependent national rule and late national rule. Here the results indicate that both types of rule have significantly lower polarization scores than the excluded category of countries with sovereign national rule in the communist era. Models 6.3 and 6.4 repeat the analysis but also substitute a dummy variable for parliamentary regimes for the initial conditions index, and the results on the variables of interest are largely unchanged.

For the most part, the economic variables provide little insight into the roots of political polarization. Only in one model does economic reform have

TABLE 6.2. *The Determinants of Polarization*

	Model			
	6.1	6.2	6.3	6.4
SovereignNational$_{it}$	5.94***	–	5.92***	–
	(1.98)		(1.97)	
DependentNational$_{it}$	–	−5.90***	–	−5.94***
		(1.82)		(1.82)
LateNational$_{it}$	–	−6.06**	–	−5.91**
		(2.62)		(2.62)
ΔGrowth$_{it}$	−.10	−.10	−.09	−.09
	(.07)	(.07)	(.07)	(.07)
Growth$_{i(t-1)}$	.08	.08	.09	.09
	(.07)	(.07)	(.07)	(.07)
ΔReform$_{it}$	−.70	−.73	−.70	−.70
	(.51)	(.79)	(.67)	(.76)
Reform$_{i(t-1)}$	−.53	−.55	−.52**	−.53
	(.33)	(.40)	(.25)	(.35)
ΔWar$_{it}$	−4.80*	−4.82*	−4.51	−4.51
	(2.87)	(2.85)	(2.91)	(2.88)
War$_{i(t-1)}$	1.25	1.21	2.00	1.99
	(1.80)	(1.79)	(1.99)	(1.98)
Oil$_{it}$	−.15	.19	−.09	−.09
	(1.45)	(1.45)	(1.68)	(1.61)
Ethnolinguistic fractionalization average, 1990–2004$_{it}$	4.66* (2.72)	4.70 (2.91)	4.51 (2.91)	2.82 (2.19)
Initial Conditions Index$_{it}$	−.55* (.31)	−.54* (.28)	–	–
Parliamentary$_{it}$	–	–	2.33**	2.32**
			(.89)	(.84)
Polarization$_{i(t-1)}$	−.31***	−.31***	−.30***	−.30***
	(.08)	(.08)	(.07)	(.07)
Constant	5.07**	11.03**	1.58	7.51**
	(2.49)	(3.75)	(1.01)	(2.62)
Dependent variable	ΔPolarization continuous	ΔPolarization continuous	ΔPolarization continuous	ΔPolarization continuous
N	334	334	334	334
R^2	.23	.23	.23	.23
Prob > χ^2	.0000	.0000	.0000	.0000

Notes: *$p < .10$, **$p < .05$, ***$p < .01$. Results reported using an error-correction model with panel-corrected standard errors in parentheses.

a statistically significant impact on the extent of political polarization.[24] The rather weak results suggest that economic outcomes are not driving political polarization.[25]

More broadly, these results are consistent with the argument that some ex-communist parties were well positioned to benefit from playing on nationalism in the postcommunist period, while others were not. Here the strength of the ex–Communist Party after 1989 depends in part on its relation to national sovereignty before 1989. Old-left parties across countries had roughly similar economic policies and constituencies, but their capacity to pursue their economic policies is in part a function of their credibility on the issue of national sovereignty, which varies across countries. These results are consistent with the observation that the initial period of transition was marked as much by demands for national autonomy as by calls for economic reform.

Of course, the structural conditions cited here account for only part of the configuration of power between old-left and right factions in the postcommunist period. One factor that has been relevant in some cases in recent years is the role of the European Union in moderating the positions of old-left parties. In the quantitative analysis, I control for initial conditions that are highly correlated with progress toward EU accession, but a comparison of the evolution of the ex-communist parties in Bulgaria and Romania, where EU membership was likely, and Ukraine and Russia, where it was not, is nonetheless instructive. When the EU integration process accelerated after 2001, the Bulgarian Socialist Party and the Party of Social Democracy in Romania moderated their economic policy stances to become more in line with EU policies (Todorov 1999).[26] In Bulgaria, the BSP became a supporter of EU integration, recognized the need for a currency board, and ultimately came to see the danger of reversing privatization (Kanev 2002).

Similarly, in Romania, the ex–communist leader President Iliescu returned to office in 2001 by campaigning on a much more economically moderate platform that included support for EU membership. After the election of 2000, Tismaneanu and Kligman (2001) noted that Iliescu was "neither Venezuela's Chavez nor Belarus's Lukashenko. But he is not Poland's Kwasniewski, either." In step with EU requirements, Iliescu's hand-chosen prime minister in July 2001 called for "a series of government programs to provide more social entitlements, but also to speed up privatization and make it more transparent; to create jobs;

---

[24] These insignificant results hold if more spare models are employed. For example, dropping variables related to economic growth or economic reform in any combination has little effect on the results.

[25] The results also hold using quadratic functions on some control variables, such as wealth per capita. I also introduced a variable measuring the miles from Vienna to the capital city in each country and its squared term with similar results. I also squared the initial conditions index, but neither component was significant in the regression analysis and their inclusion had no effect on the results.

[26] Vachudova (2005: 198–217) makes a strong case that EU integration also created a focal point for liberal economy parties to coordinate economic policies in the second half of the 1990s.

to combat corruption; to thin out the bureaucracy; to attract foreign investment and to cut taxes" in order to reduce the size of the informal economy (Pond 2001: 35).

In contrast, communist parties in Russia and Ukraine, where EU membership is unlikely in the near future, have remained far more committed to retaining the core elements of their statist economic programs. While each party has become more moderate over time, both the Communist Party of the Russian Federation and the Communist Party of Ukraine boasted economic platforms to the left of the BSP or the Party of Social Democracy (PSD) in Romania. For example, March (2002: 264–265) notes that the CPRF in the 1990s exhibited a "continued commitment to various elements of the Marxist-Leninist theoretical heritage, especially those teaching about the exploitative and divisive nature of capitalism or the colonialist nature of imperialist powers.... The CPRF programme... is Marxist-Leninist in its strategic aims." He adds that "whatever the CPRF's ideological and tactical manoeuvres, it has always sought to maintain the notion that it is an anti-system party, seeking an alternative to liberal democracy and capitalism." The Communist Party of Ukraine also retained its hard-left economic stances for the period under study. In 2000 the leader of the Communist Party noted that he had no doubts about the validity of Marxism-Leninism, and his party favored monopolizing foreign trade and safeguarding state ownership of land (Haran 2001). Moreover, the party's economic platform before the 2002 parliamentary elections emphasized state ownership of land, a guiding role for the state sector in the economy, and massive protection. The benefits of EU membership appear to have pulled ex-communist parties in Bulgaria and Romania toward the economic center. Lacking access to the EU, the ex-communist parties in Russia and Ukraine have largely preserved their distinctively leftist economic policies.

The Endogeneity of Polarization: An Instrumental Variable Approach

The final section of this chapter returns to the issue of the direction of causality between political polarization and reform outcomes. The statistical evidence cited previously provides some grounds for suggesting that polarization is driving economic outcomes rather than vice versa. This result is less surprising than it appears at first glance. First, political polarization is measured in each election year and remains constant until the next election. This built-in lag helps to ease concerns that the results are not driven by a simple form of reverse causation. Second, scholars have argued that in the early years of the transition it is difficult to determine how voters respond to the economic costs of reform. Stokes (1996, 2001a) notes that rational voters seeing a downturn in the economy after the introduction of economic reform may perceive that reforms are on track and vote for incumbents rather than turn to extremist candidates bent on derailing existing policy. Similarly, voters who see a decline in economic growth in the early years of transition may attribute this decline not to the introduction of economic reform but to decades of mismanagement by the Communist Party. This may give voters greater patience with mainstream parties than voters might have in other settings and reduce the likelihood that disappointing economic outcomes would heighten political polarization.

To assess the possibility of endogeneity between political polarization and reform outcomes more directly, it is helpful to find an instrumental variable that is highly correlated with the independent variable, in this case political polarization, but not correlated with the dependent variable, in this case economic reform (Bartels 1991; Angrist and Krueger 2001). Finding good instrumental variables is difficult under the best of circumstances, and the challenge is even more severe in the case at hand given the large number of factors that scholars have associated with economic and institutional reform. Here I use *Sovereign-National* as an instrumental variable for political polarization. A simple *t*-test finds that *SovereignNational* countries have significantly higher polarization scores than do other countries ($t = 3.5$, $p = .002$), but also that the differences between these two groups of countries in their scores on the index of economic and institutional reform and the index of inconsistent reform are not statistically significant ($t = 1.01$, 1.4, respectively). These correlations make some intuitive sense. The previous section of this chapter argued that the ability of former communist parties to play the nationalist card is an important determinant of the form and strength of that party in the postcommunist era. Yet, it is not immediately clear why the relationship of the outgoing Communist Party to national sovereignty before 1989 should have a direct effect on economic and institutional reform outcomes after 1989.[27] The dummy variable treatment using *SovereignNational* as an instrument for *Polarization* is crude, but it allows for an additional test of the relationship between political polarization and economic reform. Most importantly, it can begin to provide insights into the extent to which economic outcomes are endogenous to polarization.

In Table 6.3, I report the results of a two-stage least squares regression that uses *SovereignNational* as an instrument for the average level of political polarization during the years 1990–2004. Because the instrument does not vary over time, I use a cross-sectional analysis and run a simple two-stage least squares model using the level of economic reform in 2004 as the dependent variable in the second stage in Model 6.5. This dependent variable in the second stage reflects changes in economic and institutional reform over the period 1990–2004. To be precise, the first stage regresses *Polarization* on *Sovereign-National* and *InitialConditions*, while the second stage regresses *Reform* on *Polarization* and *InitialConditions*. The idea behind this instrumental variable approach is to identify that part of the impact of polarization on economic and institutional reform that is attributed to factors having little to do with policy choices. Doing so should help to isolate the extent to which polarization is driving economic and institutional reform rather than vice versa. I then

---

[27] I also tried various forms of geography-based instruments, such as miles from Vienna and miles from Moscow and their squared terms, but these are more highly correlated with economic reform and institutional reform than with polarization.

TABLE 6.3. *Instrumental Variable Estimate of Reform*

	Model	
	6.5	6.6
Polarization	−.038*	.025**
	(.023)	(.011)
Initial Conditions	.548***	.003
	(.128)	(.037)
War	1.367	−.123
	(1.223)	(.529)
Constant	8.974***	.439***
	(.435)	(.167)
Dependent variable (second stage)	Reform Index	Inconsistent Reform Index
N	25	25
R^2	.47	.12
Prob > f	.00	.14
RMSE	1.269	.48
F-test of excluded instruments	10.4	10.4
Hansen J	.0013	.0013

Notes: $*p < .10$, $**p < .05$, $***p < .01$. Reports results using an instrumental variable analysis (IVREG). The first-stage dependent variable is the continuous measure of *Polarization* in all analyses.

repeat the estimation using *InconsistentReform* as the dependent variable in the second stage.

Taken together, the results from Table 6.3 are generally consistent with the argument. In Model 6.5, the coefficient on *Polarization* is negative and significant and suggests that a ten-point increase in the continuous measure of polarization is associated with about a .4 drop in the index of economic and institutional reform.[28] Model 6.6 repeats the analysis using the index of inconsistent reform in 2004 in each country as the dependent variable in the second stage of the analysis. Again, the results generally support the theory. The coefficient on *Polarization* is positive and significant, indicating that a one-unit increase in political polarization is associated with a .36 increase in the inconsistency of reform, although the model fit here is higher than one might like (prob > f = .14).[29] These results comport with the argument, but it is important to bear in mind that the analysis is limited by the small number

[28] Moreover, this result is significantly affected by one outlier case, Turkmenistan, whose average score on the index of economic and institutional reform is almost three standard deviations below the mean. Dropping this case dramatically increases the predictive power of *Polarization*.

[29] Dropping *War* from this analysis has little impact on the coefficient on *Polarization* and improves the model fit.

of cases and the likelihood of measurement error in the instrumental variables analysis.[30]

Conclusion

This chapter has aimed to address concerns for reverse causation because economic outcomes may be driving political polarization rather than vice versa. In some respects, the postcommunist cases offer a useful test because initial levels of political polarization were determined by elections that preceded choices over economic and institutional reform. This sequence of events suggests that the former drove the latter at least at the start of the transformation. I used multivariate analysis to assess the possibility that the reform outcomes influenced levels of political polarization in subsequent years and found little evidence for this claim (Persson and Tabellini 2005). I also employed instrumental variable regression to begin to examine the possible endogeneity of political polarization and economic outcomes. Endogeneity problems are particularly difficult to address in cross-national studies, and the results here should be seen as only suggestive.

In addition, the chapter presented a preliminary attempt to identify the roots of political polarization across countries in the postcommunist world. It found that one aspect of the Soviet legacy – the relationship of the outgoing Communist Party to national sovereignty – is a source of political polarization in the postcommunist world. The ability of the ex-communist factions to play the nationalist card appears to have shaped the balance of partisan power in the postcommunist world in important ways.

The statistical analyses presented in the preceding four chapters permit rather precise controls for potentially confounding factors, generate estimates of the size of the impact of different variables, establish bounds of confidence for making causal claims, and allow for easy replication. Yet statistical analyses are not a panacea. One drawback to statistical analysis is that the researcher is limited to data that have been collected across a broad range of countries. Researchers often must overlook data that permit assessments of the theory but are not available for all cases. Given the difficulty of establishing relationships in social science, it is shortsighted to neglect data that might reflect on the argument but have not been collected for all countries.

The next four chapters use case studies to assess the argument and to complement the statistical analyses. Case studies have several strengths. They allow

---

[30] In an unreported analysis, I used instrumental variables regression to estimate the impact of polarization on average annual rates of economic growth. Once the outlier case of Albania is dropped from the sample, the coefficient on *Polarization* becomes significant with the correct sign, although the identification/instrumental variables relevance test falls just below acceptable levels (8.6). These results indicated that a ten-point increase in the continuous measure of *Polarization* is associated with about a 1 percent drop in the average annual growth rate. To test the robustness of this result, I dropped each country from the sample one at a time and reestimated the model, but doing so had little impact on the coefficients on *Polarization*.

one to examine other implications of the theory at hand using data that is specific to the cases. They permit greater appreciation of the context in which decision makers act and allow the researcher to trace the process of how the variables of interest shape the behavior of individuals. Focused studies of a small number of cases may also afford greater precision in measuring the variables under study and allow additional means to validate that the proxies used in the statistical analyses capture the measures at hand (Brady and Collier 2004). Moreover, they use a narrative that puts the quantitative analysis in its proper context. By tracing how changes in the partisanship of the government, the extent of polarization, and the level of democracy over time have shaped economic outcomes in Russia, Bulgaria, Poland, and Uzbekistan, the next chapters provide an additional means of assessing the argument.

7

Russia

Polarization, Autocracy, and Reform

> Fourteen years ago, Moscow's summer was filled with sheer exuberance.... On the night of Aug. 22, 1991, several construction cranes and a crowd of about 50,000 determined people gathered in central Moscow to seal that promise of something better than Soviet misery. In front of the sinister KGB building, workers rocked, cracked and then toppled the formidable statue of Feliks Dzerzhinsky. This is the man who in 1917 founded the Cheka, the "Extraordinary Commission" that terrorized the nation with the arrests and brutal executions that became known as the Red Terror.... The statue of "Iron Feliks" was relegated to an undistinguished patch of land behind the New Tretyakov Gallery.... Earlier this month, with little fanfare but plenty of dreary symbolism, Dzerzhinsky was returned to a position of honor in central Moscow. It is not the same statue, and not the same site. Instead, Iron Feliks is a few blocks away at the Interior Ministry, his bronze bust back on a pedestal in the new Russian society.
>
> *International Herald Tribune*, November 20, 2005

This chapter links variations in economic policy choices in Russia in the period under study to changes in elite partisanship, polarization, and democracy. The 1990s witnessed a highly polarized struggle for power in a setting of relatively democratic politics under a right executive. These conditions contributed to a mix of inconsistent reform, including rapid privatization, slow institutional reforms, and steep cuts in transfers. From 2000 to 2003, political polarization declined, politics remained relatively democratic, and an economically centrist president came to power. This propitious turn of political events led to a new round of economic and institutional reforms early in President Putin's first term. However, the erosion of democracy which accelerated in 2003 coincided with a slowdown in economic and institutional reform in subsequent years. That the ebbs and flows of Russia's attempts to introduce a market economy map onto changes in partisanship, political polarization, and the extent of democracy is consistent with the argument made in preceding chapters.

High Polarization and Relatively Democratic Politics, 1990–1999

Throughout the 1990s, Russia exhibited high levels of political polarization as an anticommunist president and his economically liberal supporters in the Duma squared off against a typical old-left party – the Communist Party of the Russian Federation (CPRF). Parliamentary elections in 1990, 1993, and 1995 yielded a stalemate in which the CPRF held roughly 30–40 percent of the seats and was the largest opposition party.[1] However, the CPRF faced opposition across the partisan divide from the right-wing president Boris Yeltsin, who won elections over his CPRF opponent in 1991 and 1996. This high level of political polarization in a relatively democratic setting made policy less stable and contributed to great distortions in reform.

The extent of political polarization is apparent in policy platforms pushed by the two camps. Consider the right camp headed by Boris Yeltsin, a former candidate member of the Politburo of the Communist Party of the Soviet Union (CPSU) before he was expelled in disgrace in 1988. Throughout his tenure in office, President Yeltsin favored liberal economic policies that would significantly limit the role of the state in the economy. He expressed little interest in the details of economic policy but appears to have understood its usefulness as a tool to keep the communists from returning to power. Indeed, in October 1991, as the new government prepared its major economic reform program, Yeltsin (1994: 146) noted: "The task I have set before the government is to make reform irreversible." Rather than focusing on the economic arguments in support of reform, President Yeltsin was more at home dwelling on its political benefits.[2]

The intellectual base for liberal policies in the Yeltsin administration came from his team of advisers, including his deputy prime minister, Yegor Gaidar, who had written extensively in support of radical economic reform.[3] As Russia reached independence in the fall of 1991, following the failed coup by remnants of the Communist Party of the Soviet Union and the security forces, President Yeltsin's team of liberal advisers, fearing a return of communists to power, pushed to remove price controls on almost all major goods, privatize industry at a breakneck pace, open Russia to foreign trade, and create a market economy with great speed.

---

[1] Using roll call votes by Supreme Soviet deputies from 1990 to 1993, Andrews (2002) estimates that liberal and communist camps each controlled about 30–40 percent of the seats in the parliament with the remaining delegates being largely nonaligned. She finds that these two factions were united on policies to free Russia from the Soviet Union in 1990 but became remarkably polarized over economic policy. See also Sobyanin (1994).

[2] Yeltsin's three memoirs provide little insight into his views on economic policy. The chapter entitled "Shock Therapy" in *The Struggle for Russia* quickly devolves into a discussion of political infighting among members of the government in the early 1990s. However, Yeltsin (1994: 147) does note: "Russia's trouble was never a shortage or an abundance of reformers. The trouble was an inability to adhere to a consistent policy. Whether czar or general secretary, everyone wanted to distinguish themselves in history. All of them took on an extra load, aware of their unique mission, and they turned the wheel of government sharply, about 180 degrees."

[3] For good statements of his views, see Gaidar (1990, 1997).

Next consider the Communist Party of the Russian Federation. Led by Gennady Zyuganov, a former vice chairman of the Ideology Department of the CPSU, the party consistently pursued old-left economic policies mixed with a healthy dose of Russian nationalism and great-power patriotism.[4] The CPRF was not a monolith, but its factions had much in common, particularly a penchant for old-left rather than social democratic economic policies. According to March (2002: 264–265), "CPRF leaders insist that their aim is to conserve communism, preserving historical continuity with the best of Soviet tradition, whilst eliminating its worst features" and express a "continued commitment to various elements of Marxist-Leninist theoretical heritage, especially those teachings about the exploitative and divisive nature of capitalism."

These views are reflected in campaign documents of the CPRF in the 1990s, which favored state ownership of the commanding heights of the economy and land, high levels of protection against foreign competition, and a reliance on economic nationalism. The Party Program of January 1995 called for an "end to the blackening of Russian and Soviet history, including the memory and teachings of V. I. Lenin"; a government monopoly on foreign trade of strategic goods, including raw materials, food products in short supply, and other consumer goods; the "nationalization and confiscation of property obtained in violation of the law, in the interest of the country and rights of the working class; and in its place the creation of public [*obshchenarodnoi*], or collective property." The CPRF also proudly declared itself the legal successor of the Communist Party of the Soviet Union.

One might have expected the CPRF's rhetoric to be more moderate in a two-candidate presidential campaign, given the need to win a majority of voters in a second-round runoff. But candidate Zyuganov's platform in 1996 echoed traditional old-left themes. The Communist Economic Program and Election Platform put forward in the run-up to the presidential election in June 1996 began with a critique of existing reforms as a "vulgarized version of monetarism . . . fashioned by experts from international financial organizations." After attributing the decline in Russia's production to a lack of money in the economy, it then noted that "only the state can pull our national economy out of crisis" and called for price controls including "direct state regulation ('freezing,' corridor limits) and indirect actions providing for tariff agreements among all parties involved in production and trade." The CPRF platform aimed for the state to "retain a considerable part of the national production potential, including enterprises in mining, defense and other branches of industry, transportation, and the energy sector"; opposed the buying and selling of land;

---

[4] Scholars have identified three factions within the party: "Marxist reformers," "traditional Marxist-Leninist modernizers," and "Gennady Zyuganov's nationalists" (Urban and Solovei 1997). Sakwa (1998), Flikke (1999), and March (2002) draw similar conclusions. Importantly, all of these factions bore little resemblance to European style social democratic parties, and all favored fairly traditional old-left economic policies.

favored a ban on private property in land; and supported the nationalization of private banks. To be sure, the CPRF platform included promises to cut taxes (especially for domestic producers), to respect a variety of forms of ownership, and to "create the right conditions for foreign businessmen," but these policies were vaguely described and largely at odds with the rest of the document.[5]

It is important to note that the CPRF advocated economic policies significantly to the left of their centrist ex-communist brethren in Poland, Hungary, and Lithuania. In the eyes of the CPRF, social democracy was tainted by association with Mikhail Gorbachev's attempts to reform the Soviet economy and by a belief that Russia had a unique role to play in history. As Communist Party leader Gennady Zyuganov noted in April 1996: "In Russia, social democracy of the West-European type has no chance." Indeed, McFaul (2001: 297) observes that "the CPRF leaders, in fact, emphatically rejected the label of social democrats."

In addition, voters in Russia recognized these partisan differences early on in the transformation. Treisman (1998) uses evidence from a 1993 survey to show that Russian voters were able to place parties on a left-right scale of partisanship. Moreover, voting patterns tended to fall along predictable lines. Clem and Craumer (1995: 146) found that in the 1993 Duma elections "relatively more urbanized, better educated and younger populations tended to vote in favor of Yeltsin and the reform parties, whereas rural, agricultural areas with older populations typically aligned with anti-reform parties or positions." These patterns reemerged in the elections that followed (Clem and Craumer 1996; Tucker 2006). Indeed, as Remington (2001b: 285) notes: "Throughout the 1990s, deep polarization between reform-minded and communist political camps structured parliamentary politics in Russia."

Russia's Shock Therapy

With a right president making policy in a highly polarized and relatively democratic environment, we should see rapid but inconsistent economic and institutional reform, redistribution from the dependent sector to old-economy interests, and cuts in social spending. Moreover, we should find that politicians and investors were concerned with the possibility of a reversal of economic and institutional reform.

Initial attempts to reform the economy began in earnest in late 1991 under inauspicious conditions.[6] Russia faced a high level of repressed inflation, a collapsing state, a massive debt burden, a budget deficit well in the double-digits,

---

[5] Paretskaya (1996) reports that, "during a recent campaign swing through St. Petersburg, Zyuganov said he agrees with scholars who say the optimum balance of state and private property in an economy is 61% to 39%, respectively." See Paretskaya http://archive.tol.cz/Publications/RPE/RPE.960516.html.

[6] The incoming government recognized the difficulties that it faced (Yeltsin 1994: 156).

weak control over its national currency, and an industrial structure poorly suited for a market economy.[7] In January 1992 President Yeltsin introduced a far-reaching economic reform that entailed lifting state controls on prices on about 90 percent of goods; a financial stabilization, including deep cuts in government spending and pledges to limit the expansion of the money supply; and the rapid privatization of small businesses and industrial enterprises. The hope was that sweeping price liberalization, a sound macroeconomic environment, and the transfer of assets from state to private hands would encourage domestic and foreign businesses to invest their energies and assets in the domestic economy. In October 1991 President Yeltsin finished the presentation of his economic reform program by noting: "I have to tell you frankly: today in the severest crisis we cannot carry out reform painlessly. The first step will be the most difficult. A certain decline in the standard of living will take place. It will be worse for everyone for about half a year. The prices will fall and the consumer market will be filled with goods. And toward the fall of 1992, as I promised before the elections, the economy will stabilize and the people's lives will gradually improve."

However, political polarization intervened in two ways. First, it heightened concerns about the reversal of policy, which blunted incentives for businesses to invest or restructure enterprises. In countries headed by liberal governments in less polarized settings as in Poland, managers could invest and open new businesses with confidence that reforms would not be reversed, but in Russia the threat of a policy reversal was much greater. For example, when faced with the choice of investing in their own country or sending capital abroad, businesspeople in Russia overwhelmingly chose the latter. Capital flight reigned throughout the 1990s. By some estimates, the net capital outflow in the 1990s was between $200 and $300 billion.[8] Political uncertainty also scared away many foreign investors. Among the countries of the former Soviet Union in the 1990s, only Tajikistan and Uzbekistan received less foreign direct investment per capita than did Russia (Nicholson 2004). Political instability blunted incentives to invest and engage in productive economic activity across economic sectors.

Second, political polarization undermined the government's bargaining position with the opposition across the partisan divide. In many policy areas, the government needed support from the CPRF and its allies to pass legislation.[9] Faced with the prospects of maintaining a status quo that threatened economic collapse and agreeing to policy compromises backed by groups expected to be

---

[7] All the members of the former Soviet Union who retained the ruble retained the power to print rubles. Russia's initially tight monetary policies were undermined by other former Soviet republics who continued to print rubles to finance budget deficits.

[8] Given the difficulty of measuring capital flight, caution is necessary in interpreting these figures, but there is little doubt that Russia exported capital in massive quantities in the 1990s.

[9] Before the adoption of the constitution in 1993, the decree powers of the president were conditional (Frye 1997b). After the adoption of the constitution, decree powers were expanded, but certain areas remained off-limits to presidential decrees, such as the budget. Moreover, laws passed by parliament could overturn decrees.

harmed by reform, the Yeltsin government frequently passed legislation that pushed reforms in some areas while delivering significant benefits to politically influential groups (Shleifer and Treisman 2000). These policy compromises contributed to a slower pace and less consistent economic and institutional reform than the government may have wanted. Taken together, these two effects of polarization helped to undercut efforts to reform the economy. Indeed, the economic impact of political polarization was apparent across three major areas of economic reform: market liberalization, financial stabilization, and especially industrial privatization.

The government introduced vast price liberalization on domestic goods in January 1992 but maintained extensive regulations on opening new firms, engaging in foreign trade, and the hiring and firing of workers (Aslund 1995: 68–69). This mix of price liberalization in the face of heavy regulation was a classic example of inconsistent reform. Incumbent firms could take advantage of new opportunities to increase prices, while high levels of regulation offered them protection from firms seeking to enter the market. New start-ups seeking to enter the market bore the cost of this reform, and the development of new private business was far less impressive than in less polarized settings.[10]

Attempts to stabilize the economy stumbled badly in part because of the polarization-induced credibility problems of the government. Few expected the Yeltsin administration to hold to its position of imposing hard budget constraints on firms, given the great likelihood of turnover in government. The stabilization program began in January 1992. Within days, the vice-president of Russia came out against the program and ridiculed the new government of young reformers as "little boys in pink shorts." Within four months, parliament raised a vote of no confidence in the government. Within six months, the industrial lobby dominated by managers of state-owned enterprises managed to replace three liberal ministers with candidates to their liking. Within a year, Yegor Gaidar was replaced as the head of government by Viktor Chernomyrdin, a former head of the Ministry of Oil and Gas who favored a less aggressive approach to economic reform.

Stabilization policy in this period fell victim to pressure from across the partisan divide to vastly subsidize loss-making sectors in the old economy. Moreover, given the uncertainty over future policy, few were willing to risk restructuring their firm or investing in Russia. With capital flying out of the country at a record clip, the tax base declined still further. The loose fiscal policy resulted in a massive redistribution of resources from the poor to the wealthy through the inflation tax. Inflation reached over 2,000 percent in 1992 and 1,100 percent in 1993. Estimates suggest that redistribution from the mass public to the banking sector through the inflation tax amounted to 6–9 percent of GDP (Easterly and de Cunha 1993).

---

[10] For thoughtful treatments of the tactics used to conduct economic reform in a difficult political environment, see Mau (2000) and Shleifer and Treisman (2000).

A particularly clear example of inconsistent reform occurred in the privatization of industrial enterprises. In February 1992 the government introduced rapid privatization with the stated goal of making reform irreversible, building a constituency in support of economic reform, and improving economic efficiency.[11] The designers of the privatization program viewed old-economy interests, such as industrial ministries and workers in noncompetitive enterprises, as the greatest threats to privatization and pushed hard to keep them out of the process as much as possible (Boycko et al. 1995; Blasi et al. 1997). Initial privatization plans envisaged relatively small packets of shares for managers and workers and much larger distribution to mutual funds and other outside investors. However, policy uncertainty made it very unlikely that foreign firms would buy privatized firms in Russia, and opposition in parliament from across the partisan divide watered down the proposals. The Law on Privatization that eventually passed the Supreme Soviet in June 1992 contained generous incentives for managers and workers and a limited role for mutual funds. The law offered firms three options to transfer their assets from state to private hands, and the majority of firms opted for a method of privatization that delivered 51 percent of shares to enterprise insiders. As managers quickly increased their shares by buying stocks from workers, this led to high levels of insider ownership (Blasi et al. 1997).

The rapid giveaway of state assets was accompanied by little progress in improving corporate governance. The government struggled to enforce bankruptcy legislation, to impose hard budget constraints, and to protect minority shareholder rights. In addition, the government continued to deliver benefits to the managers' lobby by accepting tax payments in kind rather than in cash and by implicitly sanctioning the widespread use of barter transactions among firms. This combination of rapid privatization with weak corporate governance delivered great benefits to industrial managers who received large ownership stakes but faced few constraints from minority shareholders or state regulators. Having received assets from privatization, enterprise insiders, particularly managers, were able to preserve soft budget constraints, first in the form of government credits, then in the form of tax breaks and offsets (Woodruff 1999). These gains came at the expense of the broader population, including the dependent sector of the population, which saw their benefits from the government shrink dramatically (Milanovic 1998; Cook 2007).

Loans for Shares

The economic perils of political polarization resurfaced in the summer of 1995 against the backdrop of upcoming parliamentary elections in December 1995 and presidential elections in June 1996. Russia was mired in an intractable

---

[11] Frye (1997a) makes the case that the Yeltsin government found a rapid privatization using vouchers attractive because it would be more difficult to reverse.

war in Chechnya, had experienced three years of economic decline, two years of hyperinflation, and massive budget deficits. The poor fiscal situation of the Russian government meant that the salaries of government workers and pensions experienced severe backlogs. It is no wonder that President Yeltsin had approval ratings in the single digits, and most observers gave the incumbent little chance in upcoming elections. One of the Russian oligarchs recounted a conversation he had in February 1996 with George Soros: "Boys, your time is over. You've had a few good years but now your time is up. His argument was that the Communists were definitely going to win. We Russian businessmen should be careful that we managed to get to our jets in time and not lose our lives" (Freeland 2000: 192).

Facing the prospects of losing power to their rivals across the partisan divide, the Yeltsin government received a proposition from a group of prominent businesspeople led by Vladimir Potanin, the head of Onexim Bank, a Russian bank with close ties to the Ministry of Foreign Trade (Lieberman and Veimetra 1996; Hoffman 2001).[12] The complicated proposal suggested that the Yeltsin government should auction the rights to manage a number of prime oil and gas companies in exchange for a loan to the government.[13] Should the government fail to repay the loans when they came due in two or three years, the winners of the auctions would retain ownership rights in the firms. After negotiations over which firms would be included in the auctions, the cash-strapped and highly unpopular Yeltsin government accepted the proposal. Moreover, the government agreed to give the banks that made the proposal the right to oversee the auctions.[14] Few expected the government to make good on the loans, and, as a result, a small group of businesspeople took control of some of the most valuable oil and metals companies in Russia at fire sale prices in exchange for political support in late 1995.

The design of what came to be known as the "loans for shares" program was complex, but the principle of the program was a simple exchange. A small group of businessmen became owners of some of Russia's most valuable firms and the government received in return much needed funds and political support. Interviewed in 2000, the head of the state body in charge of privatization, Anatoly Chubais, described the loans for shares in stark terms: "Privatization at that time, and the whole of privatization until 1997, was not an economic process. It was the process of fighting with the Communists – getting each company in the hands of private owners who kill the Communists. There is no

---

[12] For detailed discussions of the "loans for shares" program, see Lieberman and Veimetra (1996), Kokh (1998, 1999), Freeland (2000), Hoffman (2001: 296–324), and Bunich (2006).

[13] Even the notoriously fractious Russian oligarchs buried their hatchets in the six months before the election in hopes of defeating the Communist Party.

[14] International financial institutions were skeptical of the plan, particularly after foreign companies were barred from the plan. Alfred Kokh (1999: 265), a key organizer of the plan, admitted that having the banks oversee the auction was the biggest mistake in the design of the loans for shares auctions.

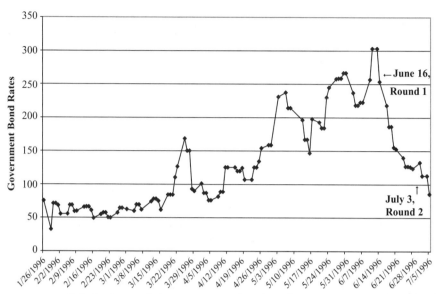

FIGURE 7.1. Polarization and the government bond market. *Source:* Central Bank of Russia.

alternative. Maybe there are better ways to sell it, but you're not always able to choose."[15]

One may take such comments by government officials and the beneficiaries of the "loans for shares" deal about the possibility of an old-left revanche as a rationalization rather than as an explanation for their behavior. Indeed, they have strong incentives to couch the loans for shares program as a necessary evil brought on by a threat from the old left. However, a more dispassionate group – players in the market for Russian bonds – behaved as though they believed the threat of a communist victory in presidential elections in June 1996 was quite high. The economic impact of political polarization in this period is evident in the market price for Russian government bonds, known as GKOs (Figure 7.1). The interest rate on GKOs peaked just before the first round of presidential elections, indicating considerable doubt about the viability of the incumbent.

[15] When asked in 2000 about the extent of the threat from the Communist Party of the Russian Federation before the presidential election of 1996, Yegor Gaidar observed: "Yes, it was a reality. There were a large number of elites who were preparing to live under the Communists. Yeltsin's popularity at the start of the year was extremely low. The Communists had just won the parliamentary elections. And based on past experience in Eastern Europe, all of us knew that the Communist Party usually won the second elections after the start of reform. We had no reason to suppose that Russia would be an exception, because reform [here] was even more confrontational, with more conflicts than there were in Eastern Europe. Of course, [there was] the domestic ideological base." See http://www.pbs.org/wgbh/commandingheights/shared/minitextlo/int_yegorgaidar.html. Vladimir Potanin (2000) made a similar comment on the loans for shares: see http://www.pbs.org/wgbh/commandingheights/shared/minitext/int_vladimirpotanin.html.

In the first round of presidential elections on June 16, President Yeltsin won 35 percent of the vote, compared to 32 percent of the vote for his nearest competitor, Gennady Zyuganov, a result that propelled both candidates into a runoff in the second round. President Yeltsin's surprisingly strong showing began to quell the markets as the price for a GKO fell from a shocking 303 percent on June 13 to "just" 186 percent on June 18. In the second round of the election, held on July 3, President Yeltsin was returned to office by a vote of 54 to 40 percent. This result again cooled the bond market somewhat as the going rate for a state treasury bond fell from 132 percent on July 1 to 86 percent on July 5. The sensitivity of the bond market to political events provides further support of how political polarization translated into economic volatility in Russia.

The design of the "loans for shares" program reflected concerns about the viability of the bargain should President Yeltsin lose the elections. The winners would receive ownership rights to the firms only after three years if the Russian government was unable to repay the loans. Underlying the sale was an assumption that the results of the auctions would be reversed should President Yeltsin lose the election. A high official in the Yeltsin government remarked: "We gave them just one of the two keys [to the property]. They would receive the second key only after the elections" (Freeland 2000: 181). Some have defended the move on economic grounds as some loans for shares firms became far more efficient than their state-owned competitors, while critics question the merits of selling valuable state assets under fire-sale conditions. Whether these sales helped President Yeltsin at the ballot box is also debatable, but they do illustrate how concerns about policy reversals influenced the choice of privatization in policy in Russia.[16]

The timing of this classic case of inconsistent reform is striking because it occurred when the political system was at its most competitive and at its most polarized. This outcome is at odds with the argument that political competition on its own inhibits inconsistent reform and promotes economic reform but is central to the argument presented in preceding chapters.

The presidential elections of 1996 not only returned President Yeltsin to office but also reproduced a high level of political polarization (White et al. 1997). An economically liberal president continued to face off against a parliament dominated by an old-left party, and this high level of political polarization was reflected in economic and institutional outcomes in the last half of the 1990s. Russia's budget deficit continued to grow and averaged more than

---

[16] Yeltsin (2000: 93) notes: "If the Communists had won the elections in 1996 the first thing they would have done is to nationalize all property. Having paid out hundreds of millions of dollars, Russian businessmen were vitally interested in the stability of the government.... That's the answer to the question, How did government and big business wind up so closely tied together. In March 1996 the businessmen came to me to help my election. Nobody asked them to do this, and nobody undertook any obligations from them. They came to defend not Yeltsin, but themselves, their businesses.... So what are our businessmen interested in most of all? Political stability."

5 percent from 1995 to 2000. To fill the government coffers, the government increasingly relied on the sale of GKOs to domestic and foreign banks rather than on tax receipts. Importantly, the private sector remained small and provided little revenue for the budget despite (or perhaps because of) high tax rates. Employment in small business – a key element of the new private economy – hovered at only about 10 to 15 percent of total employment in the 1990s (EBRD 1999). Moreover, investment, particularly direct foreign investment, remained at very low levels in large part because of political instability. With a shrinking tax base, the government skewed policy even more in favor of powerful economic interests in the banking and industrial lobbies and against the dependent sector of the population. For example, arrears on pensions reached 15 trillion rubles in 1997.

In the second half of the 1990s, economic and institutional reform faced additional difficulties beyond the reach of policy. President Yeltsin suffered a heart attack in 1996, which increased concerns about the stability of Russian economic policy, and the Asian financial crisis of 1997 caused oil prices to plummet and thereby cut sharply into Russia's revenue. Oil prices in 1997 and 1998 averaged just $17 and $12 per barrel. With its underlying fiscal problems unresolved, a yawning budget deficit, and a shrinking tax base, the Russian government soon found itself unable to finance increasingly expensive government bonds and unable to repay loans to Western banks and the International Monetary Fund. On August 17, 1998, the Russian government defaulted on its loans, devalued its currency, and stopped payments on state treasury bonds. This financial crash brought to an end the first period of economic reform in Russia.

The constant search for tax revenue compelled all levels of government to squeeze the new private sector for revenue in a variety of ways (Frye and Shleifer 1997). Russia's payroll tax of 38 percent was exceptionally high and hit new private firms hard as they had far less bargaining power with local and regional governments than did state-owned or privatized firms.[17] In addition, new private firms faced a heavy regulatory burden. For example, inspectors of various state agencies visited small private businesses in Moscow on average about nineteen times per year, while the figure for Poland was just three (Frye and Zhuravskaya 2000; Frye 2002b). Moreover, small private businesses in Russia reportedly paid bribes at a far higher rate than their counterparts in several East European countries (McMillan and Woodruff 2002). These predatory policies led to a stunted new private sector. Estimates suggest that the new private sector in the 1990s provided only about 10–15 percent of GDP per capita, while the figure for Poland was about 50 percent (EBRD 1997; Gustafson 2000).[18]

---

[17] Indeed, the World Bank estimates that payroll taxes above 25 percent spur tax evasion (World Bank 1994: 263). Not surprisingly, tax evasion was rampant (Yakovlev 2001; Easter 2006).

[18] As it is very difficult to measure the size of the new private sector with any precision, these figures should be seen as estimates.

The government repeatedly shortchanged the dependent sector of the population, including state bureaucrats, pensioners, the unemployed, and the young. Cook (2006: 134) notes: "The most socially and politically significant failure of the pension system in the 1990s was the accumulation of arrears in payments to pensioners... [which] grew from 3 percent of entitlements in 1994 to 9 percent in 1995 and 34 percent in 1996." Pension funds as a share of the budget fared relatively well as cuts in education and aid took even greater hits. Nonetheless, real pension spending fell drastically in the 1990s as scarce government resources went elsewhere and poverty levels among pensioners increased dramatically (Cook 2006: 138). Berglof et al. (2003: 122) note: "For the sake of balancing the budget, the Russian government has resorted to shrinking the size of real benefits by not indexing them adequately to interest, flattening benefits payable to different groups, and accruing benefit arrears. These changes created chaos that made the system of social programs absolutely unpredictable."

Consistent with the theoretical argument, high levels of political polarization under conditions of relatively democratic politics were associated with heightened policy instability, lower levels of investment, rapid but inconsistent reform, and few transfers. Throughout this period, the dependent sector of the population suffered considerable losses from inconsistent reforms. Unable to generate sufficient tax revenue to pay the dependent sector, the Yeltsin government experienced repeated fiscal crises that led to delays in the payment of wages to state budget workers and pensioners and ultimately to the financial collapse of August 1998.[19]

Declining Polarization amid Competitive Politics, 2000–2003

This financial crisis sharply lowered living standards for the vast majority of Russians and helped to weaken powerful vested interests grown wealthy from inconsistent reform (Frye 2006). It also promoted the rise of center-right parties that helped to moderate Russia's politics. The outcomes of parliamentary elections in December 1999 and presidential elections in March 2000 set the stage for a new round of economic reform by significantly reducing polarization and by bringing a right-nationalist president to power. Facing the end of his term, President Yeltsin nominated Vladimir Putin, then a recently named head of the Federal Security Services with a very low public profile, as prime minister in August 1999. This move signaled that the Yeltsin camp considered the new prime minister the heir apparent. In September 1999, just three months before parliamentary elections, the Yeltsin team and Russian business elites combined efforts to create a political party from scratch, called Unity, that was to serve as a vehicle for Prime Minister Putin's presidential ambitions.[20] Putin attended the founding congress of Unity, expressed

---

[19] See Zhuravskaya et al. (2005) for similar evidence from Russia's regions.
[20] See Colton and McFaul (2003), chap. 3, for a detailed account of Unity's spectacular rise.

confidence in the head of the party, and announced that he planned to vote for Unity. Putin's rising popularity rubbed off on the party, and Unity fared surprisingly well in parliamentary elections, taking just under one-quarter of the seats in the party list vote. For the first time in postcommunist Russia, a party clearly identified with the president commanded a significant position in parliament. More importantly, President Putin built a fairly reliable coalition based on Unity and several smaller factions, including Fatherland–All Russia, People's Deputy, and Russia's Regions to support his policies (Remington 2006: 287).[21]

In March 2000 President Putin won the presidential election with 54 percent of the popular vote, thereby eliminating the need for a second-round runoff.[22] Indeed, he had a 70 percent approval rating upon taking office, a rating far higher than that of his predecessor. This popularity gave the executive branch newfound leverage over powerful interest groups – particularly the tycoons and the regional governors.

Russia's rough-and-tumble politics would gradually become less democratic in the coming years, and the 1999–2000 electoral cycle exhibited many of the same biases of previous elections, including vote fraud at the margins, a strong pro-incumbent bias in the media, and little regard for campaign finance laws, but it was also marked by fierce competition between electoral blocs and vigorous coverage in the media. No major political parties were excluded from taking part. Indeed, the political spectrum was broadly represented and voters had a more complete menu of parties than in previous elections with the rise of Fatherland–All Russia, a centrist party representing a variety of regional interests headed by a former prime minister and the mayor of Moscow. Parliamentary elections occurred on schedule and, although the presidential elections occurred three months early because of President Yeltsin's resignation, the date of the presidential election was chosen according to the constitution. The Organization for Security and Cooperation in Europe (OSCE) (2000a: 2) captured the spirit of the election: "In general, and in spite of episodic challenges that could have undermined the general integrity of the process as a whole, the State Duma election marked significant progress in consolidating representative democracy." The OSCE (2000b: 3) used similar language in assessing the presidential election.[23] "In general, and in spite of episodic events that sometimes tested the system's capacity to uphold principles of fairness

---

[21] The OSCE (2000a: 9): "The 1999 election was not a struggle of political leaders teamed against the 'communist threat' which characterized the 1996 elections, but rather a struggle of personalities to guarantee their own presence on the political summit during the next four years."

[22] If no candidate wins a majority in the first round of presidential elections, a second round pits the top two vote-getters against each other. Whether a bit of ballot-box stuffing pushed Putin over the top in the second round is a subject of debate. See the reports of Borisova et al. (2000a, b) in *Moscow Times*.

[23] Reissinger (2003: 264) edited a volume dedicated to this electoral cycle and notes: "Violations of electoral law did occur, however. Still in the judgment of international observers and most

and a level playing field, the presidential election was conducted under a constitutional and legislative framework that is consistent with internationally recognized democratic standards."

Candidate Putin and Unity's policy promises on the economy were remarkably vague, but to the extent that they can be categorized, they fit more comfortably in the center than in the old-left camp. For example, Armingeon and Careja (2004) code Unity as a "social democratic party." Others referred to it as a center-right or centrist party that relied on a mix of free-market economic policies guided by a strong state (Markov 1999; Reissinger 2003). Comparisons with Pinochet were more likely than with Peron. In his discussion of economic policy, President Putin emphasized the creation of a strong state as well as the need for Russia to modernize its economy by expanding the role for markets and integrating into the global economy.[24] Shortly after coming to power, President Putin argued that private property in farmland was essential; that joining the World Trade Organization was a priority; and that government interference in the economy in Russia was excessive. Indeed, in his first few years in office, President Putin found common cause with the liberal political party, the Union of Right Forces, on economic policies, as the latter repeatedly claimed that Putin was implementing its economic policies (Remington 2000: 142; Mau 2001; author interview with Alexei Kara-Murzai 2003).[25] Remington (2001b: 287) notes that "the [economically] liberal orientation

---

of the contributors to this volume, the violations were not extensive enough to undermine the validity of the elections."

[24] Aslund (2000) noted "Putin's speeches are about market economies. He came to Moscow in 1996 at the behest of the reformer Anatoly Chubais, and his current confidants on economic policy are also Chubais allies." The journalist Andrew Jack (2005: 334) wrote that Putin's "economic vision is largely pragmatic and liberal, relatively open to the market and to foreign investment if only as the best tools to rebuild Russia's influence in the world. But his view of how to impose change remains narrow, technocratic and authoritarian." In 2000 Yegor Gaidar noted: "There are few subjects on economic policy on which he [Putin] is clear, but he has been clearest in his commitment to the protection of private property and his strong opposition to renationalization" (Desai 2006: 100).

[25] Putin's Address to the Federal Assembly on July 8, 2000, gives some impression of his views:

As of today, the state keeps interfering too actively in the field of property, business and, partially, consumption. On the contrary, the state behaves rather passively in the context of creating a common economic space, ensuring the unfailing observance of laws, as well as the protection of property rights. Economic growth is being mostly hindered by sky-high taxes, bureaucratic arbitrary rule and rampant crime. The solution of these problems depends upon the state. However, an expensive and extravagant state is unable to slash taxes. A corruption-ridden state lacking clear-cut prerogatives won't rid businessmen of bureaucratic arbitrary rule and the underworld's influence. I am absolutely sure that an ineffective state constitutes the main cause of that lengthy and profound economic crisis, whose manifestations are here for everyone to see.... Our strategic line is as follows – less administration by fiat, more free enterprise, e.g. free production, trade and investment. In a nutshell, state economic regulation should not imply the excessive use of administrative leverage as well as the state's expansion into specific sectors. We have already utilized such ineffective options. Nor should the state aim to prop up selected enterprises and market players.

of Putin's legislative agenda stands in striking contrast to the authoritarian impulses Putin has demonstrated in the political sphere."

The threat of a reversal in policy from the CPRF also declined in this period. Having failed to reach beyond its core supporters in previous electoral campaigns, the CPRF tried to attract new voters with a platform that was less radical than in previous elections. Dmitriev (1999) compared electoral platforms of the CPRF in 1995 and 1999 and noted: "If in 1995, the Communists held out the creation of a communist society as a long-term goal which included a full renationalization of industry, in its new platform, the CPRF, like all other parties, speaks of creating reliable guarantees for 'honestly obtained' private property and about the defense of shareholder rights." This shift in policy, however, did not mean that the CPRF had abandoned its roots (Dmitriev 2000). The party continued to take a hard line on revising the privatization of firms and to ban the privatization of land, while also sticking to highly protectionist trade policies. The economic policies of the CPRF in 1999–2000 remained to the left of centrist parties in Poland, Hungary, and Lithuania, but they were more moderate than in the past.[26]

The macroeconomic situation in Russia offered improved conditions for the introduction of economic and institutional reform in early 2000. The financial crash of August 1998 weakened domestic interest groups benefiting from government budget deficits, such as the banking community. In addition, the devaluation of the ruble gave temporary protection to domestic producers by raising the cost of imports and lowering the price of exports. Higher oil prices – which rose from $12 to $28 per barrel between 1998 and 2000 – coincided with President Putin assuming the reins of government. With an improved economy and a decline in polarization, the outlook for reform was much brighter than at any point in the 1990s. Berglof et al. (2003: 2) observed: "For the first time in a decade we are seeing a political and economic constellation in Russia that is conducive to the broad institutional reforms the country needs to foster sustainable economic growth."

With a center-right president in power in a relatively democratic setting, the argument suggests that the outlook for economic and institutional reform looked promising in early 2000. Indeed, shortly after taking power, President Putin put forward a number of proposals to do just that. Within two years, the new government rewrote the Tax Code and the Labor Code, overhauled the pension system, eased regulations for creating new businesses, and reformed federal-center relations. Russia adopted a substantial reform of the Tax Code, including a flat tax on income at 13 percent, the replacement of three taxes on natural resource extraction with one unified tax, a reduction in the corporate profit tax from 35 to 24 percent, and the "elimination of practically all exemptions" in corporate taxes (World Bank 2001). The government

---

[26] Moreover, given the vehemence with which the CPRF had attacked social democratic economic policies in Russia, let alone the liberal policies of the Yeltsin administration, the CPRF had difficulty convincing voters of the credibility of its newfound, more moderate economic policies.

backed its tax policy promises with action by pressing charges against some of the largest corporations that had pursued the most aggressive tax minimization schemes (Rutland 2000: 340).[27] For example, it applied pressure by leaking a memo that two large privately owned oil companies, YUKOS and Sibneft, paid substantially lower taxes than did other oil firms.[28] In July 2000 the tax police raided the offices of an oil trading firm linked to Sibneft. During a meeting with oil company executives in January 2001, President Putin displayed considerable knowledge of tax avoidance schemes then in use and threatened further action unless these practices ceased. Somewhat surprisingly, the stock market viewed these actions against these tax evaders positively (Desai et al. 2007). The announcement of charges against tax evaders and raids against trading firms involved in transfer pricing actually increased the price of Sibneft and YUKOS stocks as minority investors hoped the charges would reduce asset stripping by majority shareholders.[29]

The government passed a new Labor Code, which took effect in February 2002, that had many liberal features. The new code expanded the use of fixed-term employment agreements, increased the number of causes that could be cited for termination, extended the probationary period for some employees, and weakened the power of trade unions to influence termination decisions. The new code was not solely probusiness, as it also gave employees the right to refuse to perform tasks outside their job description, carified rules for vacation time, and increased penalties to employers for late payment of wages, but on balance, most observers considered the new code more friendly to capital than to labor (Maleva 2001; Borisova 2001; Freshfields Bruckhaus Deringer 2002). Most importantly, the code began to provide some clarity to the patchwork of legislation that previously governed business-labor relations.

The government introduced measures to cut red tape for small business. The Law on Inspections in August 2001 reduced the number of agencies that could conduct inspections and limited the number of times that state agencies could inspect a firm. In addition, the Law on Licensing, which took effect in February 2002, cut the number of activities requiring licenses and permits. Finally, the Law on Registration, which came into force in July 2002, introduced the principle of "one window" registration. If firms in the past had to visit between six and thirteen agencies to register their firms, the new legislation allowed firms to register with a single agency in many circumstances (Frye and Shleifer 1997). In combination with a simplified tax system for small businesses, these efforts reduced the regulatory burden on small firms from the very high levels of the 1990s. The Center for Economic and Financial Research

---

[27] Interros, RAO-EES, TNK, AvtoVAZ, Gazprom, LUKoil, and Sibneft were all visited by tax authorities in much publicized inspections in 2000.

[28] Desai et al. (2007).

[29] Minority shareholders had interests aligned with the state because both suffered when majority shareholders hid revenue. With increased transparency in the tax system, both the state and minority shareowners expected majority shareholders to have more difficulty skimming revenue for themselves.

(CEFIR) found that while efforts to cut red tape fell short of the government's stated goals, there was considerable improvement in the business climate for small businesses in most regions after the passage of this legislation.[30]

In December 2001 the government passed a sweeping pension reform that introduced far greater scope for market forces. In comparison to the 1990s, when pension policy was marked by "incoherence and ineffectiveness," Cook (2006: 139) notes that "since 1999 arrears have been cleared; pensions have been reliably paid throughout the Federation, and the government drafted, passed through the legislature, and began to implement a major reform of the pension system." The new policy moved Russia from a defined-benefit pension scheme to a defined-contribution pension system that included three tiers: a basic pension financed through general taxes, a notionally defined contribution (NDC) by the employee and a mandatory funded contribution by the employer, and a basic benefit (Sinyavskaya 2003). These steps marked a major change in pension policy and helped bolster a key segment of the dependent population.

Moreover, in the face of fairly strong opposition from domestic manufacturers and lukewarm support from the public at best, President Putin pushed for Russia to join the World Trade Organization. Early in his term President Putin designated WTO membership a priority and staked considerable personal capital on this issue (Moore 2001; Aslund 2003; Yudaeva 2003). While negotiations proved complex and difficult, Russia made good progress toward joining the WTO in President Putin's first term.

Finally, one often overlooked change in policy in President Putin's first term was the reduction of government spending. The Yeltsin administration spent freely in large part to buy political support from new- and old-economy interests. In the 1990s government spending averaged 43 percent of GDP, which exacerbated a budget deficit that averaged 7.5 percent in this period. Russia spent like an OECD country on the earnings of a middle-income country. However, from 2000 to 2002 Russian government spending averaged 36.2 percent of GDP, even as the government began to increase its revenue thanks to a sharp rise in oil prices. Underscoring this point, Remington (2006: 276) notes: "By my count nearly 30 percent of Yeltsin's 458 decrees in 1996 were distributive in content. In contrast in 2001 Putin issued fewer than 150 decrees (published normative decrees) and only 10 percent could be classified as distributive."

Many of these policy ideas had been discussed for years. For example, reforming the pension system and the Labor Code and joining the WTO were on the agenda in the early 1990s, but prevailing political conditions prevented the enactment of these policies. The decline in political polarization and the rise of a vaguely center-right president with strong support in parliament helped to induce these changes in policy.

Economic performance in President Putin's first term was strong in large part because of the devaluation of the ruble in 1998 and to historically high

---

[30] See http://www.cefir.org for reports on "Monitoring the Administrative Barriers to Small Business Developments in Russia."

oil prices. Once estimates of the use of transfer pricing are taken into account, between 2001 and 2004 the natural resource sectors "directly contributed more than one-third of Russian GDP growth and the oil industry alone contributed close to one-quarter" (Ahrend 2006: 5).[31] Nonetheless, heightened political stability also played a role by generating an improved business climate. Ahrend (2004: 20) notes that "the perception that property rights had become sufficiently secure was one of the factors contributing to the recovery of investment in 2001 and especially 2002, particularly in the oil sector." Investment by private oil companies increased dramatically in this period. Thanks in large part to an improved business climate, Russia experienced net private capital in-flows in 2003 for the first time in the post-Soviet period (Tompson 2004: 6).

Greater political stability in combination with credible threats by the Putin administration to punish egregious acts of malfeasance by large firms led to a shift in corporate governance practices. Boone and Rodionov (2002) note that industrial labor productivity increased by 38 percent between 1998 and 2002. Moreover, they argued that the eight largest shareholder groups who owned Russia's private blue-chip companies were taking advantage of the political stability to make their companies more efficient.[32] The most prominent turnaround in this period came from YUKOS, the largest private oil company in Russia at the time. It brought foreign management into the company, published financial data according to international accounting standards, paid substantial dividends to shareholders, and reinvested at high rates. Moreover, the company increased output by more than 30 percent between 1999 and 2004 at a time when state-owned oil companies increased output by only 14 percent (Milov and Selivakhin 2005: 26). The company's "Saul on the Road to Damascus" conversion to good governance was an especially vivid example, but the trend of improved corporate governance was fairly broad across the largest and most actively traded shareholding companies. Ratings compiled by the Moscow-based Institute for Law and Corporate Governance indicate that nineteen of the twenty-five most liquid stocks experienced an increase in their corporate governance score between 2000 and 2002.[33]

To be sure, economic reform in some sectors was halting at best. Monopolists in gas (Gazprom) and electricity (UES) remained opaque, inefficient, and a significant drain on the state budget (Boone and Rodionov 2002: 20–22). In addition, bank reform advanced in some areas, but the sector remained dominated by the poorly run state-owned giants, Sberbank and Vneshtorgbank,

---

[31] Estimates of the contribution of the private sector to GDP are even more difficult in Russia than in other settings. It is likely overstated because of the widespread practice of state-owned firms using private front companies owned by the state company. It is also understated, as the smallest private companies composed of individual proprietors (firms without legal personhood, or PBYuL) are not obliged to report their output.

[32] Boone and Rodionov estimate that these eight shareholder groups controlled about 85 percent of the top sixty-four privatized companies in Russia. More generally, see Guriev and Rachinsky (2005) on the economic role of oligarchs in Russia.

[33] See www.ILCG.RU.

which proved remarkably resistant to change (Frye 2006). Moreover, hostile takeovers were often hostile in the most basic form of the term, and many were conducted for political rather than economic goals (Barnes 2006). Even with the policy changes, it was still difficult to conduct business in Russia. But it is also safe to say that the Putin administration introduced an impressive array of reforms in its first two years in office.

That the Putin team managed to introduce these reforms was surprising. Most observers gave President Putin little chance to make headway against the industrial barons and regional governors who dominated politics in the Yeltsin era. These assumptions were quite reasonable as President Putin was a newcomer to mass politics, faced considerable opposition, and was seen as the unpopular President Yeltsin's handpicked successor (Nunn and Stuhlberg 2000; Graham 1999, 2002).[34] Many observers viewed him as at best an arbiter between factions within the Kremlin or a captive of holdovers from the Yeltsin era (Reddaway 2001, 2002; Rose et al. 2000).

It is also important to note that politics in this period remained competitive as the executive branch had to devote considerable resources to building and maintaining majority support within the parliament. Putin's popularity notwithstanding, powerful interest groups and parties in parliament left their imprint on important pieces of legislation. For example, on the bill to remove Russia from the Financial Action Task Force's Black List of Countries abetting money laundering, Finance Minister Kudrin reportedly visited the Duma almost every day for two weeks to lobby for the bill.[35] Negotiations on the Labor Code were delayed for several months by opposition from deputics from Russia's Regions concerned about their electoral prospects. Writing of Putin's first legislation session, Remington (2003: 253, 254) observed: "The executive won several notable victories.... Progress was slow, however, due to the deep conflicts over the issues within the government and the need to find separate majorities within the Duma for every piece of legislation. The government had to bargain extensively for every bill." He adds that in the budget negotiations in 2002 "the coalition of the four [parliamentary parties] succeeded in presenting a relatively united front and winning several significant concessions from the government."[36] The constraint of maintaining majority support in the parliament helped in many respects to ensure pluralism in elite bargaining over policy in this period.

---

[34] In March 2000 Graham (2000) noted that "even if Putin is a reformer, he will face opposition from regional and economic elites. In order to succeed, he will have to carefully pick his fights, pit the oligarchs against one another, and hope to create some maneuvering room for himself," adding "Russia's journey from its Soviet past is going to be long, it is going to be messy, and it is going to be uncertain."

[35] Author interview with Irina Kotelevskaya, lobbyist for the Russian Union of Industrialists and Entrepreneurs, July 20, 2003.

[36] Remington (2006: 281) notes that "overall it is probably fair to say that in the 2000–03 period ... the distributive content of legislation was much lower than in the Yeltsin period."

In an environment of declining political polarization and relatively competitive politics with a center-right executive, policy instability declined, and the government introduced a range of economic and institutional reforms, increased spending on the social sector, and created better conditions for new private businesses. The argument is consistent with policy outcomes during Putin's first three years in office.

Declining Democracy and Stalled Reforms, 2003–2004

The progress in economic and institutional reform of President Putin's first two years in office was not continued in the second half of his first term.[37] Beginning in 2003, politics became much less democratic because of a variety of exogenous and endogenous factors, including high oil prices, a perceived high terrorist threat, and the opportunism of the incumbent (Fish 2005). In this period, economic and institutional reform stagnated. The extent of the decline of democracy is difficult to assess with precision, but the drip-by-drip erosion of constraints on state power left Russia much more autocratic in 2006 than it was six years earlier (Fish 2005; Stoner-Weiss 2006). After parliamentary elections in December 2003, the OSCE (2004a: 1) noted: "While generally well administered, the election failed to meet a number of OSCE commitments for democratic elections, most notably those pertaining to unimpeded access to the media on a non-discriminatory basis, a clear separation between the State and political parties, and guarantees to enable political parties to compete on the basis of equal treatments." Its judgment of presidential elections in March 2004 (2004b:1) was equally critical. "While on a technical level the election was organized with professionalism . . . the process overall did not adequately reflect principles necessary for a healthy democratic election. The election process failed to meet important commitments concerning treatment of candidates by the State-controlled media on a non-discriminatory basis, equal opportunities for all candidates, and secrecy of the ballot."

These elections in some respects were a logical step in the gradual undermining of democracy that began shortly after President Putin took office in 2000. Over time, the government constricted freedom of the press, weakened institutions capable of providing checks on the executive, and used state power to create a political process even more tilted in favor of the executive than during the previous decade.

Changes were most apparent in the national media. Under President Yeltsin, the media was diverse, often critical of the president, and repeatedly broke major stories on corruption in high places in the government. Moreover, media outlets with private ownership were among the most influential in the country. And the private media famously rallied around the president at election time and were especially critical of the CPRF (Belin 1996). But in the Putin

---

[37] Aslund (2007a) provides similar periodization of policies.

years, state control over public sources of information, particularly television, increased dramatically, and the mass media became even more partisan and passive. In 2000 and 2001, state-owned companies with close ties to the Putin administration assumed ownership of two large private television stations that had been critical of the president. The state took control of NTV by bringing tax evasion charges against its major owner, Vladimir Gusinsky, and by using state-owned Gazprom to call in a loan previously extended to NTV. Many believed that NTV had favored Fatherland–All Russia rather than the propresidential Unity in parliamentary elections in 2000. Perhaps more importantly, its coverage of the war in Chechnya was especially critical of the government (Shevtsova 2003). The government used a similar tactic to gain ownership of Channel 1, a television station owned by former Putin supporter Boris Berezovsky, who also had grown critical of the new administration. Finally, with the government takeover of TVS in the summer of 2003, the government controlled all television stations capable of broadcasting across all of Russia. The assumption of government control over national television was quickly evident in the more favorable treatment of the president (if not the government, which was often subject to harsh criticism). Radio and print media remained more pluralistic but had less reach and political relevance. Moreover, editors and journalists reported greater pressure from state authorities under President Putin than in previous years (Fish 2005: 70–74; Tregubova 2003). In sum, from the summer of 2003 the most politically powerful sources of information about government activities were now in the hands of the government itself.

The government also made institutional changes that some argued undercut democracy. In the summer of 2000 the Putin administration moved to weaken powerful regional elites by implementing legislation preventing the governors and legislative heads of Russia's eighty-nine regions from taking seats in the Federation Council, the upper house of Russia's parliament. Previously governors and heads of legislatures held all the seats in the upper house, but new legislation required governors and legislatures to name proxies to serve in their stead. This undercut the ability of governors and legislative heads from different regions to coordinate their actions vis-à-vis the central government (Solnick 2000). In addition, the government passed legislation allowing the executive to suspend governors if they violated federal law. Reaction to these proposals at the time was mixed. Some argued that these moves would reduce the power of governors, many of whom were viewed more as feudal barons than as servants of the public. Others viewed these steps as undermining checks on executive power and significantly reducing federalism in Russia (Stoner-Weiss 2006).

Reaction to legislation passed in 2004 that made governors appointed by the president rather than elected by the citizenry was less ambiguous. This plan, which was put forward in the wake of the horrific terrorist attack on a primary school in Beslan that resulted in more than three hundred deaths in September 2004, was roundly criticized within Russia and abroad as an attempt by the Putin administration to increase its power that would have little effect on reducing terrorist activities (Freedom House 2005; Stoner-Weiss 2006). By the fall of 2004, governors in Russia had become an extension of – rather than an institutional check on – executive power.[38]

Moreover, state influence over opposition political parties and social movements gradually increased. Federal officials intervened in gubernatorial and mayoral races that led to disqualifications of those insufficiently supportive of the Kremlin (Fish 2005: 61–66). In May 2005 the Duma passed a new election law that tilted the playing field toward large parties by raising the percentage of votes needed to enter parliament from 5 to 7 percent, banning the practice of electoral coalitions between parties, tightening the requirements to register as a party, and having all candidates elected on party lists in a single nationwide constituency under proportional representation. While none of these steps by themselves struck a fatal blow to the more pluralistic politics of the 1990s, the cumulative effect of these measures amounted to a "creeping bureaucratic coup."[39] Given a high rate of economic growth, declining rates of poverty, and a dramatic increase in real income during his first term, it is hardly surprising that President Putin remained quite popular.[40] These issues aside, Russia clearly became more autocratic after Vladimir Putin assumed office in 2000, with the erosion of democracy accelerating after 2002.

The increasing authoritarianism of the period 2003–2004 coincided with a slowdown in economic and institutional reform. The clearest example of this change in course occurred in privatization as the government began to reassert state control over some of the most prized private companies in strategic sectors of the economy. Most prominently on October 25, 2003, the government arrested YUKOS owner Mikhail Khodorkovsky on a variety of charges ranging from tax evasion to violating commitments made in a privatization tender in 1994 (Tompson 2004). Found guilty on the tax evasion charges, the owners of the company faced a back-taxes bill far beyond their ability to pay. On December 19, 2004, the government auctioned off YUKOS's main assets, production facilities at Yugansk. Baikal Finance Group, a little-known company widely believed to be acting on behalf of the state-owned oil company Rosneft, won control over the company in an opaque auction and quickly sold the unit to Rosneft.

The motives behind the decision to bring charges against YUKOS are obscure, ranging from general political concerns (Khodorkovsky funded opposition parties and hinted at a future run for the presidency) to foreign policy interests (YUKOS was in discussions to sell a large stake of the company to a foreign company) to simple greed (having failed to enrich themselves during the 1990s, Putin's confidantes were taking advantage of their position) to personal motives (Khodorkovsky offended Putin by not wearing a tie during a

---

[38] It is interesting to note that this move has never been very popular with the Russia populace. See www.Levada.ru polls on the question.

[39] Attributed to Lilya Shevtsova in Wagstyl et al. (2003).

[40] Myagkov et al. (2009) use a clever method to identify much higher levels of vote fraud under President Putin than under President Yeltsin.

meeting with other businessmen) to electoral maneuvering (to bolster Unity's position in the December 2003 parliamentary election). Whatever the motives, the punishment of YUKOS for actions common among large industrial companies heightened uncertainty about the security of property rights and sparked a surge in capital flight, despite an annual economic growth rate of more than 5 percent.

Moves against YUKOS were followed by increases in state ownership in a number of large companies, including oil giant Sibneft, truck-building conglomerate KAMAZ and leading automaker AvtoVaz. State-owned banks assumed a much more aggressive lending profile, while earlier plans to privatize these banks ground to a halt. The newfound support for state ownership was largely limited to the natural resource sectors and high-profile manufacturing firms, but these steps increased concerns for the protection of private property rights against incursions by the state more generally and were emblematic of a slow-down in economic and institutional reform.

Moreover, the government made scant progress in other areas of reform. Negotiations to join the World Trade Organization slowed dramatically, even as economic reform laggards, like Albania, Armenia, Georgia, and Moldova, became members. Bank reform stalled in large part because of the dominant positions retained by the state-owned Sberbank and Vneshtorgbank (Frye 2006). Despite repeated efforts at reform, the judiciary in Russia remained riddled with corruption and favoritism. In rankings of 117 countries by the World Economic Forum in 2005, Russia fell from 85 to 106 in the extent of "favoritism in decisions of government officials" and from 84 to 102 in the degree of judicial independence. Transparency International rated Russia 126 of 159 countries in its level of corruption in 2005.

This slowdown in economic and institutional reforms is especially problematic, given the strong state of Russia's macroeconomy, thanks to historically high oil prices. Economic growth averaged more than 5 percent per year between 2000 and 2004, and the budget has been in surplus each year since 2002. Moreover, the government's hard currency reserves in 2004 exceeded $250 billion. The macroeconomic situation suggests that this would have been an especially propitious time to pursue much needed economic liberalization and institutional reform of banking, corporate governance, and competition policy, but these policies were not high on the agenda of the government.

It is difficult to analyze the relationship between politics and reform in this period, given the recent nature of these events. More perspective and research is needed to draw definitive conclusions. Moreover, it is possible that high oil prices contributed to both the slowdown in economic reform and the erosion of democratic institutions. Proponents of the resource curse argue that high oil prices undermine democracy by cutting the link between taxation and representation (Sachs and Warner 1995; Ross 2001; Fish 2005). Absent the need to extract revenue from the populace, rulers are unwilling to grant political rights. Moreover, the easy money generated by high oil prices may also blunt incentives to conduct economic reforms that may expand the tax base.

High oil prices thus correlate with both a decline in democracy and the slowing of economic reforms in recent years but offer less insight into the evolution of economic reforms in previous periods. This, too, is a topic for more research.

Conclusion

Russia's experience conducting economic and institutional reform highlights the systematic role played by elite partisanship, political polarization, and the quality of democracy. Focusing on the changes in these political factors helps to account for the pattern of economic and institutional reform in Russia. Polarized politics under high levels of political competition in the 1990s contributed to great uncertainty over policy, rapid but inconsistent reform, and deep cuts in social spending. As polarization declined following the 1999–2000 electoral cycle, a president with a vaguely center-right economic orientation pushed through an impressive range of economic and institutional reforms in his first two years in office. However, the weakening of constraints on executive power led to a decline in the quality of democracy and a subsequent slowdown in reforms.

This argument suggests that the inconsistent reforms that marked Russia in the 1990s were not primarily the result of mistaken policies, corruption, a lack of accountability, or a weak state, as is commonly argued. Instead these policies were part and parcel of attempts to retain office in polarized political settings. Like all politicians, incumbents in Russia traded economic benefits for political support. However, because they made policy in a polarized setting, they struck a worse bargain than their counterparts in less polarized settings.

It also suggests that President Putin's reform strategy has responded to changes in the political environment. Before consolidating his power, President Putin faced checks on his power from the regional governors, the Duma, and business elites, and this period saw a burst of economic and institutional reforms. However, having concentrated power and removed many institutional checks late in his first term of office, President Putin did not follow up on his earlier reforms. The decline in democracy coincided with delays in much-needed structural reforms of the economy. Thus, the argument presented can account for the significant shifts in economic policy in the Yeltsin and Putin eras.

8

Bulgaria

Polarization, Democracy, and Reform

> In 1994 Bulgaria's anti-communist government won a vociferous debate in parliament to detonate the mausoleum holding the remains of Georgi Dimitrov, the country's first communist leader. More than a ton of dynamite and several explosions, however, failed to bring down the hulking structure. One onlooker noted with sympathy for the old regime: "There is not enough ammunition to destroy our ideas." The government quickly sent in bulldozers to tear down the statue.
>
> *International Herald Tribune*, August 23, 1994

Bulgaria offers a prime illustration of the impact of political polarization and democracy on economic reform. For the first seven years of the 1990s, a parade of old-left and right governments made policy in a polarized and relatively democratic environment, and progress in economic and institutional reform was dismal, even for the postcommunist world. Policy stability was low and successive governments engaged in inconsistent reforms that provided great benefits to their supporters at the expense of the public bourse, and social spending suffered. Not surprisingly, estimates suggest that the economy shrank by about one-third between 1990 and 1996 (EBRD 1997: 115).

In late 1996 the governing old-left Bulgarian Socialist Party collapsed and parliamentary elections brought a new majority led by the right-wing Union of Democratic Forces (UDF) to power. Under IMF scrutiny, the UDF government introduced a restrictive fiscal policy based on a currency board, revamped the tax system, instituted bankruptcy procedures, privatized the banking sector, and liberalized heating and energy prices. By 2001 political polarization had declined substantially and a new consensus over economic policy emerged as the BSP became more social democratic, and a centrist party backed by the former tsar of Bulgaria took power and largely continued the economic policies of the UDF. These and other measures have produced a remarkable turnaround in the Bulgarian polity and economy since 1997. This chapter traces how political polarization influenced economic and institutional reform in Bulgaria.

TABLE 8.1. *Heads of Government, 1990–1996*

08/90–11/90	Andrei Lukanov	BSP
12/90–11/91	Dimitar Popov	Nonparty backed by BSP/UDF
11/91–10/92	Filip Dimitrov	UDF with support from MRF
10/92–08/94	Luben Berov	BSP with support from MRF
09/94–12/94	Renata Inzhova	Interim
12/94–12/96	Zhan Videnov	BSP

Bulgaria: The Background

During the Cold War, Bulgaria was seen as the "most true friend" of the Soviet Union because of its unflinching support of Moscow's foreign policy and its orthodox domestic policies. Todor Zhivkov headed the Bulgarian Communist Party from 1956 to 1989 and oversaw the transformation of Bulgaria from an agrarian to an industrial society, but he also ruthlessly persecuted dissidents, had little interest in reform socialism, and repressed the Turkish minority. As the dust of the Berlin Wall settled, then foreign minister Petar Mladenov led a coup to topple the aging Zhivkov on November 10, 1989. Mladenov led the reformist wing within the BCP that sought to reinvigorate the party along Gorbachevian lines. Public demonstrations in December 1989 pushed the Mladenov government to negotiate with an anticommunist opposition group rooted around the recently formed Union of Democratic Forces (Melone 1998). The Roundtable Agreements led to the parliamentary elections of June 1990, which were won by the successor to the BCP, the largely unreformed Bulgarian Socialist Party.

Bulgaria 1990–1996: The Roots of Political Polarization

In the first four years of the 1990s, Bulgaria saw three elections, five governments, and great turnover within cabinets. However, high levels of political polarization between the old-left Bulgarian Socialist Party and the economically liberal Union of Democratic Forces were a constant. While reform governments in Poland embarked on shock therapy, successive Bulgarian governments of old-left and liberal stripes floundered. Table 8.1 presents the series of prime ministers in Bulgaria from 1990 to 1996 and the parties that put them into office.

With the advent of the Roundtable Talks in early 1990, the Bulgarian Communist Party moved to reposition itself, while maintaining its core supporters among the rural population, import-competing firms, unskilled workers, pensioners, and state employees in the economic ministries. In the spring of 1990 the BCP held a Party Congress at which three factions emerged: a social democratic faction headed by Andrei Lukanov that represented the interests of directors of state-owned enterprises; a Marxist group headed by Aleksander

Lilov that sought a renewal of socialism that claimed to speak for workers, pensioners, and agricultural interests; and a technocratic wing led by Zhan Videnov that took a centrist position and was represented heavily by former leaders of the Communist Youth Organization.[1] At the 1990 congress, the BCP purged its most Stalinist elements, severed ties with the Communist Youth Organization, and held a referendum to change the name of the party to Bulgarian Socialist Party. The referendum passed with 86 percent approval (Melone 1998: 38). To send its message of reform, the BSP abandoned the hammer and sickle in favor of the red rose of socialism as its party symbol.

However, the newly named BSP did not completely change its spots. It confirmed its identity as the successor to the Bulgarian Communist Party, retained the assets held by its predecessor, and relied heavily on key figures from the Zhivkov era. More importantly, the BSP advocated economic policies similar to its old-left brethren. It promised a privileged role for the state in the economy, skepticism toward international economic integration, continued support for state-owned enterprises, and a gradual transition to a market economy that "remained true to socialist ideals." As it drew much of its support from voters in rural areas and on pensions, the BSP promised generous spending on agriculture and social security. The BSP resisted privatization of industry and agriculture to outsiders, as these policies would weaken supporters within state ministries that oversaw industry and agriculture.

These preferences were reflected in BSP documents. In the run-up to parliamentary elections in 1990, the BSP declared that it was not "retreating from its Marxist roots" (BSP platform, October 1990). Before parliamentary elections in 1991, it rejected a "monetarist approach to economic reform" and appealed to the "military, security personnel, and the peasantry by taking a conservative line toward reform and the economy" (Englelbrekt 1991: 7). Its 1994 platform called for "Renovating Democratic Socialism" and sought to dissociate the party from the "real socialism" that Bulgaria experienced before 1990 and the "capitalism" that Bulgaria was currently experiencing. The program promised to create an economy in which state ownership and private ownership would play equal roles in creating national wealth, criticized EU and IMF conditionality as "contrary to Bulgaria's interest," supported an evolutionary economic reform that might last 20–25 years, called for "preferential financial and credit conditions for agriculture," and aimed to unite all left-wing factions "against the neoliberal model of economic reform which aims at abolishing state intervention in the economy" (Kassayie 1998: 113–115).

Dobrin Kanev (2002: 7), a Bulgarian political scientist who later became an adviser to Socialist president Parvanov, noted the "significant difficulties in moving the party toward social democracy" early in the transformation. Writing in 1992, the leader of the reformist wing of the BSP, Andrei Lukanov, was more colorful. He dismissed "western economics," resisted the "restoration of capitalism" in Bulgaria, favored an economic strategy that embodied

---

[1] Lilov had been ideology secretary of the Bulgarian Communist Party in the communist era.

"the socialist ideals" of the former Communist Party, and denounced "neoliberalism as social sadism" and an "inhumane ideology" (Ganev 2001: 402–403). Other BSP officials were less charitable.

It is important to note that the BSP did not simply seek to preserve the pre-1989 status quo, but sought to create a new institutional equilibrium in which the state played a significant role as owner and regulator, generously rewarded the interests of the managers of state-owned enterprises, but still found a way to provide sufficient benefits to vulnerable groups of pensioners and rural residents to keep them in the fold.

The main opposition party, the Union of Democratic Forces, was formally created in December 1989 as an umbrella movement of more than sixteen groups. The thread uniting these groups was strident opposition to communism and the Bulgarian Socialist Party. The UDF was led by the former dissident Zhelyu Zhelev, a former philosophy professor who wrote a treatise called "Fascism" in the 1980s, which argued that communism and nazism were both totalitarian forms of rule. Other groups in the coalition included the independent trade group Podkrepa, the Bulgarian Social Democratic Party, the People's Union, the agrarian-based BANU–Nikola Petkov, and a variety of human rights organizations. Initially, the party saw itself as an opposition spanning the political spectrum that campaigned on the none-too-subtle slogan: "Totalitarianism or Democracy." The next decade would see a considerable winnowing of these diverse groups to form a more homogeneous, if equally fractious, party.

The 1991 UDF electoral platform called for "sweeping immediate privatization," making "a private sector that forms the backbone of the Bulgarian economy"; and implementing an "austere" fiscal policy (Engelbrekt 1991). Throughout the 1990s, it promoted the rapid privatization of industrial enterprises whenever possible through sales to outside investors, speedy liberalization of domestic prices, a quick opening of most markets to foreign competition, and restitution of land to previous owners. Moreover, the UDF proposed much stricter limits on direct and indirect loans to industrial and agricultural enterprises than did the BSP. Despite having greater internal heterogeneity than the BSP, the UDF projected a policy profile common to anticommunist parties. According to the Bulgarian political scientist Alexander Andreev (1996: 32–33), "The UDF does not possess a distinctive ideological profile. However, the policies pursued by it are definable within several basic parameters: unyielding anticommunism, commitment to speedy market reforms, pro-Western orientation, and a focus on democratic rights and the liberties of citizens."

A minor party that at times occupied a strategic position within the political system was the Movement for Rights and Freedom (MRF). Headed by Ahmed Dogan, the MRF claimed to speak for the Turkish minority population that made up about 10 percent of the population at the start of the transition. Early in the transition, the Movement for Reform and Freedom was allied with the UDF against the BSP, but this relationship became more complicated over time.

Despite the heterogeneity of the groups in each bloc, the BSP and the UDF represented clear divisions within Bulgarian society that surfaced quickly after the fall of communism. On the basis of three surveys conducted in 1991, 1993, and 1994, Shopov (1999: 187) found that "the formation and evolution of the two main political forces in post-Communist Bulgaria, the Bulgarian Socialist Party (BSP) and the Union of Democratic Forces (UDF), reveal the early emergence of a 'bi-bipolar' party configuration after the regime change in 1989." Kitschelt and several of his coauthors (1995: 143) conducted surveys in 1991 and found a similar polarization, noting that "significant aspects of political structuring may in fact appear in postcommunist polities quite early," and they located the roots of these political cleavages in individuals' prospects in the market economy. In a later work Kitschelt et al. (1999: 388) noted that "because of the organizational polarization between two major rival camps, despite their internal heterogeneity and diffuseness, citizens have little difficulty recognizing the major alternatives." Similarly, Deyanova (1996: 176) found that "the symmetric division of Bulgarian society has not changed considerably. The mirror questions whether 'a victory of the BSP (UDF) would be a total catastrophe for the country,' asked two months before the latest parliamentary elections in 1994, rendered mirror answers: 28 percent say that a BSP victory would be catastrophic, and 28 percent that a UDF victory would be catastrophic."

Others recognized the partisan differences at the elite level during this period. Kanev (2002: 9) noted the "extremely polarized political situation" in 1990, adding that the cleavage "communism-anti-communism played a significant role" early in the transition. Andreev (1996: 33) observed "the sharp opposition between the two main political forces polarized a great portion of Bulgarian society." Karasimeonov (1999: 115) argued that the balance of power between the two forces "was the basis for the persistence of a bipolar, confrontational party 'system' and determined government formation which was marked by instability and the lack of stable parliamentary majorities." Nikolov et al. (2004: 9) noted that "the collapse of the communist regime was followed by a rapid and lasting ideological polarization of the political debate."

A comparison of electoral platforms by four Bulgarian academics in Table 8.2 depicts the sharp differences in policies between the BSP and UDF. These observers note that from 1990 to 1997 "the political platforms did not register any evolution in time in their economic policy sections" (Nenova 1998: 4).

Polarization and Policy

In January 1990 the BSP and the UDF began Roundtable Talks to create a new political system for Bulgaria (Melone 1998).[2] Bulgaria's first free election since

---

[2] The BSP pushed for quick elections, hoping to take advantage of its superior organization and the popularity of some of its more prominent officials. The UDF was less united. Pointing to the experience of Poland, some groups within the UDF called for rapid elections to build on the momentum created by the fall of the Bulgarian Communist Party, while others argued in favor of elections in the fall of 1991 to give the disparate groups operating under the UDF umbrella time to organize (Melone 1998).

TABLE 8.2. *Campaign Platforms*

Policy	BSP	UDF
Development of markets	Development of markets regulated by the state	Development of a complete set of markets, price liberalization, foreign trade liberalization
Privatization	Privatization through fair (if possible equal) distribution of state property	Privatization through sales to strategic investors and active participation of managers
Restitution of property rights	Against	For a restitution of urban property and land
Economic growth promotion	Bailouts of old debts of state-owned firms	Close loss-making enterprises, applying programs for social protection of employees
Agrarian policy	Substantial state aid (noninterest loans, subsidies, price policies), land should be held by those who worked the land	Restitution of land, autonomy of the rural regions, state aid for agriculture
Social policy	State intervention by increasing transfers to pensioners and poor families, indexation of incomes, reduction in income differentiation	Social policy based on development of independent funds – social security fund, pension funds, health care insurance; funds may be state or private; inflationary indexation of incomes within reasonable limits

Source: Nenova (1998: 4).

the interwar period in June 1990 produced a strong showing for the Bulgarian Socialist Party, which won 47 percent of the popular vote and 211 of the 400 seats in parliament. The United Democratic Forces won 144 seats with 36 percent of the vote, while the Bulgarian Agrarian Union won 16 seats with 8 percent of the vote, and Movement for Rights and Freedoms won 23 seats and 6 percent of the vote. The BSP did particularly well among "the elderly, less educated, and politically inactive strata living in the small towns and villages" (Tzvetkov 1992: 34), while the UDF ran much better in the cities, among the young and the well educated.

One of the first acts of the new National Assembly was to elect a president to hold the largely ceremonial position. In July 1990 it chose Zhelyu Zhelev of the UDF as president and Attanas Semerjiev, a former interior ministry official backed by the Bulgarian Socialist Party, as his vice president. This odd marriage of a liberal former dissident and a neocommunist former apparatchik in the two top executive posts reflected the bipolar nature of Bulgarian politics.

The National Assembly elected in June gave the BSP the power to present a new government. The BSP chose as one of its leaders Andrei Lukanov, a former Politburo member and representative of the social democratic wing of the party, to head the first government. Prime Minister Lukanov called on other parties to join the government but found no takers as other parties were skeptical of the BSP government's intentions.

Lukanov's economic program was less statist than many expected but satisfied few. Hard-line elements within the BSP were unenthusiastic about its calls to open the economy and privatize sections of industry, while the UDF considered any policies pursued by the BSP as tainted by the legacy of forty years of communist rule. Promising a gradual reform that aimed to limit the social costs of the transformation, the Lukanov government moved slowly to liberalize prices, which led to increased inflation and a sharp drop in the government's popularity. Foreign support dwindled with the government's stunning decision to freeze payments on its international debt in the summer of 1990.[3] In the face of labor strikes and student demonstrations in the capital, the Lukanov government fell in November 1990.

President Zhelev then nominated Dimitar Popov, a judge without party affiliation, to the parliament. The less than stellar performance of the Lukanov government had weakened the BSP within the parliament and encouraged the UDF and the MRF to take the initiative. Popov formed a government that relied on the UDF for economic ministries, while the BSP retained control over other portfolios. The new prime minister faced the difficult task of making policy in a divided parliament headed by the BSP, which held a slim majority, and an interventionist, if formally weak president, from the UDF. Popov's broad coalition government took advantage of a brief honeymoon period and managed to gain a pledge of labor and industrial peace from the major trade unions and industrial organizations for six months (Jackson 1991: 208). With the backing of the IMF, the government liberalized some prices, unified the exchange rate, and began to open the economy to international trade in February 1991, but otherwise it made little headway on the economic front. The Popov government ultimately resigned in the run-up to elections mandated by a new constitution passed in the summer of 1991.

The parliamentary elections of October 1991 generated a turnover in government but reproduced political stalemate as neither major bloc won a majority. Operating under a new constitution that created a smaller parliament of 240 deputies and a relatively weak president and which required parties to get at least 4 percent of the vote to gain representation in parliament, the UDF and the BSP won a roughly equal share of seats, 46 and 44 percent respectively, while the MRF won 10 percent of the seats. The UDF formed a government with the support of the MRF, but the latter did not formally join the coalition. Ruling with a whisker-thin margin and heading a diverse coalition held together largely by its opposition to the BSP, the Dimitrov government was in

---

[3] The Lukanov government declared its default by faxing its creditors – hardly a move to soften the blow.

an unenviable position. The new government introduced economic reforms that removed barriers to foreign investment, promised to accelerate privatization, and laid the groundwork for restitution for land and property nationalized by the Communists. The mix of interests led to a "hastily arranged compromise," known as the 1992 Privatization Act, which emphasized sales to foreigners and restitution and left the government open to charges of "selling the country" (Bojicic-Dzelilovic and Bojkov 2002: 15).

Splits within the ruling party and poor relations with the MRF hampered efforts to pursue reforms. The constituent parts of the UDF, which ranged from labor activists of the *Podkrepa* trade union to economic liberals in the Democratic Party to the "greens" of Ecoglasnost and the Conservative Ecological Party, quickly fell out over economic policy (Andreev 1996: 29–33). In October 1992 the MRF in alliance with President Zhelev withdrew its support for the prime minister and brought down the Dimitrov government. President Zhelev then nominated Lyuben Berov, a politically unaffiliated economic historian and former economic adviser to the UDF, to form a nonparty government of technocrats and encouraged the BSP and MRF to back him. One observer noted that "Berov's government is the product of an unorthodox political compromise that may not be particularly stable" (Engelbrekt 1993: 1).

In this highly polarized environment, Berov's economic policy was muddled at best and the government spent generously to support old-economy interests in a partially liberalized environment. Successive indexations of wages and pensions based on the rate of inflation played no small role in three devaluations of the Bulgarian lev between 1993 and 1994. Wyzan (1996: 87) wrote that under the Berov government "budgetary subsidization of insolvent state enterprises was replaced by indiscriminate lending by state commercial banks to such enterprises, and the re-financing of those banks by the BNB (Bulgarian National Bank)." Berov prided himself on the consensual nature of the decision-making process of his administration, but this led to stalemate as the constituent elements of his coalition agreed on little. Failure to balance the budget sparked a currency crisis in 1994, which further undermined the incumbent government. Despite proclaiming itself "the government of privatization" upon taking office, it made little progress on this front. By the end of its tenure, "none of the main pledges that the Berov government made at the outset of the term, such as speeding up privatization and revitalizing state institutions, has been fulfilled" (Engelbrekt 1994: 20). In a word, the Berov government was no more successful than its predecessors and fell on September 18, 1994, by a vote of 219–4.[4]

The early 1990s in Bulgaria were marked by policy divisions between the old-left BSP and the rightist UDF and an environment of great uncertainty over future policy. In successive elections neither party gained sufficient political power to impose a coherent economic reform program. Kitschelt et al. (1999:

---

[4] As Prime Minister Berov told Randall Stone (2002: 214), "I never expected an agreement from only one [party faction]. I always had the consent of all three. If just one group said no, the question was closed. I tried to reach consensus on every policy."

398) noted that "government economic policies have flip-flopped with the
partisan stripes of the incumbents from social-protectionist to market-liberal
policies in 1992, back to social protectionism in 1993 and particularly after the
BSP electoral victory in 1994, and then again forward to market-liberal reform
in 1997. These policies were similar only with regard to their ineffectiveness in
turning around the Bulgarian economy."

As successive governments struggled to privatize industry and create corporate governance institutions, uncertainty over future policy was very high.
Given their short time horizons, privileged groups in state-owned enterprises
and ministers systematically looted many of Bulgaria's most valuable assets
(Ganev 2006). These spontaneous privatizations, with the tacit approval of
the BSP-led governments, enriched the few but contributed little to state coffers, and the state struggled mightily to fund social programs and to provide
institutions to support the new private sector (Stanchev 2001).

Not surprisingly, high levels of political polarization contributed to a sharp
economic decline. By 1994 the GDP in Bulgaria had fallen by more than 20 percent, annual inflation was running at almost 100 percent, and the government
budget deficit stood at almost 6 percent of GDP. Perhaps as disheartening, economic policy making was mired in difficulties as each new government took
turns raiding state coffers to buy political support.

Continued Polarization and the BSP in Power, 1994–1996

Voters returned the BSP to power by a large margin in the popular vote in elections in December 1994. The BSP won 52 percent of the seats in the National
Assembly, compared to 29 percent for the UDF, and quickly pursued a swing
to the left in economic policy. The return to power marked the rise of the
more left-wing and ideological branches of the BSP led by new prime minister
Zhan Videnov against the reputedly more social democratic wing led by ex-
prime minister Lukanov (Kassayie 1998: 121). Videnov, a former Komosom-
mol activist who at thirty-five was the youngest prime minister in Bulgarian
history, had run on a platform emphasizing his professional credentials and
promised to implement industrial policy, conduct a gradual privatization, and
protect job security, while maintaining macroeconomic stability.[5] This contradictory mix of populist policies proved ruinous.

In early 1995 the Videnov government put on hold restitution to those
who lost their property before 1989 and pushed through a mass privatization
program modeled in words, if not in deeds, on the Czech plan. The program
envisaged the privatization of 1,066 enterprises in three waves of auctions
in which the public would take part by investing privatization vouchers. In
contrast to the Czech plan, the state expected to retain a large ownership
stake, particularly in firms with more than a few hundred employees (Miller
and Petranov 2000: 228). Even in firms in which the state offered more than

---

[5] Alexander Lilov and the more ideological wing of the BSP were strong supporters of Videnov.

50 percent of shares for sale, the law allowed the state to maintain a blocking share with only 30 percent of the shares. Thus, the mass privatization program permitted the state to retain a dominant position in the management of most industrial enterprises. The change in policy delayed privatization and allowed managers of state-owned enterprises and allies within the ministries to continue to strip assets with little threat of tighter corporate governance or purchase by outsiders (Nikolov et al. 2004).

The mass privatization program created voucher funds as the major investment vehicle for the public. Regulatory and financial burdens to create voucher funds were quite high and led many to believe that the government used these funds to reward its supporters with plum management positions.[6] Evidence of collusion by managers during the voucher fund auction process was common, but competition resulting from the voucher fund auction did erode some of the bargaining power of the managers (Miller and Petranov 2000: 249; Peev 2002: 82).

The BSP also continued the use of management-employee buyouts organized by line ministries with little oversight. Most prominently, the government privatized Bulgaria's largest foreign trading company (Chimimport) in late 1994 by transferring about 60 percent of the shares to managers and workers who "paid" for the shares with credits backed by "promises of future profits" (Bojicic-Dzelilovic and Bojkov 2004: 15).

Little progress was made on industrial privatization in this period, and those transfers of property that did take place favored supporters of the government to a degree that some viewed as unseemly (Peev 2002). By the end of 1995 only about 10 percent of Bulgaria's 3,800 enterprises had been privatized, and these firms accounted for less than 3 percent of state enterprise assets (Claessens and Peters 1997: 305).

Moreover, state intervention in price making increased dramatically under the BSP. In 1992, 18 percent of prices were subject to some form of government regulation, but in 1996 the share was 45 percent (Dobrinsky 1997: 24–25). Further, the government curbed grain exports through quotas and taxes but allowed favored firms to evade those quotas and export grain at market prices (Wyzan 1998: 24). As one observer noted, "Despite the official rhetoric, reinstating some form of state socialism has been at the center of the BSP's practical measures for governing since 1995" (Kassayie 1998: 119).

The most striking outcome during this period was the solidification of collusive ties between large industrial conglomerates and the state. One of the best examples was Multigroup, a holding company established in 1990 in Lichtenstein, a country in which firms may register in the name of a local lawyer without revealing their owners. Offshoots of Multigroup were registered in Switzerland, and ultimately in Bulgaria in 1992. By the mid-1990s, it is estimated that Multigroup acquired influential stakes in more than 120 firms, including Kremikovtsi, Bulgaria's largest steel and ferrous metals producer,

---

[6] Author interview with Roumen Avramov, June 24, 2005.

and Himko, Bulgaria's largest chemical producer. Both firms held dominant positions on the local market and boasted large export operations. By 1993 Multigroup was the second-largest holding company in the country. It soon expanded its operations into collecting debts for the state bank, producing bootleg compact discs, and reselling gas for Topenergy, a company jointly owned by Russia's Gazprom and Bulgargas, which was headed by ex–prime minister and then member of parliament Andrei Lukanov. Exploiting social networks with energy-sector executives in Moscow developed during the command economy, Topenergy became the sole middleman for all gas deliveries to Bulgaria from Russia (Ganev 2006).

Elites within Multigroup had deep roots in the state and party apparatus. As Ganev (1998: 11) noted, "A look at the roster of high-ranking officials who led the corporation during the crucial 1992–1996 period reveals that the new organization relies exclusively on the expertise of former communist state officials who have occupied various sensitive positions," including the former chairman of the National Bank, the former chairman of the Privatization Agency, the former head of the National Electric Company, the former deputy minister of trade in charge of trade relations with Russia, and the former director of the state-owned monopoly of tobacco. These ties were critical in affording Multigroup access to lucrative state contracts and privatization deals.

The BSP's economic policies under Videnov could be seen as "soliciting a greater direct role for the state in the economy and restoring the all-pervasive administrative control over economic agents" (Minassian 1998). One of the main channels for state intervention was continued subsidization of loss-making state-owned enterprises under the guise of industrial policy.[7] Bulgarian economist Evgeni Peev (2002: 84) described how state resources made their way to politically well-connected firms in the mid-1990s: "Bulgarian banks pumped resources from state institutions and the state budget and transferred them as loans to 'crony private' firms and state loss makers. The latter shifted financial resources through transfer pricing or other devices to 'crony private' firms with strong political connections." Similarly, one former member of the board of directors of the Bulgarian National Bank reported regular visits from members of the BSP in his office demanding increases in credits for the economy in 1994 and 1995.[8] In the spring of 1995, Minister of Industry Kliment Vulchev

---

[7] The BSP was aware that these macroeconomic policies placed great stress on the financial system. In early 1995, the Economic Analysis and Forecasting Unit within the Ministry of Finance warned the government that mixing price controls with loose money threatened to spark a financial crisis (author interviews with Gancho Ganchev, June 24, 2005, and Lyubomir Dimitrov, June 22, 2005). That the BSP knew the risks of its policy but stayed the course indicates the importance of a structural factor like political polarization. Ruling with short time horizons, the BSP took advantage of its political position while in power to deliver great benefits to concentrated groups of supporters in the state sector.

[8] Author interview with the Central Bank Official, June 20, 2005. Avramov and Guenov (1994), Avramov and Sjard (1996), and Vincelette (2001) provide penetrating analyses of the Bulgarian banking sector.

opined that state-owned firms that had borrowed money from state-owned banks did not have to worry about paying it back as state-owned firms should support one another (Schonfelder 2005: 179).[9] To compound the problem, the Videnov government indexed pensions and industrial wages to the rate of infla-tion, which put further pressure on the budget. After modest growth in 1994 and 1995, the Bulgarian economy shrank by 10 percent and 7 percent respec-tively in 1996 and 1997, largely because of inconsistent economic policies.

In sum, an old-left government in a highly polarized political system deliv-ered vast benefits to its core supporters in state-owned firms via a very gradual privatization and weak corporate governance at the expense of new private firms and the dependent sector. The Videnov period not only marked the sub-version of economic reform through policies of inconsistent gradualism but also evinced strategic weakening of the state for partisan purposes. Through the reluctance to collect taxes, introduce corporate governance, or end soft budget constraints to politically important firms, the BSP provided massive benefits to well-connected supporters but also drove the economy to collapse.

Declining Polarization, Economic Policy, and the UDF in Power, 1997–2001

In October–November 1996, with the economy spiraling out of control, voters went to the polls to elect a president. In a sign of things to come, the voters gave a resounding victory to Petar Stoyanov, an economic liberal backed by the UDF, who promised to accelerate reforms, pursue EU membership, and reverse the policies of the BSP. In a first-round election against five rivals on October 27, Stoyanov won 44 percent of the vote. In a second-round runoff a week later against a candidate backed by the BSP, Stoyanov won 60 percent of the popular vote.

Following Stoyanov's victory, the UDF called for the immediate dissolution of parliament and new elections. These demands and the disastrous economic situation encouraged mass public demonstrations in November and December of 1996. Facing broad opposition from key social groups and dissent within the BSP, Videnov resigned in late December 1996. To complicate matters, President Zhelev had been defeated in a presidential election in November 1996 and, being a lame duck, was reluctant to nominate a new prime minister. During this interregnum, the Bulgarian economy continued its slide. In January the new UDF-backed president, Petar Stoyanov, finally took office and nominated the mayor of Sofia, Stefan Sofiyanski, to head a caretaker government. The interim government had support from members of the UDF bloc in parliament, who expected to do well in the next election. With the BSP in disarray, the Sofiyanski government cleared the way for a round of economic reform.

The parliamentary elections of April 1997 produced a landslide for the UDF, which took 57 percent of the seats, giving it a solid majority for the first time.

---

[9] Author interview with Roumen Avramov, June 24, 2005.

In contrast to previous elections where it found little support in rural areas, the UDF ran well across the country and gained more votes than the BSP in each of the country's thirty-one constituencies. The BSP won only 24 percent of seats, at the time its lowest share in the postcommunist era. Electoral defeat led more reformist elements within the BSP to leave the party and form Euroleft, a new party that promised to pursue EU integration and more social democratic policies.

This period marked the beginning of a turning point in Bulgarian politics that eventually led to a consensus around the broad contours of economic policy several years later. Polarization declined following the BSP's poor showing at the polls, but the two main blocs dominated the political systems and saw each other as their main opponents.[10] The UDF sharpened its ideological focus by shedding its more centrist elements and becoming a right-wing party.[11] The BSP also underwent change. The hard left-wing of the BSP was gravely weakened following the collapse of the Videnov government, and the social democratic segment of the BSP tried to push economic policy more toward the center, but it was far from certain that this effort would bear fruit, particularly in 1997 and 1998 (Nikolov et al. 2004: 28). In this period, the UDF dominated the political scene, but the BSP still represented the major rival across the old-left–right divide.

The UDF backed standard IMF prescriptions on the economy and used industrial privatization to weaken BSP strongholds and to entrench (and often enrich) UDF supporters. This policy mix is to be expected, given the extent of political polarization and IMF constraints.

The new majority in parliament elected longtime UDF activist and former minister of finance Ivan Kostov as prime minister. The Kostov government quickly passed a "Declaration of National Salvation" based on seven policy pledges, including, most prominently, the introduction of a currency board backed by the IMF. Other measures of the declaration obliged signators to distribute the cost of reform more equitably, to speed land restitution, to fight corruption, to accelerate lustration of Bulgarian Communist Party officials, and to promote EU and NATO membership. In a rare display of political unity, the parliament passed five of the seven measures with more than 75 percent support.

---

[10] Author interviews with UDF deputy prime minister Alexander Bozhkov, former BSP minister of foreign trade Attanas Paparizov, and BSP adviser to the president Dobrin Kanev in June 2005 indicated that all viewed the opposite camp in the UDF and the BSP as their main political opponents at this time and advocated policies based on these assumptions.

[11] As one observer noted, "The campaign produced contrasting results in the two major camps. While BSP was wracked by internal conflicts and plagued by infighting, the opposition parties continued to consolidate." "Bulgaria," *East European Constitutional Review* 6 (2–3, 1997), http://www1.law.nyu.edu/eecr/vol6num2/constitutionwatch/bulgaria.html. Similarly, a Bulgarian newspaper noted in April 1997: "The UDF not only mobilized its units, but also consolidated itself as a right-wing party/organization with an ideological platform" (*Capital*, April 24, 1997).

Under the close scrutiny of the IMF, the government established a currency board in July 1997 that fixed the price of the Bulgarian lev to the Deutschmark and served as the centerpiece of the government's economic policy. Currency boards fix the exchange rate of the domestic currency to a specified international currency. The exchange rate is supported by foreign currency reserves equal to the size of the money supply. In principle, money can be supplied only by transferring foreign currency reserves into the domestic currency. The political consensus in parliament bolstered confidence in the currency board and discouraged speculation against the lev. Inflation fell dramatically, which led to a reduction in interest rates and a drop in the fiscal deficit to manageable levels.[12]

The Kostov government pushed forward on privatization and largely met IMF requirements on this front (Stanchev 2004). Most importantly, the government and its successor privatized to foreign companies the vast majority of failing state banks and closed a number of insolvent banks. These steps helped to solidify the financial system and break close ties between the commercial banks and the public treasury.

The government's program of rapid industrial privatization produced far more equivocal results. By the end of 1999, some of the largest companies in Bulgaria, such as Balkan Airlines, Yambolen, OtK-Kardjali, Kremikovtsi, Neftochim, Petrol, and Himko, underwent privatization (EBRD 1999: 202; Peev 2002: 76). By the end of 2000, the government had sold almost 78 percent of state-owned assets (excluding infrastructure) to the public (EBRD 2001: 126). Yet the privatization program was perceived by many to be highly politicized, as would be expected given the bipolar conflict between the liberal UDF and the BSP. For example, as an opposition party, the UDF criticized management-employee buyouts (MEBOs) that allowed enterprise insiders (typically sympathetic to the BSP) to gain control over the enterprise at little cost with no infusion of capital. But as a governing party, the UDF embraced MEBOs that relied on new management teams that were reportedly sympathetic to the UDF. The UDF sponsored two amendments to the Privatization Act that lowered the percentage of workers needed to approve of privatization and allowed managers to use "investment coupons" that were essentially soft loans to purchase firms. Most privatizations conducted under the UDF were MEBOs, and there is a widespread view, although it is difficult to verify, that most of the new management teams were friendly to the UDF (Nikolov 2004). One former UDF deputy prime minister noted that "in the regions UDF leaders likely transferred firms to their supporters," and he estimated that this happened in "maybe one-quarter of the cases."[13] Other estimates were much higher. Another noted

---

[12] In September 1998 the Kostov government accepted the obligations of IMF Article VIII, which requires countries to liberalize their current account. Shortly thereafter, it raised prices for energy and for central heating in the fall of 1998 and for household electricity in early 1999 (EBRD 1999: 202).

[13] Author interview with Aleksander Bozhkov, June 23, 2005.

that "in the regions the UDF's privatization policy was a mirror image to the BSP's privatization policy." As Bulgarian economist Evgeni Peev (2002: 83) noted, "In 1998–99, the government preferred insider privatization, due to the controversial ties between policy makers and managers, a large number of privatizations were carried out through management and employee buyouts." In one of the most comprehensive studies of the topic, six Bulgarian social scientists (Nikolov et al. 2004: 36) observed:

> During the UDF rule the abuse of the dysfunctional institutional arrangements in the area of commercial privatization likely reached its peak. In this period, commercial privatization developed into an utterly clientelist system in which the ruling elite sought to provide unjustified benefits to its key political friends. But also in other areas of public regulation, such as public procurement, business permits, etc., the government openly favored its cronies. In addition, the government also reproduced the clientelistic pattern of recruitment of civil servants and party activists in the public administration.

One high-ranking UDF official is noted to have said that providing benefits to its loyalists through privatization was the only way that the party could repay its supporters because it had no other resources (Nikolov et al. 2004: 36).[14]

In some cases, the Kostov government attempted to curb the tight relations between the industrial conglomerates and the central government that emerged under the BSP. Most prominently, it took on Multigroup. Relying heavily on pressure from the Interior Ministry, the government eliminated Multigroup's privileged position as Gazprom's sole purveyor of gas in Bulgaria. The Interior Ministry then publicly accused Multigroup of evading custom duties and taxes on sugar imports and soon removed these privileges as well. The government further pressured Multigroup by exercising its ownership stakes in some of Multigroup's most prized holdings and putting these shares up for sale through privatization. In addition, the parliament made public a list of "credit millionaires," individuals who received billions of leva from various banks and never returned the money. Soon after parliament banned from entering its building five "parliamentary experts" whose names appeared on the list, including Ilya Pavlov, the head of Multigroup and an adviser to MDF leader Ahmed Dogan.[15] This comprehensive approach bore fruit. As one Bulgarian newspaper noted: "One of the reasons for Kostov's victory over Multigroup was the pressure put by state institutions on all fronts" (Nikolov 1999). These policies had both political and economic goals as they helped to reduce drains

---

[14] Bojicic-Dzelilovic and Bojkov (2004: 14) observed: "It is precisely because of their obvious abuse by the Socialists that the UDF undertook to replace enterprise management teams when it returned to power. Once a critical number of friendly managers were appointed, however, the MEBO mechanism was embraced as necessary for speeding up the privatization process, justified by the lack of foreign interest." This view was also held by Krassen Stanchev, author interview, June 24, 2005.

[15] "Bulgaria," *East European Constitutional Review* 7 (1, 1998), http://www1.law.nyu.edu/eecr/vol7num1/.

on the public fisc, while also undercutting business groups that had grown wealthy under the BSP.[16]

The government also took several steps to limit the scope of organized crime. Reportedly, the government was successful in relicensing insurance companies that often acted as fronts for organized crime and extortion groups (Schonfelder 2005: 199). After making legislative changes to the Insurance Law, four of the largest insurance companies were forced out of business (Nikolov 1999). The Kostov administration created a Unified Revenue Agency within the central government that consolidated the collection of taxes under a single roof and transferred control over borders from the Interior Ministry to the army units specifically trained in preventing smuggling (Fish and Brooks 2000).[17] These changes in policy were significant first steps in promoting institutional reforms in Bulgaria.

Some observers noted that EU accession was "only a slim prospect in the beginning of 1999" (Grozev 2000). Indeed, Azmanova (2000) cited a survey from 2000 in which only 7 percent of respondents thought it was "very likely" and only 29 percent of respondents thought it was "somewhat likely" that Bulgaria would become a full member of the EU within five years. Nonetheless, the Kostov government set Bulgaria on the path toward membership in the European Union and NATO. The government prided itself on the UDF's pro-European orientation in contrast to what it portrayed as the BSP's ambiguous stance toward Europe. These efforts paid off as in December 1999 Bulgaria was invited to start EU accession negotiations. Within eighteen months it had closed eleven chapters of the *acquis communitaire*, which outlines the legal and regulatory framework for membership in the European Union (EBRD 2001: 126). This task was made relatively easy, as all major parties were supporters of European integration.

These new institutional reforms and economic policies contributed to an economic turnaround. Growth rates averaged 3.9 percent between 1998 and 2002. In addition, inflation rates fell from more than 300 percent in 1997 to less than 22 percent in 1998 and remained in single digits, thanks in large part to a currency board arrangement backed by the IMF. The economic rebound would likely have been stronger but for factors beyond the control of the government, such as the financial crisis in Russia in 1998, the conflict over Kosovo in 1999, and a slowdown in many EU economies.

Bulgaria's economic turnaround in this period was impressive, but many problems remained. Unemployment rates, which peaked at about 20 percent

---

[16] Despite having its wings clipped, Multigroup and other business groups that profited under the BSP did not disappear. Indeed, the UDF tried to form its own business group, Olymp, but experienced only limited success (Bojicic-Dzelilovic and Bojkov 2004).

[17] Fish and Brooks (2000) noted that UDF interior minister Bogimil Bonev, himself quite a popular figure at the time, invited leaders of some of the main criminal organizations in Bulgaria to his office and threatened them with unpleasant consequences should they not move into more legitimate businesses. Schonfelder (2005: 199) cites the evolution of the business group TIM as evidence.

in 2001, were a serious concern. Despite a drop in organized crime, corruption continued to be pervasive, as many high-ranking political figures maintained close ties with business.[18] Indeed, the whiff of corruption was never far from the UDF. Government spokesman Mihail Mihailov, Minister of Industry Edith Getova, and lead EU negotiator and Kostov confidant Alexander Bozhkov were forced to resign in 2000 under charges of corruption (Nedyalkova 2001). Even the prime minister's wife was tainted. Elena Kostova admitted that a foundation that she headed had accepted an $80,000 donation from Grigory Luchansky, a Russian-born businessman with reported ties to organized crime. These unseemly problems undercut many of the economic gains that occurred on the watch of the Kostov government in the eyes of many Bulgarians.

An Emerging Consensus on Economic Policy

Parliamentary elections in June 2001 provided further evidence of a decline in political polarization and a new stability in economic policy. The campaign saw the rise of a challenger to the UDF and the BSP. The National Movement Simeon II (NSM SII), a personalist party centered on the former tsar of Bulgaria, Simeon Saxe-Coburg Gotha, formed just eleven weeks before the election but benefited from the great name recognition of its founder. Tsar Simeon initially took power in Bulgaria upon the death of his father in 1943, but was forced into exile three years later at the age of nine. Simeon Saxe-Coburg Gotha studied in Egypt and the United States, lived in Spain for many years, and returned to Bulgaria in 1996. The NSM SII ran on a vaguely center-right platform that emphasized economic issues, while promising to abandon political partisanship, unite the country, and bring a new ethics to politics (Barany 2002: 147). According to one observer, Simeon's platform "had only three planks: to reverse the negative aspects of economic reform within 800 days, to introduce a higher morality into politics, and to involve a greater number of women in public life."[19]

Moreover, in contrast to previous elections, the campaign featured a high degree of consensus among the major contenders for power. Harper (2003: 327) noted that "the campaign platforms of the three leading contenders, the UDF, the BSP's Coalition for Bulgaria, and the NSM SII, differed little on major goals. All emphasized continuing reform, economic growth, and EU membership, and unlike previous elections, all major contenders advocated NATO membership." Indeed, one observer noted that the "communist/anticommunist rhetoric which until recently dominated public discourse seems exhausted," adding that "the NSM's victory eliminates the risk of a reversal of the radical reforms launched by the previous government" (Peeva 2001). Despite the

---

[18] For a list of some of the better-known political figures and their economic holdings, see "In Search of the New Premianov," *Capital*, May 8, 1997.

[19] "Bulgaria," *East European Constitutional Review* 10(2–3, 2001), http://www1.law.nyu.edu/eecr/vol10num4/index.html.

change in power from the UDF to the NSM SII, there was far greater consensus among major political parties in comparison to the period of highly polarized politics from 1990 to 1996 and even the somewhat less polarized period of 1997–2000.

Playing effectively on dissatisfaction with the two main political parties, the ex-tsar and his movement won 43 percent of the vote, which translated into 120 of the 240 seats in parliament. The UDF fared poorly, garnering only 19 percent of the popular vote and 51 seats, while the BSP and its allies, who had formed the Coalition for Bulgaria in the run-up to the election, fared still worse and gained 17 percent of the vote and 48 seats. The NSM SII formed a coalition government with the Movement for Reforms and Freedom, a party that held 21 seats. The new government had a distinctly Western profile, as many members had been trained in Europe and most had little political experience in Bulgaria. Indeed, for the first time since 1989 the new government did not have a single minister with previous government experience (Peeva 2001).

Still constrained by the currency board, the NSM SII government largely continued the policies of its predecessor, with some exceptions. The government emphasized gaining accession to the EU, continued economic liberalization, and adherence to the currency board and other IMF conditions. It also amended the Privatization Act to curtail MEBOs, but on balance "there was a remarkable degree of continuity in the policy course after the 2001 government changeover" (Nikolov et al. 2004: 36). As before, charges of corruption over privatization deals swirled around the government, but the period saw the maintenance of economic growth, balanced budgets, and low inflation.[20] The Simeon government oversaw a drop in unemployment from 19 percent in 2001 to 11.5 percent in 2005. In addition, Transparency International scores for perceptions of corruption improved modestly from 3.5 in 2000 to 4.1 in 2004.

These gains marked the emerging consensus over economic policy because the UDF and the NSM SII, the two largest center-right parties, pursued relatively similar policies, with some exceptions. Both favored cutting state spending as a share of GDP and reducing the public sector's role in pension provision, but the former was more aggressive about cutting taxes on corporations and personal income and privatizing public utilities (*Capital*, May 20, 2005). Both have also been dogged by charges of corruption, particularly on issues of privatization.

In addition, the BSP continued to evolve in the direction of more social democratic policies in the wake of successive poor showings in parliamentary elections. The election of Georgi Parvanov to the presidency in November 2001 played a key role in marginalizing more hard-line elements within the

---

[20] One of the NSM SII government's first acts was to reduce the taxation on the "gaming industry," which many saw as a political favor to organized crime groups that may have provided campaign funds for the NSM SII (author interview with Krassen Stanchev, June 24, 2005, and Dimitar Dimitrov, June 25, 2006).

party. Parvanov became one of the most popular politicians in Bulgaria and took the BSP in a far more moderate direction. With Parvanov's backing, the BSP elected Sergey Stanishev, a thirty-nine-year-old party activist, as its leader in 2001. The BSP embraced membership in the European Union; accepted the currency board; recognized the dangers of loose fiscal policy; and, after months of intense internal debate, ultimately backed NATO membership in 2002. After a decade of rejection, the BSP finally gained admittance to the Socialist International.

Yet, in this period the BSP retained a distinct ideological profile that was further left than social democratic ex-communist parties in Poland, Hungary, or Slovenia. The top spots in the BSP party list from 2005 parliamentary elections included many figures prominent in previous BSP governments, including former foreign minister Georgi Pirinski, former trade minister Attanas Paparizov, former head of privatization Rumen Genchev, and others.[21] In addition, the BSP continued to be more partial to industrial policy, indexing salaries, and supporting rural regions than its social democratic counterparts (*Capital*, May 20, 2005). Dobrin Kanev (2002: 17) captured the position of the BSP in 2002 quite well:

The process of transformation of the Bulgarian successor party is not completed. There is no evidence at all that it is still a neocommunist party, an extreme left party, or an authoritarian socialist party. On the other hand it is hard to argue that the BSP is already a full-fledged social democratic party.... If we should imagine that the road from a communist party to a social democratic party is a continuum we can state that the BSP is much nearer to social democracy than to communism or authoritarian socialism.

The business community in Bulgaria appears to have recognized the emerging consensus over economic policy after 1996, and especially after 2001. The Bulgarian State Institute for Statistics conducts monthly surveys of business people in service, industry, construction, and retail trade and creates a weighted index of the quality of the business climate based on a five-point scale. In reviewing the trends from the period January 1997 until May 2005 in Figure 8.1, one is struck by the consistently positive balance beginning in the second half of 1997 and the relatively small variance over time. These indicate a stable and improving business climate – a result consistent with the declining political polarization during this period.

Conclusion

Bulgaria presents a challenge for several prominent theories of economic and institutional reform. For those who argue that democratic governments with high rates of turnovers are important for economic liberalization, Bulgaria should be a success. To the surprise of many, Bulgaria created a relatively

---

[21] Stanishev represents the duality of the BSP well. He is presented as the face of a generation and is often depicted riding a motorcycle, but his father was a long-serving member of the Politburo.

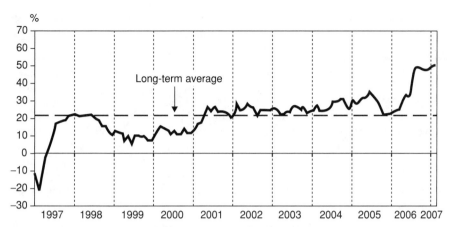

FIGURE 8.1. Business climate in Bulgaria. Percentage of positive responses to evaluations of the business climate in Bulgaria is based on a five-point scale. *Source:* Bulgarian National Institute of Statistics.

robust democracy as competitors transferred power through free and fair elections in 1991, 1994, 1997, 2001, and 2005. Similarly, government turnover was high in the early years of transition, which some argue has been an important determinant of economic reform. Five governments came to power in the first six years of the transformation in Bulgaria alone, but economic reform stumbled badly.[22] Bulgaria is relatively close to the powerful economies of the European Union, which could have been expected to serve as a motor for economic and institutional reform, but it did not do so until very late in the decade. For those who argue that geography is central to postcommunist reform, again Bulgaria should have demonstrated economic and institutional dynamism in the 1990s.

Yet none of these arguments capture the distinct phases of transformation in Bulgaria. In contrast, the argument made here comports well with variation in policy in Bulgaria. High levels of political polarization marked the first six years of the transformation as the liberal UDF and the old-left BSP had roughly equal power and presented starkly different futures for Bulgaria. This political polarization contributed to the subversion of economic and institutional reform and played no small role in the financial collapse of 1996. Only with an economic crisis that splintered the BSP and led to a UDF landslide in the April 1997 election did Bulgaria begin to introduce a more rapid, but still inconsistent, set of policies to address the crisis. Following the emergence of a broad

[22] No less surprising, Bulgaria has avoided ethnic conflict. As late as 1989, the Bulgarian government repressed ethnic minorities and conducted mass relocations of the Turkish minority, but it experienced little ethnic violence, and the main political representative of the Turkish minority, the Movement for Rights and Freedom (MRF), has achieved representation in every parliament and provided critical support for several coalition governments.

consensus on economic reform after elections in 2001, economic and institutional reforms improved dramatically. Stone (2002: 230) captures this logic well:

The BSP was much further Left than the postcommunist parties of Poland and Hungary, and its major economic policy objective was to prevent dramatic restructuring of Bulgarian industry. It was not until the financial crisis of 1996 that Bulgaria was finally able to break the cycle of partial reform. The crisis brought down the Videnov government and destroyed the BSP's electoral base. It galvanized Bulgarian elites to rally around economic reform, making it possible in 1997 – indeed, almost inevitable – for the parliament to adopt a highly restrictive currency board arrangement. The crisis allowed Ivan Kostov to build the UDF into a new political party, which for the first time had a unified program and internal discipline, which made it possible to implement politically costly reforms.

The timing of Bulgaria's turnaround is strong evidence of the importance of declining political polarization for economic reform.

Undoubtedly the currency board and IMF support played a crucial role in reversing Bulgaria's economic decline, but this policy became possible only with the resounding electoral victory of the UDF and subsequent reduction in polarization (Stone 2002). Four previous attempts by the IMF and Bulgarian governments from 1990 to 1996 failed to curb inflation and runaway budget deficits. Bulgaria's inheritance of a social structure with a strong rural sector and a weak middle class impeded progress in economic reform, but again this approach provides little leverage to account for why Bulgaria's economy improved so dramatically after 1997 (Kitschelt et al. 1999). Fish and Brooks (2000) attribute Bulgaria's turnaround to the consolidation of the UDF as a political party, but the splintering of the UDF into three rival factions in 1999 and 2000 seems at odds with this argument. The role of the EU in providing incentives certainly facilitated reform, but the EU was hesitant about offering Bulgaria membership, particularly before 1997 (Nikolov et al. 2004; Grozev 2000). The EU played a much more important role after 1999 when Bulgaria had already made significant changes in economic policy. The balance of power between partisan elites is not the only influence on policy choice, but changes in the extent of political polarization between old-left and liberal camps comport well with the evolution of economic and institutional reform in Bulgaria.

9

Poland

Robust Democracy and Rapid Reform

> But if Warsaw rose from the ashes of the War it has also been reborn from the drabness of the Stalinist era. After the fall of the Communist regime, winds of change swept through the city. New shops, hotels and a cheerful air have transformed Warsaw. Old buildings have been cleaned, and elegant boutiques are springing up. The best symbol of this rebirth is the city's tallest building, at the end of Nowy Swiat, which was once the Communist Central Committee seat and is now an expression of Poland's wanton capitalism – the stock exchange.
>
> *Hindu Business Line*, March 11, 2005

Poland provides a clear example of how robust democracy and low levels of political polarization can promote rapid economic and institutional reform. In the 1990s, a social democratic ex-communist party committed to building a market economy with a generous welfare state and a fractious liberal camp of parties committed to building a market economy with a smaller welfare state competed for power. This arrangement of political forces and institutions suggests that Poland should have experienced rapid economic and institutional reform, relatively consistent reforms, a burgeoning new private sector, and generous social welfare programs.

These expectations have largely been borne out. With little evidence of deep polarization on economic issues across the old-left–right divide, successive governments in Poland had weak incentives to conduct fire-sale privatizations or grant the types of massive tax breaks characteristic of right governments in far more polarized Russia under Yeltsin. The privatization of large industrial enterprises was conducted at a moderate pace under conditions of comparatively good corporate governance. This appears to have limited the extent of asset-stripping in large firms relative to other countries in the region and helped the government manage the decline of the state-owned industrial sector far better than in more polarized settings.

In addition, the commitment to a market economy generated a dynamic investment environment for the new private sector. The new private sector was the source of much of Poland's growth and provided a key constituency in support of liberal political parties (Jackson et al. 2003, 2005). The rapid economic growth spurred in part by the development of the new private sector helped to finance fairly generous transfers to the dependent sector of the population. Pensions in Poland in the early 1990s averaged around 13 percent of GDP, more than twice as high as in Russia (EBRD 1996). As expected, Poland's low level of political polarization and consistently promarket governments led to rapid liberalization, consistent reform, and strong economic performance relative to other countries in the region.

This is not to argue that the transformation of the economy in Poland has proceeded free of corruption, scandal, and fraud; that lobbying by powerful interests is not pervasive; or that the social costs of transformation have not been high. The wealthy in Poland often grew rich off the same type of arbitrage opportunities between state and market, seizure of state assets, and close ties with state officials found in other countries (Staniszkis 1991; Schoenmann 2005; Ganev 2006). And certainly more could be done to improve the quality of governance in Poland and bolster the performance of lagging economic regions and sectors. It is only to argue that the political environment, in particular the relatively low level of political polarization and robust democracy, has been more conducive to economic and institutional reform than elsewhere in the region.[1]

Background

Few predicted Poland's successful transformation in the 1990s, and it is easy to see why. It began the transformation with a large foreign debt, an industrial structure poorly suited for a market economy, and an agriculture sector heavily populated by very small farms. Moreover, the country's repeated failures in economic reforms under the command economy did not bode well for future success. The list of economic reforms gone awry was long and inglorious (Brus 1973; Terry 1989). Przeworski (2001: 105) notes that "the term reform itself has been worn out by the entire history of the People's Republic (of Poland)." Moreover, as the first country to introduce economic reforms in the region, Poland could not rely on the experience of its neighbors to guide policy. Finally, the key supporters of the Solidarity-led government were industrial workers who were likely to bear the brunt of economic reforms introduced by the government.[2]

---

[1] Across the region, the new wealthy tend to have close ties to the development, transit, or sale of energy. One might say that the aroma of oil pervades the new wealthy in the region.

[2] The introduction of economic reforms in January 1990 immediately removed the generous concessions earned by industrial workers at the Roundtable Talks in April 1989 (Balcerowicz 1995: 316).

Poland began the transformation with a private sector far larger than most other countries in the region, but its role in helping to build a market economy is debatable. In 1989 the private sector produced 19 percent of GDP in Poland, but 11 percent of this figure came from agriculture, in particular small and inefficient private farms. As these private farms bought their inputs from state monopolies, sold their output through state monopsonies, and transported their goods through state networks, these ostensibly private farms were very constrained by the state. In addition, private farmers were reluctant supporters of economic reforms at best, given the likelihood of increased competition from abroad. The main political vehicle for small farmers, the United Peasants Party, or PSL, was unenthusiastic about many aspects of market reforms. Finally, at the start of the transformation, only about 8 percent of GDP in Poland was produced through the nonagricultural private sector. Thus, it is easy to overstate the importance of the indigenous private sector under the command economy as a predictor of the success of economic reform.[3] Rapacki (2001: 129) noted that "with the benefit of hindsight we can say that this asset was more a figment of our imagination than real." An early study (Kondratowicz and Maciejewski 1994: 11) colorfully noted that private-sector workers under the command economy could "hardly be viewed as a group of 'Schumpeterian entrepreneurs' who survived the communist night in order to spread their wings at the dawn of the market society."

The Political Spectrum: The Centrist Parties

One advantage that Poland had was the relative consensus in the direction of economic reform demonstrated by the major political parties. Most importantly, by the start of the transformation, the successor to the Polish Communist Party, SdRP, and its electoral vehicle, the Democratic Left Alliance, or SLD, had made considerable progress toward becoming a social democratic party on the model of the Labor Party in Britain and was largely supportive of a market economy.[4] Throughout the transformation, the SdRP supported market reforms, albeit with a greater tolerance for budget deficits and a slower pace for industrial privatization than did more right-wing parties. This evolution had been a long time in coming. After taking power in 1947, the main communist party in Poland, the Polish United Workers' Party (PZPR), had great difficulty overcoming the perception that it was under the thumb of the CPSU. Moreover,

---

[3] It is perhaps helpful to note that the Czech Republic and Slovakia had much smaller private-sector economies before 1989 and have experienced economic reform trajectories similar to Poland's. Arguments linking the success of economic reform in Poland to the autonomy and power of the Catholic Church before 1989 face a similar problem. Hungary, the Czech Republic, and Slovakia had far weaker national churches, but similar economic reform outcomes in broader comparative perspective.

[4] The SdRP allied with the main official trade union from the communist era, the OPZZ, an organization that largely retained its resources and networks after 1989.

it had had few answers to revive Poland's economy (Rothschild 1989).[5] Economic crises helped to spark popular uprisings of varying strength in 1953, 1956, 1968, 1970, 1976, and (most importantly) 1980–1981. The imposition of martial law in 1981 significantly weakened the reformist elements of the party, who were discredited by their association with the military government (Korbonski 1989). With the economy unraveling in the late 1980s, the PZPR liberalized prices far beyond its past halfhearted attempts in a last-ditch effort to right the economy. In addition, it began a privatization program that allowed existing nomenklatura to take control and ownership of some of the choice assets of the Polish economy, especially in the financial sector (Zubek 1995: 276; Lewandowski 1997). It also entered into negotiations with the Solidarity labor movement in the spring of 1989, in part to hammer out the rules for sharing power and holding elections. To the surprise of many, the Polish United Workers' Party lost every seat possible in parliamentary elections in 1989.

Following this ignominious defeat, the party began to change its spots by renaming itself the Social Democratic Party of Poland to emphasize its evolution, electing a new slate of younger leaders, dismissing the most hard-line and discredited members of the party's elite, and crafting a far more centrist position on economic reform. Its 1990–1991 party program argued that by "voting for the SdRP you will support people who want radical reforms, but want to implement them with minimal social costs." To a large extent the party made good on this pledge. Grzymala-Busse's (2002: 160) close analysis of the SdRP platforms reveals that the party "consistently pursued a social democratic identity from the start." Kitschelt et al.'s (1999) four-country study of party platforms places Poland's ex-communists far closer to the center of the economic spectrum than the Bulgarian Socialist Party. Stone (2002: 111) notes that "during its long period in the political wilderness the SdRP had been compelled to reinvent itself as a moderate, responsible party of the left in order to gain respectability." Jackson et al. (2005: 43) note that the SLD consistently evolved to a more liberal position, and by the 2001 parliamentary elections it was "openly advocating support for new and small business and called one part of its platform 'Entrepreneurism Above All.'" This evolution of the SdRP into a stable social democratic party has been one of the greatest surprises of the political transition in Poland.

Somewhat greater opposition to economic liberalization came from the United Peasant Party (PSL), a holdover from the pre-1989 period that advocated subsidies for farmers and state-owned enterprises and limits on imports. In some respects, the PSL can be characterized as an old-left party, given its birth in the communist period, opposition to trade liberalization, and support for generous subsidies to agriculture. However, the PSL also was only a minor party before 1989 but helped bring down the last communist government by

---

[5] Korbonski (1984: 55) notes laconically, "except for a very brief period in 1956–57, the Communist regime did not succeed in generating popular acceptance and legitimacy and by the end of the 1960s it had lost a good deal of support among its traditional followers."

unexpectedly siding with Solidarity in 1989. It focused primarily on narrow sectarian interests of Poland's small farmers and devoted less attention to other economic interests. In addition, it was a strong proponent of private ownership of land, which makes it an odd fit for the old-left camp.[6] The Union of Labor, an anticommunist party that emerged out of the Solidarity labor movement, advocated old-left positions on economic transformation in the country but failed to attract great support save for gaining 8 percent of the seats in the 1993 parliamentary election. It ultimately merged with the ex-communist led Democratic Left Alliance in 2001. To a large extent, the old-left category was weak or vacant for much of the transformation.

Post-Solidarity Right Parties

It is more challenging to capture the changing cast of right-wing parties in Poland that seemed to enter and exit the political stage with alarming frequency. Many parties were rooted in the broad anticommunist alliance under the Solidarity umbrella that drove the PZPR from power in 1989. Having obtained power in parliamentary elections in 1989, however, differences in style, substance, and leadership began to emerge among the post-Solidarity parties. Indeed, high levels of fragmentation among right-wing parties significantly reduced the electoral clout of the camp in parliamentary elections in 1991 and 1993. Tucker (2006) characterizes the major post-Solidarity parties in two broad types. One group was the "consistently liberalizing" parties, such as the Democratic Union and the Congress of Liberal Democrats – two parties that subsequently merged to form the Freedom Union (UW). To this group could be added the Christian Democrats and the Center Alliance. A second group was the "populist leaning" parties, such as the Non-Party Movement in Support of Reforms that backed Lech Walesa and the Solidarity Electoral Alliance (AWS). To this group could be added the Polish League of Families and Law and Justice, which emerged late in the transformation. Despite differences of emphasis in speed and tactics, the economic policies of these parties would fit, broadly speaking, within the right and center-right of the political spectrum found in many countries with market economies.

Most importantly, the right-wing parties to a greater or lesser degree backed the broad outlines of a market economy as a goal. Moreover, while there was considerable party switching among right-wing parties, there was little party switching between the right and the centrist parties of the SdRP or PSL. Similarly, there is evidence voters rarely switched across the partisan divide. For example, Bell (2001: 173) notes a survey in which only 1 percent of AWS supporters said that they would vote for the SLD if they could not vote for the AWS; while no SLD supporters said that they would vote for AWS if they

---

[6] Coding the PSL as an old-left party has little impact on the substantive results. Osborn (2000) treats the PSL as a "populist" party, while Tucker (2006) removes it from his analysis on the grounds that it is primarily a party for sectarian interests.

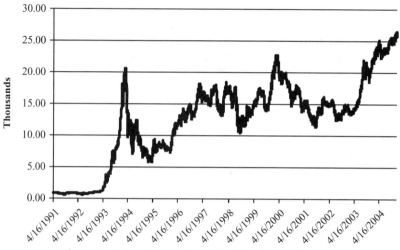

FIGURE 9.1 The main index of the Warsaw Stock Exchange, 1991–2004.

could not vote for their preferred party. This "thick line" between the parties is surprising, given the considerable overlap in economic policy positions among some of the post-Solidarity parties and the SLD (Zubek 1995: 281).[7]

Evidence from the Warsaw Stock Exchange provided in Figure 9.1 also indicates that market players recognized the general consensus among the major economic policies on political and economic reform. If in polarized Russia under President Yeltsin financial markets were quite volatile around elections, in much less polarized Poland they were not. When the SLD won elections on September 19, 1993, the stock market responded with several days of speculative activity, which pushed the index down by about 10 percent, but quickly rebounded to previous levels. Within two weeks of the election of the ex-communists to power, the Warsaw Stock Exchange reached a new high. Subsequent elections on September 21, 1997, and September 9, 2001, were met with a shrug by market players. In the three days following the 1997 election, the market gained 0.3 percent before losing 0.1 percent and 0.9 percent. Similarly, following elections in September 2001, the market fell by 1.4 percent and 1.8 percent before gaining 0.4 percent. For some perspective, the daily volatility on the Warsaw Stock Exchange from its opening on April 16, 1991, until the end of 2004 averaged 1.5 percent.

Successive governments in Poland exhibited a far greater consensus for economic and institutional reform than we find in more polarized political systems. Kitschelt et al. (1999: 251) present evidence from a survey of politicians in Poland and Bulgaria that suggests that the perceived preferences of the main ex-communist and right parties are much closer in Poland. When politicians in each country were asked to rate the parties on a twenty-point left–right scale in

---

[7] Bell (2001: 11) notes that "overall, political preferences have been surprisingly stable and radical politicians mostly marginalized."

the dimension of market economics/privatization, the difference between the major right and the former communist party in Bulgaria was 11.9, while in Poland it was only 6.6.[8] These differences were borne out on the floor of the Sejm as well. Balcerowicz (1995: 303) noted that, during the critical debates on the introduction of economic reform by the new Solidarity government in 1989 and 1990, "the distinction between the ruling parties and the opposition was not pronounced as far as the attitude to the economic program was concerned." In the early years of the transformation, the cleavage between these two camps was not primarily based in policy as the policy preferences of the Democratic Union and the SdRP had much in common. Zubek (1995: 294) notes that the two parties not only shared roots in the reformist wing of the PZPR that split from the party in the early 1980s; they also shared "tremendous ideological and programmatic similarities." The cleavage between these two major parties was largely rooted in the bitter political struggles of the 1980s, with differences in economic policies playing a lesser role. In sum, party competition among the major parties on economic policy remained in a much narrower bound than in more polarized countries such as Russia or Bulgaria.

Low Polarization and Rapid Reform

Poland's first postcommunist government was headed by Tadeusz Mazowiecki, but economic policy was largely delegated to his new minister of economics, Leszek Balcerowicz, who introduced sweeping economic reforms in the early 1990s that liberalized foreign and domestic trade, cut subsidies to industry and agriculture, and removed many obstacles to the creation of small businesses (Johnson and Kowalska 1994).[9] Inflation dropped sharply, but the economy continued to decline in 1990 and 1991 far more quickly than anticipated, and popular support for the program dropped dramatically as unemployment increased (Przeworski 2001).[10] This steep economic decline, however, was followed by positive growth in 1992 and a surge in output that lasted five years.

The remnants of the Solidarity-led government, however, failed to reap political rewards for the turnaround. The government of Prime Minister Hanna Suchocka fell because of infighting among the former Solidarity alliance in 1993 and was replaced in a close vote by a coalition of parties largely represented by the ex-communist Democratic Left Alliance and the Polish Peasant Party (Ekiert and Kubik 1998, 1999).[11] Despite some moderate concerns over the reversal of economic reform, the coalition government kept the reforms largely on track.

---

[8] More specifically, the respondents in Bulgaria gave the BSP 16.8 and the SDS a 4.9, whereas their compatriots in Poland gave the SLD a 13.7 and the Democratic Union a 7.1.

[9] For good descriptions of the period, see Dabrowski et al. (1993), Balcerowicz (1995), Stone (2002), and Johnson and Kowalska (1994).

[10] Inflation fell sharply from 1989 to 1990 but remained a stubborn problem throughout the first half of the 1990s.

[11] A new electoral law raised the threshold for gaining entrance to the parliament and punished the small, fragmented parties of the right wing.

The coalition's deputy premier and finance minister, Gregorz Kolodko, was critical of previous governments for overshooting the fiscal policy and failing to stimulate growth, but while his "Strategy for Poland" created a greater role for the state in the economy, it also continued to emphasize movement toward a market economy.[12] At a meeting of IMF officials in June 1996, Kolodko (2000: 26–27) described the government's policy stance in relation to its predecessor's policy: "It does not involve any change in target model, nor in transition speed, nor in fiscal stance.... The target remains a modern capitalism mixed economy, though with emphasis on equality and partnership between private and public sectors."[13] Indeed, while large-scale privatization slowed somewhat and agriculture received greater protection (thanks to the PSL), the coalition government did not deviate significantly from the policies of the post-Solidarity governments. Jackson et al. (2005: 43) noted that the coalition government of the PSL and SLD "altered the pace and direction of the reforms, but did not alter the basic commitment to a market economy."[14] This continuity in economic policy and continued strong economic performance helped the SLD candidate Aleksander Kwasniewski to victory in presidential elections over the incumbent and legend of the Solidarity era, Lech Walesa, in 1995.

In parliamentary elections in 1997, the SLD was rewarded at the polls with an increase of 700,000 more votes than it received in the previous election. However, this was not enough to overcome the Solidarity Electoral Alliance (AWS), a broad and unwieldy coalition of liberal and populist parties with roots in Solidarity. The AWS, whose policies were, in some respects, less supportive of the market than its centrist predecessors, formed a coalition government with the Freedom Union, a party with impeccable promarket credentials headed by former minister of economics Leszek Balcerowicz. The government managed to introduce difficult economic reforms in pensions, health care, and education (Nelson 2001; Haggard and Kaufman 2008), but political infighting and a series of high-profile corruption scandals drastically reduced the popularity of the alliance. Indeed, the main remnant of the AWS failed to obtain a single seat in the new parliament.

In parliamentary elections in 2001, power swung back to the center as the SLD returned to power. The Democratic Left Alliance, which formed a preelectoral alliance with the Union of Labor, won 41 percent of the popular vote and ultimately formed a coalition government with the PSL.[15] The main task of the coalition government was to prepare the country for accession into

---

[12] Kolodko was equally critical of attempts at gradual economic reform. Kolodko, an economist without party affiliation, replaced Marek Borowski as deputy minister in charge of economics.

[13] Stone (2002: 111) observed that the strategy for Poland "tended toward policy continuity rather than change."

[14] See also Bell (2001: 36).

[15] This alliance gave further credence to the normalization of the SLD. Despite fairly similar policies, the UP had limited cooperation with the SLD in the past because of the latter's ties to the old regime.

the European Union, and, in an irony lost on few observers, it was the ex-communist SLD that ultimately brought Poland into the European Union in May 2004.

Despite the frequent turnovers in government and the alternation in power of center and center-right political factions, the broad thrust of economic policy in Poland throughout the past decade and a half was in favor of a market economy. By the mid-1990s, when parliament finally passed a plan to privatize many of the largest and most politically sensitive firms, debates about economic policy were well within the framework that one would find in a typical middle-income market economy.

Industrial Privatization and Consistent Reform

The political incentives to conduct rapid giveaway privatization in Poland appeared weaker than in more polarized countries in the region. If in Russia the reformist government under Yegor Gaidar felt compelled to privatize as quickly as possible to reduce the likelihood of a reversal of economic reform, this pressure was much less severe in Poland. The costs to successive right and center governments of waiting to conduct privatization were much lower than in Russia, and this allowed them to delay privatization until relatively stronger institutions of corporate governance were in place.[16] By privatizing large industrial enterprises at a moderate pace while improving corporate governance institutions, successive Polish governments minimized the extent of inconsistent reform and asset stripping relative to other countries in the region.

In truth, privatization of a sort began under the last communist-era government in a parade of rather opaque transformations that allowed state bureaucrats and enterprise managers to obtain property rights of enterprises in closed-bid auctions (Tarkowski 1989; Staniszkis 1991; Zubek 1995). The first postcommunist government put the privatization of large industrial firms on the agenda in the summer of 1990, with the twin goals of making rapid progress and raising revenue for the state, but quickly realized that these two goals were in tension. "Capital" privatization included auctions of large relatively healthy firms but made slow progress and provided far less revenue than expected. Despite general agreement on the need to privatize broad swaths of industry, the post-Solidarity governments from 1990 to 1993 struggled to agree on policy and settled on a multimethod privatization that focused on the more manageable problem of small and medium-sized state enterprises. "Liquidation" privatization involved primarily small firms with fewer than 250 workers whose assets could be sold or leased to a new company on condition that the majority of the employees of the liquidated companies became owners in the new company. Under the program of "capitalization" privatization,

---

[16] This delay was in part due to the novelty of privatization on this scale, wrangling in the parliament, the technical difficulties of a proposed cash privatization, and the power of employee councils (Dabrowski et al. 1991).

firms were initially transformed into government-owned joint-stock companies and had to be privatized within two years (Wellisz et al. 1993). This method put the greatest constraints on worker management in the new company, but it also gave labor the opportunity to buy shares at a considerable discount.

Privatization of small and medium-sized state-owned enterprises proceeded at a moderate pace. In 1990 Poland had roughly 8,500 state-owned enterprises, but by the end of 1995 this figure had been cut in half (Kolodko 2000: 38).[17] The capitalization and liquidation privatization methods varied in their details but in essence allowed enterprise insiders to take ownership of state-owned enterprises at favorable prices, even as they provided little revenue for the state. Yet the economic impact of these types of privatizations appears to have helped promote restructuring over time. In many cases, enterprise insiders bought shares only to resell them to outside investors or to managers within the firms. The concentration of shares in outside investors and managers is positively associated with restructuring (Kozarzewski and Woodward 2001). Frydman et al. (1999) find that privatization to outside owners, especially foreign owners, is a robust predictor of economic restructuring in Poland.

In contrast, progress on the privatization of large industrial enterprises was slower, but given the rapid growth of the new private sector and the progress of privatization of small and medium enterprises, the economic impact of this delay was less damaging than it might have been. In June 1991 the government proposed a mass privatization plan targeted at the five hundred largest firms (in terms of sales), which accounted for about 40 percent of employment. The broad outline of the plan included free distribution of shares and the creation of private investment management funds. The Bielecki government, which came to power following the parliamentary elections of October 1991, supported the proposal but assigned it a rather low priority (Wellisz et al. 1993: 184). After much bargaining and several threats of resignation, the Suchocka government brought the mass privatization law to the floor of the Sejm in April 1993, and in a highly charged vote, the bill passed 215 to 178 with 22 abstentions. Importantly, the opposition SLD voted in favor of the proposal, which indicated its commitment to the privatization of the commanding heights of the Polish economy. Shortly after the passage of the law, the Suchocka government fell and was replaced by the SLD-PSL coalition. As the PSL was less enthusiastic about mass privatization, progress stalled. Finally, in 1996 the SLD-PSL government passed a mass privatization law to transfer into private hands the assets of the five hundred large firms that formed the backbone of Polish industry. The law included the creation of fifteen National Investment Funds (NIFs) to represent the interests of outside shareholders, many of whom were individual investors who had bought privatization vouchers sold by the state. One-third of the shares were distributed to a lead fund, 27 percent went

---

[17] These figures are taken from the Ministry of Ownership Transformation and include only privatizations that had been completed.

to other funds, 15 percent were distributed free of charge to employees, and 25 percent were retained by the Treasury.

The lead NIF played a key role in the restructuring of the firms as a concentrated outside shareholder and with a focus on debt reduction, sale of noncore assets, and expansion of distribution networks.[18] By the end of 1998, more than one-third of the firms in the NIF program had been sold to strategic investors, and roughly one-third of the strategic investors were foreign firms looking to take advantage of Poland's relatively stable politics and booming economy. Moreover, the NIFs proved remarkably successful in finding new owners of privatized assets (Blaszczyk et al. 2001: 29).

In addition, the government strengthened corporate governance institutions before the privatization of the largest industrial firms. Poland established a powerful Securities and Exchange Commission in 1991 (Grzymala-Busse 2007). Surveys of brokers indicated that Poland had far stronger corporate governance institutions than Hungary, the Czech Republic, or Russia (Kolodko 2000: 40).[19] In a detailed analysis of the Polish securities market, Glaeser et al. (2001: 855) conclude: "Poland adopted legal rules highly protective of investors, mandated extensive information disclosure by securities issues and intermediaries and created an independent and highly motivated regulator to enforce the rules.... This approach stimulated rapid development of securities markets and enabled a number of firms to raise external funds. The expropriation of investors has been modest." Poland was hardly free from corporate scandals and fraud in the 1990s, but it had strong corporate governance institutions relative to other countries in the regions. Most importantly, given the consensus over the economic direction of the country, the political gains to the government of conducting a rapid giveaway privatization with weak corporate governance were far lower than in more politically polarized settings.

The New Private Sector

Perhaps the most important response to Poland's economic reforms came from the new private sector. New firm creation was high across Poland, in part because of the program of small privatization, which was largely completed in 1992, and in part because of low barriers to entry for de novo private firms, but political factors were also important. Given the low level of political polarization on economic policy as evidenced by the broad consensus around the economic direction of the country, entrepreneurs were far more willing to risk the capital and effort to create new firms in Poland than in other more polarized settings like Russia or Bulgaria.

Data on the new private sector are often quite difficult to evaluate, given the dynamism of the sector, the size of the informal economy, and the number of unregistered workers, but by almost any measure Poland's new private sector

---

[18] *Poland International Economic Report* (1997–98): 74–75.
[19] *Central European Review* 4 (March 2, 1996): 3–4.

has been robust. In 1989 the share of employment in the private sector outside of agriculture was 13.2 percent, but it had increased to 34.4 percent by 1992 (Balcerowicz 1995: 308).[20] Indeed, by September 1991, 75 percent of retail trade was in private hands compared to only 10 percent in 1989 (Blanchard and Dabrowski 1993: 132). These figures understate the role of firms with fewer than five workers, which were not required to report financial data to the state statistical agency for much of the transformation. Nor did it capture those working in the gray economy, which accounted for about 17 percent of all employees in small private enterprises (Polska Agencia Rozwoju Regionalnego [PARR] 1999: 33).[21] By the end of 1992, if agriculture is included in the calculation, half of the workforce in Poland was in the private sector (Blanchard and Dabrowski 1993: 131). Frydman et al. (1999) found that between 1990 and 1997 more than 90 percent of gross job creation occurred in the new private sector in Poland.

Jackson et al. (2005: 20) note that "the distinguishing feature of the Polish economy during the 1990s is the high rate of job creation among new firms which provides an important counter to the job destruction among the large state-owned enterprises at the start of the transformation." Similarly, Slay (2000: 33) observed: "The creation and expansion of the indigenous private sector in the Polish transition has been much more important than the privatization of state enterprises and property. Poland's economic recovery began in early 1992, when privatization was essentially limited to small and medium-sized state firms, and well before mass privatization began."

The robust new private sector had important political as well as economic implications for Poland's transition. The creation of new private firms exhibited strong agglomeration effects as new private firms tended to be created in regions with many other new private firms.[22] This concentration of new firms helped to bolster the political power of the new private sector at the ballot box as this group proved to be an important constituency for centrist and liberal parties. On the basis of a unique dataset of new private firms in Poland, Jackson et al. (2005: 165) found that in parliamentary elections in 1991, 1993, and 1997 "higher rates of de novo firm creation increase the votes for liberal economic parties, which are also the most centrist parties." Survey evidence from 2001 parliamentary elections produces similar results.

---

[20] This figure excludes cooperatives, which, if they are included, raise the figure to 44.4 percent. These data are from GUS (1993).

[21] Macieja (2001: 146) notes that the number of new private businesses increased from around 840,000 in 1990 to 2.1 million in 1998. These figures likely included many firms that were no longer active but had not informed GUS of their closure. One estimate suggests that the number of active firms in the small and medium enterprises was about 1.7 million (Polska Agencia Rozwoju Regionalnego [PARR] 1998: 32). See also Belka (2001).

[22] The political importance of the new private sector has been consistently underestimated in the transformation, because observers expected new private firms to be too dispersed to have much of an effect on politics. Thus, the agglomeration effects noted by Jackson et al. (2005) provide an important corrective to the literature.

State-Owned Firms

Given the long history of failed reform efforts, many observers predicted that state-owned firms would respond sluggishly to the policies of the Solidarity-led government and continue to raise wages, hoard labor, and hope for financial help from the government. Indeed, without major restructuring many, but far from all, state-owned firms were unlikely to survive in a market economy, given their product mix, geography, and capital stock. In contrast to reform plans put forward by the PZPR, however, the political conditions made a reversal of economic reform much less likely, and many firms in the state sector responded to the new economic policies. A study of seventy-five state-owned enterprises in five manufacturing sectors that included numerous interviews with managers between 1989 and 1992 found that many small and medium-sized state-owned firms adjusted rather quickly to the new policies, even if their long-term outlook was rather cloudy (Pinto et al. 1993: 255). When asked whether the government would stay the course and maintain hard budget constraints, fifty of fifty-nine respondents agreed, and only nine expected some dilution of hard budget constraints (Pinto et al. 1993). Only eight of fifty-nine respondents expected their firm to remain state-owned in the near future, forty-three expected privatization soon, five expected to be offered managerial contracts, and three were already privatized by the conclusion of the study. They attributed this rapid restructuring to the government's commitment to economic reform and the low probability that reform would be reversed. Pinto (1993: 4) notes that "the government's 'no bailout' signal has been consistent and unambiguous right from the start." On the basis of this strong signal, "managers believe that good performance will be rewarded at the time of privatization and that their reputation, and hence compensation, will be dependent upon their performance today. This is a major factor why state-owned enterprises managers have been more farsighted than expected" (Pinto et al. 1993: 255). Dabrowski et al. (1991: 413–14) concur. According to a study of fifty state-owned firms conducted in 1990 and data from the state statistical agency, they found that "contrary to the extremely pessimistic assessments of state firms by reformers, many firms, especially small and medium enterprises, have adjusted dynamically." These studies are important because systematic evidence at this very early stage of the transformation is scarce.

One tool that the Solidarity government instituted to push firms from the state to the private sector was a tax on excess wages that applied only to state-sector firms (Dabrowski et al. 1993; Easter 2002: 6). Seen as a temporary measure to fight inflation by keeping wages in check and to provide an incentive for state-owned firms to undergo privatization, the *popiwek* raised significantly more tax revenue than expected from 1990 to 1993 before being scrapped in 1994.

Of course, far from all state-owned firms adjusted to the new market conditions, and loss-making state-owned firms occupied the attention of policy makers in the 1990s, as successive governments sought to minimize the damage to the budget of lending to the state-owned firms (Dabrowski et al. 1993). In addition, the state-owned giants of Polish industry, such as URSUS and the Gdansk Shipyard, presented a far greater challenge, and these firms were a persistent drain on state finances. Yet small and medium-sized state-owned firms proved to be much less of a barrier to economic transformation than many anticipated, as managers responded relatively quickly to the hard budget constraint imposed by the state in many cases.

Social Policy

The argument suggests that democracies with low levels of political polarization not only should experience more rapid and more consistent economic and institutional reform but should also provide relatively generous social programs. Indeed, even as Poland was introducing one of the most radical economic liberalizations in the region, it was also preserving and expanding key elements of the socialist welfare state.[23] Social transfers as a share of GDP increased from 25.2 percent of GDP in 1989 to 32.1 percent in 1991 and remained relatively constant through 1995 (Adam 1999: 128). Within this mixture of policies, health expenditures remained roughly constant, but spending on pensions increased. These increases were in part driven by a surge in the raw number of pensioners, as the government used generous payouts to lure older workers into retirement. The number of pensioners increased by almost 35 percent between 1989 and 1996, and this increase put a significant strain on public finance, but the government raised real spending on pensions above the level necessary to accommodate the larger number of pensioners entering the program, indicating other motives were at work as well (Muller 1999: 96–101).

These transfers were part of a political strategy to ensure support for the program from Poland's emerging middle class. Keane and Prasad (2000: 4) note that a "substantial portion of pensions was in fact directed not toward households at the bottom of the income distribution, but toward the middle class and via the increased generosity of pensions to older workers who were potentially big losers in terms of employment and earnings during the transition." Pieralla et al. (2004) make a similar argument using household budget data. This strategy helped to increase the political benefits gained through transfers by including a broader portion of the electorate in the program. Rather than focusing transfers solely as a means to alleviate poverty, incumbents in Poland also directed transfers toward the middle class to help bolster their political position (Keane and Prasad 2001, 2002).

The generous transfers through pensions appear to have helped improve the living standards of pensioners despite the popular view that pensioners were among the big losers from the transformation (Kramer 1997). Bell (2001: 153) observed that "during the 1990s the real value of pension payments was

---

[23] While many argue that economic liberalization offers a trade-off between efficiency and equity, the argument made here suggests that the two should go hand in hand.

preserved or increased, even though the number of claimants rocketed during the first few years of the transition. On average, pensioners increased their consumption of food and consumer goods and improved their income even in relation to 1990 deflated incomes."

Of course, spending on social transfers, including pensions, produced a great burden on the budget, and plans to rationalize the system were a frequent subject of discussion in the 1990s. Despite recognition of the problem, the crowded reform agenda and the political sensitivity and technical difficulties of the project led to slow progress.[24] After much internal debate and in cooperation with the World Bank, Poland reformed its pension system in 1999, moving to a multitier system that included a dominant mandatory pay-as-you-go tier, an employer-funded tier managed by pension funds, and a tier for voluntary additional insurance. Even after pension reform, however, spending remained quite generous.[25] Haggard and Kaufman (2008: 314) note that "despite strong pressures for liberalization of the pension system, the new system guaranteed protection of the elderly and left a number of entitlements from the socialist period intact." Thus, even after rationalizing the pension system, the fiscal position of the Polish government was sufficiently strong to maintain relatively generous spending levels.

Political polarization, partisanship, and democracy were not the whole story behind the rapid progress in economic reform. Certainly, the lure of joining the European Union played no small role, particularly after 1997 (Vachudova 2005). Poland began cooperating with the EU in December 1991, and the EU did not commit itself to inviting Poland until after Poland had stabilized the economy and conducted significant economic reforms. It could just as easily be argued that Poland's favorable political conditions and broad-based commitment to economic reform made it an especially attractive country for the EU to court. As noted elsewhere, untangling the direction of causation between the pull of the EU and the push of domestic factors in promoting economic reform is a challenge.[26]

In addition, the role of the International Monetary Fund in promoting economic stabilization should not be overlooked (Stone 2002). IMF conditionality helped to keep Poland's economic reform on track in the early 1990s. In

---

[24] Postcommunist Poland inherited a pension system that included a bewildering array of categories, exceptions, and benefits for political groups. Interest groups benefiting from these separate programs, such as the military and the police, complicated efforts to reform the pension system (Inglot 2008).

[25] Muller (1999: 112–113) notes that the SLD-PSL government passed the first half of legislation on pension reform before elections in September 1997 and the right-wing UWS-UW government passed the second half of the reform after the election. This suggests the broad consensus in favor of pension reform even among the most competitive blocs in Poland. This type of cooperation would be hard to imagine in more polarized countries like Russia or Bulgaria in the 1990s.

[26] Haggard and Kaufman (2008: 350) are skeptical that the impact of the EU on social policy was especially important and note that "social protection in Eastern Europe could be explained largely by domestic political factors associated with socialist welfare legacy rather than external influence or emulation."

addition, the IMF seal of approval likely helped to attract investors and facilitate the renegotiation of Poland's debt with Western creditors in 1991. But, as with the EU, it is difficult to divine the direction of causation. The IMF may have been especially likely to devote resources to Poland, given its favorable domestic political conditions.

Conclusion

Low levels of political polarization and robust democracy shaped economic and institutional reform as expected. Successive governments in Poland pursued rapid and consistent reform and created conditions in support of the new private sector. Somewhat surprisingly, but in line with the theoretical argument, Poland also spent generously on social programs. The case of Poland comports well with the theory developed in preceding chapters.

10

Uzbekistan

Autocracy and Inconsistent Gradualism

> In September 1993 President Karimov dedicated a statue to Timur (Tamerlane) on the site where a monument to Karl Marx had previously stood in the centre of Tashkent.... The new Timur is thus the centerpiece of an Uzbek national ideology based on the idea that the Uzbeks have been, since time immemorial, the dominant political and cultural force in Central Asia. Parallels between Karimov and Timur have frequently been drawn in the Uzbekistani press.
>
> Melvin (1999: 46)

Throughout the period under study Uzbekistan has been ruled by an old-left executive in a nonpolarized autocracy. As expected, Uzbekistan pursued a mix of inconsistent gradual policies emphasizing state-led development, slow privatization, and vast state intervention in the economy to support the executive's core constituency in state-owned industry and agriculture. Fifteen years into the transformation, land was state owned, companies producing the largest export commodities, cotton and gold, were largely in state hands, protection against foreign goods was vast, and economic policy was widely perceived to be subject to arbitrary changes. High market prices for gold and cotton in the first half of the 1990s helped to prop the Uzbek economy and provide fairly generous transfers, but ultimately, the country's inconsistent gradual policies failed to generate sufficient growth to maintain high levels of transfers.

Before assessing how well the argument fits the facts, it is important to recognize some difficulties in studying this case. Uzbekistan began the transformation much poorer, more agricultural, and with different institutional and cultural legacies than countries in the previous case studies. In the statistical chapters, one can control for many differences that may influence policy choice, but this is more difficult to do in a narrative case study. Case selection can help rule out potential competing explanations, but this is often a blunt tool, particularly in this case where Uzbekistan differs from other cases on multiple dimensions.

In addition, the quality of data is much lower in this case. Throughout the period under study, Uzbekistan's autocratic government maintained tight controls on official data. Many types of economic data, including household budget surveys and reliable public opinion polls, are simply unavailable. Not surprisingly, scholars have also expressed some doubts on official economic data reported by the Uzbek state (Broadman 2000; Pomfret 2006).

Finally, the secondary literature on Uzbekistan is less extensive than for other countries in the region. Several major works on contemporary Uzbekistan have been published in recent years, but the number of scholars studying the country is much smaller than for the previous cases.[1] The presence of foreign businesses and international organizations has been much smaller in Uzbekistan, which removes other potentially valuable sources of information. While the quality of economic and political data in the postcommunist region is generally better than in other regions of the world, we simply know much less about Uzbekistan than we do about other postcommunist countries, despite the best efforts of scholars. Thus, the conclusions drawn from the qualitative evidence are more tentative than in the preceding cases.

Background

Uzbekistan as a political entity was created by the Bolsheviks in the 1920s from a mixture of local religious communities based in Khiva and Bukkhara (Rumer 1989). Soviet power sought to foster an Uzbek national identity as a counterbalance to pan-Turkic or Islamic identities by promoting the Uzbek language and by creating a history for Uzbekistan distinct from its Central Asian neighbors (Fierman 1997: 362). Communist Party rule helped to increase literacy and raise standards of living in Central Asia above those of neighboring countries outside the Soviet orbit. In 1990 citizens of Uzbekistan had relatively longer life expectancy and higher levels of education than countries at similar levels of income, but Uzbekistan nonetheless began the transition as a poor, largely agrarian, double-landlocked country with civil wars raging in neighboring Tajikistan and Afghanistan and a host of serious environmental problems bequeathed by the Soviet regime.

Many in Uzbekistan greeted the end of Soviet power in 1991 with little fanfare. Nationalist mobilization in Central Asia was far lower than in any other region, and Uzbekistan was no exception (Beissinger 2002: 73–74). In the March 1991 referendum on a new union treaty that promised to reform center-republic relations, but also to preserve the USSR, Uzbeks voted in favor of preserving the union. Uzbekistan was also slow to declare independence and introduce a national currency. Given the country's dependence on markets within the former Soviet Union and on economic assistance from Moscow, this stance is perhaps not surprising.

Throughout the Soviet period, Uzbekistan was one of the least industrialized economies in the region and was highly dependent on agriculture, in

---

[1] Among others, see Jones Luong (2002), Collins (2006), Weinthal (2002), Pomfret (2006), Gleason (2003), and Yalcin (2002).

particular cotton. Folk wisdom portrays Uzbekistan as "two-thirds desert, one-third cotton." In the 1990s cotton provided about 40 percent of state revenue and 50 percent of exports (Pomfret 2000: 280). Uzbekistan also produced gold, minerals, and enough oil to avoid being dependent on neighboring states for energy. Manufacturing is concentrated in light industry, again with a bent toward machine building for the cotton industry. Ironically, Uzbekistan's relatively low level of industrialization may have helped minimize damage caused by the collapse of the command economy (Zettelmeyer 1999). Uzbekistan also began the 1990s with significant environmental problems, most dramatically signified by the desiccation of the Aral Sea (Weinthal 2002).

Political Setting: An Old-Left Autocracy

The dominant figure in the transformation of postcommunist Uzbekistan is Islam Karimov. Having spent his pre-1991 career in the Uzbek state and Communist Party apparatus, Karimov is a classic old-left political leader, albeit one with a strong penchant for personal rule. Born in Samarkand in 1938, Karimov joined the CPSU when he was twenty-six. He worked in the Uzbek branch of the State Planning Committee from 1966 to 1983 under the tutelage of Sharaf Rashidov, the long-serving first secretary of the Uzbek Communist Party, whose reign became synonymous with the corruption and cronyism of the late Soviet period. Rashidov died in 1983, and the decade saw massive turnover in the Uzbek party apparatus as Moscow and local elites struggled for control.[2] Between 1981 and 1986, more than three-quarters of the Uzbek Central Committee was replaced (Fierman 1997: 366). In an effort to weaken the Rashidov group, Gorbachev moved many cadres to Uzbekistan, but these efforts made little headway (Collins 2006: 128). In June 1989 Gorbachev named Karimov head of the Uzbek Communist Party, and the new leader moved quickly to consolidate and expand his power in the republic. Indeed, the departures of Gorbachev appointees allowed Karimov to stock the state and party apparatus with his supporters.

By training and career path, Karimov appeared likely to favor a statist approach to the economy.[3] He was a minister of economics and finance in Uzbekistan, but spent most of his career in the Uzbek State Planning Committee. Collins (2006: 192) characterizes Karimov as "a classic communist party apparatchik; he had risen to power and prominence through the rank and file of the CPSU as well as through his connection with Ismoil Surchakov and the Rashidov clan by virtue of his birthplace, Samarkand." While Karimov

[2] Carlisle (1994) suggests that almost sixty thousand officials were replaced in the Uzbek Communist Party through this program.
[3] A comparison here with Askar Akayev in neighboring Kyrgyzstan is perhaps appropriate. Akayev, an academic and former official in the Kyrgyz Academy of Sciences, came to power from outside the Communist Party and the state apparatus and quickly introduced a range of economic reforms.

demonstrated little commitment to communist ideology and the Communist Party as an organization, there is little doubt that his economic views were shaped by his experience within Soviet planning.[4]

Shortly after coming to power, Karimov laid out five principles to guide Uzbekistan:

(1) The economy should prevail over politics and all necessary conditions be created to develop entrepreneurship. (2) The state should be the main instigator of reform throughout the transition period and should initiate the process of reform in the interests of the nation.... (3) To achieve tangible results in the economic transformation, the entire process of renewal and progress should be founded on adjusted and practically applicable laws. (4) A strong social policy should be implemented, one that takes into account the demographic situation and the existing living standards of the people. (5) The establishment of new economic market relations should be introduced without past "revolutionary leaps," but with careful consideration, stage by stage.

Karimov consistently referenced the Chinese economic development strategy as a source of inspiration, although the resemblance is more in rhetoric than in practice. Pomfret (2000: 279) notes that Karimov's reforms "may come to resemble China's at a superficial level" but currently provide much weaker incentives to increase output and rely to a far greater extent on state intervention. In addition, policy in Uzbekistan has lacked the consistency of Chinese economic reforms. Pomfret and Anderson (1997: 20) characterize Uzbek economic policy as "inconsistent gradualism."

Perhaps as importantly, Karimov headed constituencies with deep roots in the state and party apparatus, groups unlikely to favor market-oriented policies that would undercut their interests. Karimov relied heavily on relations developed during his twenty years in the Uzbek bureaucracy and on clan ties from his native Samarkand to staff high positions with supporters. Indeed, while Karimov disbanded the Communist Party of Uzbekistan shortly after the coup of 1991, he turned to a variety of former Communist Party officials to head key posts. Ten of the twelve regional governors (hoakim) appointed by Karimov in 1992 held high positions in the Uzbek Communist Party (Pribylovsky 2003: 171; Fierman 1997: 384). Similarly, Karimov created the People's Democratic Party of Uzbekistan in November 1991 largely from the remnants of the Uzbek Communist Party.[5] As Jones Luong (2002: 130) notes, "Karimov and his supporters successfully assimilated the organizational and numerical strength of the former Communist Party of Uzbekistan into a new governmental party apparatus and eliminated any opposition to its monopoly on political power." Given his career path and bases of support, it is hardly surprising that Karimov has favored a state-led economy.

---

[4] Karimov backed the coup by Soviet leaders in August 1991 (Collins 2006: 162).
[5] Karimov left the party in 1996 on the grounds that the president should be above party politics (Fierman 1997).

Karimov has headed one of the least democratic and most repressive states in the postcommunist world.[6] While neighboring Kyrgyzstan and Kazakhstan had periodic bouts of mild political liberalization, Uzbekistan remained staunchly autocratic. Freedom House has placed Uzbekistan in the "not free" camp throughout the past twenty years. The OECD consistently reports that elections are neither free nor fair. State agencies tightly control the mass media and brook few deviations from the progovernment line. Moreover, foreign media have been subject to surveillance and harassment. For example, the country director of the Institute for War and Peace Reporting was labeled a terrorist and forced to flee the country following her reporting on an uprising in the city of Andijon.[7]

Uzbekistan stands out even among the autocratic regimes of the former Soviet Union for its level of repression, particularly following a bombing in Tashkent in 1999 that may have been meant for President Karimov. Amnesty International reports that torture is regularly practiced on political opponents, adding that the "criminal justice system is seriously flawed by widespread corruption and the failure of courts to investigate allegations of torture."[8] Political opponents have regularly been harassed, arrested, and on occasion beaten.[9] Rivals within the state, including many former Karimov allies, were thought to pose even greater threats to the incumbent and received similarly rough treatment. The government of Uzbekistan received widespread international condemnation for quelling a 2005 uprising in Andijon with excessive force. Details of the incident are unclear, but Uzbek troops fired upon a gathering of citizens, leaving between two hundred and five hundred dead.[10]

President Karimov centralized political power early in the transformation and has jealously guarded his prerogatives.[11] He was the first head of a republic of the USSR to propose the creation of a republic-level presidency and was elected president by the Uzbek parliament without facing an opposition candidate in March 1990. Reportedly, this move was opposed by Gorbachev (Collins 2006: 128). He solidified his position in a popular election on

[6] Fierman (1997: 385) noted that Karimov once justified repressing the political opposition by observing: "It is necessary to straighten out the brains of 100 people in order to preserve the lives of thousands."

[7] International Crisis Group (2006: 4).

[8] http://web.amnesty.org/report2005/uzb-summary-eng.

[9] For example, in April 2005, an opposition group called the Sunshine Coalition called for faster economic and political reforms. Within nine months, both leaders of the movement, Sanjar Umanov, a wealthy businessman, and Nigora Hidoyotova, acting head of the Free Farmers' Party, were arrested. Moreover, Hidoyotova's sister was arrested and her husband was murdered under suspicious circumstances in Kazakhstan (International Crisis Group 2006).

[10] *Human Rights Watch*, June 2005. The Russian Human Rights Group Memorial published the names of 185 people killed in Andijon.

[11] Collins (2006) argues that Karimov initially came to power as an arbiter between two rival clans in Uzbekistan. As such, in her view he was more constrained early in his rule than other observers suggest.

December 31, 1991, in which he was elected with 86 percent of the vote. Karimov then extended his tenure in office through popular referenda in 1995 and 2000. In each case, the government reported that the referenda were approved with 99 percent of eligible voters both turning out and voting in favor (Melvin 1999: 34).

Karimov moved quickly to neutralize the Supreme Soviet by reducing the number of delegates from 450 to 225 in the early 1990s. Moreover, in December 1992 he pushed through a constitution with broad presidential powers, including the right to issue decrees, to suspend any acts by a regional governor, and to dissolve the parliament at any time with the concurrence of the Constitutional Court. The Karimov government has also maintained tight control over the electoral process. While there were multiple candidates in the December 1994 elections to the Uzbek parliament, it was "next to impossible for a candidate opposed to the government to gain a place on the ballot" (Fierman 1997: 391). Importantly, the president retained the power to appoint hoakim (Jones Luong 2002).

Politics in Uzbekistan has exhibited low levels of polarization as defined here. Karimov has held power uninterrupted since 1990, and opposition movements from across the partisan divide have been minimal at best. Two small opposition movements, Birlik (Unity) and Erk (Freedom), provided token opposition early in the transformation on platforms of respect for human rights, protection of the environment, and a stronger sense of Uzbek nationalism. Both movements were banned from taking part in politics in 1993 (Melvin 1999: 36). Leaders of these now unregistered movements have been subject to harassment and arrest and proved to be no match for the Karimov regime. While repressing these groups, President Karimov co-opted their nationalist agenda but little else.

The main political challenge for Karimov has been to balance the various clan and regional interests lodged within the state apparatus. Indeed, former allies within the state and their various regional and clan bases of power have been cited as his most prominent threats. For example, at various times over the past fifteen years, Zokirjan Almatov, the long-standing director of the Interior Ministry, Rustam Inoyatov, the head of the Security Services, and Prime Minister Shavkat Miziyoyev were thought to be potential rivals with substantial resources within the state.[12] In sum, the partisanship of the government, the level of polarization, and the regime type have remained constant throughout the period under study as President Karimov has used the powers of the state to ward off political change from below and to centralize autocratic power in the executive branch.

---

[12] The daughter of President Karimov, Gulnara Karimova, has become a prominent businessperson with interests in media and energy. A former student at the Harvard Business School, she reportedly has favorable relations with the Russian energy giant Gazprom and with Western businesses operating in Uzbekistan (International Crisis Group 2006: 3).

Economic Policy

In line with its partisan bent, the old-left government of Uzbekistan pursued a gradual transformation that featured state-led development, import-substitution industrialization relying on cotton sales, and an emphasis on self-sufficiency in energy and food. These policies, however, have not been pursued with great consistency, and high levels of state intervention have contributed to uncertainty over property rights. Initially, Uzbekistan relied on buoyant prices for cotton and gold to keep transfers to the dependent sector relatively high, but it struggled to maintain this level of social expenditures when international prices fell.

Facing an end to subsidies from Moscow, political instability in neighboring countries, an industrial structure not well suited for a market economy, and low prices for its main export, Uzbekistan began the transition in perilous conditions. The government responded by temporizing for much of 1992–1996 before embarking on a gradual transformation of the command economy, relying heavily on import-substitution industrialization in 1995–1996.

The privatization of the few large industrial enterprises in Uzbekistan has proceeded at a glacial pace. Despite governmental promises to accelerate privatization of industrial enterprises in 1996, 1999, and 2002, progress on this front has been very slow. The government created a State Privatization Committee in 1992, but this body initially focused on the "easy reforms" of small privatization and housing privatization. In late 1996, after several delays, Uzbekistan began a mass privatization program but still had difficulty shedding state ownership. The privatization program typically reserved 25 percent of shares for the state, 26 percent for the workers collective, and made 49 percent available to the general public.[13] However, the shares available to the public were typically transferred to other state structures, such as sectoral ministries and state-owned banks (EBRD 1997: 211). Thus, many industrial firms that went through the privatization process remained largely controlled by state bodies.

In strategic sectors of the economy, such as cotton, oil, and autos, the government has created large state holding companies that provide concentrated benefits for Karimov loyalists. Broadman (1999) noted these holding companies are opaque and control large swaths of the Uzbek economy even if their ownership stakes in individual firms are not large. For example, Uzkhlopkopromsbyt, the trade association in the cotton processing and marketing sector, is the successor to the ministry of cotton and unites 130 cotton ginneries whose members employ about seventy thousand people. As Uzkhlopkopromsbyt did not make its budget publicly available, it is difficult to analyze its performance. It is, however, known that it provides credit to cotton producers from a special fund established by presidential decree and buys cotton at predetermined prices

---

[13] The government hardly encouraged the secondary market by prohibiting managers from buying shares in their own companies in 1998 (EBRD 1998: 198).

that are much lower than world prices (Broadman 1999: 12). The company represents state interests on the boards of the ginneries and is therefore well placed to pressure producers through its control of the purchase of cotton. Equally opaque trade associations dominate the oil and gas sector (Uzbekneftegaz) and auto and transportation services (Uzavtotrans).

Slow privatization has been accompanied by weak corporate governance. Industrial firms have benefited from a variety of indirect subsidies. As the EBRD (1997: 211) noted, "While industrial enterprises are not experiencing explicit subsidies, they continue to benefit from access to commercial credits at relatively low (sometimes negative) interest rates, the ability to accumulate payment arrears, and access to foreign exchange at the official rate." Similarly, an August 1998 presidential decree allows state representatives to delay the implementation of any decision of the shareholders meeting if the change in policy is deemed to be contradictory to state interests (World Bank 1999: 63). Moreover, state attorneys were added as members of the board for any company in which the state owns at least one-quarter of the shares. Rather than creating strong corporate governance institutions, the government prefers to rely on direct ownership and extensive intervention in management decisions.

While Uzbekistan possesses a comparative advantage in agriculture, the reform of large farms has been carried out in word more than in deed. The government renamed the Soviet-era collective farms, *shirkhats*, but did little to encourage more efficient use of resources. The *shirkhats* are largely farmed by extended families, each of whom oversees a subdivision of state-owned land. A 1998 Land Code enshrined state ownership as preeminent and banned the sale of land except in rare circumstances. Throughout the 1990s, governors continued to appoint managers and staff at *shirkhats*. State orders have remained on strategically important products such as cotton and wheat. Pressure from the IMF and good harvests allowed the government to lower state procurement in 2002 and 2003, but state procurements for cotton remained at about 90 percent of the harvest in 2002 (EBRD 2003: 212).

More generally, Uzbekistan transferred great resources from cotton to industrial sectors competing with imports. Borrowing from the logic of import substitution, Uzbekistan taxed cotton exports through a variety of mechanisms, including compulsory sales through state marketing boards, to fund investments in manufacturing, many of which were of dubious economic quality. Cotton farmers were required to sell much of their output at below-market prices to the state, which then sold the cotton at higher prices on the international market with the difference between the two prices remaining with the government. Since 1992, the state has required cotton farmers to sell between 30 and 75 percent of their crop through state marketing boards, but these figures significantly understate the extent of state procurement, as they are based on planned rather than actual output. As the former typically exceed the latter, the great majority of cotton is sold at below-market prices to the state (Spoor and Khaitov 2002: 69). This arrangement does little to encourage farmers to work productively and increase exports.

An overvalued exchange rate and the compulsory resale of hard currency earnings to the state at below-market prices further increased transfers from agriculture to manufacturing. By some estimates, the government transferred about 10 percent of GDP from the cotton sector in the mid-1990s alone (Auty 1999). This strategy reduced incentives for exporters to produce.

One of the least reformed areas of the economy was the foreign trade system, which relied on a multiple exchange rate system that seriously distorted incentives to export. Following a balance-of-payment crisis in 1996, the government required exporters to sell hard currency to the state at below-market prices, while also allowing selected importers to buy foreign exchange from the state at below-market prices. This system remained in place until 2003, when the Uzbek government, under pressure from the IMF, unified the exchange rate.

The multiple foreign exchange rates were a considerable disincentive for foreign investors, who frequently complained of discrimination as they were forced to exchange dollars for *som* at disadvantageous rates. In addition, the Uzbek government placed severe bureaucratic restrictions on withdrawal of funds by foreign companies from local banks. A 2004 report by the Office of the U.S. Trade Representative noted: "American investors unanimously complain that they do not control their corporate bank accounts. . . . Every routine banking operation requires official permission." For much of the 1990s, investments of more than $20 million required approval by the cabinet minister (UNCTAD 1999).

Policy over foreign direct investment was also quite unpredictable. As one lawyer (Newman 1999: 3) noted, "A primary complaint of foreign investors is the legal uncertainty caused by the remarkable frequency with which the Uzbek government adopts new laws and repeals old ones." In 2003 the U.S. trade representative wrote that "companies are particularly concerned with the consistent and fair application of the Foreign Investment Law."

As suggested by the argument, foreign direct investment in Uzbekistan has been minimal. From 1990 to 2002, Uzbekistan had the lowest annual average of foreign direct investment of any economy in the postcommunist world, including several countries that had experienced bitter civil conflict.[14] Much of the investment accrued in a small number of large joint-venture projects in the tobacco sector (British American Tobacco), the gold sector (Newmont Industries and Oxus), and autos (UzDaewoo). However, few investments bore fruit. In 2005 the government pressured the Korean auto giant Daewoo to sell its majority shares to the state and used a similar strategy against Oxus, the British mining company. In 2006 the Uzbek government accused the U.S. gold mining firm Newmont, the largest foreign investor in Uzbekistan, of tax evasion and eventually declared the firm bankrupt (Nones 2006).[15]

---

[14] World Bank (2003).

[15] Smaller foreign firms generally fared less well. See, for example, Bukharbaeva (2000). The decision to move against Newmont occurred in the wake of a serious downturn in U.S.-Uzbek relations in which the former ultimately lost basing rights in the latter.

To be sure, Uzbekistan's economy in the twenty-first century is not a replica of the Soviet-era command economy, and some "easy" types of economic reforms have made progress (Spechler 2008). Most importantly, the Uzbek government quickly reoriented the export of cotton from Russia to other markets. By 1995 more than half of exports were to countries outside the Commonwealth of Independent States (CIS) – a policy in keeping with the Uzbek government's emphasis on self-reliance (Roy 2000: 193).[16] The government also managed to become self-sufficient in food and energy, although this came at the cost of transferring resources from more productive sectors.

In addition, prices on most goods (apart from cotton, wheat, and energy) were liberalized in 1994 and have remained relatively unfettered, save for great distortions in the exchange rate. Small privatization began slowly but became rather extensive by the end of the decade despite persistent barriers to entry. In the 1990s small businesses trading at bazaars became an integral part of the economy, and the government's small privatization program was proceeding apace. Housing privatization has also been extensive and was largely complete by the mid-1990s. In these areas, Uzbekistan is similar to many other postcommunist countries that have pursued these relatively easy reforms. However, in the main, economic reform has been gradual, with the state playing a dominant role. Pomfret (2006: 26) captures the main thrust of economic reforms in Uzbekistan: "The hallmark of Uzbekistan's economic policies was a cautious recognition that change was inevitable, and a commitment to gradual reform in order to minimize negative or disruptive consequences of change."

Economic Performance

To the surprise of many, Uzbekistan experienced the shallowest output drop of any country in the former Soviet Union in the 1990s.[17] It was the first former republic of the USSR to reach its 1990 level of GDP. For the period 1990–2004, Uzbekistan's average annual growth rate was 1.1, which placed it in the middle of the twenty-five countries under study. There is some debate over the sources of Uzbekistan's economic performance. To account for Uzbekistan's economic growth, the International Monetary Fund (2000) placed greater emphasis on initial conditions, such as the relatively rich resource endowment, the dominance of agriculture in the economy, the low level of industrialization, and low level of energy imports. It also pointed to the buoyant prices for Uzbekistan's two main exports, cotton and gold, in the first half of the 1990s. While not

---

[16] The government shifted resources from the cotton sector to also achieve self-sufficiency in wheat and energy. The former achievement is, however, rather dubious given the relative abundance of foodstuffs in the region.

[17] The World Bank (1993: xx) noted: "In the absence of comprehensive reform, the few scattered and partial reforms that the government is implementing would have no major impact. This failure to adjust would lead to a supply-led contraction of the level of economic activity, reduction in savings and investment, and unnecessary hardship on the population in the medium term by a decline in consumption per capita of no less than 30 percent."

neglecting these factors, Taube and Zettelmeyer (1998) and Zettelmeyer (1999) also give some credit to policy choices in Uzbekistan, including relatively high levels of social spending that may have helped Uzbekistan avoid the cataclysmic drop in economic growth of neighboring countries in the 1990s.

Uzbekistan's economic fortunes have depended to a considerable extent on international markets. From 1990 to 1996, economic growth was relatively strong, as the country benefited from high prices on cotton and gold, but Uzbekistan's economy was vulnerable to economic shocks, given its reliance on a small number of export products.[18] When cotton and gold prices fell in 1996–1997, Uzbekistan experienced its first economic crisis in the postcommunist era as the budget deficit ballooned to 15 percent of GDP in the fourth quarter of 1996. From 1996 to 2004, the economy continued to grow but at a slower rate than many peer countries in the region. Low prices for cotton did not help, but the distortions in economic policy rooted in the import-substitution strategy became more apparent. The overvalued exchange rate, currency controls, and heavy taxation on exports reduced incentives to engage in international trade, at least in the formal economy, and encouraged bribery, particularly at the border. The economy stumbled in 2003 and 2004, even as prices for cotton began to increase. The government's response was predictably heavy-handed, including new restrictions on small and medium-sized enterprises and changes in the legal code that gave local authorities greater control over small business (Pomfret 2006: 35).

State Revenue and Social Spending

For all the economic distortions induced by an unpredictable and highly interventionist state, Uzbekistan initially protected its sources of revenue and levels of expenditure relatively well, thanks largely to high prices for its main commodities. Whereas many transition countries struggled in vain to protect their fiscal base, Uzbekistan retained control over its sources of revenue in the 1990s. Saidova and Cornia (2005: 87) note that the "experience of Uzbekistan differs from that of other CIS economies as it avoided the revenue implosion and collapse in the provision of essential public goods and social safety nets suffered by many CIS countries." To monitor tax payments and collect taxes, the government relied on state-owned banks – a strategy that impeded the development of the banking sector as a conduit between borrowers and savers but helped the government to remain relatively solvent in the early years of the transition. For example, Table 10.1 indicates that the Uzbek revenue as a share of GDP has been higher than in other countries in Central Asia, although these data tell us little about how well these revenues are put to use.

While economic reforms have been slow across almost all dimensions, there is evidence that Uzbekistan largely sidestepped the worst aspect of inconsistent

---

[18] The strong export performance of the Uzbek economy in the first half of the 1990s also appears to have encouraged the government to spend more freely than it might otherwise have done.

TABLE 10.1. *Revenue as a Share of GDP*

	1995	1996	1997	1998	1999	2000	2001	2002
Uzbekistan	38	37	39	36	33	35	35	36
Kazakhstan	20	22	24	22	20	23	28	25
Kyrgyzstan	22	21	20.5	22.4	20.7	18.7	21	23

Source: EBRD (2009).

reform by maintaining control over the cotton and gold sectors in the first half of the 1990s. Benefiting from high cotton and gold prices in this period, Uzbekistan had weaker incentives to buy political support using tax breaks and fire-sale privatizations. As Pomfret (2000: 9) notes, "Uzbekistan has avoided the pitfalls of rapid reform in Russia and Kazakhstan without falling into the trap of nonreform as in Turkmenistan. In particular, Uzbekistan avoided alienation of natural resource rents, which gave the government an important continuing source of revenue." Zettelmeyer (1999) argues that Uzbekistan's "growth puzzle" has less to do with what the government has done than with what it has not done. In his view, it did not allow extensive value-destroying predation by state and private actors in the cotton and gold sectors. During this period, Uzbekistan maintained relatively high levels of spending on education and health, 7.2 and 3.3 percent of GDP, respectively, in the 1990s (Alam and Bannerji 2001). Alam and Sundberg (2002) provide data in Table 10.2 that suggest that Uzbekistan devoted a higher share of its gross domestic product to education and social protection than other countries in the region in the late 1990s. Education spending is also high, in large part, because of the relative youth of the Uzbek population.

Indeed, while generally critical of Uzbek economic policies, the World Bank (1999: 71, 86) reported that, "despite an overall contraction in expenditures, the government has protected health and education expenditures in relative terms, consistent with its social objective of investing in human resources." In addition, "both in absolute and relative terms, pensions have been well defended in recent years."

One important institution in Uzbek social policy is the mahalla, or community. A traditional Uzbek social institution based on groups of families headed by an elder, the mahalla dispenses social aid to the less well-off in the

TABLE 10.2. *Public Expenditure as a Percentage of GDP in the 1990s*

	Education	Health	Social Protection
Central Europe/Baltics	4.6	5.1	13.3
CIS countries	4.6	3.6	7.4
Uzbekistan	7.4	2.6	12.5[a]

[a] Includes expenditures on pension spending, which account for more than 85 percent of this figure. Saidova and Cornia (2005: 96).

community. In 1994 the government began to provide financing to mahallas to increase their role in the implementation of social policy. The government was sufficiently pleased with the mahallas to expand their duties, and by 1999 they provided a range of services, such as overseeing a local budget for sanitation, monitoring environmental matters, distributing land plots, and mediating domestic disputes (Kamp 2004: 39). Mahallas are run by groups of families that elect a chairman and a committee of elders, who make most decisions. One of their primary responsibilities is to judge petitions to receive social assistance. Representatives of the local state bodies may also serve on this committee. Mahallas may include from 150 to 1,500 households and are designed to tap local knowledge of the petitioner's need and resources. The difficulty of verifying "need" in a transition economy suggests that local groups with more information and monitoring capacity than a typical state agency may be better placed to oversee these programs.

Research on the effectiveness of mahallas is scarce. Official data from the Uzbek government indicate that 9 percent of households received a benefit from a mahalla in 1994, 21 percent in 1995, 15 percent in 1996, and 17 percent in 1997 (Coudouel et al. 1998: 4). A 1995 survey from three regions in Uzbekistan suggests that less well-off households were more likely to receive a benefit from a mahalla than were better-off households. In addition, female-headed households and households with children were also more likely to get aid (Coudouel et al. 1998). This suggests that mahallas are directing resources to the more needy segments of the population. However, the size of benefits appears to be unrelated to need. Moreover, mahallas appear to favor residents from rural areas and of Central Asian descent (Coudouel and Marnie 1999). These studies come from the mid-1990s, so caution is necessary in interpreting the results.

These organizations also serve an important political function as social policy is used for partisan purposes. Decision making within mahallas is opaque, and these organizations serve as a means for the Uzbek government to co-opt local elites by giving them resources and the power to allocate them with little accountability (Kamp 2004: 51). Mahalla committee members receive a state salary and work closely with state officials. In addition, there is a concern that women and non-Uzbek minorities may be reluctant to use the system (Coudouel and Marnie 1999). Perhaps as important, the mahalla functions as a means of social control for the state as well (Sievers 2000). By including state and local elites on the mahalla committee, the state can extend its reach deep into society (Melvin 1999: 32–33).

It is difficult to determine the impact of social policy because of data constraints. There is partial evidence suggesting that it has had some positive effects. Harry Broadman of the World Bank (1999) in a largely critical review from the late 1990s commended Uzbekistan's social policy.[19]

---

[19] Pomfret (2006: 133) reaches a roughly similar conclusion on the basis of a household budget survey conducted in Tajikistan, Kyrgyzstan, and one region (Fergana) in Uzbekistan. He notes

While data inadequacies seriously hamper a complete assessment of social and living standards in Uzbekistan, anthropomorphic data, and health and education outcomes – low prevalence of stunting and wasting, average life expectancy of over 70 years, infant mortality of 30 per 1000 live births, maternal mortality of 12 per 100,000 births, literacy rates of almost 100 percent, high enrollments, and little gender differentials in schooling – are good and compare favorably with other countries with comparable income levels.

Yet, more recent data that capture the post-1996 decline in cotton prices paint a less positive picture. Saidova and Cornia (2005: 37) find that income inequality continued to increase throughout the 1990s. Indeed, the increase in income inequality occurred during the last half of the 1990s when the government pursued its import-substitution strategy rather than during the first half of the decade when the government was focused on reacting to the collapse of the command economy. Between 1991 and 1999, the gini coefficient of income inequality increased from .26 to .39 by their account.

Evidence of the effectiveness of social spending at the individual level is subject to debate, given the lack of quality data. Data on poverty, inequality, and unemployment are difficult to evaluate and subject to manipulation by political authorities. But there appears to be a general decline in the provision of social services after world prices for cotton and gold turned against Uzbekistan in 1996. Indeed, economic mismanagement and sluggish growth after 1998 have strained the social safety net, as the government's import-substitution policies did little to generate economic growth that could help fund generous social welfare programs. Social expenditures declined from 4 percent to 2 percent of GDP between 1996 and 2002 (Saidova and Cornia 2005: 95). After 1998, the government's shift toward value-added taxes, excise payroll taxes, and fees helped to make the tax system much more regressive and placed additional burdens on the poor (Saidova and Cornia 2005).[20] The crony statist policy mix of gradual reforms, weak corporate governance, and an overvalued exchange rate failed to generate the self-sustaining economic growth needed to generate generous social transfers.

Conclusion

Evidence from Uzbekistan is largely consistent with the argument. An old-left executive in a nonpolarized autocracy pursued gradual and inconsistent reforms across a wide variety of policies. While international prices helped to generate revenue for relatively generous social policies in the early years of the

that household expenditures increase with the presence of a pensioner in the household in Uzbekistan but not in Tajikistan or Kyrgyzstan. This insight is qualified by the small sample size and the absence of data from other regions in Uzbekistan but suggests that the government has maintained social commitments relatively well in Uzbekistan.

[20] Moreover, the introduction of regulations to more tightly control the retail trade conducted at bazaars in 2003 may more than offset relatively strong social spending, because small business has served as an important means for the poor to supplement their income.

transition, the failure to generate self-sustaining growth prevented Uzbekistan from maintaining these commitments after international prices for cotton and gold fell. Uzbekistan is clearly a dictatorship and far from a benign one at that. The government's penchant for gradual reform and import-substitution policies brought significant distortions in the economy that may be difficult to undo. Highly opaque state-owned firms dominate the economy, while the state bureaucracy does little to promote the private sector. Perhaps a better metaphor than the benign dictator is Olson's (1993) roving bandit.

11

Conclusion

For fourteen months in the late 1980s, I traveled to six cities in the USSR as a guide on a cultural exhibit sponsored by the United States Information Agency that drew several thousand visitors a day. In the industrial city of Magnitogorsk, a middle-aged woman approached my stand and declared: "An American. A real live American. I never thought I would see a real live American." This comment, made just over twenty years ago, gives some sense of the magnitude of the challenges that have confronted postcommunist societies over the past two decades. One cannot overstate the difficulty of taking societies with political and economic institutions designed to shutter society from the outside world into the twenty-first century.

To put the scope of this challenge in further perspective, it is helpful to consider the response of the advanced economies to the global financial crisis of 2008. Countries with long-standing market economies have debated the size of economic assistance needed to stimulate economic activity, whether to take shares in bankrupt financial institutions, and how to create sterner regulatory institutions that make a future financial collapse less likely while retaining the dynamism of the market. These changes have no doubt been painful in many countries, but they are mere tinkering in comparison to the overhaul of economic and political institutions in the postcommunist world, where the agenda included lifting price controls on almost all goods, moving complex industrial assets from state to private hands, and exposing firms sheltered from international competition for decades into a rapidly expanding global economy.

In accounting for variation in the success and failures of economic and institutional transformation across countries and over time, this book offers an argument that differs in many respects from more popular accounts. It is not a tale of "white hat" reformers against "black hat" rent seekers, as the argument assumes that both old- and new-economy interests prefer to grow rich off rents rather than to undertake the hard work of investing. It is not a story of enlightened political leaders and technocrats selflessly making policy without consideration for their political fate, as politicians have the more banal goals of holding onto their office and maximizing revenue as they do in most countries most of the time. It is also not primarily a narrative of Western powers imposing their institutions and values on prostrate societies, as domestic political and economic interests in the postcommunist region are the major actors in my argument. It is also not an account that emphasizes the confusion and disorganization of transition, as politicians and citizens recognize their interests sufficiently well to map strategies that often fail and sometimes succeed but are at least intuitively plausible, given the constraints before them. Finally, it is not simply a narrative of thieving politicians and businesspeople raiding the state, as sometimes they do and sometimes they do not. In many respects, this is a more prosaic story of politicians seeking to retain office, businesses trying to protect their economic interests, and dependent sectors attempting to preserve their livelihood, but under different types of political and economic constraints.

This book began by marveling at the tremendous diversity of economic and political outcomes across the postcommunist states before developing a theory that tries to account for this variation. The theory emphasizes that democracy and partisan power are critical to understanding policy choice across the region. It argues that under democracy politicians seek to stay in office by satisfying their core constituents but also must find revenue to buy the political support of other groups in society. When political polarization is low in democracies, policy makers can make credible policy promises and productive sectors in society can invest confident that current policy is unlikely to be reversed in the future. Incumbent politicians can then tax this investment and buy sufficient political support from the dependent sector of society to retain office. In contrast, autocratic governments and democratic governments confronted with high levels of political polarization are less able to make credible commitments to economic and institutional reforms, face greater uncertainty over future policy and induce weaker responses to reform from producers, and receive less tax revenue. Anticipating this loss of revenue (and hence political support), incumbent governments use policy to reward narrow interest groups in hopes of staying in power rather than to pursue broad-based economic reforms that may jeopardize their political future. This policy choice leads to slower and less consistent economic and institutional reform in autocracies and polarized democracies.

One policy implication for improving the performance of markets and state institutions that flows from this analysis is the benefit of a two-pronged strategy that focuses on promoting democratic institutions and reducing economic inequality. The promotion of democratic institutions on its own may have disappointing results if income inequality is high and is reflected in political polarization. Indeed, the results suggest that polarized democracies fare much worse than their less polarized counterparts in promoting economic and institutional reform.

Democracy and Reform

The theoretical argument and empirical tests help us understand the great variation in economic outcomes across the postcommunist world but also contribute to broader debates. Perhaps as importantly, the argument and evidence raise questions that point to potentially fruitful areas for research.

Does democracy promote economic reform? Debates on this question have been as hotly contested as they have been inconclusive (cf. Haggard and Webb 1993, 1994; Haggard and Kaufman 1995; Przeworski 1991; Hellman 1998). This work seeks to offer some nuance to these debates by identifying conditions under which democracy has a greater or a lesser impact on reform. More precisely, democracies conducted more rapid and consistent reforms and provided more generous social transfers when polarization was absent, but each increment of polarization reduced the positive impact of democracy on reform and on transfers. By recognizing the conditional impact of democracy on economic and institutional reform, this book hopes to make more precise predictions about the relationship between democratic institutions and policy choice than are often made in the literature.

Refining the conditions under which democracy shapes policy outcomes is important because institutional arguments on their own often make indeterminate predictions about policy choice. Many have made plausible arguments for why democracy should promote economic reform, but equally plausible arguments suggest the opposite. While democratic governments may be more accountable, they also may be more prone to gridlock as powerful groups struggle to advance competing policies. Because it is difficult to determine which of these effects will dominate, arguments about the impact of democracy on policy choice are often indeterminate. More generally, the claims advanced here suggest the importance of developing arguments that explore how institutions interact with power relations and partisan strategies in hopes of generating sharper predictions about policy.

In addition, the argument identifies a different logic by which democracy may promote economic and institutional reform. Many have noted the correlation between democracy and reform in the postcommunist world, but few have made persuasive arguments about precisely how democracy influences policy choice. In this work democracy promotes economic and institutional reform by making politicians rely on revenue generated by keeping reforms on track to buy the support of the dependent sector. The interaction of polarization and democracy can account for why incumbents collude with powerful firms to create inconsistent reforms at the expense of the dependent sector in some cases but ally with the dependent sector against challengers in the opposing political camp in other cases.

One question for future research is whether differences within autocracies also influence economic and institutional reform.[1] I have explored how polarized and nonpolarized democracies made different choices over economic and institutional reforms but have not discussed how distinctions within autocracies may influence policy. Do personalist or one-party autocracies pursue different

---

[1] One promising line of research examines variation in the ability of autocratic regimes to make credible commitments over time (Haber et al. 2003; Besley and Kudamatsu 2007; Gehlbach and Keefer 2008).

reform strategies? Do resource-rich and resource-poor autocracies take different reform paths? This line of research could be especially fruitful as recent research in the broader comparative politics literature suggests that differences within autocracies can lead to systematic variation in policy (Gehlbach and Keefer 2008; Magaloni 2006; Ghandi 2008).

Another area of future research could try to endogenize the direct impact of democracy on policy choice. Here I have taken democracy as exogenous to the argument and explored the conditional impact of democracy under different levels of polarization. Based on the assumption that the impact of the omitted variables linking democracy and reform is at work in both low- and high-polarization environments, this approach permits a test for the differential impact of democracy on policy under varying levels of polarization without the simple form of endogeneity bias that typically plagues studies of the direct effects of democracy on reform (Grosjean and Senik 2007, 2008; Denisova et al. 2009). However, the level of democracy likely changes for both exogenous and endogenous reasons, and it would be helpful to decompose these effects (Przeworski et al. 2000; Boix and Stokes 2003). This step would help advance empirical studies of the impact of democracy on economic outcomes. Future work could also try to make the impact of democracy on policy more endogenous on a theoretical level by identifying conditions under which politicians and social interests prefer abandoning democracy rather than using revenue to buy political support from groups outside of core constituents (Boix 2003; Acemoglu and Robinson 2006).

States and Markets

This work aims to determine the conditions under which the building of states and markets goes hand in hand and when these processes work at cross-purposes. Recent studies emphasize that state building is a deeply political process. Therefore, it is essential to determine when politicians have incentives to weaken or strengthen the state (Geddes 1994; Carpenter 2001; O'Dwyer 2006; Grzymala-Busse 2007; Gehlbach 2008). The argument in this book aims to provide some microfoundations for the decision to make state institutions more or less capable. Ironically, in nonpolarized democracies, incumbent politicians can bolster state institutions by conducting economic and institutional reforms that induce economic activity and allow the government to reap more revenue through taxation. Doing so helps incumbents stay in power. Indeed, the expansion of economic and institutional reform in nonpolarized democracies goes hand in hand with more consistent reform, more generous transfer payments to the dependent sector, and more capable state institutions. In this case, economic reform does not advance by pitting the state against the market, but, rather, under these conditions markets and states develop hand in hand. Here the attention paid to social welfare comes less from a popular backlash by groups harmed by the expansion of markets than by a cold calculation about how best to buy political support (Polanyi 1944).

Incumbents in autocratic governments or polarized democracies have stronger incentives to weaken state institutions as they introduce economic reforms. By weakening the power of state institutions strategically, incumbents can deliver substantial benefits to the producing sectors in society at the expense of providing transfers to those who rely on the state for their incomes, including bureaucrats, pensioners, and the unemployed. This formula too can keep incumbents in power, at least until the economic consequences of allowing private actors to prey on the state become too onerous (Ganev 2006). In this setting, market building and state building work at cross-purposes.

This argument casts literature about the role of state institutions in economic transition and development in a somewhat different light. Recent work has tended to focus on the capture of state institutions by powerful interests within society (Hellman et al. 2003). In this view, it is narrow interest groups that dictate policy to politicians who are too weak to fend off the advances of lobbying groups. In contrast, this work suggests that under some conditions politicians have incentives to deliver benefits to narrow interest groups at the expense of the broader public – even in the absence of well-organized and powerful interest groups.[2]

This argument seems more consistent with the evidence in part because interest groups at the start of the transition were fairly similar across countries, owing to the many institutional similarities in the command economy. In general, managers of industrial enterprises were politically powerful, whereas workers and pensioners were not. New private-sector firms were politically weak, whereas bureaucrats in industrial ministries were strong. In all countries economic actors sought to capture the state, but their ability to do so depended in large part on the extent to which politicians benefited by granting them influence over policy.

Politicians across the postcommunist region faced different incentives and adopted different strategies to stay in office. In nonpolarized democracies, politicians were better positioned to fend off demands by narrow interest groups by relying on support from the dependent sector of the population. However, when polarization was high in democracies, politicians often were more than willing to be captured by narrow interest groups when the alternative meant losing office. This supply-side treatment of state capture is somewhat closer to Stigler's (1971) original formulation of the concept.

In addition, this work hopes to advance the important debate on the sources of state capacity by endogenizing the decision to strengthen or weaken state institutions. The strategic weakening of the state is not the first choice of politicians in polarized democracies or autocracies. Instead, incumbents in democracies are induced to weaken the state by the threat of losing office. In autocracies they weaken the state because of a limited capacity to commit to economic reforms that will raise revenue for the state. Many observers

---

[2] Gehlbach (2008) presents a similar argument about how politicians shape markets for their political advantage in the postcommunist world.

have made sweeping arguments that politicians in the postcommunist world have largely been interested in weakening or strengthening the state without identifying more precisely the conditions under which we should expect the former rather than the latter.

One potentially productive line of research is whether the interaction of state building and market building analyzed here has echoes in other parts of the world at other times.[3] The theoretical argument makes general predictions about policy choice, and it may be useful to think about how the argument applies in other settings. The political logic that incumbent politicians pursue slower and less consistent reforms under autocracy and polarized democracy may resemble attempts to conduct economic reforms in other settings. For example, Murillo (2009) finds that partisanship and political polarization have been important determinants of the implementation of privatization policy in Latin America in recent years. Given the high degree of income inequality in many countries in Latin America, incumbent politicians would likely be hard-pressed to create a stable policy environment that would provide a steady stream of revenue for the state. As such, politicians may have strong incentives to conduct inconsistent reforms in this setting that provide narrow benefits to powerful groups among the productive elements of society at the expense of the dependent sectors. Indeed, Schamis (1999) and Murillo (2009) provide considerable evidence that economic reform in Latin America along one dimension is often undermined by policy decisions along other dimensions. The combination of rapid privatization and weak state institutions described in this work should be familiar to the Latin American ear.

However, this is not to deny the important differences that mark economic transformation in the postcommunist world from other regions. The scope of state control of the economy at the start of the transition was significantly greater in the postcommunist world than in other regions. Politicians in the postcommunist world at the start of the transformation were redistributing the vast majority of productive assets in society. This gave politicians tremendous opportunities to use the power of the state to reward supporters and punish opponents. Privatization in other regions of the world is much narrower in scope and now typically involves public utilities, telecommunications, and large energy firms. The logic of the argument may have relevance in other settings, including where politicians squeezed for revenue because of commitment problems subvert economic and institutional reform for political gain, but this is a subject for future research.

Partisanship and Policy

This work differs from much existing literature on the politics of economic reform by emphasizing the importance of executive partisanship. For the most part, existing literature on postcommunist transformation has downplayed the

---

[3] See Pop-Eleches (2009: 7–8) for a nice discussion of the value of cross-regional comparisons.

impact of government partisanship on policy choice. Many have suggested that initial structural conditions, the pull of the European Union, IMF conditionality, and the hegemony of neoliberalism compelled politicians of different partisan stripes to pursue similar policies (De Melo et al. 2001; Vachudova 2005; Appel 2004). Others argue that patronage concerns overwhelm considerations of partisanship (Hale 2006; Way 2005). Still others suggest that political competition and the fragmentation of political power by themselves are sufficient to promote economic reform regardless of the partisanship of government (Hellman 1998).

In contrast, this work has argued that executive partisanship and political polarization are important determinants of economic policy and institutional reforms. To neglect these factors in accounting for policy choice is to implicitly agree that economic agents are largely indifferent as to whether an old-left, center, or right politician controls the executive. However, the intensity of political struggles to capture the seat of power indicates that they care deeply about the matter. But partisanship is only part of the story. Because the partisanship of the government does not always translate directly into policy outcomes, it is important to identify the constraints facing politicians pursuing partisan interests.

Yet this hardly exhausts the possibilities of studying the relationship between partisanship and reform. Examining the impact of differences among groups within the three camps of partisans analyzed here might be a productive area for future research. Lumping political actors into three broad partisan camps, as I have done here, is common in the literature on policy making, but is clearly a simplification. In future work, it would be helpful to examine how institutions or structural conditions make coordination among groups within a particular camp more or less likely. In addition, the impact of partisanship may differ in times of economic crisis and in times of normal politics (Pop-Eleches 2008, 2009). Finally, it would be helpful to examine whether different types of partisan governments vary in their choice of policy. For example, do the policy choices of personalist old-left governments, such as those in Kazakhstan, Azerbaijan, and Belarus, differ from more party-based old-left governments, such as those in Bulgaria or Moldova? Answers to this question would be of interest to scholars interested in partisan effects on policy more generally.

The Dynamics of Political Polarization

This work identified, albeit somewhat tentatively given the nature of the data, economic inequality as a social base for political polarization. This step is helpful because not all social cleavages map easily into politics on a one-to-one basis, and studies that rely on social indicators of political polarization that are not translated into politics risk misspecification (Posner 2004). Moreover, because scholars have identified a range of social factors as possible sources of political polarization, it is helpful to find a link between economic inequality and political polarization.

One topic for future work would explore the dynamics of political polarization, considering, for example, how economic crises induced by inconsistent reform can lead to a new political equilibrium. This logic appears to have been at play following economic crises in Russia in 1998, Bulgaria in 1996, and Romania in 1996. In each of these cases, the government used inconsistent reforms to deliver significant benefits to narrow interest groups, but these policies put government finances under duress and eventually led to an economic crash when the government lacked the revenue to pay its bills. Similar financial setbacks in more authoritarian settings such as Kyrgyzstan in 1998 and Belarus in 1998 failed to produce similar changes in policy.

Similarly, it would be helpful to explore how the pull of the European Union and democracy may have shaped political polarization in the cases at hand. The possibility of EU accession may have altered the incentives of politicians to moderate their policies somewhat and move toward the center of the political spectrum, especially among old-left political parties, in Bulgaria and Romania, as noted in Chapter 6. In addition, while I have emphasized that the incentives to engage in partisan politics are quite strong during transition, the slow boring of democratic competition and the pull of the median voter over time may constrain the extent to which politicians can fully cater to partisan supporters.

Finally, it would be useful to explore whether other social cleavages could be used to generate polarization on economic issues. Recent years have seen a rise in populist parties in the postcommunist world, as Bulgaria, Romania, Poland, Latvia, and Slovakia have elected governments whose leaders fit this admittedly vague term and as populist parties have significantly increased their vote shares in Latvia, Lithuania, and Slovenia. For the most part, these populist parties have not made dramatic departures from the economic policies of their predecessors but have instead focused on social and cultural issues, especially anticorruption (Krastev 2007). This relative continuity in economic policy is perhaps not surprising as economies in the region experienced a prolonged boom in the past decade. However, the financial crash of 2008 may alter the incentives of populist parties and lead them to adopt more antireform policies. To the extent that the cultural and social issues that brought the populist parties to power overlap with groups facing economic insecurity, there may be room for heightened polarization around economic issues in the future.

Institutional Legacies, Path Dependence, and Increasing Returns

This study found that institutional legacies shape reform outcomes as countries with better initial conditions experienced more rapid and consistent economic and institutional reforms. More surprising, however, was the weakness of the evidence that the impact of bad initial conditions on economic and institutional reform was increasing or decreasing over time. Despite the expectation that initial conditions would drive a wedge between countries with better and worse starting points, the empirical evidence presented in Chapter 3 suggests that a simple version of path dependence that emphasizes the "lock-in" effect of initial conditions does not seem to be present in the reform outcomes in the cases at hand. In contrast, there is some evidence that countries with bad initial conditions can catch up to countries with good initial conditions over time as argued in Chapter 4. Indeed, while countries with poor initial conditions experienced a deep economic decline early in the transition, they experienced faster economic growth than countries with better initial conditions in subsequent years.

More generally, this work suggests the value of analyzing the interaction of institutional legacies and time-trend variables to explore whether the influence of institutions on policy outcomes has increasing or decreasing returns. Recent scholarship has emphasized the possibility of path-dependence and feedback processes in economic outcomes as initial policy choices and initial institutional configurations make path-departing change harder to accomplish. Initial policy choices and institutional legacies may empower some groups that are then better able to defend their interests in the political arena, or they may contain technical features that raise the costs of reversing course (North 1990). This dynamic has been identified most prominently in the study of economic growth (North 1990), the welfare state (Pierson 1994, 2004), and corporate governance (Bebchuk and Roe 1999). The notion that initial choices and institutions lock policies into specific paths that are increasingly resistant to change is intuitively appealing but is often difficult to demonstrate empirically (Page 2006). By interacting a measure of initial conditions with a time-trend variable, it is possible to gain some empirical leverage on whether the impact of initial conditions on policy takes a simple form of increasing or decreasing returns.

The Value of Microfoundations

Finally, this work has argued for the importance of providing evidence at the individual level to support arguments about national-level outcomes. A great deal of work in comparative political economy examines how national-level variables influence national-level outcomes. For example, scholars have produced influential lines of research exploring whether trade openness undermines social spending, resource wealth promotes economic growth, or democratization makes a country more prone to war (cf. Garrett 1998; Sachs and Warner 1995; Mansfield and Snyder 2005). Cross-national regressions remain an essential element of the social science tool kit, but they tell us little about whether the individuals often depicted in our arguments actually behave as we claim that they do. To help put our arguments on firmer footing, it is important to provide individual-level analyses that complement cross-national analyses using national-level variables. This work used survey data from twenty-three countries to demonstrate that businesspeople in countries with higher levels of political polarization viewed policy as less stable and invested at lower rates than their counterparts in countries with lower levels of polarization. These findings were consistent with broader claims generated by the argument and helped to provide stronger microfoundations for the theory. In general, there is a great deal of work to be done in exploring whether individual-level data underpin or undermine arguments made using national-level variables.

Final Remarks

I have tried to push the argument to make it as clear as possible and to assess my claims against a broad range of data, but it is important to recognize that any single work can offer only a narrow slice of the postcommunist transformation. The building of states and markets in a postcommunist context is an extraordinarily complex undertaking that in some respects is still unfolding. Undoubtedly scholars will pore over memoirs, analyze available statistical data, and dig deeper into the archives to better understand the creation of markets and states in the region for many years to come. The argument put forward here tries to make the great postcommunist transformation comprehensible, but it is equally important to retain the exquisite wonder of the events of the past twenty years in the region as well. There is still much more to be learned about variation in the creation of markets, states, and democracies in the postcommunist region.

Two central debates in comparative politics motivate this book. The first examines whether democracy promotes reform and the second explores whether state building and market building work at cross-purposes or go hand in hand. Here I have tried to contribute to these debates by identifying the conditions under which democracy promotes the reform of the economy and the reform of the state. In the end, I found that the answer to these grand questions is: "It depends." Undoubtedly, this response will leave some scholars wanting for more. Hopefully, it will encourage them to push this research agenda further.

References

Abdelal, Rawi. 2001. *National Purpose in the World Economy: Post-Soviet States in Comparative Perspective.* Ithaca, NY: Cornell University Press.

Acemoglu, Daron, Simon Johnson, and James Robinson. 2001. "The Colonial Origins of Comparative Development: An Empirical Investigation." *American Economic Review* 91 (December): 1369–1401.

Acemoglu, Daron, and James Robinson. 2006. *The Economic Origins of Dictatorship and Democracy.* Cambridge: Cambridge University Press.

Achen, Christopher. 2000. "Why Lagged Dependent Variables Can Suppress the Explanatory Power of Other Independent Variables." Paper presented at the annual meeting of the Political Methodology Section of the APSA, Los Angeles.

Adam, Jan. 1999. *Social Costs of Transformation to a Market Economy in Post-Socialist Countries.* New York: St. Martin's Press.

Aghion, Philippe, and Olivier Blanchard. 1994. "On the Speed of Transition in Central Europe." *NBER Macroeconomics Annual* 9 (March): 283–330.

Aghion, Philippe, and Peter Howitt. 1998. *Endogenous Growth Theory.* Cambridge, MA: MIT Press.

Ahrend, Rudiger. 2004. "Accounting for Russia's Post-Crisis Growth." OECD Economics Department Working Paper no. 404. Paris: OECD.

———. 2006. "Russia's Post-Crisis Growth: Its Sources and Prospects for Continuation." *Europe-Asia Studies* 58 (1): 1–24.

Alam, Asad, and Arup Bannerji. 2001. "Uzbekistan and Kazakhstan: A Tale of Two Transition Paths." Unpublished manuscript, World Bank, Washington, DC.

Alam, Asad, and Mark Sundberg. 2002. "A Decade of Fiscal Transition." World Bank, Washington, DC.

Aldrich, John. 1983. "A Downsian Spatial Model with Party Activists." *American Political Science Review* 77 (3): 974–990.

Alesina, Alberto, and Allen Drazen. 1991. "Why Are Stabilizations Delayed?" *American Economic Review* 81: 1170–1189.

Alesina, Alberto, and Dani Rodrik. 1994. "Distributive Politics and Economic Growth." *Quarterly Journal of Economics* 109 (2): 465–490.

Alesina, Alberto, and Howard Rosenthal. 1995. *Partisan Politics, Divided Government, and the Economy.* Cambridge: Cambridge University Press.

Alexandrova, Galina, and Miglena Mancheva. 1999. "Dispute over Petrol and Neftochim Brings to Light Buyers' Lobbies." *ISI Emerging Markets Data*, July 30. http://www.securities.com/cgibin/split/94dec/Data/BG/News/../kptl990128e.html? KPTL.

Alstadt, Audrey L. 1997. "Azerbaijan's Struggle toward Democracy." In Karen Dawisha and Bruce Parrott, eds., *Conflict, Cleavage, and Chance in Central Asia and the Caucasus*, 110–155. Cambridge: Cambridge University Press.

Amsden, Alice, Jacek Kochanowicz, and Lance Taylor. 1994. *The Market Meets Its Match: Restructuring the Economies of Eastern Europe*. Cambridge, MA: Harvard University Press.

Anderson, Christopher, and Yulia Tverdova. 2003. "Corruption, Political Allegiances, and Attitudes toward Government in Contemporary Democracies." *American Journal of Political Science* 41: 91–109.

Andreev, Alexander. 1996. "The Political Changes and Political Parties." In Marie Zloch-Christy, ed., *Bulgaria in a Time of Change: Political and Economic Dimensions*, 25–43. Avebury: Aldershot.

Andrews, Josephine. 2002. *When Majorities Fail: The Russian Parliament, 1990–1993*. Cambridge: Cambridge University Press.

Angrist, Joshua, and Alan B. Krueger. 2001. "Instrumental Variables and the Search for Identification: From Supply and Demand to Natural Experiments." *Journal of Economic Perspectives* 15 (4): 69–95.

Appel, Hillary. 2004. *A New Capitalist Order: Privatization and Ideology in Russia and Eastern Europe*. Pittsburgh: University of Pittsburgh Press.

Armingeon, Klaus, and Roman Careja. 2004. "Comparative Political Data-Set II." Bern, Switzerland: University of Bern.

Armingeon, Klaus, Romana Careja, Pajatos Potolidis, Marlene Gerber, and Philipp Leimgrubber. 2008. "Comparative Political Data Set III, 1990–2006." Bern, Switzerland: University of Bern.

Aron, Leon. 2000. *Yeltsin: A Revolutionary Life*. New York: St. Martin's Press.

Aslund, Anders. 1995. *How Russia Became a Market Economy*. Washington, DC: Brookings Institution.

———. 2000. "Meeting Report." Carnegie Endowment for International Peace, January 6. Washington, DC.

———. 2002. *Building Capitalism: The Transformation of the Former Soviet Bloc*. Washington, DC: Brookings Institution.

———. 2003. "WTO Entry: No Time to Lose." *Moscow Times*, February 3, 10.

———. 2007a. *Russia's Capitalist Revolution: Why Market Reform Succeeded and Democracy Failed*. Washington, DC: Petersen Institute for International Economics.

———. 2007b. *How Capitalism Was Built*. Cambridge: Cambridge University Press.

Aslund, Anders, Peter Boone, and Simon Johnson. 1996. "How to Stabilize: Lessons from Post-Communist Countries." *Brookings Papers on Economic Activity* 1: 217–311.

Aslund, Anders, and Georges de Menil. 2000. *Economic Reform in Ukraine: The Unfinished Agenda*. Armonk, NY: M. E. Sharpe.

Auty, Richard M. 1999. "The IMF Model and Resource-Abundant Transition Economies: Kazakhstan and Uzbekistan." United Nations University, Working Papers no. 169. November.

Avramov, Roumen, and Kamen Guenov. 1994. "The Rebirth of Capitalism in Bulgaria." Unpublished manuscript, Sofia.

Avramov, Roumen, and Jerome Sjard. 1996. "Bulgaria: From Enterprise Indiscipline to Financial Crisis." Centre d'Etudes Prospectives et d'Informations Internationales, Paris.

Azmanova, Albena. 2000. "Bulgaria." *East European Constitutional Review* 9 (4). http://www1.law.nyu.edu/eecr/vol9num4/features/EUarticle5.html.

Balcerowicz, Leszek. 1994. "Poland." In John Williamson, ed., *Political Economy of Policy Reform*, 155–177. Washington, DC: Institute for International Economics.

———. 1995. *Socialism, Capitalism, Transformation*. Budapest: Central European University Press.

Barany, Zoltan. 2002. "Bulgaria's Royal Elections." *Journal of Democracy* 13 (April): 141–155.

Barnes, Andrew. 2006. *Owning Russia: The Struggle over Factories, Farms and Power*. Ithaca, NY: Cornell University Press.

Barro, Robert. 1991. "Economic Growth in a Cross Section of Countries." *Quarterly Journal of Economics* 106 (2): 407–443.

Bartels, Larry. 1991. "Instrumental Variables and 'Quasi-Instrumental' Variables." *American Journal of Political Science* 35 (3): 777–800.

———. 2008. *Unequal Democracy: The Political Economy of the New Gilded Age*. Princeton: Princeton University Press.

Bates, Robert. 1990. "Macropolitical Economy in the Field of Development." In Kenneth Shepsle and James Alt, eds., *Perspectives on Positive Political Economy*, 31–55. Cambridge: Cambridge University Press.

Bearce, David. 2007. *Monetary Divergence: Domestic Policy Autonomy in the Post-Bretton Woods Era*. Ann Arbor: University of Michigan Press.

Bebchuk, Lucian Arye, and Mark J. Roe. 1999. "A Theory of Path Dependence and Corporate Governance and Ownership." *Stanford Law Review* 52: 127–170.

Beck, Nathaniel, and Jonathan Katz. 1995. "What to Do (and Not to Do) with Time-Series Cross-Sectional Data." *American Political Science Review* 89 (3): 634–647.

———. 2001. "Throwing Out the Baby with the Bath Water: A Comment on Green, Kim and Yoon." *International Organization* 55 (2): 487–495.

———. 2004. "Time-Series-Cross-Section Issues: Dynamics, 2004." 35 pp. Unpublished manuscript, New York.

Beck, Thorsten, George Clarke, Alberto Goff, Philip Keefer, and Patrick Walsh. 2001. "New Tools in Comparative Political Economy: The Database of Political Institutions." *World Bank Economic Review* 15 (1): 165–176.

———. 2004. Update to Database of Political Institutions. http://econ.worldbank.org/WBSITE/EXTERNAL/EXTDEC/EXTRESEARCH/0,,contentMDK:20649465~pagePK:64214825~piPK:64214943~theSitePK:469382,00.html.

Beissinger, Mark. 2002. *Nationalist Mobilization and the Collapse of the Soviet State*. Cambridge: Cambridge University Press.

Belin, Laura. 1996. "Private Media Comes Full Circle." *Transition* 2 (21): 62–65.

Belka, Marek. 2001. "Lessons on the Polish Transformation." In George Blazyca and Ryszard Rapacki, eds., *Poland into the New Millennium*. 13–32. Northampton, MA: Edward Elgar.

Bell, Janice. 2001. *The Political Economy of Reform in Post-Communist Poland*. Cheltenham: Edward Elgar.

Berg, Andrew, Eduardo Borensztein, Ratna Sahay, and Jeromin Zettelmeyer. 1999. "The Evolution of Output in Transition Economies." IMF Working Paper, no. 99/73. Washington, DC: International Monetary Fund.

Berglof, Erik, and Patrick Bolton. 2002. "The Great Divide and Beyond – Financial Architecture in Transition." *Journal of Economic Perspectives* 16 (1): 77–100.

Berglof, Erik, Andrey Kounov, Julia Shvets, and Ksenia Yudaeva. 2003. *The New Political Economy of Russia*. Cambridge, MA: MIT Press.

Besley, Timothy. 2006. *Principled Agents: The Political Economy of Good Government*. Oxford: Oxford University Press.

Besley, Timothy, and Masayuki Kudamatsu. 2007. "Making Autocracy Work." LSE STICERD Research Paper no. DEDPS 48.

Bewley, R. A. 1979. "The Direct Estimation of the Equilibrium Response in a Linear Dynamic Model." *Economic Letters* 3: 357–361.

Bialer, Seweryn. 1982. *Stalin's Successors: Leadership, Stability and Change in the Soviet Union*. Cambridge: Cambridge University Press.

Biberaj, Elez. 1998. *Albania in Transition: The Rocky Road to Democracy*. Boulder, CO: Westview Press.

_____. 2000. "The Albanian National Question: The Challenges of Autonomy, Independence, and Separatism." In Michael Mandelbaum, ed., *The New European Diasporas*, 214–288. New York: Council on Foreign Relations.

Birch, Sarah. 2000. *Elections and Democratization in Ukraine*. Basingstoke, UK: Macmillan.

Black, Duncan. 1958. *The Theory of Committees and Elections*. Cambridge: Cambridge University Press.

Blanchard, Olivier. 1997. *The Economics of Post-Communist Transition*. Clarendon: Oxford University Press.

Blanchard, Olivier, Maxim Boycko, Marek Dabrowski, Rudiger Dornbusch, Richard Layard, and Andrei Shleifer. 1994. *Postcommunist Reform: Pain and Progress*. Cambridge, MA: MIT Press.

Blanchard, Olivier, and Marek Dabrowski. 1993. "The Progress of Restructuring in Poland." In Olivier Blanchard et al., eds., *Postcommunist Reform: Pain and Progress*, 109–150. Cambridge, MA: MIT Press.

Blasi, Joseph, Maya Kroumova, and Douglas Kruse. 1997. *Kremlin Capitalism: Privatizing the Russian Economy*. Ithaca, NY: Cornell University Press.

Blaszczyk, Barbara, M. Gorzynski, T. Kaminski, and B. Paczoski. 2001. "Secondary Privatization in Poland (Part II): Evolution of Ownership Structure and Performance in National Investment Funds and Their Portfolio Companies." Case Report no. 48. Warsaw: Center for Economic Research.

Bohle, Dorothee, and Béla Greskovits. 2006. "The Variety of Socio-Economic Regimes in Central and Eastern Europe." Paper prepared for Post-Communist Political Economy and Democratic Politics Conference, Duke University, April.

Boix, Carles. 1998. *Political Parties, Growth, and Equality: Conservative, Social Democratic Economic Strategies in the World Economy*. Cambridge: Cambridge University Press.

_____. 2003. *Democracy and Redistribution*. Cambridge: Cambridge University Press.

Boix, Carles, and Susan Stokes. 2003. "Endogenous Democratization." *World Politics* 55 (4): 517–549.

Bojicic-Dzelilovic, Vesna, and Victor Bojkov. 2004. "Informality in Post-Communist Transition: Determinants and Consequences of the Privatization Process in Bulgaria." IBEU Working Paper 3.2.

Boone, Peter, and Denis Rodionov. 2004. "Rent Seeking in Russia and the CIS." Unpublished manuscript, UBS Warburg, Moscow.

Borisova, Yevgeniya. 2001. "Compromise Labor Code over First Hurdle." *St. Petersburg Times*, July 6.

Borisova, Yevgeniya, Gary Peach, Nonna Chernyakova, and Mayerbeck Nunayev. 2000a. "Baby Boom or Dead Souls." *Moscow Times*, September 9. www.MoscowTimes.com.

———. 2000b. "How Many Forgeries?" *Moscow Times*, September 9. www.MoscowTimes.com.

Boycko, Maxim, Andrei Shleifer, and Robert Vishny. 1995. *Privatizing Russia*. Cambridge, MA: MIT Press.

Bozoki, Andras. 2002. "The Hungarian Socialists: Technocratic Modernizationism or New Social Democracy?" In Andras Bozoki and John T. Ishiyama, eds., *The Communist Successor Parties of Central and Eastern Europe*, 98–115. Armonk, NY: M. E. Sharpe.

Bozoki, Andras, and John Ishiyama, eds. 2002. *The Communist Successor Parties of Central and Eastern Europe*. Armonk, NY: M. E. Sharpe.

Brader, Ted, and Joshua Tucker. 2001. "The Emergence of Mass Partisanship in Russia, 1993–1995." *American Journal of Political Science* 45 (1): 69–83.

Brady, Henry, and David Collier. 2004. "Refocusing the Discussion of Methodology." In Henry Brady and David Collier, eds., *Rethinking Social Inquiry: Diverse Tools, Shared Standards*, 3–20. Lanham, MD: Rowman and Littlefield.

Breslauer, George W. 2002. *Gorbachev and Yeltsin as Leaders*. Cambridge: Cambridge University Press.

Broadman, Harry G. 1999. "Uzbekistan: Social and Structural Policy Review, August 25, Poverty Reduction and Economic Management Unit." World Bank, Washington, DC.

———. 2000. "Competition, Corporate Governance, and Regulation in Central Asia: Uzbekistan's Structural Reform Challenges." World Bank Policy Research Working Paper no. 2331. May.

Brooks, Sarah. 2008. *Social Protection and the Market in Latin America: The Transformation of Social Security Institutions*. Cambridge: Cambridge University Press.

Brubaker, Rogers. 1996. *Nationalism Reframed: Nationhood and the National Question in the New Europe*. Cambridge: Cambridge University Press.

Brus, Wolodimierz. 1973. *The Economics and Politics of Socialism*. London: Routledge and Paul Kegan.

Bryant, Fred B., and Rebecca L. Guilbault. 2002. "'I Knew It All Along' Eventually: The Development of Hindsight Bias in Reaction to the Clinton Impeachment Verdict." *Basic and Applied Social Psychology* 24 (1): 27–41.

Bugajski, Janusz. 2002. *Political Parties of Eastern Europe: A Guide to Politics in the Post-Communist Era*. Armonk, NY: M. E. Sharpe.

Bukharbaeva, Galima. 2000. "Investors Shun Uzbekistan." *Institute for War and Peace Reporting*, May 25.

Bulgarian Socialist Party. 1994. *Documents of the 41st Congress of the Bulgarian Socialist Party, June 3–6, 1994*. Sofia: Bulgarian Socialist Party.

Bunce, Valerie. 1984–1985. "The Empire Strikes Back: The Evolution of the Eastern Bloc from a Soviet Asset to a Soviet Liability." *International Organization* 39: 1–46.

———. 1999a. *Subversive Institutions; The Design and Destruction of Socialism and the State*. Cambridge: Cambridge University Press.

_____. 1999b. "The Political Economy of Postsocialism." *Slavic Review* 58: 756–793. Special issue on "Ten Years in Transition."

Bunich, Andrei. 2006. *Osen' oligarkhov*. Moscow: Yauza Publishing House.

Butora, Martin, and Zora Butorova. 1999. "Slovakia's Democratic Awakening." *Journal of Democracy* 10 (1): 80–95.

Cameron, David. 1978. "The Expansion of the Public Economy: A Comparative Analysis." *American Political Science Review* 72 (4): 1243–1261.

Campos, Nauro. 1999. "Back to the Future: The Growth Prospects of Transition Economies Reconsidered." Cerge-EI Working Paper Series 146. Czech Republic.

Campos, Nauro, and Fabricio Corricelli. 2002. "Growth in Transition: What We Know, What We Don't and What We Should." *Journal of Economic Literature* 40 (3): 793–836.

Campos, Nauro, and Roman Horvath. 2007. "Reform Redux: Measurement, Determinants and Reversals." Unpublished manuscript, Brunel University, London.

Campos, Nauro, and Vitaliy Kizuyev. 2007. "On the Dynamics of Ethnic Fractionalization." *American Journal of Political Science* 51 (3): 620–639.

Capital. 1997. "In Search of the New Premianov." *ISI Emerging Markets Data*, July 30. http://www.securities.com/cgi-bin/split/94dec/Data/BG/News.../kptl970508e.html?KPTL.

Carlisle, D. S. 1991. "Uzbekistan and the Uzbeks." *Problems of Communism* 40 (5): 23–44.

_____. 1994. "Islam Karimov and Uzbekistan: Back to the Future?" In Timothy. J. Colton and Robert. C. Tucker, eds., *Patterns of Post-Soviet Leadership*, 191–216. Boulder, CO: Westview Press.

Carpenter, Daniel. 2001. *The Forging of Bureaucratic Autonomy: Networks, Reputations and Policy Innovation in Executive Agencies, 1862–1928*. Princeton: Princeton University Press.

Chotiner, Barbara Ann. 1999. "The Communist Party of the Russian Federation: From the Fourth Congress to the Summer of 1998 Government Crisis." In John T. Ishiyama, ed., *Communist Successor Parties in Post-Communist Politics*, 101–130. Commack, NY: Nova Science Publishers.

Claessens, Stijn, and R. Kyle Peters. 1997. "State Enterprise Performance and Soft Budget Constraints." *Economics of Transition* 5 (2): 305–322.

Clem, Ralph S., and Peter R. Craumer. 1995. "The Politics of Russia's Regions: A Geographical Analysis of the Russian Election and Constitutional Plebiscite of December 1993." *Post-Soviet Affairs* 36 (2): 67–86.

_____. 1996. "Roadmap to Victory: Boris Yeltsin and the Russian Presidential Elections of 1996." *Post-Soviet Geography and Economics* 27 (6): 335–354.

Collins, Kathleen. 1999. "Clans, Pacts, and Politics: Understanding Regime Transition in Post-Soviet Central Asia." Ph. D. dissertation, Stanford University.

_____. 2006. *The Logic of Clan Politics in Central Asia: Its Impact on Regime Transformation*. Cambridge: Cambridge University Press.

Colton, Timothy J. 2000. *Transitional Citizens: Voters and What Influences Them in the New Russia*. Cambridge, MA: Harvard University Press.

Colton, Timothy J., and Michael McFaul. 2003. *Popular Choice and Managed Democracy*. Washington, DC: Brookings Institution.

Connor, Walter. 1990. "When Is a Nation?" *Ethnic and Racial Studies* 13 (1): 92–103.

Cook, Linda. 2006. "State Capacity and Pension Provision." In Timothy Colton and Stephen Holmes, eds., *The State after Communism: Governance in the New Russia*, 121–154. Lanham, MD: Rowman and Littlefield.

————. 2007. *Postcommunist Welfare States: Reform Politics in Russia and Eastern Europe*. Ithaca, NY: Cornell University Press.

Coudouel, Aline, and Sheila Marnie. 1999. "From Universal to Targeted Assistance: An Assessment of the Uzbek Experience." *Most'-Most* 9: 443–458.

Coudouel, Aline, Sheila Marnie, and John Micklewright. 1998. "Targeting Social Assistance in a Transition Economy: The Mahallas in Uzbekistan." Innocenti Occasional Papers Series, no. 63.

Cox, Gary. 2001. *Making Votes Count: Strategic Coordination in the World's Electoral System*. Cambridge: Cambridge University Press.

Cox, Terry, and Bob Mason. 1999. *Social and Economic Transformation in East Central Europe*. Cheltenham: Edward Elgar Press.

Crowther, William. 1997. "The Politics of Democratization in Post-Communist Moldova." In Karen Dawisha and Bruce Parrott, eds., *Democratic Changes and Authoritarian Reactions in Russia, Ukraine, Belarus, and Moldova*, 282–299. Cambridge: Cambridge University Press.

Dabrowski, Janusz, M. Michal Federowicz, Tytus Kaminski, and Jan Szomburg. 1993. "Privatisation of Polish State-Owned Enterprises: Progress, Barriers, Initial Effects." Third Report, 1–103. Warsaw-Gdansk: Gdansk Institute for Market Economics.

Dabrowski, Janusz, M. Michal Federowicz, and Anthony Levitas. 1991. "Polish State Enterprises and the Properties of Performance: Stabilization, Marketization, Privatization." *Politics and Society* 19 (4): 403–437.

Darden, Keith. 2009. *Economic Liberalism and Its Rivals: The Formation of International Institutions among the Post-Soviet States*. Cambridge: Cambridge University Press.

Darden, Keith, and Anna Grzymala-Busse. 2007. "The Great Divide: Pre-Communist Schooling and Post-Communist Trajectories." *World Politics* 59 (1): 83–115.

De Boef, Susanne, and Luke Keele. 2008. "Taking Time Seriously: Dynamic Regression." *American Journal of Political Science* 52 (1): 184–200.

De Melo, Martha, Cevdet Denizer, and Alan Gelb. 1996. "From Plan to Market: Patterns of Transition." World Bank Policy Research Paper. Washington, DC.

De Melo, Martha, Cevdet Denizer, Alan Gelb, and Stoyan Tenev. 2001. "Circumstances and Choice: The Role of Initial Conditions and Policies in Transition Economies." *World Bank Economic Review* 15 (1): 1–31.

de Menil, Georges. 2000. "From Hyperinflation to Stagnation." *Russian and East European Finance and Trade* 36 (1): 28–58.

Deirmeier, Daniel, Joel Ericson, Timothy Frye, and Steve Lewis. 1997. "Credible Commitment and Property Rights: The Role of Strategic Interaction between Political and Economic Actors." In David Weimer, ed., *The Political Economy of Property Rights*, 20–42. Cambridge: Cambridge University Press.

Denisova, Irina, Markus Eller, Timothy Frye, and Ekaterina Zhuravskaya. 2009. "Who Wants to Revise Privatization: The Complementarity of Institutions and Market Skills." *American Political Science Review* 103 (2): 284–304.

Desai, Mihir, Alexander Dyck, and Luigi Zingales. 2007. "Theft and Taxes." *Journal of Financial Economics* 84 (3): 591–623.

Desai, Padma. 2006. *Conversations on Russia: Reform from Yeltsin to Putin*. Oxford: Oxford University Press.

Dewatripont, Matthias, and Gerard Roland. 1995. "The Design of Reform Packages under Uncertainty." *American Economic Review* 85 (5): 1207–1223.

Deyanova, Lilyana. 1996. "The Battles for the Mausoleums." In Jacque Coenen-Huther, ed., *Bulgaria at the Crossroads*, 175–186. New York: Nova Science Publishers.

Djankov, Simeon, and Peter Murrell. 2002. "Enterprise Restructuring in Transition: A Quantitative Survey." *Journal of Economic Literature* 40 (3): 739–792.

Dmitriev, Mikhail. 1999. "Parlamentskie vybory v Rossii: Ekonomicheskie programmy vedushchikh partii i blokov" (Parliamentary elections in Russia: Economic programs of the leading parties and blocs). *Brifing* 11 (1, November): 4. Carnegie Moscow Center.

———. 2000. "Evolutsiia ekonomicheskikh programm vedushikh politicheskikh partii i blokov Rossii." *Voprosy Ekonomiki* 2000 (1): 1–14.

Dobozi, Istvan. 1995. "Real Output Decline in Transition Economies: Forget GDP, Try Power Consumption." *Beyond Transition* 6 (January–February): 17–18.

Dobozi, Istvan, and Gerhard Pohl. 1995. "Real Output Decline in Transition Economies – Forget GDP, Try Power Consumption Data!" *Transition* 6 (1–2): 17.

Dobrinsky, Rumen. 1997. "Transition Failures: Anatomy of the Bulgarian Crisis." Unpublished manuscript, WIIW, Vienna.

Doyle, Michael W. 1986. "Kant's Perpetual Peace." *American Political Science Review* 80 (4): 1115–1169.

Dunteman, George H. 1989. *Principal Components Analysis*. London: Sage.

Easter, Gerald. 1997. "Preference for Presidentialism: Postcommunist Regime Change in Russia and the NIS." *World Politics* 49 (2): 282–308.

———. 2002. "Politics of Revenue Extraction in Post-Communist States: Poland and Russia Compared." *Politics and Society* 30 (4): 599–627.

———. 2006. "Building Fiscal Capacity." In Timothy J. Colton and Stephen Holmes, eds., *The State after Communism: Governance in the New Russia*, 21–52. Lanham, MD. Routledge.

Easterly, William, and Paulo Viera de Cunha. 1993. *Financing the Storm: Macroeconomic Crises in Russia, 1992–1993*. Washington, DC: World Bank.

Ekiert, Gregorz, and Jan Kubik. 1998. "Contentious Politics in New Democracies: East Germany, Hungary, Poland and Slovakia, 1989–1993." *World Politics* 50 (4): 547–581.

———. 1999. *Rebellious Civil Society: Popular Protest and Democratic Consolidation in Poland, 1989–1993*. Ann Arbor: University of Michigan Press.

Elster, Jon. 1983. *Explaining Technical Change: A Case Study in the Philosophy of Science*. Cambridge: Cambridge University Press.

———. 1993. "The Necessity and Impossibility of Simultaneous Economic and Political Reform." In Douglas Greenberg, Stanley Katz, Melanie Beth Oliviero, and Steven C. Wheatley, eds., *Constitutionalism and Democracy: Transition in the Contemporary World*, 267–274. New York: Oxford University Press.

———. 1998. "A Plea for Mechanisms." In Peter Hedstrom and Richard Swedberg, eds., *Social Mechanisms: An Analytical Approach to Social Theory*, 45–73. Cambridge: Cambridge University Press.

Engelbrekt, Kjell. 1991. "Bulgaria: Cracks in the Union of Democratic Forces." *RFE/RL Report on Eastern Europe* 2 (20): 1–8.

———. 1993. "Bulgaria's Communists: Coming or Going?" *Radio Free Europe/Radio Liberty* 21: 1–5.

———. 1994. "Bulgaria's Political Stalemate." *Radio Free Europe Research Report*, June 24, 20–22.

Epperly, Brad. 2008. "Institutions and Legacies: Electoral Volatility in Eastern Europe and the Former Soviet Union." Paper presented at the annual meeting of the MPSA Annual National Conference, Chicago, April 3.

Ericson, Richard E. 1991. "The Classical Soviet-Type Economy: Nature of the System and Implications for Reform." *Journal of Economic Perspectives* 5 (4): 11–27.

———. 1992. "Economics." In Timothy J. Colton and Robert Legvold, eds., *After the Soviet Union: From Empire to Nations*, 49–83. New York: W. W. Norton.

Esping-Andersen, Gosta. 1990. *Three Worlds of Welfare Capitalism*. Princeton: Princeton University Press.

Esteban, Joan Maria, and Debraj Ray. 1994. "On the Measurement of Polarization." *Econometrica* 62 (4): 819–851.

European Bank for Reconstruction and Development (EBRD). Various years. *Transition Report*. London: EBRD.

Evans, Geoffrey. 2006. "The Social Bases of Political Divisions in Postcommunist Eastern Europe." *Annual Review of Sociology* 32: 245–270.

Falcetti, Elisabetta, Tatiana Lysenko, and Peter Sanfey. 2006. "Reforms and Growth in Transition. Re-examining the Evidence." *Journal of Comparative Economics* 34 (3): 421–445.

Falcetti, Elisabetta, Martin Raiser, and Peter Sanfey. 2002. "Defying the Odds: Initial Conditions, Reforms and Growth in the First Decade of Transition." *Journal of Comparative Economics* 30 (2): 229–250.

Fidrmuc, Jan. 2000. "Economics of Voting in Postcommunist Countries." *Electoral Studies* 19: 199–217.

———. 2003. "Economic Reform, Democracy, and Growth during Postcommunist Transition." *European Journal of Political Economy* 19: 583–604.

Fierman, William. 1997. "Political Development in Uzbekistan: Democratization?" In Karen Dawisha and Bruce Parrott, eds., *Conflict, Cleavage and Change in Central Asia and the Caucasus*, 360–408. Cambridge: Cambridge University Press.

Fiorina, Morris. 1996. *Divided Government*. Boston: Alwyn Bacon.

Fischer, Stanley, Ratna Sahay, and Carlos Végh. 1996. "Stabilization and Growth in Transition Economies: The Early Experience." *Journal of Economic Perspectives* 10: 45–66.

Fischer, Stanley, and Ratna Sahay. 2000. "The Transition Economies after Ten Years." IMF Working Paper 00/30. Washington, DC: International Monetary Fund.

Fischhoff, B. 1975. "Hindsight ≠ Foresight: The Effect of Outcome Knowledge on Judgment under Uncertainty." *Journal of Experimental Psychology: Human Perception and Performance* 104 (2): 288–299.

Fish, M. Steven. 1998. "The Determinants of Economic Reform in the Postcommunist World." *East European Politics and Society* 12 (1): 37–78.

———. 2005. *Democracy Derailed in Russia: The Failure of Open Politics*. Cambridge: Cambridge University Press.

Fish, M. Steven, and Robin Brooks. 2000. "Bulgarian Democracy's Organizational Weapon." *East European Constitutional Review* 9: 69–77.

Flikke, Geir. 1999. "Patriotic Left-Centrism: The Zigzags of the Communist Party of the Russian Federation." *Europe-Asia Studies*, 51 (2): 275–298.

Foxley, Alejandro. 1983. *Latin American Experiments in Neoconservative Economics*. Berkeley: University of California Press.

Franzese, Robert. 2002. *Macroeconomic Policies of Developed Democracies*. Cambridge: Cambridge University Press.

Freedom House. Annual Survey of Freedom Country Scores. www.Freedomhouse.org.

Freeland, Christia. 2000. *The Sale of the Century: Russia's Wild Ride from Communism to Capitalism*. New York: Crown Books.

Freeman, John R., ed. 1994. *Political Analysis*. Ann Arbor: University of Michigan Press.

Freshfields Bruckhaus Deringer. 2002. "Changes to Russian Labour Legislation." Briefing Paper, February. Moscow.

Frydman, Roman, Cheryl Gray, Merell Hasek, and Andrzej Rapaczynski. 1999. "When Does Privatization Work? The Impact of Private Ownership on Corporate Performance in the Transition Economics." *Quarterly Journal of Economics* 114 (4): 1153–1191.

Frye, Timothy. 1997a. "Russian Privatization and the Limits of Credible Commitment." In David Weimer, ed., *The Political Economy of Property Rights: Institutional Change and Credibility in the Reform of Centrally Planned Economies*, 84–108. Cambridge: Cambridge University Press.

———. 1997b. "A Politics of Institutional Choice: Postcommunist Presidencies." *Comparative Political Studies* 30 (5): 523–552.

———. 2000. *Brokers and Bureaucrats: Building Market Institutions in Russia*. Ann Arbor: University of Michigan Press.

———. 2002a. "The Perils of Polarization: Economic Performance in the Postcommunist World." *World Politics* 54 (3): 308–337.

———. 2002b. "Private Protection in Russia and Poland." *American Journal of Political Science* 46 (3): 572–584.

———. 2003. "Markets, Democracy and New Private Business in Russia." *Post-Soviet Affairs* 19 (1): 24–45.

———. 2006. "Governing the Banking Sector." In Timothy Colton and Stephen Holmes, eds., *The State after Communism: Governance in the New Russia*, 155–186. Lanham, MD: Rowman and Littlefield.

Frye, Timothy, Joel Hellman, and Joshua Tucker. 2000. "Data Base on Political Institutions in the Post-Communist World." Unpublished Data Set. Ohio State University.

Frye, Timothy, and Edward D. Mansfield. 2003. "Fragmenting Protection: The Political Economy of Trade Policy in the Post-Communist World." *British Journal of Political Science* 33: 635–657.

———. 2004. "Timing Is Everything: Elections and Trade Liberalization in the Post-Communist World." *Comparative Political Studies* 37 (4): 371–398.

Frye, Timothy, and Andrei Shleifer. 1997. "The Invisible Hand and the Grabbing Hand." *American Economic Review Papers and Proceedings* 87 (May): 554–559.

Frye, Timothy, and Ekaterina Zhuravskaya. 2000. "Rackets, Regulation, and the Rule of Law." *Journal of Law, Economics, and Organization* 16 (2): 478–502.

Gaddy, Clifford G., and Barry W. Ickes. 2002. *Russia's Virtual Economy*. Washington, DC: Brookings Institution.

Gaidar, Yegor. 1990. *Ekonomicheskie reformy i ierarkhicheskie struktury*. Moscow: Nauka.

———. 1997. *Yegor Gaidar: Sochinenie v dvukh tomakh*. Moscow: Evraziia.

Ganev, Venelin. 1998. "State and Networks in Post-Communist Bulgaria." Paper presented at the annual conference of the American Political Association, Boston, September 2–6.

———. 2001. "The Separation of Party and State as a Logistical Problem: A Glance at the Causes of State Weakness in Post-Communism." *East European Politics and Societies* 15 (2): 389–420.

———. 2006. *Preying on the State: Political Capitalism in Bulgaria*. Ithaca, NY: Cornell University Press.

Garrett, Geoffrey. 1998. *Partisan Politics in the Global Economy.* Cambridge: Cambridge University Press.

Garton-Ash, Timothy. 1993. *The Magic Lantern: The Revolution of '89 Witnessed in Warsaw, Budapest, Berlin, and Prague.* New York: Random House.

Geddes, Barbara. 1994. *Politician's Dilemma: Building State Capacity in Latin America.* Berkeley: University of California Press.

———. 1995. "A Comparative Perspective on the Leninist Legacy in Eastern Europe." *Comparative Political Studies* 28 (2): 239–274.

———. 2003. *Paradigms and Sand Castles: Theory Building and Research Design in Comparative Politics.* Ann Arbor: University of Michigan Press.

Gehlbach, Scott. 2008. *Representation through Taxation: Revenue, Politics, and Development in Postcommunist States.* Cambridge: Cambridge University Press.

Gehlbach, Scott, and Philip Keefer. 2008. "Investment without Democracy: Ruling-Party Institutionalization and Credible Commitment in Autocracies." Unpublished manuscript, Washington, DC, and Madison, WI.

Gehlbach, Scott, and Edmund Malesky. 2008. "The Role of Veto Players in Economic Reform." Unpublished manuscript, Madison, WI, and San Diego, CA.

Gelman, Andrew, and Jennifer Hill. 2007. *Data Analysis Using Regression and Multilevel/Hierarchical Models.* Cambridge: Cambridge University Press.

Ghandi, Jennifer. 2008. *Political Institutions under Dictatorship.* Cambridge: Cambridge University Press.

Gilbert, Daniel. 2007. *Stumbling on Happiness.* New York: Vintage Press.

Glaeser, Edward, Simon Johnson, and Andrei Shleifer. 2001. "Coase Versus the Coasians." *Quarterly Journal of Economics* 116 (3): 853–899.

Gleason, Gregory. 1994. "Uzbekistan: From Statehood to Nationhood." In Ian Bremmer and Ray Taras, eds., *National Politics in the Soviet Successor States,* 331–360. Cambridge: Cambridge University Press.

———. 2003. *Markets and Politics in Central Asia: Structural Reform and Political Change.* London: Routledge.

Graham, Thomas. 1999. "From Oligarchy to Oligarchy: The Structure of Russia's Ruling Elite." *Demokratizatsiya* 7: 325–340.

———. 2000. "Meeting Report." Carnegie Endowment for International Peace, January 6. Washington, DC.

———. 2002. "Fragmentation of Russia." In Andrew Kuchins, ed., *Russia after the Fall,* 39–61. Washington, DC: Carnegie Endowment.

Greene, Donald P., Soo Yeon Kim, and David H. Yoon. 2001. "Dirty Pool." *International Organization* 55 (2): 441–468.

Greene, William H. 1993. *Econometric Analysis.* 2d ed. Englewood Cliffs, NJ: Prentice Hall.

Groseclose, Timothy, and Nolan McCarty. 2000. "The Politics of Blame: Bargaining before an Audience." *American Political Science Review* 45 (1): 33–50.

Grosjean Pauline, and Claudia Senik. 2007. "Should Market Liberalization Precede Democracy? Causal Relations between Political Preferences and Development." IZA Discussion Paper 2889. London and Paris.

———. 2008. "Why Populist Democracy Promotes Market Liberalization." IZA Discussion Paper 3257. London and Paris.

Grossman, Sanford, and Elhanan Helpman. 1994. "Protection for Sale." *American Economic Review* 84 (4): 833–850.

Grozev, Kostadin. 2000. "Out with the Old, In with the New." *Bulgaria: Annual Report, 1999. Transitions on Line,* January 10. http://archive.tol.cz/countries/bulgaroo.html.

Grzymala-Busse, Anna. 2002. *Redeeming the Communist Past: The Regeneration of Communist Parties in East Central Europe.* Cambridge: Cambridge University Press.

―――. 2007. *Rebuilding Leviathan: Party Competition and State Exploitation in Post-Communist Democracies.* Cambridge: Cambridge University Press.

Guriev, Sergei, and Andrei Rachinsky. 2005. "The Role of Oligarchs in Russian Capitalism." *Journal of Economic Perspectives* 19 (1): 131–150.

GUS. 1993. *Informacja o situacii spoleczno-gospodarczej kraju. Rok 1992.* Warsaw: GUS.

Gustafson, Thane. 2000. *Capitalism Russian Style.* Cambridge: Cambridge University Press.

Haber, Stephen, Armando Razo, and Noel Maurer. 2003. *The Politics of Property Rights: Political Instability, Credible Commitments, and Economic Growth in Mexico, 1876–1929.* Cambridge: Cambridge University Press.

Haggard, Stephan, and Robert Kaufman. 1995. *The Political Economy of Democratic Transitions.* Princeton: Princeton University Press.

―――. 2008. *Revising Social Contracts: Social Spending in Latin America, East Asia, and the Former Socialist Countries, 1980–2000.* Princeton: Princeton University Press.

Haggard, Stephan, and Steven B. Webb. 1993. "What Do We Know about the Political Economy of Economic Policy Reform?" *World Bank Policy Research Observer* 8: 143–167.

―――. 1994. Introduction. In Stephan Haggard and Steven B. Webb, eds., *Voting for Reform: Democracy, Political Liberalization, and Economic Adjustment,* 1–8. New York: Published for the World Bank, Oxford University Press.

Hale, Henry. 2006. *Why Not Parties in Russia: Democracy, Federalism and the State.* Cambridge: Cambridge University Press.

Hanley, Sean. 2002. "The Communist Party of Bohemia and Moravia after 1989. Subcultural Party to Neocommunist Force." In Andras Bozoki and John T. Ishiyama, eds., *The Communist Successor Parties of Central and Eastern Europe,* 141–155. Armonk, NY: M. E. Sharpe.

Hanson, Stephen. 1995. "The Leninist Legacy and Institutional Change." *Comparative Political Studies* 28 (2): 306–314.

Haran, Olexiy. 2001. "Can Ukrainian Communists and Socialists Evolve to Social Democracy?" *Demokratizatsiya* 9 (1). http://www.demokratizatsiya.org/html/Vol9-no1.html.

Harper, M. A. G. 2003. "The 2001 Parliamentary and Presidential Elections in Bulgaria." *Electoral Studies* 22: 325–395.

Haughton, Tim. 2001. "HZDS: The Ideology, Organisation and Support Base of Slovakia's Most Successful Party." *Europe-Asia Studies* 53 (5): 745–769.

Havrylyshyn, Oleh. 2001. "Recovery and Growth in Transition Economies." *IMF Staff Papers* 48 (special issue): 53–87.

Havrylyshyn, Oleh, Ivailo Izvorski, and Ron van Rooden. 1998. "Recovery and Growth in Transition Economies, 1990–1997: Stylized Regression Analysis." IMF Working Paper 98/141. Washington, DC: International Monetary Fund.

Havrylyshyn, Oleh, and Ron van Rooden. 2003. "Institutions Matter in Transition, but So Do Policies." *Comparative Economic Studies* 45: 2–24.

Hedstrom, Peter, and Richard Swedberg, eds. 1998. "Social Mechanisms: An Introductory Essay." In Peter Hedstrom and Richard Swedberg, eds., *Social Mechanisms: An Analytical Approach to Social Theory,* 1–31. Cambridge: Cambridge University Press.

Hellman, Joel S. 1998. "Winners Take All: The Politics of Partial Reform." *World Politics* 50 (2): 203–234.

Hellman, Joel S., Geraint Jones, and Daniel Kaufman. 2003. "Seize the State, Seize the Day." *Journal of Comparative Economics* 31 (4): 751–773.

Hellman, Joel S., Geraint Jones, Daniel Kaufmann, and Mark Schankerman. 2000. "Measuring Governance and State Capture: The Role of Bureaucrats and Firms in Shaping the Business Environment." European Bank for Reconstruction and Development Working Paper no. 51. London: European Bank for Reconstruction and Development.

Hendley, Kathryn, Barry W. Ickes, Peter Murrell, and Randi Ryterman. 1997. "Observations on the Use of Law by Russian Enterprises." *Post-Soviet Affairs* 13 (1): 19–41.

Hendley, Kathryn, Peter Murrell, and Randi Ryterman. 2000. "Law, Relationships and Private Enforcement: Transactional Strategies of Russian Enterprises." *Europe-Asia Studies* 52 (4): 627–656.

———. 2001. "Law Works in Russia: The Role of Legal Institutions in the Transactions of Russian Enterprises." In Peter Murrell, ed., *Assessing the Value of the Rule of Law in Transition Economies*, 56–93. Ann Arbor: University of Michigan Press.

Henisz, Witold Jerzy. 2004. "Political Institutions and Policy Volatility." *Economics and Politics* 16 (1): 1–27.

Herrera, Yoshiko. 2008. *Transforming Bureaucracy: Conditional Norms and the International Standardization of Statistics in Russia*. Ithaca, NY: Cornell University Press.

Hewett, Ed. 1988. *Reforming the Soviet Economy: Efficiency and Equity*. Washington, DC: Brookings Institution.

Heybey, Berta, and Peter Murrell. 1999. "The Relationship between Economic Growth and the Speed of Liberalization during Transition." *Journal of Policy Reform* 3 (2): 121–137.

Hirsch, Francine. 2005. *Empire of Nations: Ethnographic Knowledge and the Making of the Soviet Union*. Ithaca, NY: Cornell University Press.

Hoff, Karla, and Joseph Stiglitz. 2004. "The Transition from Communism." World Bank Research Paper. Washington, DC.

———. 2008. "Exiting Lawlessness." *Economic Journal* 118 (531): 1474–1497.

Hoffman, David E. 2001. *The Oligarchs: Wealth and Power in the New Russia*. New York: Public Affairs.

Holmes, Stephen. 1995. "Conceptions of Democracy in the Draft Constitutions of Postcommunist Countries." In Beverly Crawford, ed., *Markets, States, and Democracy: The Political Economy of Postcommunist Transition*, 71–80. Boulder, CO: Westview Press.

———. 1996. "Cultural Legacies or State Collapse?" In Michael Mandelbaum, ed., *Perspectives on Postcommunism*, 22–76. New York: Council on Foreign Relations.

Horowitz, Donald. 1985. *Ethnic Groups in Conflict*. Berkeley: University of California Press.

Horowitz, Shale, and Eric C. Browne. 2008. "Party Systems and Economic Policy Change in Postcommunist Democracies." *Comparative Politics* October 41 (1): 21–39.

Hsiao, Cheng. 2003. *Analysis of Panel Data*. Cambridge: Cambridge University Press.

Huber, John, Georgia Kernell, and Eduardo L. Leoni. 2005. "Institutional Context, Cognitive Resources, and Party Attachments across Democracies." *Political Analysis*, special issue, 13 (4): 365–386.

Hunter, Shireen. 1993. "Azerbaijan: Search for Identity and New Partners." In Ian Bremmer and Ray Taras, eds., *Nations and Politics in the Soviet Successor States*, 225–260. Cambridge: Cambridge University Press.

Huskey, Gene. 1994. "Kyrgyzstan: The Politics of Demographic and Economic Frustration." In Ian Bremmer and Ray Taras, eds., *Nations and Politics in the Soviet Successor States*, 398–418. Cambridge: Cambridge University Press.

Inglot, Tomasz. 2008. *Welfare States in East Central Europe, 1919–2004*. Cambridge: Cambridge University Press.

International Crisis Group. 2006. "Uzbekistan: In for the Long Haul." Policy Briefing no. 45. February 16, 1–16.

International Monetary Fund. 2000. *Republic of Uzbekistan: Recent Economic Developments*. IMF Staff Country Report, 00/36. Washington, DC: International Monetary Fund.

Ishiyama, John. 1995. "Communist Parties in Transition: Structures, Leaders, and Processes of Democratization in Eastern Europe." *Comparative Politics* 27 (2): 147–166.

———. 1997. "The Sickle or the Rose? Previous Regime Type and the Evolution of Ex-Communist Parties." *Comparative Political Studies* 30 (3): 299–330.

———, ed. 1999. *Communist Successor Parties in Post-Communist Politics*. Commack, NY: Nova Science Publishers.

Islam, Nazrul. 1995. "Growth Empirics: A Panel Data Approach." *Quarterly Journal of Economics* 110 (4): 1127–1170.

Jack, Andrew. 2005. *Inside Putin's Russia: Can There Be Reform without Democracy*. Oxford: Oxford University Press.

Jackson, John E., Jacek Klich, and Krzystyna Poznanska. 2003. "Democratic Institutions and Economic Reform: The Polish Case." *British Journal of Political Science* 33 (1): 85–108.

———. 2005. *The Political Economy of Poland's Transition: New Firms and Reform Governments*. Cambridge: Cambridge University Press.

Jackson, Marvin. 1991. "The Rise and Decay of the Socialist Economy in Bulgaria." *Journal of Economic Perspectives* 5 (4): 203–209.

Janusauskiene, Diana. 2002. "The Metamorphosis of the Communist Party of Lithuania." In Andras Bozoki and John T. Ishiyama, eds., *The Communist Successor Parties of Central and Eastern Europe*, 224–239. Armonk, NY: M. E. Sharpe.

Jensen, Nathan M. 2003. "Rational Citizens against Reform: Poverty and Economic Reform in Transition Economies." *Comparative Political Studies* 36 (9): 1092–1111.

Johnson, Simon, Daniel Kaufmann, and Andrei Shleifer. 1997. "The Unofficial Economy in Transition." *Brookings Papers on Economic Activity* 2: 159–239.

Johnson, Simon, and Marzena Kowalska. 1994. "Poland: The Political Economy of Shock Therapy." In Stephen Haggard and Steven B. Webb, eds., *Voting for Reform: Democracy, Political Liberalization, and Economic Adjustment*, 185–241. New York: Oxford University Press.

Jones Luong, Pauline. 2002. *Institutional Change and Political Continuity in Post-Soviet Central Asia: Power, Perceptions, and Pacts*. Cambridge: Cambridge University Press.

Jowitt, Kenneth. 1992. *New World Disorder: The Leninist Extinction*. Berkeley: University of California Press.

Judson, Ruth A., and Ann L. Owen. 1999. "Estimating Dynamic Panel Data Models: A Practical Guide for Macroeconomists." *Economics Letters* 65 (1): 9–15.

Kam, Cindy D., and Robert J. Franzese. 2007. *Modeling and Interpreting Interactive Hypotheses in Regression Analysis*. Ann Arbor: University of Michigan Press.

Kamp, Marianne. 2004. "Between Women and the State: Mahalla Committees and Social Welfare in Uzbekistan." In Pauline Jones Luong, ed., *The Transformation of Central Asia: States and Societies from Soviet Rule to Independence*, 29–58. Ithaca, NY: Cornell University Press.

Kanev, Dobrin. 2002. "The Bulgarian Socialist Party: The Long Road of Transformation." Unpublished manuscript, Sofia.

Kapstein, Ethan B., and Branko Milanovic. 2000. "Dividing the Spoils: Pensions, Privatization and Reform in Russia's Transition." World Bank Policy Research Paper no. 2292. Washington, DC.

Karasimeonov, Georgi. 1999. "Past and New Cleavages in Post-Communist Bulgaria." In Kay Lawson, Andrea Rommele, and Georgi Karasimeonov, eds., *Cleavages, Parties and Voters: Studies from Bulgaria, the Czech Republic, Hungary, Poland, and Romania*, 109–121. Westport, CT: Praeger.

Kassayie, Berhanu. 1998. "The Evolution of Social Democracy in Reforming Bulgaria." *Journal of Communist Studies and Transition Politics* 14 (3): 109–125.

Katznelson, Ira. 2003. "Periodization and Preferences: Reflections on Purposive Action in Comparative Historical Social Science," In James Mahoney and Dietrich Rueschemeyer, eds., *Comparative Historical Analysis in the Social Sciences*, 270–304. Cambridge: Cambridge University Press.

Kaufman, Robert R., and Alex Segura-Ubiergo. 2001. "Globalization, Domestic Politics, and Social Spending in Latin America: A Time-Series Cross-Section Analysis, 1973–1997." *World Politics* 53 (2): 553–588.

Keane, Michael, and Eswar S. Prasad. 2000. IMF Working Paper 00/117, June. Washington, DC: International Monetary Fund.

_____. 2001. "Poland: Inequality, Transfers, and Growth in Transition." *Finance and Development* 38 (1): 1–8.

_____. 2002. "Poland: Inequality, Transfers, and Growth in Transition: New Evidence from the Economic Transition in Poland." *Review of Economics and Statistics* 84 (2): 324–341.

Keefer, Philip, and Stephen Knack. 2002. "Polarization, Politics, and Property Rights: Links between Inequality and Growth." *Public Choice* 111: 127–154.

Kenyon, Thomas, and Megumi Naoi. 2007. "Policy Uncertainty in Hybrid Regimes: Evidence from Firm-Level Surveys." Unpublished manuscript, World Bank, Washington, DC.

Kiewiet, Roderick, and Mikhail Myagkov. 1998. "The Emergence of the Private Sector: A Financial Market Perspective." *Post-Soviet Affairs* 14: 23–47.

King, Gary, Robert Keohane, and Sydney Verba. 1994. *Designing Social Inquiry: Scientific Inference in Quantitative Research*. Princeton: Princeton University Press.

Kitschelt, Herbert. 2003. "Accounting for Postcommunist Regime Diversity: What Counts as a Good Cause?" In Grzegorz Ekiert and Stephen E. Hanson, eds., *Capitalism and Democracy in Central and Eastern Europe*, 49–86. Cambridge: Cambridge University Press.

Kitschelt, Herbert, Dimitar Dimitrov, and Assen Kanev. 1995. "The Structuring of the Vote in Post-Communist Party Systems: The Bulgarian Example." *European Journal of Political Research* 27: 143–160.

Kitschelt, Herbert, and Edmund Malesky. 2000. "Constitutional Design and Post-Communist Economic Reform." Paper presented at the annual meeting of the Midwest Political Science Association, Chicago, April 28.

Kitschelt, Herbert, Zdenka Mansfeldova, Radoslaw Markowski, and Gabor Toka. 1999. *Post-Communist Party Systems: Competition, Representation, and Inter-Party Cooperation*. Cambridge: Cambridge University Press.

Kokh, Alfred. 1998. *The Selling of the Russian Empire*. New York: Liberty Publishing.

———. 1999. "Gosudarstvo Prodavets." In Anatolii Chubais, ed., *Privatizatsiia porossiiski*, 247–269. Moscow: Vagrius.

Kolodko, Grzegorz. 2000. *Post-Communist Transition: The Thorny Road*. Rochester, NY: University of Rochester Press.

Kondratowicz, Andrzej, and Wojciech Maciejewski. 1994. *Small and Medium Private Enterprises in Poland*. Warsaw: Adam Smith Research Centre.

Kono, Daniel. 2008. "Democracy and Trade Discrimination." *Journal of Politics* 70 (4): 942–955.

Kopstein, Jeffrey S., and David Reilly. 2000. "Geographic Diffusion and Transformation of Post-Communist Europe." *World Politics* 53 (1): 1–30.

Korbonski, Andrzej. 1984. "Soviet Policy toward Poland." In Sarah M. Terry, ed., *Soviet Policy in Eastern Europe*, 61–92. New Haven: Yale University Press.

———. 1989. "The Politics of Economic Reforms in Eastern Europe: The Last Thirty Years." *Soviet Studies* 41 (1): 1–19.

Kornai, Janos. 1990. *The Road to a Free Economy*. New York: W. W. Norton.

———. 1992. *The Socialist System: The Political Economy of Communism*. Princeton: Princeton University Press.

Kotkin, Stephen. 2000. *Armageddon Averted: The Soviet Collapse, 1970–2000*. Oxford: Oxford University Press.

Kozarzewski, Piotr, and Richard Woodward. 2001. "Evolution of Ownership Structure and Corporate Performance in Firms Privatized by Employee Buyout." Secondary Privatization in Poland, Part I. Case Reports, 47. Warsaw.

Kramer, Mark. 1997. "Social Protection Policies and Safety Nets in East-Central Europe." In Ethan Kapstein and Michael Mandelbaum, eds., *Sustaining the Transition*, 46–123. New York: Council on Foreign Relations.

Krastev, Ivan. 2007. "The Strange Death of the Liberal Consensus." *Journal of Democracy* 18 (4): 56–63.

Kreps, David. 1990. "Corporate Culture and Economic Theory." In James Alt and Kenneth Shepsle, eds., *Perspectives on Positive Political Economy*, 90–144. Cambridge: Cambridge University Press.

Krueger, Gary, and Marek Ciolko. 1998. "A Note on Initial Conditions and Liberalization during Transition." *Journal of Comparative Economics* 26 (4): 117–149.

Kurtz, Marcus J., and Sarah M. Brooks. 2008. "Embedding Neoliberal Reform in Latin America." *World Politics* 60 (2): 231–281.

Kurzer, Paulette. 1993. *Business and Banking*. Ithaca, NY: Cornell University Press.

Laitin, David. 1998. *Identity in Formation: The Russian-Speaking Populations in the Near Abroad*. Ithaca, NY: Cornell University Press.

Lane, David, and Cameron Ross. 1999. *The Transition from Communism to Capitalism: Ruling Elites from Gorbachev to Yeltsin*. New York: St. Martin's Press.

Lane, Jan-Erik, David McKay, and Kenneth Newton. 1997. *Political Data Handbook: OECD Countries*. Oxford: Oxford University Press.

Levine, Ross, and David Renelt. 1992. "A Sensitivity Analysis of Cross-Country Growth Regressions." *American Economic Review* 82 (4): 942–963.

Lewandowski, Janusz. 1997. "Poland's Privatization Process: A View from the Inside." *Journal of International Affairs* 50 (2): 573–580.

Lewis, Paul. 2000. *Political Parties in Post-Communist Eastern Europe*. London: Routledge.

Lieberman, Ira, and Rogi Veimetra. 1996. "The Rush for State Shares in the 'Klondyke' of Wild East Capitalism: Loans for Shares Transactions in Russia." *George Washington Law School Review of International Law and Economics* 29: 737–768.

Lieven, Anatol. 1993. *The Baltic Revolution: Estonia, Latvia, Lithuania and the Path to Independence*. New Haven: Yale University Press.

Lindblom, Charles E. 1959. "The Science of Muddling Through." *Public Administration Review* 19 (Spring): 79–88.

———. 1977. *Politics and Markets: The World's Political-Economic Systems*. New York: Basic Books.

Linz, Juan J., and Alfred Stepan. 1996. *Problems of Democratic Transition and Consolidation: Southern Europe, South America, and Post-Communist Europe*. Baltimore: Johns Hopkins University Press.

Lipton, David, and Jeffrey Sachs. 1990. "Creating a Market Economy in Eastern Europe: The Case of Poland." *Brookings Papers on Economic Activity* 1: 75–147.

Macieja, Jan. 2001. "Public and Private Sector: New and Old Patterns of Entrepreneurship." In George Blazyca and Ryszard Rapacki, eds., *Poland into the New Millennium*, 142–160. Cheltenham: Edward Elgar.

Magaloni, Beatriz. 2006. *Voting for Autocracy: Hegemonic Party Survival and Its Demise in Mexico*. Cambridge: Cambridge University Press.

Mahoney, James. 2003. "Knowledge Accumulation in Comparative Historical Analysis: The Case of Democracy and Authoritarianism." In James Mahoney and Dietrich Rueschemeyer, eds., *Comparative Historical Analysis in the Social Sciences*, 131–174. Cambridge: Cambridge University Press.

Malesky, Edmund. 2003. "Making Better Use of Business Survey Data: Thoughts on Overcoming the Anchoring and Nested Data Problems in Interpreting Business Survey Results." Paper presented at the annual meeting of the American Political Science Association, Philadelphia.

Maleva, Tatyana. 2001. "The New Labor Code: Victory or Defeat?" *Briefing Papers* 3 (2): 1–5. Carnegie Center, Moscow.

Mandelbaum, Michael. 1997. Introduction. In Ethan B. Kapstein and Michael Mandelbaum, eds., *Sustaining the Transition*, 1–9. New York: Council on Foreign Relations.

Mansfield, Edward D., and Jack Snyder. 2005. *Electing to Fight: Why Emerging Democracies Go to War*. Cambridge, MA: MIT Press.

March, Luke. 2002. *The Communist Party in Post-Soviet Russia*. Manchester: Manchester University Press.

Marese, Muchael, and Jan Vanous. 1983. *Soviet Subsidization of Trade with Eastern Europe: A Soviet Perspective*. Berkeley: Institute for International Studies, University of California at Berkeley.

Markov, Sergei. 1999. "The Kremlin's Last Gasp." Unpublished manuscript, Moscow.

Martin, Terry. 2001. *The Affirmative Action Empire: Nations and Nationalism in the Soviet Union, 1923–1939*. Ithaca, NY: Cornell University Press.

Mattli, Walter, and Thomas Plumper. 2002. "The Demand-Side Politics of EU Enlargement: Democracy and the Application for EU Membership." *Journal of European Public Policy* 9 (4): 550–574.

Mau, Vladimir. 2000. *Russian Economic Reforms as Seen by an Insider: Success or Failure?* London: Chatham House.

————. 2001. "Ekonomicheskaia politika: Rossiia v nachale novoi fazy." *Voprosy Ekonomiki* 72 (3): 10–21.

McCarty, Nolan, Keith T. Poole, and Howard Rosenthal. 2006. *Polarized America: The Dance of Ideology and Unequal Riches*. Cambridge, MA. MIT Press.

McFaul, Michael. 2001. *Russia's Unfinished Revolution: From Gorbachev to Putin*. Ithaca, NY: Cornell University Press.

McGregor, James. 1994. "The Presidency in East Central Europe." *RFE/RL Research Report* 3 (2): 23–31.

McKinnon, Ronald. 1991. *The Order of Economic Liberalization: Financial Control in the Transition to a Market Economy*. Baltimore: Johns Hopkins University Press.

McMillan, John, and Christopher Woodruff. 2002. "The Central Role of Entrepreneurs in Transition Economies." *Journal of Economic Perspectives* 16 (3): 153–170.

Melone, Albert P. 1998. *The Transition to Democracy in Bulgaria*. Columbus: Ohio State University Press.

Melvin, Neil. 1999. *Uzbekistan: Transition to Authoritarianism on the Silk Road*. London: Taylor and Francis.

Mencinger, Joze. 1993. "The Slovene Economy." *Nationalities Papers* 21 (1): 81–89.

Milanovic, Branko. 1998. *Income, Inequality, and Poverty during the Transition from Planned to Market Economy*. Washington, DC: World Bank.

Miller, Jeffery, and Stefan Petranov. 2000. "The First Wave of Mass Privatization in Bulgaria and Its Immediate Aftermath." *Economics of Transition* 8 (1): 225–250.

Milov, Vladimir, and Ivan Selivakhin. 2005. "Problemy energeticheskoi politiki." Issue 4, Working Papers. Carnegie Center, Moscow.

Minassian, Garabed. 1998. "The Road to Economic Disaster in Bulgaria." *Europe-Asia Studies* 50 (2): 331–349.

Moore, Mike. 2001. "Russia, the International Economy and the World Trade Organization." March 30. www.wto.org/English/news_e/spmmm.

Motyl, Alexander. 1988. *The Turn to the Right: The Ideological Origins and Development of Ukrainian Nationalism, 1919–1929*. Boulder, CO: East European Monographs.

————. 1989. *Will the Non-Russians Rebel? State, Ethnicity, and Stability in the USSR*. Ithaca, NY: Cornell University Press.

Muller, Katharina. 1999. *The Political Economy of Pension Reform in Central-Eastern Europe*. Cheltenham: Edward Elgar.

Murer, Jeffrey Stevenson. 1999. "Challenging Expectations: A Comparative Study of the Communist Successor Parties of Hungary, Bulgaria and Romania." In John Ishiyama, ed., *Communist Successor Parties in Post-Communist Politics*, 179–221. Commack, NY: Nova Science Publishers.

Murillo, M. Victoria. 2001. *Labor Unions, Partisan Coalitions, and Market Reforms in Latin America*. Cambridge: Cambridge University Press.

————. 2009. *Political Competition, Partisanship and Policy Making*. Cambridge: Cambridge University Press.

Murphy, Kevin, Andrei Shleifer, and Robert Vishny. 1992. "The Transition to a Market Economy: The Pitfalls of Partial Reform." *Quarterly Journal of Economics* 107 (August): 889–906.

Murrell, Peter. 1992. "Evolution in Economics and in the Economic Reform of the Centrally Planned Economies." In Christopher Clague and Gordon C. Rausser, eds., *The Emergence of Market Economies in Eastern Europe*, 35–53. Cambridge, MA: Blackwell.

Myagkov, Mikhail, Peter C. Ordeshook, and Dmitry Shakin. 2009. *The Forensics of Election Fraud: Russia and Ukraine*. Cambridge: Cambridge University Press.

Nahaylo, Bohdan, and Victor Swoboda. 1990. *Soviet Disunion: A History of the Nationalities Problem in the USSR*. New York: Free Press.

Nedyalkova, Yordanka. 2001."Breaking Spells." *Transitions On Line*, January 17. http://www.tol.cz/look/knowledgeNet/tolprint.tpl?IdLanguage=1&IdPublication= 12&NrIssue=14&NrSection=15&NrArticle=4814&ST1=body&ST_T1=knreport& ST_AS1=1&ST_max=1.

Nelson, Joan. 1993. "The Politics of Economic Transformation: Is the Third World Experience Relevant in Eastern Europe?" *World Politics* 45 (3): 433–463.

———. 2001. "The Politics of Pension and Health-Care Reforms in Hungary and Poland." In Janos Kornai, Stephan Haggard, and Robert Kaufman, eds., *Reforming the State*, 235–266. Cambridge: Cambridge University Press.

Nenova, Tatyana. 1998. "Bulgaria." Unpublished manuscript, European Bank for Reconstruction and Development, London.

Newman, Alisa. 1999. "Investing in Uzbekistan: A Rough Ride on the Silk Road." *Law and Policy in International Business* 30 (3, Spring): 553–567.

Nicholson, Alex. 2004. "Foreign Capital Sinks to New Low." *Moscow Times*, January 12.

Nikolov, Boyko, Nikolay Markov, Nasko Dochev, Dimitar Dimitrov, Rumyana Kolarova, and Rumen Dobrinsky. 2004. "Understanding Reform: A Country Study for Bulgaria." Global Development Network: Centre for Economic and Strategic Research. WIIW (October): 1–54.

Nikolov, Yovo. 1999. "War with Criminal Groups Turns into Battle for Interior Ministry." ISI Emerging Markets Data, July 30. http://www.securities.com/cgi-bin/ split/94dec/Data/BG/News.../kptl990114e.html?KPTL1.

Nissman, David. 1993."Turkmenistan: Just Like Old Times." In Ian Bremmer and Ray Taras, eds., *Nations and Politics in the Soviet Successor States*, 384–397. Cambridge: Cambridge University Press.

Nones, Jon A. 2006. Newmont Loses Control of Zarafshan JV in Uzbekistan. *Resource Investor*, August 11. http://www.resourceinvestor.com/News/2006/8/ Pages/Newmont-Loses-Control-of-Zarafshan-JV-in.aspx.

North, Douglass. 1990. *Institutions, Institutional Change, and Economic Performance*. Cambridge: Cambridge University Press.

———. 1993. "Institutions and Credible Commitment." *Journal of Institutional and Theoretical Economics* 149 (1): 11–23.

North, Douglass C., and Barry R. Weingast. 1989. "Constitutions and Commitment: The Evolution of Institutions Governing Public Choice in Seventeenth Century England." *Journal of Economic History* 59 (4): 803–832.

Nunn, Sam, and Adam N. Stuhlberg. 2000. "The Many Faces of Modern Russia." *Foreign Affairs* 79 (2, March–April): 45–62.

O'Dwyer, Conor. 2006. *Runaway State-Building: Patronage Politics and Democratic Development*. Baltimore: Johns Hopkins University Press.

Offe, Claus. 1991. "Capitalism by Democratic Design: Democratic Theory Facing the Triple Transition in East-Central Europe." *Social Research* 58 (4): 865–892.

Olcott, Martha Brill. 1995. *The Kazakhs*. Palo Alto: Stanford University Press.

———. 1997. "Democratization and the Growth of Political Participation." In Karen Dawisha and Bruce Parrott, eds., *Conflict, Cleavage, and Change in Central Asia and the Caucasus*, 201–241. Cambridge: Cambridge University Press.

Olson, Mancur. 1993. "Dictatorship, Democracy, and Development." *American Political Science Review* 87 (3): 567–557.

Orenstein, Mitchell. 2001. *Out of the Red: Building Capitalism and Democracy in Postcommunist Europe.* Ann Arbor: University of Michigan Press.

Osborn, Elizabeth. 2000. "Popular Support for Privatization: Do Political Orientations Matter?" In Kazimierz M. Slomczynski, ed., *Social Patterns of Being Political: The Initial Phase of Post-Communist Transition in Poland*, 113–128. Warsaw: IFiS Publishers.

OSCE. 2000a. Russian Federation Elections to the State Duma, 19 December 1999. Office of Democratic Institutions and Human Rights. Warsaw.

——. 2000b. Russian Federation Presidential Election, 29 March 2000. Office of Democratic Institutions and Human Rights. Warsaw.

——. 2004a. Russian Federation Elections to the State Duma, 7 December 2003. Office of Democratic Institutions and Human Rights. Warsaw.

——. 2004b. Russian Federation Presidential Election, 14 March 2004. Office of Democratic Institutions and Human Rights. Warsaw.

Pacek, Alexander. 1994. "Macroeconomic Conditions and Electoral Politics in East Central Europe." *American Journal of Political Science* 38 (3): 723–744.

Page, Scott. 2006. "Path Dependence." *Quarterly Journal of Political Science* 1 (1): 87–115.

Paretskaya, Anna. 1996. *Radio Free Europe/Radio Liberty Daily Report*, May 3. http://archive.tol.cz/Publications/RPE/RPE.960516.html.

Parker, George. 2003. "New EU Members Warned against Rush to Euro." *Financial Times*, September 4. http:financialtimes.com.

Peev, Evgeni. 2002. "Ownership and Control Structures in Transition to 'Crony' Capitalism: The Case of Bulgaria." *Eastern European Economics* 40 (5): 73–91.

Peeva, Ralitsa. 2001. "Electing a Czar: The 2001 Elections and Bulgarian Democracy." *East European Constitutional Review* 10 (4). http://www.law.nyu.edu/eecr/vol1onum4/focus/peeva.html.

Persson, Torsten, and Guido Tabellini. 1994. "Representative Democracy and Capital Taxation." *Journal of Public Economics* 55 (1): 53–70.

——. 2005. *The Economic Effects of Constitutions.* Cambridge, MA: MIT Press.

Petersen, Roger. 2002. *Understanding Ethnic Violence: Fear, Hatred, Resentment in Twentieth-Century Eastern Europe.* Cambridge: Cambridge University Press.

Pettai, Vello, and Marcus Kreuzer. 1999. "Party Politics in the Baltic States: Social Bases and Institutional Context." *East European Politics and Society* 13 (1): 148–189.

Pieralla, Paci, Marcin J. Sasin, and Jos Verbeek. 2004. "Economic Growth, Income Distribution and Poverty in Poland during Transition." World Bank Policy Research Paper no. 3467. Washington, DC.

Pierson, Paul. 1994. *Dismantling the Welfare State: Reagan, Thatcher and the Politics of Retrenchment.* Cambridge: Cambridge University Press.

——. 2004. *Politics in Time: History, Institutions, and Social Analysis.* Princeton: Princeton University Press.

Pinto, Brian. 1993. "Brian Pinto Explains Why Polish State Firms Are Restructuring." *World Bank/PRDTM* 4 (7): 4–5.

Pinto, Brian, Marek Belka, and Stefan Krajewski. 1993. "Transforming State Enterprises in Poland: Evidence on Adjustment." *Brookings Papers on Economic Activity* 1: 213–270.

Pipes, Richard. 1954. *The Formation of the Soviet Union: Communism and National-ism, 1917–1923*. Cambridge, MA: Harvard University Press.

Plumper, Thomas, and Vera Troeger. 2007. "Efficient Estimation with Time-Invariant Variables in Finite Sample Panel Analyses with Fixed Effects." *Political Analysis* 15 (2): 124–139.

Polanyi, Karl. 1944. *The Great Transformation: The Political and Economic Origins of Our Time*. Boston: Beacon Press.

Polska Agencia Rozwoju Regionalnego – PARR (Polish Agency for Regional Develop-ment). 1998. *Regional Development in Poland – Basic Facts*. Warsaw: PARR.

_____. 1999. *Regional Development in Poland – Basic Facts*. Warsaw: PARR.

Pomfret, Richard. 2000. "The Uzbek Model of Economic Development, 1991–1999." *Economics of Transition* 8 (3): 733–748.

_____. 2006. *The Central Asian Economies since Independence*. Princeton: Princeton University Press.

Pomfret, Richard, and Kathryn Anderson. 1997. "Uzbekistan: Welfare Impact of Slow Transition." United Nations University World Institute for Development Eco-nomics Research (UNU/WIDER WP135), Helsinki. http://citeseer.ist.psu.edu/richard97uzbekistan.html.

Pond, Elizabeth. 2001. "Better Late Than Never." *Washington Quarterly* 24 (2): 35–43.

Pop-Eleches, Grigore. 2007. "Historical Legacies and Post-Communist Regime Change." *Journal of Politics* 69 (4): 908–926.

_____. 2008. "Crisis Is in the Eye of the Beholder: Economic Crisis and Partisan Politics in Latin America and East European IMF Programs." *Comparative Political Studies* 41 (9): 1179–1211.

_____. 2009. *From Economic Crisis to Reform: IMF Programs in Latin America and Eastern Europe*. Princeton: Princeton University Press.

Popov, Vladimir. 2000. "Shock Therapy versus Gradualism: The End of the Debate Explaining the Magnitude of the Transformational Recession." *Comparative Eco-nomic Studies* 42 (1): 1–57.

Posner, Daniel. 2004. "Measuring Ethnic Fractionalization in Africa." *American Jour-nal of Political Science* 48 (4): 849–863.

Potanin, Vladimir. 2000. http://www.pbs.org/wgbh/commandingheights/shared/minitext/int_vladimirpotanin.html.

Pritchett, Lant. 1998. "Patterns of Economic Growth: Hills, Valleys, and Plateaus." World Bank Policy Research Paper no. 1047. Washington, DC.

Prohaska, Maria, and Plamen Tchipev. 2000. "Establishing Corporate Governance in an Emerging Market: Bulgaria." CSD Reports. Sofia: Center for the Study of Democracy.

Pribylovsky, Vladimir. 2003. *Rukovoditeli gosudarstv na territorii byvshego SSSR*. Moscow: Panorama.

Przeworski, Adam. 1991. *Democracy and the Market: Political and Economic Reforms in Eastern Europe and Latin America*. Cambridge: Cambridge University Press.

_____. 2001. "Public Support for Economic Reform in Poland." In Susan C. Stokes, ed., *Public Support for Market Reforms*, 103–130. Cambridge: Cambridge University Press.

Przeworski, Adam, et al. 1995. *Sustainable Democracy*. Cambridge: Cambridge Uni-versity Press.

Przeworski, Adam, Michael E. Alvarez, Jose A. Cheibub, and Fernando Limongi. 2000. *Democracy and Development: Political Institutions and Well-Being in the World*. Cambridge: Cambridge University Press.

Rakhmanin, Serhii, and Yulia Mostovaya. 2002. "Ukrainian Political Parties. Part IV. The Socialist Party of Ukraine." *Zerkalo Nedel* 9 (384, March 8–15). http://www. mw.ua/1000/1550/34078.

Rapacki, Ryzsard. 2001. "Economic Performance, 1989–1999, and Prospects for the Future." In George Blazyca and Ryszard Rapacki, eds., *Poland into the New Millennium*, 107–141. Northampton, MA: Edward Elgar.

Reddaway, Peter. 2001. "Will Putin Be Able to Consolidate Power?" *Post-Soviet Affairs* 17 (1): 23–44.

———. 2002. "Is Putin's Power More Formal Than Real?" *Post-Soviet Affairs* 18 (1): 31–40.

Reissinger, William. 2003. "The 1999–2000 Elections and Russia's Prospects for Democracy." In Vicki L. Hesli and William Reissinger, eds., *The 1999–2000 Elections in Russia: Their Impact and Legacy*, 261–274. Cambridge: Cambridge University Press.

Remington, Thomas F. 2000. "Putin's Agenda." *Brown Journal of World Affairs* 3 (1): 135–145.

———. 2001a. *The Russian Parliament: Institutional Evolution in a Transitional Regime, 1989–1999*. New Haven: Yale University Press.

———. 2001b. "Putin and the Duma." *Post-Soviet Affairs* 17 (4): 285–308.

———. 2003. "Coalition Politics in the New Duma." In Vicky L. Hesli and William Reissinger, eds., *The 1999–2000 Elections in Russia: Their Impact and Legacy*, 232–257. Cambridge: Cambridge University Press.

———. 2006. "Democratization, Separation of Power and State Capacity." In Timothy Colton and Stephen Holmes, eds., *The State after Communism: Governance in the New Russia*, 261–298. Lanham, MD: Rowman and Littlefield.

Remmer, Karen. 2002. "The Politics of Economic Policy and Performance in Latin America." *Journal of Public Policy* 22 (1): 29–59.

Rigby, T. H. 1990. *Political Elites in the USSR: Central Leaders and Local Cadres from Lenin to Gorbachev*. Northampton, MA: Edward Elgar.

Rinegold, Deana. 1999. "Social Policies in Postcommunist Europe." In Linda Cook, Mitchell A. Orenstein, and Marilyn Rueschemeyer, eds., *Left Party and Social Policy in Postcommunist Europe*, 11–46. Boulder, CO: Westview Press.

Rodrik, Dani. 1989. "Promises, Promises: Credible Policy Reform via Signalling." *Economic Journal, Royal Economic Society* 99 (397): 756–772.

———. 1996. "Understanding Economic Policy Reform." *Journal of Economic Literature* 34 (1): 9–41.

———. 1998. "Why Do More Open Economies Have Bigger Governments?" *Journal of Political Economy* 106 (5): 997–1032.

———. 1999. "Where Did All the Growth Go? External Shocks, Social Conflict and Growth Collapses." *Journal of Economic Growth* 4: 385–412.

———. 2005. "Why We Learn Nothing from Regressing Economic Growth on Policies." Unpublished manuscript, Cambridge, MA.

Roeder, Philip G. 1991. "Soviet Federalism and Ethnic Mobilization." *World Politics* 43 (2): 196–232.

Roland, Gerard. 2000. *Transition and Economics: Politics, Markets, and Firms*. Cambridge, MA: MIT Press.

Rosato, Sebastian. 2003. "The Flawed Logic of Democratic Peace Theory." *American Political Science Review* 97 (4): 585–602.

Rose, Richard, Neil Monro, and Stephen White. 2000. "How Strong Is Vladimir Putin's Support?" *Post-Soviet Affairs* 16 (4): 287–312.

Ross, Michael. 2001. "Does Oil Impede Democracy?" *World Politics* 53: 325–361.

Rothschild, Joseph. 1974. *Eastern Europe between the Wars*. Seattle: University of Washington Press.

———. 1989. *Return to Diversity: A Political History of East Central Europe since World War II*. New York: Oxford University Press.

Roy, Olivier. 2000. *The New Central Asia: The Creation of Nations*. New York: NYU Press.

Rumer, Boris Z. 1989. *Soviet Central Asia: A Tragic Experiment*. London: Unwin Hyman.

Rutland, Peter. 1985. *The Myth of the Plan: Lessons from the Soviet Planning Experience*. London: Hutchinson.

———. 2000. "Putin's Rise to Power." *Post-Soviet Affairs* 16 (4): 313–354.

Sachs, Jeffrey D. 1993. *Poland's Jump to a Market Economy*. Cambridge, MA: MIT Press.

———. 1994a. "Life in the Economic Emergency Room." In John Williamson, ed., *On the Political Economy of Policy Reform*, 501–524. Washington, DC: Institute for International Economics.

———. 1994b. "Russia's Struggle with Stabilization: Conceptual Issues and Evidence." Paper prepared for the World Bank Annual Conference on Development Economics. World Bank, Washington DC.

———. 1996. "The Transition at Mid-Decade," *American Economic Review Papers and Proceedings* 86 (May): 128–133.

Sachs, Jeffrey D., and Boris Pleskovic. 1993. "Political Independence and Economic Reform in Slovenia." In Olivier Blanchard, Kenneth A. Froot, and Jeffrey D. Sachs, eds., *The Transition in Eastern Europe*, vol. 1: *Country Studies*, 57–80. Chicago: University of Chicago Press.

Sachs, Jeffrey D., and Andrew Warner. 1995. "Economic Reform and Process of Global Integration." *Brookings Papers on Economic Activity* 1: 1–95.

Saidova, Galina, and Giovanni Andrea Cornia. 2005. *Linking Macroeconomic Policy to Poverty Reduction in Uzbekistan*. Tashkent: Center for Economic Development and United Nations Development Program.

Sakwa, Richard. 1998. "Left or Right? The CPRF and the Problem of Democratic Consolidation in Russia." *Journal of Communist Studies and Transition Politics* 14 (1): 128–158.

Sartori, Giovanni. 1976. *Parties and Party Systems*. Cambridge: Cambridge University Press.

Schamis, Hector. 1999. "Distributional Coalitions and the Politics of Economic Reform in Latin America." *World Politics* 51 (2): 236–268.

Schoenmann, Roger. 2005. "Captains or Pirates? State Business Relations in Post-Socialist Poland." *East European Politics and Society* 19 (1): 40–75.

Schonfelder, Bruno. 2005. "Bulgaria's Long March towards Meaningful Credit Contracts." *Post-Communist Economies* 17 (2): 173–204.

Schroeder, Gertrude. 1998. "Economic Transformation in the Post-Soviet Republics: An Overview." In Bartlomiej Kaminski, ed., *Economic Transition in Russia and the New States of Eurasia*, 11–41. Armonk, NY: M. E. Sharpe.

Selowsky, Marcelo, and Ricardo Martin. 1997. "Policy Performance and Output Growth in the Transition Economies." *American Economic Review Papers and Proceedings* 87: 349–358.

Sheahan, John. 1987. *Patterns of Development in Latin America: Poverty, Repression and Economic Strategy*. Princeton: Princeton University Press.

Shevtsova, Lilia. 2003. *Putin's Russia*. Washington, DC: Carnegie Endowment for International Peace.

Shleifer, Andrei, and Daniel Treisman. 2000. *Without a Map: Political Tactics and Economic Reform in Russia*. Cambridge, MA: MIT Press.

Shleifer, Andrei, and Robert Vishny. 1998. *The Grabbing Hand*. Cambridge, MA: Harvard University Press.

Shopov, Vladimir. 1999. "How the Voters Respond in Bulgaria." In Kay Lawson, Andrea Rommele, and Georgi Karasimeonov, eds., *Cleavages, Parties and Voters: Studies from Bulgaria, the Czech Republic, Hungary, Poland, and Romania*, 187–202. Westport, CT: Praeger.

Shvetsova, Olga. 2003. "Resolving the Problem of Pre-election Coordination: The Parliamentary Election as an Elite Presidential 'Primary.'" In Vicki L. Hesli and William Reissinger, eds., *The 1999–2000 Elections in Russia: Their Impact and Legacy*. Cambridge: Cambridge University Press.

Simmons, Beth. 1999. "The Internationalization of Capital." In Herbert Kitschelt et al., eds., *Continuity and Change in Contemporary Capitalism*, 36–69. Cambridge: Cambridge University Press.

Sinyavskaya, Oxana. 2003. "Pension Reform in Russia: A Challenge of Low Pension Age." PIE Discussion Paper Series. Moscow.

Slay, Ben. 2000. "Polish Economic Transition: Outcome and Lessons." *Communist and Postcommunist Studies* 33 (1): 49–70.

Smith, Graham, Vivien Law, Andrew Wilson, Annette Bohr, and Edward Allworth. 1998. *Nation-Building in the Post-Soviet Borderlands: The Politics of National Identities*. Cambridge: Cambridge University Press.

Snijders, Tom A. B., and Joel R. Bosker. 1999. *Multilevel Analysis: An Introduction to Basic and Advanced Multilevel Modeling*. London: Sage.

Sobyanin, Alexander. 1994. "Political Cleavages among the Russian Deputies." In Thomas Remington, ed., *Parliaments in Transition*, 181–203. Boulder, CO: Westview Press.

Solnick, Steven L. 1998. *Stealing the State: Control and Collapse in Soviet Institutions*. Cambridge, MA: Harvard University Press.

————. 2000. "Federalism and State-Building: Post-Communist and Post-Colonial Perspectives." In Andrew Reynolds, ed., *The Architecture of Democracy: Constitutional Design, Conflict Management and Democracy*, 171–205. Oxford: Oxford University Press.

Sonin, Konstantin. 2003. "Why the Rich May Favor Poor Protection of Property Rights." *Journal of Comparative Economics* 31 (4): 715–731.

Spechler, Martin. 2008. *The Political Economy of Reform in Central Asia*. Abingdon, UK. Routledge.

Spiller, Pablo, and Mariano Tommasi. 2003. "The Institutional Foundations of Public Policy: A Transactions Approach with Application to Argentina." *Journal of Law, Economics, and Organization* 19 (2): 281–306.

Spoor, Max, and Aktam Khaitov. 2002. "Agriculture, Rural Development and Poverty." http://www.undp.org/poverty/docs/sppr/docs-propoor/uzbekistan-report/Ch%205%20.

Staehr, Karsten. 2005. "Reforms and Economic Growth in Transition Economies: Complementarity, Sequencing and Speed." *European Journal of Comparative Economics* 2 (2): 177–202.

Stallings, Barbara. 1992. "International Influence on Economic Policy: Debt, Stabilization and Structural Reform." In Stephan Haggard and Robert Kaufman, eds., *The Politics of Economic Adjustment*, 41–88. Princeton: Princeton University Press.

Stanchev, Krassen. 2001. "The Path of Bulgarian Economic Reform." *East European Constitutional Review* 10 (4). http://www.law.nyu.edu/eecr/vol10num4/focus/stanchev.html.

———. 2004. "Political Economy of De-etatization in Bulgaria." Unpublished manuscript, Sofia.

Staniszkis, Jadwiga. 1991. "Political Capitalism in Poland." *East European Politics and Society* 5 (1): 127–141.

Stark, David, and Laszlo Bruszt. 1998. *Post-Socialist Pathways: Transforming Politics and Property in East Central Europe*. Cambridge: Cambridge University Press.

Stasavage, David. 2003. *Public Debt and the Birth of the Democratic State: France and Great Britain, 1688–1789*. Cambridge: Cambridge University Press.

Steenbergen, Marco R., and Bradford S. Jones. 2002. "Modeling Multilevel Data Structures." *American Journal of Political Science* 46 (1): 218–237.

Stigler, George. 1971. "The Theory of Economic Regulation." *Bell Journal of Economics and Management Science* 2: 3–21.

Stiglitz, Joseph. 2000. "Whither Reform." In *Annual Bank Conference on Development Economics, 1999*, 27–56. Washington, DC: World Bank.

Stokes, Gale. 1993. *The Walls Came Tumbling Down*. Oxford: Oxford University Press.

Stokes, Susan C. 1996. "Public Opinion and Market Reforms: The Limits of Economic Voting." *Comparative Political Studies*, special issue 29 (5): 499–519.

———, ed. 2001a. *Public Support for Market Reforms in New Democracies*. Cambridge: Cambridge University Press.

———. 2001b. *Mandates and Democracy: Neoliberalism by Surprise*. Cambridge: Cambridge University Press.

———. 2007. "Political Clientelism." In Carles Boix and Susan Stokes, eds., *The Oxford Handbook of Comparative Politics*, 604–627. Oxford: Oxford University Press.

Stone, Randall. 1996. *Satellites and Commissars: Strategy and Conflict in the Politics of Soviet-Bloc Trade*. Princeton: Princeton University Press.

———. 2002. *Lending Credibility: The International Monetary Fund and the Post-Communist Transition*. Princeton: Princeton University Press.

Stoner-Weiss, Kathryn. 2006. *Resisting the State: Reform and Retrenchment in Post-Soviet Russia*. Cambridge: Cambridge University Press.

Strange, Susan. 1996. *The Retreat of the State: The Diffusion of Power in the World Economy*. Cambridge: Cambridge University Press.

Suny, Ronald Grigor. 1993. *The Revenge of the Past: Nationalism, Revolution, and the Collapse of the Soviet Union*. Stanford: Stanford University Press.

———. 1995. "Elite Transformation in Transcaucasia." In Timothy J. Colton and Robert C. Tucker, eds., *Patterns in Post-Soviet Leadership*, 141–168. Boulder, CO: Westview Press.

Svejnar, Jan. 2002. "Transition Economies: Performance and Challenges." *Journal of Economic Perspectives* 16 (Winter): 3–28.

Svensson, Jakob. 1998. "Investment, Property Rights and Political Instability: Theory and Evidence." *European Economic Review* 42: 1317–1341.

Tarkowski, Jacek. 1989. "Old and New Patterns of Corruption in Poland and the USSR." *Telos* 80: 51–63.

Taras, Ray, ed. 1997. *Postcommunist Presidents*. Cambridge: Cambridge University Press.

Taube, Gunther, and Jeromin Zettelmeyer. 1998. "Output Decline and Recovery in Uzbekistan: Past Performance and Future Prospects." IMF Working Paper 98/132. Washington, DC: International Monetary Fund.

Terry, Sarah Miekljohn. 1989. "The Future of Poland: Perestroika or Perpetual Crisis." In William E. Griffith, ed., *Central and Eastern Europe: The Opening Curtain*, 178–218. Boulder, CO: Westview Press.

Thames, Frank. 2005. "Searching for Party Effects in Ukraine." *Communist and Post-Communist Studies* 38: 89–108.

Thelen, Kathleen. 1999. "Historical Institutionalism in Comparative Politics." *Annual Review of Political Science* 2: 369–404.

Tismaneanu, Vladimir, and Gail Kligman. 2001. "Romania's First Postcommunist Decade: From Iliescu to Iliescu." *East European Constitutional Review* 10 (1). http://www.law.nyu.edu/eecr/vol10num1/features/romaniafirstpostcomdecade.html.

Todorov, Antony. 1999. "The Role of Political Parties in Bulgaria's Accession to the EU." CSD Reports. Sofia: Center for the Study of Democracy.

Tompson, William. 2004. "Putin and the 'Oligarchs': A Two-Sided Commitment Problem." *Royal Institute for International Affairs* (London): 1–20.

Tregubova, Elena. 2003. *Baiki kremlevskogo diggera*. Moscow: Ad Marginem.

Treisman, Daniel. 1998. "Between the Extremes: Moderate Reformist and Centrist Blocs." In Timothy Colton and Jerry F. Hough, eds., *Growing Pains: The 1993 Russian Duma Election*, 141–176. Washington, DC: Brookings Institution.

———. 2000. "The Causes of Corruption." *Journal of Public Economics* 76 (3): 399–457.

Tsebelis, George. 1995. "Decision Making in Political Systems: Veto Players in Presidentialism, Parliamentarianism, Multicameralism, and Multipartyism." *British Journal of Political Science* 25 (3): 289–326.

Tucker, Joshua. 2006. *Regional Economic Voting: Russia, Poland, Hungary, Slovakia, and the Czech Republic*. Cambridge: Cambridge University Press.

Tworzecki, Hubert. 2003. *Learning to Choose: Electoral Politics in East Central Europe*. Stanford: Stanford University Press.

Tzvetkov, Plamen. 1992. "The Politics of Transition in Bulgaria: Back to the Future?" *Problems of Communism* 41 (3): 34–43.

Urban, Joan Barth, and Valery Solovei. 1997. *Russia's Communists at the Crossroads*. Boulder, CO: Westview Press.

UNCTAD. 1999. "Investment Policy Review of Uzbekistan," July, 1–65. New York and Geneva: United Nations.

Vachudova, Milada. 2005. *Europe Undivided: Democracy, Leverage, and Integration after Communism*. Oxford: Oxford University Press.

Valev, Neven. 2004. "No Pain, No Gain: Market Reform, Unemployment, and Politics in Bulgaria." *Journal of Comparative Economics* 32: 409–425.

Verdery, Katherine. 1993. "Nationalist and National Sentiment in Post-socialist Romania." *Slavic Review* 52 (2): 179–203.

Vincelette, Gallina Andronova. 2001. "Bulgarian Banking Sector Development, Post-1989." *Southeast European Politics* 2 (1): 4–23.

Vujacic, Veljko. 1996. "Gennady Zyuganov and the 'Third Road.'" *Post-Soviet Affairs* 12 (2): 118–154.

Wagstyl, Stefan, Andrew Jack, and Arkady Ostrovsky. 2003. "A Creeping Bureaucratic Coup." *Financial Times*, November 3.

Warner, Andrew. 2001. "Is Economic Reform Popular at the Polls?" *Journal of Comparative Economics* 29: 448–465.

Wawro, Gregory. 2003. "Estimating Dynamic Panel Data Models in Political Science." *Political Analysis* 10 (1): 25–49.

Way, Lucan A. 2005. "Rapacious Individualism and Political Competition in Ukraine, 1992–2004." *Communist and Post-Communist Studies* 38: 191–205.

Weingast, Barry. 1997. "The Political Foundations of the Rule of Law." *American Political Science Review* 91 (January): 245–264.

Weinthal, Erika. 2002. *State Making and Environmental Cooperation: Linking Domestic and International Politics in Central Asia.* Cambridge, MA: MIT Press.

Wellisz, Stanislaw, Henryk Kokoszczynski, and Andrzej Kondratowicz. 1993. "The Polish Economy, 1989–1991." In Henryk Kokoszczynski, Marek Okolski, and Stanislaw Wellisz, eds., *Stabilization and Structural Adjustment in Poland,* 29–66. London: Routledge.

Wernke, Michael. 2001. *Everything You Want to Hear and Nothing They Mean: Policy Switching in Post-Communist Democracies, a Senior Honors Thesis.* Columbus: Ohio State University Press.

Weyland, Kurt. 2005. "Theories of Policy Diffusion: Lessons from Latin American Pension Reform." *World Politics* 57 (January): 262–295.

White, Stephen, Richard Rose, and Ian McAlister. 1997. *How Russia Votes.* Chatham, NJ: Chatham House.

Willerton, John P. 1992. *Patronage and Politics in the USSR.* Cambridge: Cambridge University Press.

Williamson, John. 1994. "In Search of a Manual for Technopols." In John Williamson, ed., *The Political Economy of Policy Reform,* 1–28. Washington, DC: Institute for International Economics.

Wintrobe, Ronald. 1998. *The Political Economy of Dictatorship.* Cambridge: Cambridge University Press.

Wittenberg, Jason. 2006. *Crucibles of Political Loyalty: Church Institutions and Electoral Continuity in Hungary.* Cambridge: Cambridge University Press.

Woldendorp, J. 1998. "Party Government in 20 Democracies: An Update (1990–1995)." *European Journal of Political Research* 33 (1): 125–164.

Woodruff, David. 1999. *Money Unmade: Barter and the Fate of Russian Capitalism.* Ithaca, NY: Cornell University Press.

World Bank. 1993. *Uzbekistan: An Agenda for Economic Reform.* Washington, DC: World Bank.

———. 1994. *Averting the Old Age Crisis.* Washington, DC: World Bank.

———. 1997. *Annual Development Report.* Washington, DC: World Bank.

———. 1999. "Uzbekistan Social and Structural Policy Review, August 25." World Bank Report no. 19626.

———. 2000. *Balancing Protection and Opportunity: A Strategy for Social Protection in Transition Economies.* Washington, DC: World Bank.

———. 2001. *Russian Federation: Russian Economic Report.* May. http://go.worldbank.org/LPMH7GDTY0.

———. 2003. *World Development Indicators, 2003.* http://go.worldbank.org/BDEXK5OE00.

World Bank Governance Website. www.worldbank.org/wbi.governance.

Wyzan, Michael. 1996. "Stabilization and Anti-inflationary Policy." In Iliana Zloch-Christy, ed., *Bulgaria in a Time of Change: Economic and Political Dimensions,* 77–105. Aldershot: Avebury.

————. 1998. "The Political Economy of Bulgaria's Peculiar Post-Communist Business Cycle." *Comparative Economic Studies* 40 (1): 5–42.

Yakovlev, Andrei. 2001. "Black Cash: Disincentives to Invest in the Formal Economy." *Europe-Asia Studies* 53 (January): 33–55.

Yalcin, Resul. 2002. *The Rebirth of Uzbekistan: Politics, Economy and Society in the Post-Soviet Era.* Reading, UK: Ithaca Press.

Yeltsin, Boris. 1994. *The Struggle for Russia.* London: Times Books.

————. 2000. *Midnight Diaries.* New York: Public Affairs.

Yudaeva, Ksenia. 2003. "Effects of WTO Accession on the Russian Economy." Carnegie Endowment, Moscow, May 28.

Zettelmeyer, Jeromin. 1999. "The Uzbek Growth Puzzle." *IMF Staff Papers* 46 (3): 274–292.

Zhuravskaya, Ekaterina, Irina Slinko, and Elena Yakovleva. 2005. "Laws for Sale: Evidence from Russia's Regions." *American Law and Economic Review* 3 (1): 284–318.

Zielinski, Jakub. 2002. "Translating Social Cleavages into Party Systems: The Significance of New Democracies." *World Politics* 54 (2): 184–211.

Zinnes, Clifford, Yair Eliat, and Jeffrey Sachs. 2001. "The Gains from Privatization in Transition Economies: Is 'Change of Ownership' Enough?" *IMF Staff Papers*, special issue, 48: 146–170.

Zubek, Voytek. 1995. "The Phoenix Out of the Ashes: The Rise to Power of Poland's Post-Communist SdRP." *Communist and Post-Communist Politics* 28 (3): 275–306.

Index

Abdelal, Rawi, 146, 156
Acemoglu, Daron, 7, 38, 247
Adam, Jan, 226
Adreev, Alexander, 196, 199
Aghion, Phillipe, 106, 137
Agrarian Party of Moldova, 52, 63, 68
Ahrend, Rudiger, 185
Akaev, Askar, 3, 50, 68, 231
Alam, Asad, 240
Albania, 37, 54, 57, 68, 79, 147, 154, 155, 156, 166, 190
Aldrich, John, 24
Alesina, Alberto, 7, 14, 24, 25, 26, 40, 57, 58, 123, 126
Aliev, Heydar, 3, 49, 66, 67, 151
Alliance for Democratic Left (Poland), 63
Allworth, Edward, 150
Almatov, Zokirjan, 234
Alvarez, Michael E., 247
Anderson, Christopher, 133
Anderson, Kathryn, 232
Andreev, Alexander, 195
Andrews, Josephine, 169
Angrist, Joshua, 164
Appel, Hillary, 14, 24, 250
Arellano-Bond correction, 115
Armenia, 19, 55, 68, 79, 109, 146, 152, 190
Armingeon, Klaus, 49, 51, 53, 63, 181
Aron, Leon, 68

Asian financial crisis, 178–179, 207
Aslund, Anders, 7, 12, 13, 41, 66, 106, 107, 109, 111, 118, 119, 123, 173, 181, 184, 187
autocracy
  and credible commitment, 29–30, 33–34
  legislative gridlock, 125
  polarization, 33–34
  policy unpredictability, 125, 134–136
Auty, Richard M., 237
Avramov, Roumen, 201, 202, 203
AvtoVAZ, 183, 190
Azerbaijan, 19, 49, 56, 57, 66, 79, 90, 145, 150, 151, 250
Azmanova, Albena, 207

Baikal Finance Group, 189
Balcerowicz, Leszek, 87, 214, 219, 220, 224
Bannerji, Arup, 240
bank reform. *See* institutional reform
BANU–Nikola Petkov, 195
Barany, Zoltan, 208
Barnes, Andrew, 186
Barro, Robert, 111
Bartels, Larry, 26, 164
Bates, Robert, 18
Bearce, David, 26
Bebchuk, Lucian Arye, 252
Beck, Nathaniel, 77, 78, 84, 112
Beck, Thorsten, 54, 86

BEEPS Data Set
  descriptive results, 130–132
  methodology of, 129, 130
  variable definitions, 141
  weaknesses in, 130
Beissinger, Mark, 148, 153, 230
Belarus, 16, 72, 74, 90, 138, 150, 162,
  250, 251
Belin, Laura, 187
Belka, Marek, 225
Bell, Janice, 217, 218, 220, 226
Berezovsky, Boris, 188
Berg, Andrew, 107, 111
Berglof, Erik, 4, 179, 182
Berov, Lyuben, 199
Besley, Timothy, 36, 246
Bewley technique, 83, 84, 93, 94, 103,
  115
Bewley, R. A., 83, 115
Bialer, Seweryn, 154, 155
Biberaj, Elez, 155, 157
Bielecki, Jan, 222
Birch, Sarah, 68
Birlik (Unity-Uzbekistan), 234
Black, Duncan, 24
Blanchard, Olivier, 106, 107, 224
Blasi, Joseph, 174
Blaszczyk, Barbara, 223
Bohle, Dorothee, 72
Bohr, Annette, 150
Boix, Carles, 7, 26, 38, 247
Bojicic-Dzelilovic, Vesna, 199, 201, 205,
  207
Bojkov, Victor, 199, 201, 205, 207
Bolton, Patrick, 4
Boone, Peter, 13, 107, 111, 120, 185
Borisova, Yevgeniia, 180, 183
Borensztein, Eduardo, 107, 111
Bosker, Joel R., 132, 133
Boycko, Maxim, 106, 174
Bozoki, Andras, 52, 67, 146, 156, 157
Brader, Ted, 25
Brady, Henry, 20, 167
Breslauer, George W., 39
Broadman, Harry G., 230, 235, 236,
  241
Brooks, Robin, 207, 212
Brooks, Sarah, 17, 85, 107
Browne, Eric C., 13, 41

Brubaker, Rogers, 148, 154
Brus, Wolodimierz, 214
Bruszt, Laszlo, 6, 16, 24, 107
Bryant, Fred B., 56
Bugajski, Janusz, 50, 66
Bulgargas, 202
Bulgaria
  bank reform, 199, 205
  competition policy, 199, 205–207
  corporate governance, 200
  corruption, 200–202, 205–206
  currency board, 205, 209
  European Union, 207, 210–211
  large privatization, 194, 195, 198–199,
    200–201, 205–206, 209
  party platforms and polarization, 194,
    195, 208–209
  price liberalization, 195, 198, 201
  recognition of polarization, 195–196
  small privatization, 198–199
  tax policy, 203, 207
  trade and currency liberalization,
    198–199, 201
Bulgarian Communist Party, 66
Bulgarian Socialist Party, 6, 49, 54, 66,
  159, 192, 193–195, 196, 197, 216
Bunce, Valerie, 147, 148, 149, 152, 153,
  154
Bunich, Andrei, 175

Cameron, David, 127
Campos, Nauro, 60, 73, 108, 111, 112,
  120, 160
Careja, Romana, 49, 51, 53, 63, 181
Carlisle, D. S., 149, 151, 231
causal depth, 18–19, 144–145
causal mechanisms, 10–11, 18–19,
  127–128
Center Alliance, 217
centrist faction
  classification of, 67–68. *See also*
    political faction, classification
    scheme
  examples of, 64–65
  preferences, 4–5
  reform under autocracy, 33–34
  reform under high polarization, 32–33
  reform under low polarization, 31
  support base, 26–27

challenger producer, 28–30. *See also* producer sector

Channel 1 (Russia), 188

Chavez, Hugo, 53, 162

Chechnya, 175, 188

Cheibub, Jose A., 247

Chernomyrdin, Viktor, 70, 173

Chernyakova, Nonna, 180

Chotiner, Barbara Ann, 156

Christian Democratic Union (Croatia), 63

Christian Democrats, 217

Chubais, Anatoly, 175, 181

Ciolko, Marek, 111

Civic Democratic Party (Czech Republic), 68

Civic Forum, 68

Claessens, Stijn, 201

Clarke, George, 54, 86

Clem, Ralph S., 171

Collier, David, 20, 167

Collins, Kathleen, 39, 68, 150, 151, 230, 231, 232, 233

Colton, Timothy, 25, 52, 179

COMECON, 147, 148, 154

communist bloc, 147–148

communist party. *See* old-left faction

Communist Party of the Russian Federation, 6, 68, 157, 163, 169, 170, 176

Communist Party of Ukraine, 66, 68, 157, 163

Communist Party of Uzbekistan, 66

Comparative Political Data Set, 49–52, 53, 63, 181

competition policy. *See* institutional reform

Congress of Liberal Democrats (Poland), 217

Connor, Walter, 150

consistent reform, 2–3, 87–88. *See also* state building
  findings, 90–94
  measurement of, 72–73, 88–90
  robustness checks on findings, 94–95

Cook, Linda, 96, 123, 174, 179, 184

Cornia, Giovanni, 239, 240, 242

corporate governance. *See* institutional reform

Corricelli, Fabricio, 108

Coudouel, Aline, 241

Cox, Gary, 39, 127, 160

Craumer, Peter R., 171

credible commitment
  autocracy, 33–34
  democracy with high polarization, 32–33
  democracy with low polarization, 30–31
  and investment, 23, 32–33
  and taxes, 32–33

credible commitment, for parties. *See* political faction

Croatia, 52, 152

Croatian Democratic Union, 51

Crowther, William, 52

Czech Republic, 60, 89, 146, 153, 159, 215, 223

Czechoslovakia, 9, 147, 154, 159

Dabrowski, Janusz, 219, 221, 225, 226

Dabrowski, Marek, 224

Darden, Keith, 10, 18, 145, 146, 156

De Boef, Suzanna, 77, 78, 83, 85

de Cunha, Paulo Viera, 173

De Melo, Martha, 16, 17, 72, 79, 86, 107, 111, 120, 160, 250

de Menil, Georges, 7, 66, 123

Deirmeier, Daniel, 21, 25, 34, 35, 37

democracy, 9–11
  findings, 80, 82–93, 97–99
  legislative gridlock, 125
  measurement of, 78–79
  polarization, 30–33. *See also* polarization
  policy unpredictability, 125, 134–136
  and reform, 245–247
  robustness checks on findings, 84–86, 94–95
  substantive effects of polarization and, 80–84, 93–94

Democratic Convention (Romania), 68

Democratic Forum (Hungary), 68

Democratic Labor Party (Lithuania), 66

Democratic Left Alliance (Poland), 215, 217, 219, 220

Democratic National Salvation Front (Romania), 157

Democratic Party (Albania), 68

Democratic Union (Poland), 217
Denisova, Irina, 8, 78, 247
Denizer, Cevdet, 17, 120
dependent national model. *See*
    nationalism
dependent sector, 4, 26–27
    effects of polarization on, 5
    preferences, 26–27, 29, 43
Desai, Mihir, 183
Desai, Padma, 181
Dewatripont, Matthias, 87, 88
Dimitrov, Dimitar, 196, 201, 204, 205,
    206, 209, 212
Djankov, Simeon, 129
Dmitriev, Mikhail, 182
Dobozi, Istvan, 109, 118
Dobrinsky, Rumen, 196, 201, 204, 205,
    206, 209, 212
Dochev, Nasko, 196, 201, 204, 205, 206,
    209, 212
Doyle, Michael W., 127
Drazen, Allen, 40, 58, 123
Dunteman, George H., 74
Dyck, Alexander, 183

Easter, Gerald, 12, 29, 151, 178, 225
Easterly, William, 173
economic growth
    data, 108–109
    debates on rapid versus gradual
        reform, 106–107
    findings, 112–115
    polarization, 105–106
    reverse causality vis-à-vis polarization,
        159–160
    robustness checks on findings,
        116–118
economic inequality
    findings, 60–61, 62–63
    measurement of, 59–60
    polarization, 58–59
    robustness checks on findings, 62
economic liberalization. *See* economic
    reform
economic reform, 2, 72, 73, 106–107
    competition policy, 219, 237
    globalization, 13–14, 23, 249–251
    large privatization, 3, 22, 24, 28,
        31–32, 34, 73, 88–90, 111, 162,

170, 172–176, 182, 187–188, 190,
    194–195, 198–201, 205–206, 209,
    216, 220–223, 235–236
    measurement of, 72–73, 88–90
    polarization, 88–90
    price liberalization, 22, 24, 73, 111,
        169–170, 172–173, 195, 198, 201,
        216, 238
    small privatization, 22, 24, 28, 31–32,
        34, 73, 88, 111, 162, 172, 198–199,
        221–223, 235, 238
    trade and currency liberalization, 22,
        24, 73, 88, 111, 169–170, 173, 182,
        184, 198, 201, 205, 219, 235–237,
        239
    and transfers, 36
economic reform, globalization. *See*
    political faction, policy convergence
economic shock, 22, 40
Ekiert, Gregorz, 219
elections
    order of play, 27, 43–44
    role of uncertainty, 5, 29–30, 33
Eliat, Yair, 87, 88, 120
Eller, Markus, 8, 78, 247
Elster, Jon, 9, 18, 128
endogeneity, 18–19. *See also* reverse
    causality
    democracy, 8
    democracy and polarization, 85–86
    democracy and reform, 8, 78
    growth and polarization, 118
    growth and reform, 115
    polarization and reform, 159–166
Engelbrekt, Kjell, 195, 199
Epperly, Brad, 54
Ericson, Joel, 21, 25, 34, 35, 37
Ericson, Richard, 71
Erk (Freedom-Uzbekistan), 234
error-correction model, 77–78, 80, 90,
    112, 160
Esping-Andersen, Gosta, 72
Esteban, Joan Maria, 58
Estonia, 1, 71, 72, 74, 146, 152
Estonian National Independence Party,
    51, 63
ethnolinguistic fractionalization, 60, 160
European Bank for Reconstruction and
    Development, 9, 10, 72, 75, 87, 89,

99, 110, 112, 178, 192, 205, 207, 214, 235, 236
European Union. *See* initial conditions
Evans, Geoffrey, 52
executive, 3, 53
    general preferences, 27–28
    role, 4–6

Falcetti, Elisabetta, 120
Fatherland-All Russia Party, 180, 188
Federation Council (Russia), 188
Federowicz, M. Michal, 219, 221, 225, 226
FIDESZ (Hungary), 3, 50, 68
Fidrmuc, Jan, 25, 52
Fierman, William, 230, 231, 232, 233, 234
Fifth Republic Movement (Venezuela), 53
Fiorina, Morris, 58
firm. *See* producer sector
Fischer, Stanley, 88, 107, 111, 120
Fischhoff, B., 56
Fish, M. Steven, 13, 41, 187, 188, 189, 190, 207, 212
Flikke, Geir, 157, 170
Former Yugoslav Republic of Macedonia, 57, 63, 68, 152
Foxley, Alejandro, 9
Franzese, Robert, 56, 77, 79, 112
Freedom House, 24, 55, 79, 86, 102, 124, 125, 127, 134, 141, 188, 233
Freedom Union (Poland), 50, 68, 217, 220
Freeland, Christia, 175, 177
Frydman, Roman, 50, 222, 224
Frye, Timothy, xii, 8, 10, 12, 21, 24, 25, 34, 35, 37, 39, 49, 50, 52, 56, 78, 123, 125, 127, 129, 172, 174, 178, 179, 183, 186, 190, 247

Gaddy, Clifford G., 16, 118
Gaidar, Yegor, 25, 169, 173, 176, 181, 221
Ganev, Venelin, 12, 94, 195, 200, 202, 214, 248
Garrett, Geoffrey, 24, 26, 252
Garton-Ash, Timothy, 153
Gazprom, 183, 188, 202, 206

Geddes, Barbara, 107, 247
Gehlbach, Scott, 16, 29, 33, 34, 39, 41, 130, 246, 247, 248
Gelb, Alan, 17, 120
Gelman, Andrew, 132
generalized linear latent and mixed model (GLLAMM), 132–133
General-Method of Moments (GMM), 115
Georgia, 55, 146, 152, 153, 190
Gerber, Marlene, 51
Ghandi, Jennifer, 247
Gilbert, Daniel, 56
gini coefficient. *See* economic inequality, measurement of
GKO State Treasury Bonds (Russia), 176, 178
Glaeser, Edward, 223
Gleason, Gregory, 151, 230
Goff, Alberto, 54, 86
Gorbachev, Mikhail, 66, 147, 171, 193, 231, 233
Gorzynski, M., 223
Graham, Thomas, 186
Gray, Cheryl, 50, 222
Greene, Donald P., 84
Greskovits, Bela, 72
Groseclose, Timothy, 123
Grosjean, Pauline, 247
Grossman, Sanford, 37
Grozev, Kostadin, 212
Grzymala-Busse, Anna, 6, 10, 15, 16, 18, 41, 50, 66, 67, 145, 146, 153, 156, 159, 185, 247
Guenev, Kamen, 202
Guilbault, Rebecca, 56
Guriev, Sergei, 185
Gusinsky, Vladimir, 188
Gustafson, Thane, 178

Haber, Stephen, 33, 246
Haggard, Stephan, 7, 9, 58, 75, 96, 220, 227, 246
Hale, Henry, 14, 25, 250
Hanley, Sean, 159
Hanson, Stephen, 107
Haran, Olexiy, 157, 163
Harper, M. A. G., 208
Hasek, Merell, 50, 222

Havrylyshyn, Oleh, 111, 112, 120
Hedstrom, Peter, 128
Hellman Joel, 2, 3, 9, 10, 39, 41, 59, 60, 87, 88, 125, 129, 130, 246, 248, 250
Helpman, Elhanan, 37, 123
Hendley, Kathryn, 129
Henisz, Witold, 125
Herrera, Yoshiko, 109
Hewett, Ed, 16, 71
Heybey, Berta, 107, 111, 120
Hill, Jennifer, 132
hindsight bias, 56
Hirsch, Francine, 148
Hoff, Karla, 10, 16, 87, 88
Hoffman, David, 175
Holmes, Stephen, 12, 13, 39
Horowitz, Donald, 157
Horowitz, Shale, 13, 41
Horvath, Roman, 111, 112
Howitt, Peter, 137
Hoxha, Enver, 155
Hsiao, Cheng, 77
Huber, John, 136, 143
Hungarian Democratic Forum, 68
Hungarian Socialist Party, 63, 67
Hungary, 1, 19, 50, 51, 53, 66, 71, 72, 74, 146, 147, 153–154, 159, 171, 182, 210, 215, 223
Hunter, Shireen, 150
Huskey, Gene, 149, 151
HZDS (Slovakia), 63

Ickes, Barry W., 16, 118, 129
Iliescu, Ion, 157, 162
IMRO (Macedonia), 63, 68
inconsistent reform, 2–3
  as rents, 26
  result of, 4, 87–88, 183, 213, 221
initial conditions, 15–18, 107–108
  command economy, 71
  European Union, 15–16, 162–163, 210–211, 227
  findings, 116
  measurement of, 79
  path dependence, 17–18, 86–87, 95
  structural features, 16–17
Inoyatov, Rustam, 234
institutional reform, 2, 72, 73

bank reform, 10, 73, 88–90, 185–186, 199, 202–203, 205, 207
competition policy, 10, 31, 73, 88–90, 111, 170, 173–174, 182–184, 199, 205–207, 225, 236
corporate governance, 3, 10, 28, 31, 73–90, 174, 185, 190, 200–203, 207, 221, 223, 235–236
globalization, 13–14, 23, 249–251
measurement of, 88–90
property rights, 184–185, 189, 235, 236
regulation, 11–13, 34, 184–185
securities market reform, 10, 31, 73, 88–90, 223
institutional reform, globalization. *See* political faction, policy convergence
institutional reform, pace of reform. *See* pace of reform
instrumental variables approach
  applied to democracy and reform, 85–86
  applied to polarization and economic reform, 163–166
  applied to polarization, democracy, and reform, 93
International Monetary Fund (IMF), 108, 178, 192, 194, 198, 204, 205, 207, 209, 212, 220, 227, 228, 236–238, 250
investment
  assumptions, 35, 36
  autocracy, 5–6, 33–34
  and changes to order of play, 36
  democracy, 5, 30–31, 32–33
  findings, 138
  measurement of, 104–105, 137
  order of play, 43–44
  under high polarization, 29, 32–33
  under low polarization, 29, 30–31
investment, producers' strategies. *See* producer sector
Ishiyama, John, 6, 50, 58, 66, 67, 146, 153, 156, 157
Islam, Nazrul, 109

Jack, Andrew, 181, 189, 224
Jackson, John E., 50, 52, 214, 216, 220, 224

Jackson, Marvin, 198
Janusauskiene, Diana, 66
Jensen, Nathan, 16, 130
Johnson, Simon, 12, 13, 107, 111, 120, 129, 219, 223
Jones, Bradford S., 18, 132, 133
Jones, Geraint, 129, 130, 248
Jones Luong, Pauline, 39, 66, 150, 151, 230, 232, 234
Judson, Ruth A., 109, 115

Kam, Cindy D., 79
KAMAZ, 190
Kaminski, Tytus, 219, 221, 223, 225, 226
Kamp, Marianne, 241
Kanev, Assen, 196
Kanev, Dobrin, 162, 194, 196, 210
Kapstein, Ethan B., 26, 27, 43, 96
Karasimeonov, Georgi, 196
Karimov, Islam, 49, 66, 151, 231–234, 235
Kassayie, Berhanu, 194, 200, 201
Katz, Jonathan, 77, 78, 84, 112
Katznelson, Ira, 128
Kaufman, Robert R., 7, 9, 57, 58, 75, 96, 220, 227, 246
Kaufmann, Daniel, 129, 130, 248
Kazakhstan, 56, 67, 79, 150, 233, 240, 250
Keane, Michael, 226
Keefer, Philip, 33, 34, 40, 54, 58, 86, 105, 115, 246, 247
Keele, Luke, 77, 78, 83, 85
Kenyon, Thomas, 134
Keohane, Robert, 8
Kernell, Georgia, 136, 143
Khaitov, Aktam, 236
Khodorkovsky, Mikhail, 189
Kiewiet, Roderick, 56
Kim, Soo Yeon, 84
King, Gary, 8
Kitschelt, Herbert, 6, 17, 18, 25, 52, 66, 67, 107, 144, 146, 159, 196, 200, 212, 216, 218
Kizuyev, Vitaliy, 60, 160
Klaus, Vaclav, 68
Klich, Jacek, 50, 52, 214, 216, 220, 224
Kligman, Gail, 162

Knack, Stephen, 40, 58, 105, 115
Kokh, Alfred, 175
Kokoszcynski, Henryk, 222
Kolarova, Rumyana, 196, 201, 204, 205, 206, 209, 212
Kolodko, Gregorz, 220, 222, 223
Kondratowicz, Andrzej, 222
Kono, Daniel, 79, 83
Kopstein, Jeffrey S., 10, 15
Korbonski, Andrzej, 216
Kornai, Janos, 16, 71, 106
Kostov, Ivan, 204–208
Kotkin, Stephen, 108
Kounov, Andrey, 179, 182
Kowalska, Marzena, 219
Kozarzewski, Piotr, 222
Krajewski, Stefan, 225
Kramer, Mark, 226
Krastev, Ivan, 251
Kreps, David, 35, 37, 46
Kroumova, Maya, 174
Krueger, Gary, 111
Kruse, Douglas, 174
Kubik, Jan, 219
Kuchma, Leonid, 68
Kudamatsu, Masayuki, 246
Kurtz, Marcus J., 85
Kurzer, Paulette, 13, 23
Kwasniewski, Aleksander, 162, 220
Kyrgyzstan, 19, 50, 56, 60, 68, 89, 150, 159, 231, 233, 251

Labor Code (Russia), 182–183, 184, 186
Laitin, David, 146, 155
Lane, David, 152, 154
large privatization. *See* economic reform
late-national model. *See* nationalism
Latvia, 152, 153, 251
Latvia's Way, 68
Law, Vivien, 150
Law and Justice Party (Poland), 217
Law on Inspections (Russia), 183
Law on Licensing (Russia), 183
Law on Privatization (Russia), 174
Law on Registration (Russia), 183
legislative gridlock, 123
    macrofindings, 125
    predictions, 123–124
Leimgrubber, Philipp, 51

Leoni, Eduardo L., 136, 143
Levine, Ross, 110
Levitas, Anthony, 221, 225
Lewandowski, Janusz, 216
Lewis, Paul, 52
Lewis, Steve, 21, 25, 34, 35
Liberal Democratic Party (Slovenia), 68
Lieberman, Ira, 175
Lieven, Anatole, 152
Lilov, Aleksander, 194
Limongi, Fernando, 247
Lindblom, Charles E., 71
Linz, Juan, 107, 160
Lipton, David, 12, 106
Lithuania, 51, 66, 67, 146, 152, 153, 171, 182, 251
loans for shares (Russia), 174–177
long-run multiplier (LRM), 80, 83, 90, 93
losers from reform. *See* dependent sector; old-economy interests; and old-left faction
Lukanov, Andrei, 193, 194, 198, 200, 202

Macedonia. *See* Former Yugoslav Republic of Macedonia
Macieja, Jan, 224
Magaloni, Beatriz, 247.
Mahalla, 240–241
Mahoney, James, 17
Malesky, Edward, 17, 129
Maleva, Tatyana, 183
Mandelbaum, Michael, 96
Mansfeldova, Zdenka, 6, 25, 52, 66, 146, 159, 196, 200, 212, 216, 218
Mansfield, Edward D., 10, 24, 39, 125, 252
March, Luke, 157, 163, 170
Marese, Michael, 147
market building, 11–13, 247–249. *See also* economic reform
Markov, Nikolay, 196, 201, 204, 205, 206, 209, 212
Markov, Sergei, 181
Markowski, Radoslaw, 6, 25, 52, 66, 146, 159, 196, 200, 212, 216, 218
Marnie, Sheila, 241
Martin, Raiser, 120
Martin, Ricardo, 109, 118, 120

Mattli, Walter, 15, 16
Mau, Vladimir, 39, 53, 59, 106, 122, 123, 126, 173, 181
Maurer, Noel, 33, 246
Mazowiecki, Tadeusz, 219
McAlister, Ian, 177
McCarty, Nolan, 39, 53, 59, 122, 123, 126
McFaul, Michael, 68, 171, 179
McGregor, James, 127
McKinnon, Ronald, 9
McMillan, John, 178
Meciar, Vladimir, 51, 63
media curtailment (Russia), 187–188
median voter theorem. *See* political faction, policy convergence
Melone, Albert P., 193, 194, 196
Mencinger, Joze, 67
Micklewright, John, 241
microfoundations, 127–128, 252–253
Milanovic, Branko, 26, 27, 43, 59, 60, 96, 174
Miller, Jeffery, 200, 201
Milov, Vladimir, 185
Minassian, Garabed, 202
Miziyoyev, Shavkat, 234
Moldova, 1, 57, 60, 152, 190, 250
Monro, Neil, 186
Moore, Mike, 184
Morales, Evo, 53
Mostovoya, Yulia, 66
Motyl, Alexander, 147, 156
Movement for a Democratic Slovakia, 51
Movement for Rights and Freedoms (Bulgaria), 195, 197, 211
Movement toward Socialism (Bolivia), 53
Muller, Katharina, 96, 226, 227
Multigroup, 201–202, 206–207
Murer, Jeffrey Stevenson, 157
Murillo, M. Victoria, 2, 26, 57, 249
Murphy, Kevin, 2, 3, 87
Murrell, Peter, 106, 107, 111, 120, 129
Myagkov, Mikhail, 56, 189

Nahaylo, Bohdan, 147, 152
Naoi, Megumi, 134
National Investment Funds (Poland), 222–223

National Movement Simeon II (Bulgaria), 208
National Salvation Front (Romania), 49, 66
nationalism
   dependent national model, 151–153
   findings, 159–162
   and foreign policy autonomy, 152–153, 154–155
   and institutional legacies, 147
   late national model, 149–151
   and layers of the communist bloc, 148–149
   and opposition parties, 150, 153, 156
   polarization, 145–146, 150–151, 153, 156
   sovereign national model, 153–158
   timing of national identity formation, 149, 150–152, 153–154
nationalist faction, 51, 68. *See also* rightist faction
Nazarbaev, Nursultan, 67
Nedyalkova, Yordanka, 208
Nelson, Joan, 13, 220
Nenova, Tatyana, 196, 197
Nerlove, Marc, 115
New Azerbaijan Party, 66
new-economy interests, 4–5, 26
Newman, Alisa, 237
Nicholson, Alex, 172
Nikolov, Boyko, 196, 201, 204, 205, 206, 209, 212
Nikolov, Yovo, 206, 207
Nissman, David, 151
Nones, Jon A., 237
Non-Party Movement in Support of Reforms (Poland), 217
North, Douglas C., 14, 17, 107, 252
NTV (Russia), 188
Nunn, Sam, 186

O'Dwyer, Conor, 41, 54, 247
Olcott, Martha Brill, 67
old-economy interests, 4–5, 26
old-left faction
   classification of, 66–67
   examples of, 64–65
   preferences, 4–5
   reform under autocracy, 33–34

reform under high polarization, 32–33
reform under low polarization, 30
support base, 26
old-left faction, classification of. *See* political faction, classification scheme
Olson, Mancur, 34, 243
Onexim Bank, 175
ordered logit model, 133
Ordeshook, Peter C., 189
ordinary least squares (OLS) regression, 77, 112
Orenstein, Mitchell, 68
Organization for Security and Cooperation in Europe, 180, 187
Osborn, Elizabeth, 217
Ostrovsky, Arkady, 189
Owen, Ann L., 115

pace of reform, 2, 9–11. *See also* state building
   findings, 78–84, 115
   growth, 106–107
   measurement issues vis-à-vis growth, 112
   measurement of, 72–73
   robustness checks on findings, 84–86
Pacek, Alexander, 52
Page, Scott, 17, 252
Paretskaya, Anna, 171
parliamentary system
   consistency and pace of reform in, 95
   polarization, 55
partial reform. *See* inconsistent reform
partisanship, 52–53, 171, 195–197. *See also* political faction
Party of the Democratic Left (Slovakia), 66
Parvanov, Georgi, 194, 209, 210
Paszoski, B., 223
path dependence. *See* initial conditions
Peach, Gary, 180
Peev, Evgeni, 201, 202, 205, 206
Peeva, Ralitsa, 208, 209
People's Democratic Party (Uzbekistan), 232
People's Deputy Party (Russia), 180
Peoples Union (Bulgaria), 195
Persson, Torsten, 8, 166

Peters, R. Kyle, 201
Petersen, Roger, 152
Petranov, Stefan, 200, 201
Pieralla, Paci, 226
Pierson, Paul, 17, 107, 252
Pinto, Brian, 225
Pipes, Richard, 147, 151
Pleskovic, Boris, 67
Plumper, Thomas, 15, 16, 85
Pohl, Gerhard, 118
Poland, 146
  competition policy, 219, 225
  corporate governance, 221, 223
  and the dependent sector, 226–227
  European Union, 221, 227
  large privatization, 216, 221–223
  new private sector of, 223–224
  party platforms and polarization,
    215–218
  price liberalization, 216
  private sector, 215
  privatization, 224
  recognition of polarization, 218
  securities market reform, 223
  small privatization, 221–223
  state-owned firms, 225–226
  trade and currency liberalization,
    219
Polanyi, Karl, 15, 247
polarization, 3
  alternative measurement of, 58
  and bond markets, 56, 176
  democracy, 78–84, 90–93
  ethnicity as a source of, 58, 60–61
  firm level decision making, 136–138
  growth, 112–115
  inequality as a source of, 58–59, 60–63
  and investment, 29–33, 105–106,
    136–138
  legislative gridlock, 125
  measurement of, 74–75
  nationalism as a source of, 145–146,
    150–151, 153, 156, 159–162
  policy unpredictability, 125, 134–136
  regionalism as source of, 58
  religion as a source of, 58
  transfers, 97–99
polarization, and firms. *See* producer
  sector

polarization, endogeneity. *See*
  endogeneity
polarization, policy unpredictability. *See*
  policy unpredictability
polarization, reverse causality. *See* reverse
  causality
policy making
  costs of switching (investors), 35
  costs of switching (politicians), 35
  under autocracy, 33–34
  under democracies with low
    polarization, 32
  under democracy with high
    polarization, 29–33
policy reversal
  endogenous reversal, 22–23
  exogenous reversal, 22
  measurement of, 124
policy reversal, investment. *See*
  investment
policy unpredictability
  effects of, 5, 29–30, 123
  findings, 134–136
  growth, 105–106
  macrofindings, 125
  measurement of, 130–132
  predictions, 123
Polish League of Families, 217
Polish Peasant Party, 219
Polish United Workers' Party, 215–216
political faction, 49
  classification scheme, 49–53, 57,
    63–66, 68
  examples of classification, 64–65
  level of organization, 25
  policy convergence, 23–26, 249–251
  preferences, 27–30
political faction, credible commitment.
  See credible commitment
Pomfret, Richard, 230, 231, 232, 238,
  239, 240
Pond, Elizabeth, 163
Poole, Keith T., 39, 53, 59, 122, 123, 126
Pop-Eleches, Grigore, 13, 18, 41, 249,
  250
Popov, Dimitar, 198
Popov, Vladimir, 107, 111
Potanin, Vladimir, 175, 176
Potolidis, Pojatos, 51

Poznanska, Krzystyna, 50, 52, 214, 216, 220, 224
Prasad, Eswar S., 226
presidential system
  consistency and pace of reform in, 95
  executive party affiliation, 55–56
  polarization, 55
  and policy making, 39
price liberalization. *See* economic reform
Pritchett, Lant, 116
privatization. *See* economic reform
Privatization Act (Bulgaria), 199, 205, 209
privatization law (Russia), 174
producer sector
  assumptions about, 35
  under autocracy, 33–34
  under democracy with high polarization, 32–33
  under democracy with low polarization, 30–31
  investment, 138
  and policy reversal, 23
  preferences, 28–29, 42
Przeworski, Adam, 9, 12, 13, 15, 214, 219, 246, 247
Putin, Vladimir, 179–189

Rachinsky, Andrei, 185
Rakhmanin, Serhii, 66
Rapacki, Ryzsard, 215
Rapaczynski, Andrzej, 50, 222, 224
Ratna, Sahay, 88, 107, 111, 120
Ray, Debraj, 58
Razo, Armando, 33, 246
Reddaway, Peter, 186
Reilly, David, 10, 15
Reissinger, William, 180, 181
Remington, Thomas F., 123, 171, 180, 181, 184, 186
Remmer, Karen, 13, 23, 26, 57
Renelt, David, 110
reverse causality
  democracy and reform, 8
  polarization and reform, 159–166
Rigby, T. H., 154
Right Democratic Party (Lithuania), 63

rightist faction
  anticommunism, 50–51
  classification of, 68. *See also* political faction, classification scheme
  examples of, 64–65
  preferences, 4–5
  reform under autocracy, 33–34
  reform under high polarization, 32–33
  reform under low polarization, 30
  support base, 26
Rinegold, Deanna, 96
Robinson, James, 7, 38, 247
Rodionov, Denis, 185
Rodrik, Dani, 7, 15, 35, 58, 79, 87, 106, 111, 125
Roe, Mark J., 252
Roeder, Philip G., 147, 148
Roland, Gerard, 3, 15, 26, 87, 88, 106
Roman, Horvath, 73
Rosato, Sebastian, 128
Rose, Richard, 49, 177, 186
Rosenthal, Howard, 14, 24, 25, 26, 39, 53, 57, 59, 122, 123, 126
Rosneft, 189
Ross, Cameron, 152, 154
Ross, Michael, 190
Rothschild, Joseph, 152, 154, 155, 159, 216
Roy, Olivier, 238
Rumer, Boris Z., 230
Russia
  bank reform, 185–186
  and bond markets, 176
  commodity prices, 178, 182, 184–185, 187, 190–191
  competition policy, 173, 174
  corporate governance, 174, 185, 190
  dependent sector, 173–174
  inflation, 171
  large privatization, 172, 174, 175–176, 177, 182, 190
  loans for shares program. *See* loans for shares (Russia)
  media control, 187–188
  and nationalism, 153–154
  oligarchs, 175–176, 177, 189–190
  party platforms and polarization, 169–171, 181–182
  price liberalization, 169, 170, 173

Russia (*cont.*)
  private sector, 178
  renationalization, 187–188
  reversal of privatization, 189–190
  and shock therapy. *See* shock therapy
  small privatization, 172
  stabilization programs, 171–172, 173
  tax policy, 173–174, 178–179,
    182–183
  trade and currency liberalization, 169,
    170, 172, 173, 182
  transfers, 178–179
Russia's Regions Party, 180, 186
Rutland, Peter, 71, 183
Ryterman, Randi, 129

Sachs, Jeffrey D., 1, 12, 16, 25, 51, 67,
  87, 88, 106, 120, 190, 252
Sahay, Ratna, 107, 111
Sakwa, Richard, 157, 170
Sanfey, Peter, 120
Sartori, Giovanni, 39, 49
Sasin, Marcin J., 226
Saxe-Coburg Gotha, Simeon, 208
Sberbank, 185, 190
Schamis, Hector, 2, 9, 249
Schankerman, Mark, 129, 130, 248
Schoenmann, Roger, 214
Schroeder, Gertrude, 109
Securities and Exchange Commission
  (Poland), 223
securities market reform. *See* institutional
  reform
Segura-Ubiergo, Alex, 57
Selivakhin, Ivan, 185
Selowsky, Marcelo, 109, 118, 120
Senik, Claudia, 247
Shakin, Dmitry, 189
Shevtsova, Lilia, 189
shirkhats, 236
Shleifer, Andrei, 2, 3, 12, 87, 106, 129,
  173, 174, 178, 183, 223
shock therapy, 106–107, 171–174
Shopov, Vladimir, 196
Shvets, Julia, 179, 182
Shvetsova, Olga, 188
Sibneft, 183, 190
Simmons, Beth, 13
Sinyavskaya, Oxana, 184

Sjard, Jerome, 202
Slay, Ben, 224
Slinko, Irina, 179
Slovakia, 51, 60, 63, 66, 146, 153, 215,
  251
Slovenia, 51, 66, 68, 74, 89, 98, 146,
  152, 210, 251
small privatization. *See* economic reform
Smith, Graham, 150
Snijders, Tom A. B., 132, 133
Snyder, Jack, 252
Social Democratic Party of Albania, 49
Social Democratic Party of Bulgaria, 195
Social Democratic Party of Croatia, 68
Social Democratic Party of Poland, 216
Social Democratic Party of the Czech
  Republic, 52, 63, 68
Socialist Party of Albania, 54, 157
Sofiyanski, Stefan, 203
Solidarity, 214, 216–217, 219–220, 225
Solidarity Electoral Alliance (AWS), 217,
  220
Solnick, Steven, 23, 94, 188
Solovei, Valery, 170
Sonin, Konstantin, 10, 87
sovereign national model. *See* nationalism
Soviet Union, 79–80, 146, 147, 148–150,
  152, 153
Spechler, Martin, 238
Spiller, Pablo, 22
Spoor, Max, 236
Staehr, Karsten, 107, 111, 120
Stalin, Joseph, 51, 155
Stallings, Barbara, 24
Stanchev, Krassen, 200, 205, 209
Staniszkis, Jadwiga, 214, 221
Stark, David, 16, 107
Stasavage, David, 4, 7, 10–11, 22, 39
state building, 40
  and market building, 5, 11–13,
    247–249
state capture, 10–11, 201–202, 205–206
State Privatization Committee
  (Uzbekistan), 235
state-owned enterprise, 199, 200,
  202–203
Steenbergen, Marco R., 18, 132, 133
Stepan, Alfred, 107
Stigler, George, 248

Stiglitz, Joseph, 3, 10, 16, 60, 87, 88, 106
Stokes, Gale, 153
Stokes, Susan, 13, 14, 35, 57, 118, 163, 247
Stone, Randall, 24, 41, 50, 147, 199, 212, 216, 219, 220, 227
Stoner-Weiss, Kathryn, 187, 188
Stoyan, Tenev, 17
Stoyanov, Petar, 203
Strange, Susan, 23
Stuhlberg, Adam N., 186
Suchocka, Hanna, 219, 222
Sundberg, Mark, 240
Suny, Ronald Grigor, 147, 148, 149, 150, 152
survivor bias, 130
Svensson, Jakub, 22, 40, 59, 105, 115
Swedberg, Richard, 128
Swoboda, Victor, 147, 152
Szomburg, Jan, 219, 221, 225, 226

Tabellini, Guido, 8, 166
Taras, Ray, 39
Tarkowski, Jacek, 23, 221
Taube, Gunther, 239
Tax Code (Russia), 182
tax revenue
    under autocracy, 33–34
    in democracy with low polarization, 30–31
Tenev, Stoyan, 120
Terry, Sarah Miekljohn, 214
Thelen, Kathleen, 17
Tismaneaunu, Vladimir, 162
Todorov, Antony, 162
Toka, Gabor, 6, 25, 52, 66, 146, 159, 196, 200, 212, 216, 218
Tommasi, Mariano, 22
Tompson, William, 185, 189
trade and currency liberalization. *See* economic reform
transfers
    as electoral strategy, 29
    in democracies with high polarization, 33
    in democracies with low polarization, 30–31
    measures of, 97
    size, 29, 97–99

and taxes, 26
    timing of, 36, 43–44
Tregubova, Elena, 188
Treisman, Daniel, 107, 171, 173
Troeger, Vera, 85
Tsebelis, George, 39
Tucker, Joshua, 25, 50, 52, 171, 217
Tudjman, Franjo, 51, 63
Turkmenistan, 19, 74, 79, 109, 150, 151, 165, 240
Tverdova, Yulia, 133
Tworzecki, Hubert, 68
Tzvetkov, Plamen, 197

UES, 185
Ukraine, 7, 16, 56, 57, 108, 123, 127, 134, 154–156, 162–163
UNCTAD, 237
Union of Democratic Forces (Bulgaria), 50, 68, 192, 195–196, 200, 208–209, 211–212
Union of Labor (Poland), 217, 220
Union of Right Forces (Russia), 181
United Peasant Party (PSL-Poland), 215, 216–217, 220–221, 222
United People's Party (Kazakhstan), 67
Unity Party (Russia), 179–181, 188, 190
Urban, Joan Barth, 170
Uzavtotrans, 236
Uzbekistan
    and autocratic consolidation, 234
    commodity prices, 238–240
    competition policy, 237
    corporate governance, 235, 236
    foreign direct investment climate, 237
    import substitution strategy, 235–236, 239, 242
    Land Code, 236
    large privatization, 235–236
    and nationalism, 151
    price liberalization, 238
    role of commodities, 231
    ruler's orientation, 232
    small privatization, 235, 238
    tax policies, 239–240
    trade and currency liberalization, 235–237, 239
    transfers, 240–242
Uzbekistan, Mahalla. *See* Mahalla

Uzbekneftegaz, 236
Uzkhlopkopromsbyt, 235

Vachudova, Andrew, 50
Vachudova, Milada, 15, 162, 227, 250
van Rooden, Ron, 111, 120
Vanous, Jan, 147
Végh, Carlos, 88, 107, 111, 120
Veimetra, Rogi, 175
Verba, Sydney, 8
Verbeek, Jos, 226
Verdery, Katherine, 157
veto points, 39, 125–127
  effects of, 123
  fragmentation, 253
Videnov, Zhan, 54, 194, 200, 202, 203,
  204
Vishny, Robert, 2, 3, 12, 87, 106, 174
Vneshtorgbank, 185, 190
voters, 27, 42
voucher privatization, 87, 174, 200–201,
  222–223
Vujacic, Veljko, 144

Wagstyl, Stefan, 189
Walsh, Patrick, 54, 86
Warner, Andrew, 16, 190, 252
Warsaw Pact, 147, 154, 159
Wawro, Greg, 77
Way, Lucan A., 250
Webb, Steven B., 9, 246
Weingast, Barry R., 14
Weinthal, Erika, 230, 231
Wellisz, Stanislaw, 222
Wernke, Michael, 25
Weyland, Kurt, 13
White, Stephen, 177, 186
Willerton, John P., 150

Williamson, John, 13, 14, 15, 24
Wilson, Andrew, 150
winners from reform. *See* new-economy
  interests
winners take all, 9–11
Wintrobe, Ronald, 34
Wittenberg, Jason, 145
Woldendorp, J., 57
Woodruff, Christopher, 129
Woodruff, David, 174
Woodward, Richard, 222
World Bank, 54, 72, 86, 97, 182, 236,
  240
World Trade Organization, 72, 181, 184,
  190
Wyzan, Michael, 199, 201

Yakovlev, Andrei, 178
Yakovleva, Elena, 179
Yalcin, Resul, 230
Yeltsin, Boris, 6, 25, 50, 55–56, 68, 169,
  171–173, 175, 177–180, 184,
  186–187, 191, 213, 218
Yoon, David H., 84
Yudaeva, Ksenia, 179, 182, 184
YUKOS, 183, 185, 189–190

Zettelmeyer, Jeromin, 107, 108, 111,
  231, 239, 240
Zhivkov, Todor, 193, 194
Zhuravskaya, Ekaterina, 8, 37, 78, 129,
  178, 179, 247
Zielinski, Jakub, 14, 54, 145
Zingales, Luigi, 183
Zinnes, Clifford, 87, 88, 120
Zubek, Voytek, 216, 218, 219, 221
Zyuganov, Gennady, 56, 170, 171,
  177

+401

Other Books in the Series (*continued from page iii*)

Catherine Boone, *Political Topographies of the African State: Territorial Authority and Institutional Change*

Michael Bratton and Nicolas van de Walle, *Democratic Experiments in Africa: Regime Transitions in Comparative Perspective*

Michael Bratton, Robert Mattes, and E. Gyimah-Boadi, *Public Opinion, Democracy, and Market Reform in Africa*

Valerie Bunce, *Leaving Socialism and Leaving the State: The End of Yugoslavia, the Soviet Union, and Czechoslovakia*

Daniele Caramani, *The Nationalization of Politics: The Formation of National Electorates and Party Systems in Europe*

John M. Carey, *Legislative Voting and Accountability*

Kanchan Chandra, *Why Ethnic Parties Succeed: Patronage and Ethnic Head-counts in India*

José Antonio Cheibub, *Presidentialism, Parliamentarism, and Democracy*

Ruth Berins Collier, *Paths toward Democracy: The Working Class and Elites in Western Europe and South America*

Christian Davenport, *State Repression and the Domestic Democratic Peace*

Donatella della Porta, *Social Movements, Political Violence, and the State*

Alberto Diaz-Cayeros, *Federalism, Fiscal Authority, and Centralization in Latin America*

Thad Dunning, *Crude Democracy: Natural Resource Wealth and Political Regimes*

Gerald Easter, *Reconstructing the State: Personal Networks and Elite Identity*

Margarita Estevez-Abe, *Welfare and Capitalism in Postwar Japan: Party, Bureaucracy, and Business*

M. Steven Fish, *Democracy Derailed in Russia: The Failure of Open Politics*

Robert F. Franzese, *Macroeconomic Policies of Developed Democracies*

Roberto Franzosi, *The Puzzle of Strikes: Class and State Strategies in Postwar Italy*

Geoffrey Garrett, *Partisan Politics in the Global Economy*

Scott Gehlbach, *Representation through Taxation: Revenue, Politics, and Development in Postcommunist States*

Miriam Golden, *Heroic Defeats: The Politics of Job Loss*

Jeff Goodwin, *No Other Way Out: States and Revolutionary Movements*

Merilee Serrill Grindle, *Changing the State*

Anna Grzymala-Busse, *Rebuilding Leviathan: Party Competition and State Exploitation in Post-Communist Democracies*

Anna Grzymala-Busse, *Redeeming the Communist Past: The Regeneration of Communist Parties in East Central Europe*

Frances Hagopian, *Traditional Politics and Regime Change in Brazil*

Henry E. Hale, *The Foundations of Ethnic Politics: Separatism of States and Nations in Eurasia and the World*

Mark Hallerberg, Rolf Ranier Strauch, and Jürgen von Hagen, *Fiscal Governance in Europe*

Gretchen Helmke, *Courts under Constraints: Judges, Generals, and Presidents in Argentina*

Yoshiko Herrera, *Imagined Economies: The Sources of Russian Regionalism*

J. Rogers Hollingsworth and Robert Boyer, eds., *Contemporary Capitalism: The Embeddedness of Institutions*

John D. Huber and Charles R. Shipan, *Deliberate Discretion? The Institutional Foundations of Bureaucratic Autonomy*

Ellen Immergut, *Health Politics: Interests and Institutions in Western Europe*

Torben Iversen, *Capitalism, Democracy, and Welfare*

Torben Iversen, *Contested Economic Institutions*

Torben Iversen, Jonas Pontussen, and David Soskice, eds., *Unions, Employers, and Central Banks: Macroeconomic Coordination and Institutional Change in Social Market Economies*

Thomas Janoski and Alexander M. Hicks, eds., *The Comparative Political Economy of the Welfare State*

Joseph Jupille, *Procedural Politics: Issues, Influence, and Institutional Choice in the European Union*

Stathis Kalyvas, *The Logic of Violence in Civil War*

David C. Kang, *Crony Capitalism: Corruption and Capitalism in South Korea and the Philippines*

Junko Kato, *Regressive Taxation and the Welfare State*

Robert O. Keohane and Helen B. Milner, eds., *Internationalization and Domestic Politics*

Herbert Kitschelt, *The Transformation of European Social Democracy*

Herbert Kitschelt, Peter Lange, Gary Marks, and John D. Stephens, eds., *Continuity and Change in Contemporary Capitalism*

Herbert Kitschelt, Zdenka Mansfeldova, Radek Markowski, and Gabor Toka, *Post-Communist Party Systems*

David Knoke, Franz Urban Pappi, Jeffrey Broadbent, and Yutaka Tsujinaka, eds., *Comparing Policy Networks*

Allan Kornberg and Harold D. Clarke, *Citizens and Community: Political Support in a Representative Democracy*

Amie Kreppel, *The European Parliament and the Supranational Party System*

David D. Laitin, *Language Repertoires and State Construction in Africa*

Fabrice E. Lehoucq and Ivan Molina, *Stuffing the Ballot Box: Fraud, Electoral Reform, and Democratization in Costa Rica*

Mark Irving Lichbach and Alan S. Zuckerman, eds., *Comparative Politics: Rationality, Culture, and Structure, second edition*

Evan Lieberman, *Race and Regionalism in the Politics of Taxation in Brazil and South Africa*

Pauline Jones Luong, *Institutional Change and Political Continuity in Post-Soviet Central Asia*

Julia Lynch, *Age in the Welfare State: The Origins of Social Spending on Pensioners, Workers, and Children*

Doug McAdam, John McCarthy, and Mayer Zald, eds., *Comparative Perspectives on Social Movements*

Beatriz Magaloni, *Voting for Autocracy: Hegemonic Party Survival and Its Demise in Mexico*

James Mahoney and Dietrich Rueschemeyer, eds., *Historical Analysis and the Social Sciences*

Scott Mainwaring and Matthew Soberg Shugart, eds., *Presidentialism and Democracy in Latin America*

Isabela Mares, *The Politics of Social Risk: Business and Welfare State Development*

Isabela Mares, *Taxation, Wage Bargaining, and Unemployment*

Anthony W. Marx, *Making Race, Making Nations: A Comparison of South Africa, the United States, and Brazil*

Bonnie M. Meguid, *Party Competition between Unequals: Strategies and Electoral Fortunes in Western Europe*

Joel S. Migdal, *State in Society: Studying How States and Societies Constitute One Another*

Joel S. Migdal, Atul Kohli, and Vivienne Shue, eds., *State Power and Social Forces: Domination and Transformation in the Third World*

Scott Morgenstern and Benito Nacif, eds., *Legislative Politics in Latin America*

Layna Mosley, *Global Capital and National Governments*

Wolfgang C. Müller and Kaare Strøm, *Policy, Office, or Votes?*

Maria Victoria Murillo, *Labor Unions, Partisan Coalitions, and Market Reforms in Latin America*

Ton Notermans, *Money, Markets, and the State: Social Democratic Economic Policies since 1918*

Aníbal Pérez-Liñán, *Presidential Impeachment and the New Political Instability in Latin America*

Roger Petersen, *Understanding Ethnic Violence: Fear, Hatred, and Resentment in Twentieth-Century Eastern Europe*

Simona Piattoni, ed., *Clientelism, Interests, and Democratic Representation*

Paul Pierson, *Dismantling the Welfare State? Reagan, Thatcher, and the Politics of Retrenchment*

Marino Regini, *Uncertain Boundaries: The Social and Political Construction of European Economies*

Marc Howard Ross, *Cultural Contestation in Ethnic Conflict*

Lyle Scruggs, *Sustaining Abundance: Environmental Performance in Industrial Democracies*

Jefferey M. Sellers, *Governing from Below: Urban Regions and the Global Economy*

Yossi Shain and Juan Linz, eds., *Interim Governments and Democratic Transitions*

Beverly Silver, *Forces of Labor: Workers' Movements and Globalization since 1870*

Theda Skocpol, *Social Revolutions in the Modern World*

Regina Smyth, *Candidate Strategies and Electoral Competition in the Russian Federation: Democracy without Foundation*

Richard Snyder, *Politics after Neoliberalism: Reregulation in Mexico*

David Stark and László Bruszt, *Postsocialist Pathways: Transforming Politics and Property in East Central Europe*

Sven Steinmo, Kathleen Thelen, and Frank Longstreth, eds., *Structuring Politics: Historical Institutionalism in Comparative Analysis*

Susan C. Stokes, *Mandates and Democracy: Neoliberalism by Surprise in Latin America*

Susan C. Stokes, ed., *Public Support for Market Reforms in New Democracies*

Duane Swank, *Global Capital, Political Institutions, and Policy Change in Developed Welfare States*

Sidney Tarrow, *Power in Movement: Social Movements and Contentious Politics*

Kathleen Thelen, *How Institutions Evolve: The Political Economy of Skills in Germany, Britain, the United States, and Japan*

Charles Tilly, *Trust and Rule*

Daniel Treisman, *The Architecture of Government: Rethinking Political Decentralization*

Lily L. Tsai, *Accountability without Democracy: Solidary Groups and Public Goods Provision in Rural China*

Joshua Tucker, *Regional Economic Voting: Russia, Poland, Hungary, Slovakia, and the Czech Republic, 1990–1999*

Ashutosh Varshney, *Democracy, Development, and the Countryside*

Jeremy M. Weinstein, *Inside Rebellion: The Politics of Insurgent Violence*

Stephen I. Wilkinson, *Votes and Violence: Electoral Competition and Ethnic Riots in India*

Jason Wittenberg, *Crucibles of Political Loyalty: Church Institutions and Electoral Continuity in Hungary*

Elisabeth J. Wood, *Forging Democracy from Below: Insurgent Transitions in South Africa and El Salvador*

Elisabeth J. Wood, *Insurgent Collective Action and Civil War in El Salvador*